INSIGHT GUIDE

MonTReaL

DISCOVERY
CHANNEL

APA PUBLICATIONS L

Part of the Langenscheidt Publishing Group

ABOUT THIS BOOK

Editorial

Project Editor
Julia Roles
Managing Editor
Donna Dailey
Editorial Director
Brian Bell

Distribution

UK & Ireland
GeoCenter International Ltd
The Viables Centre, Harrow Way
Basingstoke, Hants RG22 4BJ
Fax: (44) 1256-817988

United States
Langenscheidt Publishers, Inc.
46–35 54th Road, Maspeth, NY 11378
Fax: (1) 718 784-0640

Canada
Thomas Allen & Son Ltd
390 Steelcase Road East
Markham, Ontario L34 1G2
Fax: (1) 905 475 6747

Australia
Universal Press
1 Waterloo Road
Macquarie Park, NSW 2113
Fax: (61) 2 9888 9074

New Zealand
Hema Maps New Zealand Ltd (HNZ)
Unit D, 24 Ra ORA Drive
East Tamaki, Auckland
Fax: (64) 9 273 6479

Worldwide
Apa Publications GmbH & Co.
Verlag KG (Singapore branch)
38 Joo Koon Road, Singapore 628990
Tel: (65) 865-1600. Fax: (65) 861-6438

Printing

Insight Print Services (Pte) Ltd
38 Joo Koon Road, Singapore 628990
Tel: (65) 865-1600. Fax: (65) 861-6438

©2001 Apa Publications GmbH & Co.
Verlag KG (Singapore branch)
All Rights Reserved
First Edition 1991
Third Edition 2001

CONTACTING THE EDITORS
We would appreciate it if readers
would alert us to errors or out-
dated information by writing to:
Insight Guides, P.O. Box 7910,
London SE1 1WE, England.
Fax: (44) 20 7403-0290.
insight@apaguide.demon.co.uk

www.insightguides.com

This guidebook combines the interests and enthusiasms of two of the world's best-known information providers: Insight Guides, whose titles have set the standard for visual travel guides since 1970, and Discovery Channel, the world's premier source of nonfiction television programming.

The editors of Insight Guides provide both practical advice and general understanding about a destination's history, culture, institutions and people. Discovery Channel and its website, www.discovery.com, help millions of viewers explore their world from the comfort of their own home and also encourage them to explore it first hand.

This fully updated edition of *Insight Guide: Montreal* is carefully structured to convey an under standing of the city and its culture as well as to guide readers through its sights and activities:

◆ The **Features** section, indicated by a yellow bar at the top of each page, covers the history and culture of the city and region in a series of informative essays.

◆ The main **Places** section, indicated by a blue bar, is a complete guide to all the sights and areas worth visiting. Places of special interest are coordinated by number with the maps

◆ The **Travel Tips** listings section, with an orange bar, provides information on travel, hotels, shops restaurants and more An index to the section is on the back flap.

The contributors

An experienced team of writers and editors worked hard to update and expand the previous edition of *Insight Guide: Montreal*. The project editor was **Julia Roles**, an English editor now living in Canada, who also project edited *Insight Guide: Cyprus* and worked on Insight Guides to Egypt and Oman & the UAE. **Donna Dailey** coordinated and supervised the project at Insight Guides' London office and worked with **Tom Le Bas** on the picture edit.

Freelance journalist **Paul Karr** wrote several new features, including Montreal Cuisine, the Needle Trade, Famous Montrealers, Arts Desire, The Young and the Restless and Anatomy of the Plateau, along with the picture stories on Ethnic Montreal, Architecture and the St Lawrence River. He also updated the Places and Features sections and Travel Tips. Karr has been resident in Montreal since 1993 and speaks fluent French. He spends a lot of time roaming around Canada, Europe and his native United States on writing projects, which include chapters of *Insight Guide: USA On the Road* and updates for *Atlanta*, *Austria* and *Switzerland*.

The section on Quebec City was written by **Matthew Parfitt**, with additions by Paul Karr. Parfitt wrote about the province of Quebec for *Insight Guide: Canada* and also produced several chapters for the original edition of this guide, including Bohemian Montreal, The Jazz Scene and Stadiums and Gardens.

Other contributors to previous editions whose work survives in the new *Insight Guide: Montreal* include **Lysiane Gagnon**, who wrote A Tale of Two Solitudes; **Mark Kingwell**, whose contributions range from History to Ice Hockey; **Emil Sher**, who wrote about Jewish life in his native Montreal; **Charles Foran** and **Mary Ladky**, who wrote several of the Places and Features chapters; **Louise Legault** who wrote about Festivals, **Nancy Lyon**, who wrote the Excursions; **Katherine Snyder**, who compiled the Travel Tips; and editors **Joanna Ebbutt, Stephen Scharper** and **Hilary Cunningham**.

The photography in this guide is largely the work of **Carl** and **Ann Purcell**, an internationally known photographic and writing team, and **Jackie Garrow**, a Toronto-based photographer who also shot the Insight Compact Guides to Montreal and Toronto.

The book was proofread by **Pam Barrett** and the index was compiled by **Isobel McLean**.

Map Legend

— ·· —	International Boundary
— — —	State Boundary
— · —	National Park/Reserve
— — —	Ferry Route
Ⓜ	Metro
✈ ✈	Airport: International/Regional
🚌	Bus Station
ⓘ	Tourist Information
✉	Post Office
† †	Church/Ruins
†	Monastery
☾	Mosque
✡	Synagogue
🏰	Castle/Ruins
∴	Archaeological Site
∩	Cave
👤	Statue/Monument
★	Place of Interest

The main places of interest in the Places section are coordinated by number with a full-colour map (e.g. ❶), and a symbol at the top of every right-hand page tells you where to find the map.

Insight Guide Montreal

Contents

Maps

Montreal City **122**

Old Montreal **126**

Downtown **156**

Latin Quarter and
Plateau **178**

Westmount and
Outremont **194**

Stadiums and Gardens **210**

Ile Ste-Hélène and
Ile Notre-Dame **214**

Excursions **225**

Quebec City **246**

A map of Montreal is on the
inside front cover

A map of Quebec City is on
the inside back cover

Plans of the Montreal Métro
and the Montreal
Underground City face the
inside back cover

Introduction

The French Connection **15**

History

Decisive Dates **18**
The River and the Mountain .. **21**
Coming of the British **33**
Conflict and Confederation **43**
Modern Montreal **51**

Features

Tale of Two Solitudes **65**
The Montrealer **73**
The Jews of Montreal **79**
Politics, Language, Identity **89**
Montreal Cuisine **101**
The Needle Trade **104**
Why Ice Hockey Matters **107**

Latin
Quarter
roof line

Insight on ...

Ethnic Montreal 86
Architecture 152
The St Lawrence 218

Information panels

Religious Roots 30
Habitants 40
The Quiet Revolution 58
Brain vs Brawn 92
Pierre Trudeau 96
A Living Language.............. 132
Famous Montrealers 144
Grand Dame 160
Art's Desire 173
The Young and the Restless 180
The Jazz Scene.................. 187
Parc du Mont-Royal............ 196
Outremont Cafés 201

Places

Introduction 121
Old Montreal 125
Downtown 155
Bohemian Montreal 177
Anatomy of The Plateau 188
Westmount and Outremont .. 193
St Joseph's Oratory 203
Stadiums, Gardens, Islands 209
Excursions 223
Quebec City 245

Travel Tips

Getting Acquainted . . 258
Planning the Trip 259
Practical Tips 261
Getting Around 264
Where to Stay 267
Restaurants 270
Nightlife 275
Culture & Other
Attractions 276
Festivals 277
Shopping 278
Sport 280
Language 282
Further Reading 287

Full Travel Tips Index
is on page 257

THE FRENCH CONNECTION

The largest francophone city after Paris, Montreal combines

Old World style with North American modernity

Despite the political tensions that constantly seem to threaten to rip it apart, you will rarely find a city happier than Montreal at remaining just what it is: a place of good food and drink, close-knit families, and the unending stimulation of shops, bars, cafés, festivals, immigrants and the arts.

It is a beautiful town, of Second Empire, Orthodox and Anglican architecture that has mostly been left to stand. It is a vibrant town of 3 million people (including the many suburbs) with – say tourist officials – more restaurants per capita than any major city in the world, plus a healthy share of writers, painters, dancers and musicians.

It is also astonishingly tolerant. Racial and violent crime is almost unknown, and alternative lifestyles go about their business without disruption: one of the continent's largest gay parades takes place each summer to the cheers of local residents, for instance, and vegetarian restaurants and health-food shops are more prevalent than in any comparable North American city.

This tolerance goes back to the American Civil War, when Montrealers found themselves welcoming both escaping slaves and the fleeing fathers of Southern secession. Immigrants today find the place welcoming, and most quickly pick up French and English to add to their Spanish or Portuguese or Vietnamese. But it retains its French values – you can reliably locate excellent bread, wine, croissants, cigarettes and a noisy discotheque in any part of the city.

Such is the *joie de vivre* in Montreal that sometimes it's hard to imagine that secessionist troubles still brew (occasionally turning violent), or that there are large poor quarters in the city's east end, or that government and public services run with bumptious inefficiency, just well enough to survive but never better.

And what of the weather? The average winter temperature here, after all, fights to reach –10°C (15°F), fierce winds and storms often blow in off the Laurentians or Adirondacks, and snow isn't unheard of in May. When summer finally does come, it comes with a suddenness and uncomfortable humidity borne of the city's valley position and proximity to so much water.

"We do not fight winter," says one local. "We invite it, play with it, welcome it."

Indeed, that is the attitude here. Play. Welcome. *Bienvenue.*   ❏

PRECEDING PAGES: Raymond Mason's *Illuminated Crowd* sculpture on avenue McGill College; Montreal winter; *calèches*; fun at La Ronde.
LEFT: parade on St-Jean-Baptiste Day.

Decisive Dates

1535: French navigator Jacques Cartier visits a Huron village, Hochelaga, later to become the site of Montreal.

1608: Samuel de Champlain, the French explorer, establishes Quebec City, the first permanent settlement in Canada.

1611: Samuel de Champlain explores Montreal and builds a wall, the island's first European construction, near the St-Pierre River.

1615: First Catholic mass in North America is celebrated on the island of Montreal.

1642: The first colonists arrive, establish a tiny colony and name it Ville Marie.

1643: After a severe flood, the commander of Ville Marie, Paul de Chomedey, Sieur de Maisonneuve, erects a wooden cross on Mont Royal.

1658: Montreal's first schoolteacher, Marguerite Bourgeoys, begins teaching in a stable located in Ville Marie.

1672: The first streets are laid out and named by Dollier de Cassons: among them is Notre-Dame, in honour of the Virgin Mary, the patron saint of the colony.

1716: The French decide to build a wall around Montreal to fortify it.

1754–63: While the Seven Years' War rages in Europe, tensions between the French and English escalate in North America.

1759: General James Wolfe attacks French forces near Quebec City and, after three months, defeats them on the Plains of Abraham. Montreal is captured by General Jeffery Amherst in 1760. The surrender of New France is signed in Montreal and British troops take over the town, which has 60,000 inhabitants.

1763: Under the Treaty of Paris, the French give most of their land in Canada to the British. They keep two tiny islands south of Newfoundland: St-Pierre and Miquelon.

1774: The Quebec Act is enacted: it extends Quebec's borders and guarantees the use of French language and freedom of religion.

1775: As the American revolution begins, United Empire Loyalists come north.

1776: Benjamin Franklin, Samuel Chase and the Jesuit Charles Caroll visit Montreal in an attempt to convince French Canadians to join the American revolutionary cause against England. English troops arrive in June and the Americans withdraw from the city.

1778: The first issue of *Gazette du Commerce et Littéraire pour la ville et le district de Montréal* is printed. It later becomes *The Montreal Gazette*.

1792: Montreal is divided into east and west, with boulevard Saint-Laurent as the dividing line.

1801–20: The stone walls around Montreal are demolished.

1809: Canada's first steamboat sails the St Lawrence River from Montreal to Quebec City.

1812–14: The Americans attempt to invade Canada but are eventually repelled. The Treaty of Ghent ends the war.

1832: Montreal is incorporated as a city.

1833: Jacques Viger is elected the first mayor of Montreal. On July 19, the city adopts the coat of arms and the motto *Concordia Salus*.

1837–38: French Canadians lead a rebellion against the Château Clique; one leader, Louis Joseph Papineau, flees to the United States.

1843: The first classes are held at McGill University. Under the Act of Union, Montreal (briefly) becomes the capital of the united provinces of Upper and Lower Canada (Ontario and Quebec).

1852: After the Great Fire in Montreal, 9,000 people are left homeless.

1867: Canada and the Atlantic Provinces of Nova Scotia and New Brunswick become the Dominion of Canada.

1885: The Canadian Pacific Railway, based in

Montreal, completes Canada's first continental railroad.

1886: Canada's first transcontinental railway train leaves Montreal for Vancouver.

1889: First automobile arrives in Montreal.

1914: World War I army conscription divides French and English Canadians.

1924: Cross on Mont Royal is illuminated.

1928: 22,000 people attend the opening of Montreal Stadium.

1929: Stock market crashes and the Great Depression ravages the city's finances. The bridge across the St Lawrence River is completed. It is named after Jacques Cartier in 1934.

1940: Montreal Mayor Camillien Houde urges French Canadians to defy a government plan for conscription during World War II. Most French Canadians oppose the military draft. Federal authorities put Houde in a prison camp until 1944.

1954: Jean Drapeau is elected mayor for the first time.

1959: Britain's Queen Elizabeth II and the president of the United States, Dwight D. Eisenhower, open the St Lawrence Seaway.

1963: The terrorist Front de Libération de Québec (FLQ) joins the Quebec separatist movement. Between 1963 and 1968, the FLQ claims responsibility for hundreds of bombings and armed robberies in the Montreal area.

1967: Opening of the World's Fair, Expo '67, in Montreal. More than 50 million people attend.

1970: In October the FLQ kidnaps British Trade Commissioner James R. Cross and Quebec Labour Minister Pierre Laporte. Prime Minister Pierre Trudeau sends federal troops to Montreal. Laporte is murdered. Cross is released after the government guarantees his kidnappers safe passage to Cuba.

1976: The Parti Québécois wins the provincial election; Olympic Games are held in Montreal.

1980: Voters defeat a proposal to give provincial leaders the right to negotiate Quebec's political independence from Canada.

1982: Marguerite Bourgeoys is canonized.

1985: The Liberals gain control of the provincial legislature and Robert Bourassa becomes premier of Quebec.

1987: Meech Lake Accord acknowledges Quebec's separate and distinct culture".

1990: Amid threats of Quebec's separation from Canada, the Meech Lake Accord fails to be ratified.

1992: The 350th anniversary of Montreal's founding is celebrated.

1993: The separatist Bloc Québécois, led by Lucien Bouchard, becomes the Official Opposition party in Canada's federal parliament.

1994: Robert Bourassa hands over the Quebec Liberal Party reins to Daniel Johnston, who leads the party to an electoral defeat. Jacques Parizeau's Parti Québécois party wins a resounding victory.

1995: Federally-minded voters in Quebec narrowly defeat a referendum proposal in favour of Quebec's independence. Parizeau resigns.

1996: Lucien Bouchard takes over the leadership of the Parti Québécois.

1998: Quebecker Jean Charest takes over as leader of Quebec's demoralized Liberal party. In November Bouchard calls a sudden provincial election. Although the PQ wins, the Liberals retain 43.7 percent of the popular vote. The Ice Storm hits Montreal and Quebec.

1999: An American businessman, Jeffrey Loria, purchases the Montreal Expos baseball club.

2000: Pierre Trudeau and hockey star Maurice Richard die. Trudeau's state funeral, in Basilique Notre-Dame in Old Montreal, is the largest in Canada's history. Quebecker Jean Chrétien wins third term as Liberal prime minister. ❑

PRECEDING PAGES: Montreal's maritime past.
LEFT: spring cleaning, pioneer style. **RIGHT:** Jacques Parizeau, leader of the Parti Québécois, until 1995.

THE RIVER AND THE MOUNTAIN

From Native Canadians to French to British, the story
of Montreal has always been closely tied to its landscape

Each in its way symbolizes the influences which have shaped the city. The mountain, ancient symbol of man's spiritual journey, dramatizes the missionary faith which founded the first European settlement here. The river, flowing past the island on which the city stands, created the highway which made Montreal such a natural centre for trade and commerce.
—Aline Gubbay, urban historian

The fortunes of Montreal have been varied and spectacular – sketchy Indian settlement, French missionary outpost and trading centre, throbbing industrial port, tourist destination. Through all this, two facts have remained constant: the broad flow of a river and the upward thrust of a mountain.

In Montreal, understanding history begins with understanding geology. For here, in a time before history, hot lava from beneath the earth's crust forced its way to the surface and created the volcanic mountain whose burnt-out remains Jacques Cartier was to claim, millennia later, for King Francis I of France. At 230 metres (755 ft) Cartier's Mont Royal is hardly in the class of the Rockies, but its hardened cone of volcanic basalt nevertheless withstood the glacial ice that scoured the rest of this region more than 10,000 years ago.

Those same glaciers, receding sheets of ice 3 to 5 km (2 or 3 miles) thick, forged the complex waterways and thousands of islands that mark the fertile valley of the St Lawrence River. The island now known as Montreal is situated near the confluence of two powerful rivers, the St Lawrence and the Ottawa, whose waters meet in violent confrontation before heading east to the Atlantic. With its flat, fertile expanse and single conspicuous peak, the island is a peaceful contrast to the turbulent rapids that surround it.

The river and the mountain serve to frame the dual aspect of the city's unique history.

LEFT: totem pole at the McCord Museum of Canadian History in downtown Montreal.
RIGHT: the ambitious King Francis I of France.

Montreal's early mixture of contradictory impulses – the first French settlers traded as assiduously for furs as they did for souls – has characterized the city through the centuries. It is a place where opposites not only attract, but marry. French and English, wealthy and destitute, radical and conservative, federalist and

separatist – all have found a place, sometimes an uneasy one, in this rich human settlement.

The history of Montreal is therefore a narrative in two dimensions, a history that mirrors its fortuitous location. Horizontally, it is one of arduous co-existence, conquest, uneasy reconciliation and assimilation. That story continues today as Montrealers struggle to maintain a common life when their cultural and linguistic differences threaten to pull them apart.

Vertically, the story of Montreal is a story of individual visions – political, commercial and religious – that drive men and women to these shores to carve out ideal cities that appear in their dreams. But other dreams have always persisted, and Montreal can neither boast nor mourn any single vision of itself. It is no city on a hill, no new Jerusalem. Instead it has been, and is, many cities, a place where successive generations of dreamers have come to try and turn their dreams into reality.

Early inhabitants

The earliest settlers of the island now known as Montreal were, of course, Indians, mainly of the Huron, Algonquin and Montagnais tribes. There is no way of telling how long these peoples had been residing on the island when the first European, Jacques Cartier, set foot here on

October 2, 1535. His account speaks of an island already criss-crossed with Indian trails and possessing one apparently permanent settlement, Hochelaga ("at the place of the beaver dam"). This was a circular, palisaded village inhabited by Algonquin and Hurons living in communal long houses. The site is probably close to where McGill University now stands.

Though the inhabitants appeared filthy and ignorant to Cartier, they enjoyed the benefits of a disease-free, complex society. It was governed by a closely guarded oral history, sophisticated natural pantheism, and a consensual form of rule in which senior men of the settlement would meet to agree on policy, division of

labour and war measures. The tribes existed as loose associations of many far-flung settlements and roving bands. Together, the Algonquin, Huron, Iroquois and Montagnais nations occupied most of the St Lawrence River Valley, the Great Lakes, and what is now New England.

Among the Indians, meat was not consumed every day, and in addition to the fruits of the hunt, many Indians subsisted on a paste of cold cornmeal and animal fat that later became known to the French as *sagamité*. The Hurons turned their efforts to cultivating the land. Beans, squash and corn were their staples and were mashed into pastes or boiled to make soups. This semi-agricultural way of life made for settlements more permanent than those of the Algonquin or the Iroquois, and it was probably Hochelaga Hurons whom Cartier encountered in the early months of 1535.

Cartier's mission

Jacques Cartier was a professional sailor from the town of St-Malo, a proud Frenchman in an age whose most accomplished naval men were Italian and Iberian. His king, Francis I, had charged him with a simple task: "To discover islands and countries where they say there is a lot of gold." King Francis was a man of limited imagination but boundless ambition, and the voyage on which he sent Cartier was only the first of many undertaken at his behest.

In these early days of the Age of Discovery, France's influence in North America became unparalleled, driven by the cupidity and religious aspirations of French monarchs, and realized by the unusual versatility and capabilities of their subjects. Cartier was one of these men, a brilliant navigator and a surprisingly deft diplomat. As a geographer, he was unfortunately limited by the ignorance of his times. Like everyone else, Cartier thought that North America was Asia, and that the rumoured mountains of gold and unlimited supplies of spice and silk were within his grasp. He sailed his convoy of three ships, led by the flagship *Grande Hermine*, as far as he could up the St Lawrence until, near the north shore of an island, his progress was stopped by impassable rapids.

It was here that the fateful encounter between European and Indian, the beginnings of Montreal, took place. Cartier dressed himself "gorgeously" for his first formal call on Hochelaga and upon entering the village saw the horse-shoe-shaped stockade that was typical of a Huron village. He was shown their settlement and taken to meet Agouhanna, the chief of Hochelaga.

Agouhanna decided to show him the local sights. Cartier was conveyed to the summit of the island's small mountain, and from this vantage he could see the river winding its way east for hundreds of miles. Here, thought Cartier, was the route to the Orient! He planted a cross, claimed the site for King Francis as the Hurons

A MINOR DEITY

The Hurons were friendly to Cartier, and being impressed by his "floating island" and his strange dress, they took him to be a travelling minor deity.

sailing, he reached France to report to King Francis and have the samples of "gold" and "diamonds" analyzed. They turned out to be iron pyrite (fool's gold) and quartz crystal.

But Cartier had also brought with him another gift from Agouhanna, a different kind of treasure, and one that was to fuel much of the exploration and colonization of Montreal – and Canada. It was the pelt of the Canadian beaver, an intelligent herbivore native to North America and possessed of a rich warm coat.

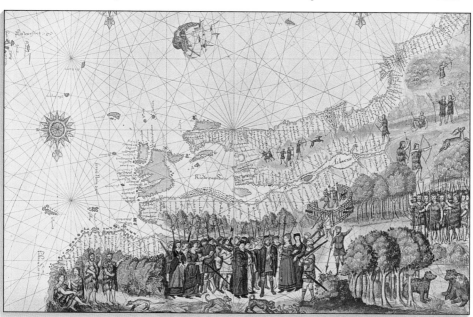

looked on baffled, and pronounced the site "Mont Royal". The derivative of this – Montreal, did not come into general usage until a century later.

Fool's gold and beaver pelts

Cartier also asked Agouhanna if he knew where to find the "shining rocks" he had heard were to be found in the area. The chief cheerfully supplied him with some rock samples and Cartier hurried back to his ship. After a brutal winter's

LEFT: Jacques Cartier, the first European to set foot on Montreal soil. **ABOVE:** a 16th-century depiction of Cartier's landing with colonists.

Over the next two centuries, European demand for the pelts, which could be made into fashionable hats and garments, would explode. During this same period, many of the Indians, who found the pelts could be traded for weapons and implements, came to view the beaver as a powerful animal deity whose merits they had failed to recognize. Their desire for the products of European technology – pots, guns, alcohol – allowed profit-driven Europeans to exploit their canoeing and trapping skills. The value of goods traded for pelts was far below the price they would bring in Europe.

Cartier revisited Montreal in 1541, but did not linger long, and the general settlement of

New France was now centred on what were to become the Canadian provinces of Nova Scotia and New Brunswick. By 1604, the new French king, Henry IV, a devout Huguenot (Protestant), had granted to his Huguenot friend, the Sieur de Monte, a monopoly on all the furs in New France.

Father of New France

Without manpower, such a monopoly was worthless, but one of Monte's closest friends was a tireless figure who possessed the drive and imagination needed to settle New France and allow the fur trade to flourish. His name

was Samuel de Champlain, a man of unusual resourcefulness who would become known as "the Father of New France". Champlain, an accomplished soldier and scholar, made several journeys to New France in the early years of the 17th century, and he founded settlements in Acadia (part of what is now Nova Scotia) and Quebec.

In 1611 he visited the island of Montreal and found that the Hochelaga settlement mentioned in Cartier's account had disappeared. He ordered his men to clear an area by the river bank and called it "Place Royale", a name the area possesses to this day. Champlain also took a fancy to the small island offshore from Montreal and

used the dowry of his teenage wife, Hélène Boulé, to buy it. Like many Montreal place names, it was informally canonized when Champlain's wife was long dead: it is known today as Ile Ste-Hélène, and is part of the permanent park erected when the World's Fair, Expo '67, was held in Montreal.

Champlain's main settlement was in Quebec City, which he founded on July 3, 1603. But he visited Montreal again in 1615, this time on the north shore of the island, and here happened to meet two priests of the Récollet (Franciscan Minor) Order, Denis Janet and Joseph le Caron, both arrived from France.

Momentous Mass

Together with Champlain's men, these two performed the first Catholic Mass in North America on June 24, 1615. The setting was not auspicious for this momentous event, nothing more than a clearing and some rough wooden tables, but Champlain knelt with the two tough little priests. Many, many more masses would be said in New France.

Champlain, known to the Indians as Agnonha, was a colonial governor who was devout and warlike by turns. He had earned the enduring enmity of the Iroquois by killing more than 300 of them at Ticonderoga, matching European technology – primitive firearms known as arquebuses – against bow and arrow. His allies, the Hurons and Algonquins, also feared and hated him. Yet they bowed to his attempts at regulating the fur trade. He was not a man lightly crossed.

While Champlain was consolidating his power in Quebec City, the energetic Récollet priests were doing their best to consolidate God's power further upstream. Not surprisingly, the Indians proved unwilling converts. The continuing aggression of the Iroquois against Place Royale created many early Christian martyrs among the Récollets and the Jesuits, known to the Indians as Black Robes. The priests were sometimes befriended by the Hurons or Algonquins, but were more often despised and feared as bizarre sorcerers who refused to have sex, share their belongings, or live communally.

Conversions were recorded, especially by the Jesuits, but they were of dubious theological validity and cost a high price in French lives. Jesuit priests were tortured and then gruesomely killed by the Indians, who believed that signs of weakness in conquered enemies made the conquerors stronger.

Graphic accounts of these events, written by the Jesuits and circulated in France, inspired a general religious zeal. In 1627, the French prime minister was the Machiavellian figure, Armand Jean du Plessis (better known as Cardinal Richelieu) who, seeking tirelessly to make France the preeminent power in the world, controlled the court of Louis XIII with a mixture of guile and terror.

At Richelieu's urging, Louis granted title to

> **HAPLESS HEATHENS**
>
> In France, the name "Mont Royal" became synonymous with a forlorn heathen place in need of salvation.

common missionary passion for converting "heathen" Indians, and determined to start a permanent mission at Montreal.

They could not help viewing their meeting as providential. Pooling their resources, they set off in 1641 with a group of 50 missionary members of their newly created "Société de Notre Dame de Montréal" under the leadership of Paul de Chomedey, Sieur de Maisonneuve. The new mission was to be established for the sole purpose of converting Indian souls to Catholicism, and Olier spec-

all land in New France to a group of shrewd French businessmen known as the Company of One Hundred Associates. Unable to exploit all the territory themselves, the Associates granted subleases to likely settlers. The title to the island of Montreal was granted by the Associates to two fervent believers, Jean-Jacques Olier, later founder of the Order of St Sulpice, and Jerome de la Royer de la Dauversière, a tax collector from Anjou. Olier and Dauversière had met by chance in Paris, discovered a

LEFT: Samuel de Champlain, the city's first developer, in 1611. **ABOVE:** portrait of Armand Jean du Plessis, better known as Cardinal Richelieu.

ified that the Notre Dame settlers "should have nothing to do with the fur trade". There would be difficulty enough, they cautioned Maisonneuve, in "planting the banner of Christ in an abode of desolation and a haunt of demons".

Religious fervour

Maisonneuve, a tough ex-soldier and Knight of Malta now driven by religious fervour, founded his colony, "Ville Marie", on Champlain's Place Royale site after a hard Atlantic crossing. On reaching the shore, he fell on his knees and gave thanks. A rough palisade was quickly erected, and Mass was said on August 18, 1642.

The consecrated host was displayed all day

on the altar to show that this place had been claimed for Christ.

Life was extraordinarily hazardous and arduous for the newly arrived settlers, who were fortified by their belief that they were doing God's work. Attacks by Indians were a constant danger, their crops refused to take in the soil, and the melting snow caused disastrous annual floods. In December 1642, the confluence of the St Lawrence and St Peter rivers rose violently, lapping at the

a defensive posture. Nevertheless, Iroquois ambushes, often of workers returning to the palisades after a day in the fields, killed more than 50 people between 1643 and 1650 – this in a community that numbered fewer than 150.

To guard against ambushes, the settlers employed guard dogs who warned the French of stalking Iroquois warriors and prevented many deaths. Most famous of these was Maisonneuve's dog, Pilote, whose keen nose frequently detected the

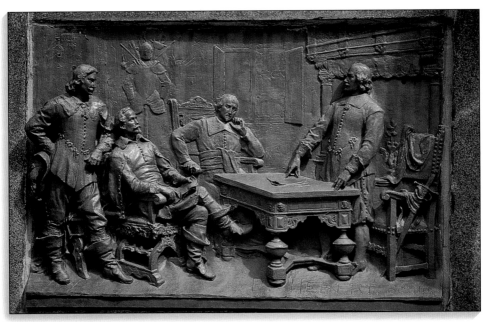

edges of the fledgling settlement. Maisonneuve, in great fear, planted a cross on the threatened bank and vowed that he would erect another on Mont Royal if the waters receded – which indeed they did, on Christmas Day. On the feast of Epiphany (on January 6) a procession, with a grateful Maisonneuve himself at the rear bearing a heavy wooden cross, scaled the hill and planted this token of thanks for God's mercy.

Costly conversions

The Iroquois raids were a more constant and nagging danger and, until his men learned canoeing skills sufficient to meet the Indians on the water, Maisonneuve was forced to adopt

approaching Indian warriors before they were visible. The dog is immortalized along with Maisonneuve in a statue located in old Montreal.

The first baptism of an Algonquin child occurred at Ville Marie in 1642, and this was a great victory for the embattled missionaries. After all, conversion of the pagans was their reason for enduring the hardships of life in New France. But as they gathered around the rough baptismal font, their thoughts may have turned to the great cost of salvation. How many more would die so that a few Indian souls could be saved? So many of the Indians did not want them there at all, and many others simply did not find the prospect of eternal life with God a joyful one. Would this first native Christian child find itself an outcast, or an apostate, in later life? The devout could banish such doubts, but not all of the Ville Marie company were as stout in their faith as the ascetic Récollet priests and the grim Maisonneuve himself.

In 1644, fed up with the continual Indian harassment of the settlement, Maisonneuve walked out like a Western gunslinger to meet the leader of the Iroquois in single combat. It wasn't by any means a fair fight, Maisonneuve having armed himself with two pistols. He succeeded in killing the chief at what is now known as Place d'Armes. The statue of Maisonneuve and his dog (plus other prominent figures in Montreal's early history) stands there today.

Strong women

Despite the religious fervour of some at Ville Marie, the settlement flourished more as a French outpost than a centre of conversion. The quick wealth of the fur trade brought more people, including the so-called *filles du roi* – young Frenchwomen transported to Montreal to marry the male settlers. With a larger population came the need for new services. In 1644 the young nurse Jeanne Mance opened Montreal's first hospital, l'Hôtel Dieu, which was also the first building outside the palisades. Mance, who had almost died on the voyage from France, regained her strength to tend to those less fortunate.

The schoolmistress Marguerite Bourgeoys, another deceptively frail Frenchwoman, founded the settlement's first chapel, Notre-Dame-de-Bon-Secours – still standing, after several rebuildings, on its original site in Old Montreal. Bourgeoys's order of nuns, Le Congrégation de Notre-Dame-de-Bon-Secours, was authorized by Louis XIV in 1671, the first native Canadian religious order. The Notre-Dame Congregation was, until well into the 20th century, one of North America's most influential institutions for the education of Catholic women, and Bourgeoys was raised to sainthood in 1982 by Pope John Paul II.

Montreal was now North America's premier Roman Catholic city and remained so for almost two centuries. Dominated in the early

days by Franciscans and Jesuits, the city later welcomed Jean-Jacques Olier's St-Sulpice fathers, and the so-called Grey Sisters (more formally known as Les Soeurs de la Charité de l'Hôpital Général de Montréal), who tended to the poor and destitute. The Oblates, Christian Brothers and Sacred Heart Sisters also found their way to the city.

Mountain of churches

All the schools of Montreal and many of its most impressive buildings are the result of the church's great hold on Montrealers. When the Notre-Dame Cathedral of Montreal was built

in 1829, it drew visitors from across Canada and the United States; it was then the largest church in North America and remained so until St Patrick's Cathedral was built in New York in 1879.

In 1874 there were 74 churches of all denominations in Montreal – one for every 2,000 inhabitants. Even at this date they were still largely Catholic, but with several tasteful additions from the Church of Scotland and the Anglican Church. Harriet Beecher Stowe, author of *Uncle Tom's Cabin*, wrote in 1860 that "Montreal is a mountain of churches", while Mark Twain took a more jaundiced view: "This is the first time I was ever in a city," he

LEFT: Paul de Chomedey, Sieur de Maisonneuve, lays down the law.
RIGHT: an early Quebec winter.

wrote in 1881, "where you could not throw a brick without breaking a church window."

Muscular Christianity

During the 1660s, the governing spirit of Ville Marie was the energetic Superior of the Sulpicians and keen amateur historian François Dollier de Cassons (1632–1702). He was a strapping, 2.2-metre (6½-ft) ex-soldier who, with his cassock tucked up for greater freedom of movement, surveyed the town's first street plan, planned a canal to bypass the Lachine rapids, and built the first parish church and a seminary for the Sulpicians, the order that

was still the official owner of the island.

In 1663, however, Louis XIV took formal possession of all the land and trade of New France, and land parcels and trading licences henceforth were granted only by the Crown and its representatives at Quebec.

Division of the spoils

The island of Montreal was divided into land packets known as *seigneuries*; the owners, or *seigneurs*, subdividing their land into long and narrow tenant parcels known as *rangs*, which were farmed by *habitants*.

For a nominal rent the *habitant* was given the land to work, on which he built a dwelling for himself and maintained a road. He also had to pay to grind his grain at the *seigneur*'s mill.

Seigneuries were typically divided up into long strips rather than chunks in order that every *habitant* could have some river access. This division is still evident in Quebec estates. The *habitant*, with his dyed wool cap *(toque bleu)*, blanket-cloth coat and tasselled sash, remains a ubiquitous, if somewhat clichéd, symbol of rural Quebec. *(Bonhomme*, the snowman symbol of Quebec City's annual winter festival, also wears the toque and sash of the *habitant*.)

The landowners themselves built grand stone houses on estates away from the river-bank. Named after their owners, some of these *châteaux* are still standing: Château de Ramezay, one of the first, served later as the seat of Montreal's government; De La Salle House can be found in the suburb of Lachine (named rather hopefully as a stage on the road to *La Chine*, French for China).

Sustained attacks

But while Ville Marie seemed to be gaining a foothold on the island, the Indian threat did not lessen. On August 4, 1689, the worst Iroquois raid yet left 200 residents of Lachine dead. Another 100 were captured and never returned.

There followed 10 years of sustained fighting with the Iroquois, which effectively halted the fur trade on which Montreal's prosperity depended. The city entered the 18th century on a pensive note, but the diplomatic new Governor-General of Montreal, Hector de Callières, managed to negotiate a peace treaty with the Indians. In 1701 more than 1,300 Indians, representatives of 40 different nations, were persuaded to come to Montreal and camp outside the city's walls for peace talks. De Callières, skilled in smoothing over old grievances, circulated among the assembled chiefs and hammered out a deal all could accept. Surveying the hundreds of tents, camp fires and milling Indians and Frenchmen, de Callières cried: *"Voici la paix. Oublions le passé"* (Peace is here, let us forget the past).

Peace had come, yes. But it was not destined to last for long. ❏

LEFT: tranquillity in 1791. **RIGHT:** Jean de Brébeuf, a Jesuit priest who worked among the Hurons, is tortured to death by the Iroquois.

Religious Roots

Perhaps more than any other North American city, Montreal exudes the ambience of a community where church and state were long and enduring bedfellows. As you pass by Montreal's numerous churches, centuries-old hospitals, and houses for various religious communities, pause for a moment just to recall the lives affected so irrevocably by 17th-century Catholicism.

The religious fervour of 17th-century France, which was marked by the creation of numerous religious orders and evangelizing groups, spilled

over into New France, which rapidly became populated by both old and new religious congregations.

As history painfully shows, however, colonies do not live by faith alone. In Montreal, Catholicism combined with fur and the *fleur-de-lis* to form the defining triptych of the city's early history, and this medley led to an ecclesiastical power and control unprecedented in North America, a power that remained relatively undiminished until the "Quiet Revolution" deep in the 20th century.

Ever since Sieur de Maisonneuve planted a towering crucifix in thanksgiving for Ville Marie's survival of a flood at the end of 1642 *(see page 26)*, Montreal has struggled to integrate its political and religious interests.

New France was envisioned as both a source of wealth for France and as a North American beachhead for the Counter (or Catholic) Reformation – an attempt by the Roman Catholic church to respond to the rapid and lasting emergence of the Protestant reformers.

The Jesuits were among the first missionary orders to brave the frigid but fertile colony of New France. Their missions in South America, Ethiopia, Russia, India and China were well-known, and their fame led not only to a steady flow of vocations, but also to handsome donations from well-endowed patrons.

Called "Black Robes" by the Native Americans, the Jesuits sought converts among the Iroquois and Huron peoples. Unfortunately they had not received a formal invitation from the objects of their conversion, and for many of these missionaries their vocations ended in martyrdom. During the 1650s, the Iroquois attacked Quebec City, Trois-Rivières and Montreal, the three centres of the French fur trade along the St Lawrence River. Montreal, which was a natural "command centre" for the fur trade, was saved from being virtually wiped out by the efforts of Adam Dollard and 16 companions, who perished in a stand against several Iroquois war parties on the Ottawa River.

Upon learning of these attacks, the "Sun King" Louis XIV bestowed his radiance upon his valuable but besieged outpost. In 1661, he declared the small community of under 2,000 settlers a royal province, and dispatched 1,000 troops to protect the colony.

All public appointments were, from 1663, handled by the crown. The governor – the "intendant" (who maintained the royal authority and oversaw economic development) – joined with the Roman Catholic bishop to form the Sovereign Council, which meant that in New France, unlike the British colonies, cross and sword united to block any embryonic democratic initiatives; the separation of church and state was unthinkable.

Bishop Laval was quite happy to pick up the political mantle that was proffered him by the king. As chief prelate from 1649 to 1688, this ascetic cleric secured vast lands for the church. He also established a seminary (the forerunner of Quebec's Laval University) and controlled education in the colony.

Another major figure in the ecclesiastical educational system of Montreal was Marguerite Bourgeoys (1620–1700), who was to become Canada's first female saint. A dramatic amalgam of courage, compassion, and conviction, Marguerite set sail for Montreal in 1657 with Sieur de Maisonneuve, 100 men, and a handful of girls and women. During the undulating passage, she served as nurse, prelate, and mortician, nursing the eight men who died of plague during the voyage and preparing them for watery graves.

Marguerite, who eventually founded the Congrégation de Notre-Dame, counselled, catechized, and cared for many of the 1,000 *filles du roi* who streamed to New France between 1665 and 1673. In a French colonial version of "Here Come the Brides", King Louis XIV sponsored the migration of these young girls to the colony, to help populate New France.

In a further effort to increase the number of French settlers on its small snowy domain, the crown granted baby bonuses, penalized bachelors, and provided handsome pensions for fecund parents. Parents were also required by law to have their sons married by the age of 18 or 19, and their daughters had to be betrothed by 14 or 15.

In many ways, the church was attempting to build a more Catholic France in North America, a new "city on the hill" that would somehow be more pristine than its European counterpart. Marguerite Bourgeoys was the trump card played by the church in this enterprise.

Dubbed "mother of the colony", Marguerite, in addition to chaperoning the *filles du roi*, recruited French and Canadian girls as teachers, organized a boarding school and established a school for Indian girls on the Sulpician reserve of La Montagne, as well as a domestic arts school. As a guardian of virgins, Marguerite was well aware of the dangers of the opposite sex in a colony where women were a scarce and precious resource. Although Bishop Laval refused to allow her and her co-workers to take religious vows, they were eventually permitted in 1671 to become a non-cloistered religious community. Although she was widely considered by her peers to be a saint when she died in 1700, Marguerite was not officially canonized by the church until October 1982.

Today you can see where Marguerite welcomed the king's wards at Maison Saint-Gabrielle (on rue Favard). Built in 1688, this served as a farm centre, an elementary school and, finally, as the first school of domestic arts for young women in New France. Part of the present-day structure dates back to 1698.

Perhaps no-one more epitomized the strength of the missionary church than Abbé François Dollier de Cassons, Superior of the Sulpicians in Montreal. A towering figure *(see page 28)* he could apparently lift two men simultaneously, one in each hand. While praying on his knees one evening by the Bay of Quinté, it is said, Dollier de Cassons was harangued by a young Indian, who mocked him with obscenities. Without getting up, the forceful cleric shot out his right arm and sent the brave sprawling. He finished his prayers uninterrupted.

Dollier de Cassons built the Sulpician Seminary

at Place d'Armes. Begun in 1680, this is the oldest building in Montreal and one of the oldest in North America. It is now a retirement home for the religious community.

The work of religion – in education at every level, and in ministry to the sick, the impoverished, orphans and the elderly – has been of central importance to Montreal's history. Throughout the city, religious schools, hospitals and seminaries are among the oldest, most enduring institutions.

The tenacious grip of medieval Christendom on Montreal eventually began to relax, however, after 1950 when Government intervention in the areas of health and education was followed by the effects of the "Quiet Revolution" *(see page 58).* ❏

LEFT: Montreal has a rich heritage of religious statuary. **RIGHT:** Tiffany window in the Erskine and American United Church, built in 1863.

THE COMING OF THE BRITISH

Montreal was always seen as a prize by both the British and Americans.
As a result, the British mark on this French city is unmistakable today

After the peace of 1701 between the French and the Indians, Montreal rebuilt itself, dropped the name of Ville Marie, and concentrated on becoming the trading centre its location seemed always to promise. The pursuit of the beaver pelts was furious, sometimes unscrupulous, and almost always at the expense of Indians on the lookout for European liquor, guns and utensils. Traders typically exchanged goods for pelts at far below market price, reserving the massive profits for themselves and exploiting the Indian trappers who had risked life and limb to bring in the pelts.

The lure of quick wealth was too much for most early Montrealers to resist, and "everyone turns trader", a contemporary traveller noted. The aging Dollier de Cassons wrote of the fur trade gloomily, describing "the diabolical attractions" of quick wealth and the resulting *"perdition générale"* of Montreal. Even Montreal's clergymen ventured out to the trading stalls beyond the city gates to barter their utensils and equipment for furs that would bring massive profits in Europe.

The Indians, however, were not the only ones to pursue the beavers into their habitat. Toughened *coureurs de bois* – French woodsmen skilled in the arts of paddling and trapping – steered fur-heavy canoes into Montreal harbour and looked for a good price. Some of these hardy souls had "gone native" and barely appeared French to the civilized denizens of Montreal. Their supplies sold off, they and the Indians would proceed to get roaring drunk on cheap liquor, collapsing in dirty heaps or copulating, fighting and drinking until dawn.

In 1721, the town fortifications were improved with 5.5-metre (18-ft) stone walls, bastions, a citadel and more cannons. The wooden buildings inside the walls, always at risk of fire, were replaced in accordance with building regulations that called for stone walls

and roofs of slate, tile, or tin. "The town has suffered by fire very materially at different times," the traveller Isaac Weld wrote some time later, "and the inhabitants have such a dread of it, that all who can afford it cover the roofs of their houses with tin-plates instead of shingles. By law they are obliged to

have one or more ladders, in proportion to the house, always ready on the roofs."

Drama and dancing

For almost five decades the little town boomed, its *seigneurs* and traders gradually becoming wealthier as the demand for beaver furs grew in Europe. In the long winter months, leisure time was unlimited and the Ramezays, Vaudreuils, and other prosperous families of Montreal enjoyed amateur theatricals, dancing, and so-called sugaring-off picnics in which a festive party sledded out to the maple forests to collect sap for maple syrup. The more prosaic *habitants*, at least as portrayed by sentimental

LEFT: Wolfe's troops attacking the city of Quebec in 1759. **RIGHT:** fur trappers and traders were lured by the promise of quick wealth.

artists such as Cornelius Krieghoff (1812–72), loved to dance, play cards (a pursuit officially banned by the church), and drink heavily. Krieghoff is perhaps the best known of the artists who chronicled the scenes of daily life in early Quebec. His paintings are seen frequently on posters, postcards and, memorably, the label of a brand of Canadian whisky.

End of the peace

It was 1756 when the Seven Years' War brought an end to the prosperous peace. Armed conflict, this time between French and English, once more ruptured Montreal. The English, long machinations that prevented an all-out effort on the part of France to keep its colonies. Richelieu's influence was long gone, and the desire for imperial might was waning in a France wracked by internal difficulties and facing battles with English and Prussian soldiers on its own land. (The satirist Voltaire conveyed one prominent attitude to France's colonial adventure when, in *Candide*, he famously dismissed New France as "a few acres of snow".)

French defeat at Quebec City

The English and French forces met in a decisive battle in Quebec City in 1759. The French com-

eager to get a foothold in North America and the riches it promised, ran up against the well-oiled imperial designs first proposed by Richelieu. Neither side had any illusions about their colonial ambitions, despite the rhetoric of religious conversion habitually used by the French.

The English, after several abortive attempts to oust the French, massed their efforts in the middle of the 1750s, attacking first at Ticonderoga. Louis-Joseph, Marquis de Montcalm, ruled the French forces from his headquarters in Montreal and scored an impressive short-handed victory at this first battle site.

The English forces were superior, however, and they were not hampered by the political mander, Montcalm, defending a stout fort, did not reckon on a flanking manoeuvre. The English went upriver past the city, scaled the cliffs, and surprised the French forces from the rear. Montcalm was defeated and killed on the Plains of Abraham by the British general, James Wolfe, who also died there.

Montreal surrenders

In September 1760, the British general Lord Jeffrey Amherst entered Montreal through the Récollet gate and was met by Vaudreuil, the governor of New France, who formally surrendered. The British flag flew over Montreal for the first time on September 9, 1760. In

1763, under the Treaty of Paris, France ceded its territories to Britain, ending the era of French control in Montreal.

Despite this enormous change in political direction, daily life did not alter much for the average Montreal inhabitant. The British governors were sensitive to the fact that several generations of Frenchmen were responsible for whatever European civilization, trade and development the colony enjoyed. No land was stripped from the *seigneurs*, and the Quebec Act

> ### UNDERGROUND RAILWAY
> From this time on, and especially in the decades immediately befoe the American Civil War, Montreal was a frequent destination of slaves trekking to freedom on the so-called Underground Railway.

Montreal was still a boom town, on whose streets leather-clad *coureurs de bois* (woodsmen), fresh from the river portages and Indian camps, rubbed shoulders with Scottish merchants, English soldiers, and aristocratic French *seigneurs*.

New civil regulations also marked the influence of English bureaucrats on Montreal. In 1765, the price of a four-pound white loaf of bread (a "brick") was fixed at eight coppers; bakers could not charge more than 10 coppers for the heavier brown loaf.

of 1774 accepted the French language and Roman Catholic religion as essential parts of Quebec culture.

A cosmopolitan mix

But by this time one could hear a broad Scottish burr on the streets of Montreal, and the haughty bleat of English nobility. The demographics of the city changed radically during the next generation as the population exploded with an exuberant commercial eagerness.

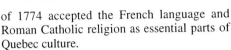

LEFT: the *Habitants*, portrayed by Cornelius Krieghoff. **ABOVE LEFT:** the death of Wolfe at the battle for Quebec City. **ABOVE RIGHT:** toe-tapping amusement.

Slavery was also a prevailing concern, and the governors thought it best to distance themselves officially from the buying and selling of humans so widely prastised in parts of the republic to the south. It was decreed that "no tavern, alehouse or innkeeper do receive, harbour, or entertain any bond or servant slave or slaves, drinking, gaming or loitering in their houses, under a penalty of £5".

Desirable target

The strategic position of Montreal – Dollier de Cassons had called it "the dyke of Canada" – made it a desirable military target, and during the American Revolution (1775–83) the city once again came under attack. The first American overture was a failure. In 1775 the garrison at Montreal heard that Ethan Allen and his famous "Green Mountain Boys" were marching along the Longue Pointe road, just east of the city.

A small force of English and French soldiers advanced to challenge the invaders, and Allen was easily defeated and captured. The garrison commandant, an old soldier called Prescott, threatened to cane the arrogant Allen, and he had to be dragged off by his men. Allen was imprisoned on board the ship *Gaspé*, moored in harbour, and Montrealers rejoiced at having

Americans failed to reckon with other ideas of freedom; Montrealers were happy and prosperous under the British, and mocked the American deliverance and its agents. The Americans, on the other hand, found Canadian notions of liberty "monstrously ill-digested" and soon regarded the Montrealers as "rascals and enemies" and even "dam'd Tories".

Peace breaks out

Benjamin Franklin arrived in 1776 to smooth over these rough spots and court possible annexation. He tried to convince French Canadians to join the American revolutionary cause

"caged the great New Hampshire incendiary".

However, the jubilation was short-lived, for in the autumn of 1775 General Richard Montgomery advanced towards the city with a much larger force, and the governor, Sir Guy Carleton (later Lord Dorchester), was compelled to surrender without resistance.

American occupation

The attitude of the Americans was that the occupied people should be overjoyed to be freed from the shackles of colonial rule. Montrealers were invited to "seize the opportunity presented to you by Providence itself" and join the not-quite-Continental Congress. But the

against England, but his overtures were rejected and he withdrew.

The Americans finally left in 1783 when Britain massed a large army near Montreal, and a peace treaty was signed with the new United States republic the same year.

Perhaps the only palpable benefit of the American occupation was that one of Franklin's associates, a propagandist called Fleury de Mesplet, decided to stay on and ply his printing trade in Montreal.

In a shop on rue de la Capital, a narrow lane off rue St-François-Xavier, he began producing Canada's first newspaper, *La Gazette du Commerce et Littéraire*. In 1788 the paper was printed in English as well as French, a concrete indication that English had arrived in the city.

Scottish influence

Many other commercial enterprises began in these decades to serve the needs of the wealthy fur traders and their employees, and at the same time the influx of United Empire Loyalists fleeing the anti-monarchist revolution to the south swelled Montreal's population. The focus of the town shifted away from the harbour and toward what is now downtown Montreal.

NEWS IN ENGLISH

You can still pick up a copy of the *Gazette* today – founded in 1788, it is now Montreal's main English-language daily newspaper.

In 1783 a group of them founded the North-West Company, a fur-trading cooperative begun in order to challenge the hegemony of England's Hudson's Bay Company. The Nor-Westers were absorbed by the Hudson's Bay Company in 1821, but for decades it raced them to the fur trade in the west and north of Canada.

Just as their names would go down in history on the maps of the region, the Nor-Westers left their mark on their home base of Montreal. The city's main English-speaking university is built on land bequeathed by Edin-

The city's new aristocracy was largely Scottish in origin, and it included many enterprising rogues who had taken advantage of the wide-open colonial life to make their vast fortunes in fur trading.

Simon McTavish, Joseph Frobisher, William McGillivray, James McGill and Simon Fraser were the stars in Montreal's social and commercial firmament in this era. Their names also dot the rivers and regions of western Canada, which they were the first to explore.

LEFT AND ABOVE: Montreal continued to boom in the decades after the Treaty of Paris, and trade was brisk in such commodities as ice blocks and timber.

burgh University graduate James McGill, who wanted the colony to have "an English college on a liberal scale".

With $10,000 and the 18 hectares (45 acres) of land known as Burnside, nestled at the foot of Mont Royal, the oldest of Montreal's four universities was founded in 1821.

The original building on the campus still stands at the end of the drive. Now the Arts Building, this austere neoclassical structure designed by architect John Ostell, was McGill University's only building for three decades.

When classes commenced the college site was still countryside, and its 20 hardy students tramped across fields full of crops and grazing cattle to reach the fount of wisdom. They had to dress "in plain, decent and comely clothes, without superfluous ornament" and wear gowns to their lectures on medicine, classics and mathematics. Throughout the century the institution was one of the brightest jewels of Montreal's Scottish bourgeoisie and is still one of Canada's finest educational establishments.

Beaver Hall Hill, site of Canada's first men's club, also owes its name to the Nor-Westers. Membership in the Beaver Club was restricted to those who had wintered in Canada's wilderness, *le pays d'en haut*, and during the long Montreal winters the adventurers would gather

here to tell tall stories, drink whisky and sing the canoeing songs of the old *voyageurs*, paddling away for all they were worth with their walking sticks, fire tongs or dress swords. The minutes of one dinner meeting, for February 28, 1809, recorded that the 24 attending members drank 38 bottles of wine as well as 26 bottles of beer in what must surely have been an extremely rowdy evening.

The grand houses of the new fur lords, dwarfing the châteaux of the early *seigneurs*, were sited away from the town in the elevated environs of Westmount and Mont Royal itself. The name Westmount is still synonymous with privilege and old money in Montreal society.

Biculturalism

While these Scottish "lords of lake and forest", the "hyperborean nabobs" of the fur trade (as Washington Irving had enthusiastically called them), spoke English among themselves, most were bilingual, the result of necessary traffic with their *voyageur* paddlers and, in some cases, of Scotland's Auld Alliance with France against the English.

Many of these Scots, including McTavish, McGill and Frobisher, also married French Canadians. They were models of biculturalism in action, happy in a city still essentially French. It was not until the spring of 1786 that an English play, Goldsmith's *She Stoops to Conquer*, was performed in Montreal by a professional troupe from Albany, New York. No other play is mentioned in the history of Montreal for almost 13 years, so presumably English-style drama did not appeal to the tastes of these northern hearties.

Molson's brewery opens

In the same year, 1786, the Englishman John Molson opened his brewery on the banks of the St Lawrence. He also established a small shipping line that was to expand quickly during the next 50 years. Molson, who was a great favourite among the French *habitants* along the river, is an appropriate emblem for this golden age of commercial Montreal. Starting out with almost nothing in the new colony, he made his vast fortune by working hard to meet the simple needs of its inhabitants. He is reputed to have said that "An honest brew makes its own friends" – a slogan found on his family's beer bottles to this day. When the brewery opened, a bottle of strong beer cost 5 cents while mild ale went for 7 cents.

Molson also built Montreal's first hotel and its first commercial theatre, the Théâtre Royale.

Molson's brewery was the first to be built in North America and, while the steamship line that used to run his two ships – the *Accommodation* and the *Swiftsure* – between Quebec and Montreal is long gone, you can still enjoy Molson's lager or ale in any Canadian tavern. The Molson family continues to play a prominent, if less visible, role in Montreal. ❑

LEFT: society women in 18th-century New France.
RIGHT: British troops took decisive control after Wolfe won Quebec and General Amherst entered Montreal.

Habitants

Imagine yourself a very long way from home, so far away that the prospect of returning is next to impossible. You are in a strange land, known for its fierce winters and covered by a tenacious, seemingly impenetrable forest. You will be the first to settle the new colony – you will plan your settlement without really knowing much about the country, taking risks, experimenting, and desperately hoping that all will turn out well.

You will give birth to your children on the kitchen table, perhaps, but not always, with the help of a

midwife, and each day you will toil to provide the necessities of life: preparing meals, making soap and candles, mending and washing clothes.

At the end of your days your face will betray the marks of a rough life outdoors and of bearing too many children, and your hands will show the scars of many harvests.

But you will have lived an honest life, even a prosperous life – the life of a French Canadian *habitant* or *habitante*.

No one could possibly envy the hardships the first French Canadians faced in their new land – the bitter and lonely winters, unpredictable crops, the relentless necessity of becoming self-reliant. These were all things every Canadian pioneer con-

fronted. But the French managed to settle along the St Lawrence in a unique fashion and, in so doing, founded a truly distinct society.

New France's first permanent homesteads (evidence of which can still be seen today) were uniquely linked to the available and so-crucial water sources. The original plots were very long, narrow strips of land with one end facing the St Lawrence River. In the original settlements, this water frontage was usually 200–250-metres (655–820-ft) wide, with the plot stretching away from the river to a depth of several kilometres.

Following a French feudal model, colonization in French Canada used *seigneurs* – usually merchants, soldiers, priests and gentlemen farmers – as principal real estate agents for frontier properties. Usually a large tract was granted to a *seigneur* who promised the French crown he would settle the land. Once *habitants* (farmers) were found, they were given tenancy on the land and the responsibility to build a house, harvest crops each year, pay rent (*cens*) and fringe benefits (usually a yearly ham or a tub of butter) to the *seigneur,* as well as agreeing to the *corvée* (a feudal service) that most often involved construction and road work. In return, the *seigneur* erected a mill and oven, handled disputes, and tried to nurture an environment of bucolic prosperity.

The narrow plots along the river became the fundamental social unit of early French Canadian culture, and they profoundly influenced the way in which New France emerged. The linear settlement pattern with houses clustered along the waterfront established a compelling solidarity among the *habitants*. Few other colonies in Canada developed this kind of built-in interdependency. As one historian has noted, the uniformity of these narrow lots created a "peculiar social equality among households" with mutual assistance playing a key role in the community. As a result, French Canada never suffered from the rise of the large estate and the divisive social stratification associated with it. (This was seen as recently as 1998, when a punishing ice storm shut down the city *(see page 53).*

One institution reflecting the importance of neighbours was the *premier voisin* (first neighbour), usually the head of the next-door family. Invited to most family functions and included in all important decisions, the *premier voisin* helped out with any major project and was called upon for help when any emergency arose. In return, his family always received a loaf of bread on baking day or a slab of meat during the slaughtering season.

The life of the farmer in France was, in many ways, remarkably suited to Canada. Both France and the St Lawrence region were good dairy countries with few milk-souring heat waves and possessed soils suitable for growing *légumes*, root crops, hay and fruits rather than cereals. The core diet of the *habitants* strongly echoed the typical fare of a French peasant, with a few changes: peas and pork became central ingredients in many dishes, particularly in the form of a daily staple: pea soup.

One 18th-century trader recorded the recipe for this now famous French Canadian dish: "The tin kettle in which they [a group of fur traders] cook their food would hold eight to ten gallons. It was hung over the fire, nearly full of water, then nine quarts of peas – one quart per person, the daily allowance – were put in; and when they were well bursted, two or three pounds of pork, cut into strips, for seasoning, were added, and allowed to boil or simmer until daylight when the cook added four biscuits, broken up, to the mess, and invited all hands to breakfast. The swelling of the peas and biscuits had now filled the kettle to the brim, so thick that a stick would stand upright in it... The men now squatted in a circle, the kettle to the mouth, with almost electric speed, soon filled every cavity" (from Edith Fowke's *Folklore of Canada*).

In New France, the *habitants* could supplement their diet with game, particularly wild hare and venison, as well as an abundant supply of fish from the St Lawrence River.

Eels, which were considered a delicacy in France, were more readily available and were eaten raw, smoked, dried and stewed.

The folklorist Edith Fowke notes that the *habitants,* following an old French recipe, would simmer the molluscs in cream along with cider, salted pork and onions. British colonists to the south imported this recipe, where it was to become New England clam chowder.

In the new colony, milk became a core part of the French peasant's diet and was used in the preparation of almost every meal. In one popular dish, milk was boiled, then chunks of bread were thrown into it along with great quantities of maple sugar. The soggy mixture was spooned out into bowls and eaten as a kind of bread pudding in the evening. These game and milk dishes were

rounded out by wild berries, garden vegetables, especially carrots, onions, cabbage, turnips and eventually potatoes.

Cabbage dishes were also popular because, according to French folk medicine, cabbage cured venereal diseases, increased a mother's milk, and prevented hair from falling out.

The *habitants'* daily menu consisted of a breakfast of pancakes, bread, salted pork and cider (until replaced by coffee and tea). A noontime lunch of pea soup with fried potatoes and a garden vegetable followed.

At around 4 o'clock in the afternoon, leftovers from lunch would be consumed, accompanied by a

cucumber salad and bread smeared with either pork fat or butter. The final meal of the day was eaten at eight or nine o'clock in the evening, when a bowl of bread cooked in milk and sugar would be served along with cider.

Although today's French Canadian diet has changed drastically from that of the *habitants*, many of the old foods associated with holidays are still remarkably popular: *tortières*, meatball stew, sausages, onion sauce, maple sugar candies and doughnuts among them. Even by today's health-conscious standards, Canada's first European settlers had a healthy diet that was well balanced in calories and protein and, with few exceptions, pleasing to the average palate. ❑

LEFT AND RIGHT: the French Canadian *habitants* and *habitantes* settled along the St Lawrence in a unique fashion, founding a truly distinct society.

CONFLICT AND CONFEDERATION

Canada's two contentious cultures inevitably clashed –
and eventually made peace – in Montreal

With the ambitious Americans to the south, peace was unlikely to endure in Montreal. War came once more in October 1813, when 5,000 troops under Major-General Hampton advanced on Montreal from the west. A decisive battle was fought at Chateauguay, where fewer than 1,000 Canadians, commanded by Lieutenant-Colonel Charles de Salaberry, defeated the Americans.

Although Montreal was the first city of Canada, both commercially and strategically, the main battles of the War of 1812–14 were fought in Ontario. But Montreal did feel the effects, if only psychological ones, of the unrest in the threat of "Fenian raids".

The Fenians, Irish Americans whose name comes from the Irish motto *Sinn Fein* (which translates as "Ourselves Alone" and is today the name of the Irish Republican Army's political wing), harassed settlers all along Canada's southern border during the 1812–14 war and after America's bloody Civil War (1861–65).

The sallies of the Fenians never amounted to anything like an invasion, though Montrealers lived in daily fear of having their throats cut by savage Irishmen.

One of their marching songs gives a better idea of their motives and mien:

We are the Fenian brotherhood, skilled in
  the arts of war
And we're going to fight for Ireland, the
  land that we adore,
Many battles we have won, along with the
  boys in blue
And now we're going to conquer Canada –
  because we ain't got nothing else to do.

But the Fenians did have some bite, as Canadians learned in the early morning of April 7, 1868. Thomas d'Arcy McGee, one of the Fathers of Confederation, was on his way home from an all-night meeting when he was shot and killed outside his house in Ottawa by

agents who claimed to be connected with the Fenian cause. This had the dubious distinction of being the first political assassination in Canadian history. As news of the murder travelled, a huge crowd of mourners gathered to wait for the arrival of d'Arcy McGee's body at Montreal's Bonaventure Station.

Post-war progress

A salutary effect of the War of 1812 was that its threat to Canada's economy hastened the founding of the colony's first bank, the Bank of Montreal, which was chartered in 1817.

The war had also indicated the very real danger of moving men and supplies past the Lachine Rapids when time was of the essence; nobody had successfully navigated the rapids that had stopped Cartier, and they remained extremely arduous. In 1821, with money "panhandled" from the provincial and British governments, the Lachine Canal was completed – almost 200 years after it had first been suggested by the far-sighted Dollier de Cassons.

Left: the men's snowshoe club turned essential winter footwear into an excuse for social activity.
Right: John Macdonald, Canada's first prime minister.

Improvements were also evident on the city streets, lit from 1815 onward with gas lamps. The purpose of this innovation appeared to be mostly social – a decree said the lamps were installed so "that ladies might be induced to visit their friends much more frequently".

Also in this period (1832), the City of Montreal was incorporated, and its first mayor, Jacques Viger, was elected the following year. Viger completed a grand term in office, performing Montreal's first census and donating the land for Viger Square, Montreal's most popular park, between the 1860s and 1890s.

Montreal's first mayor also coined the city motto, *Concordia Salus* (Health lies in Concord), giving it the distinctive coat of arms that conjoins the national symbols of France, England, Scotland and Ireland. The Societies of St Jean-Baptiste, St Andrew, St Patrick and St George were all founded at this time. "Concordia Salus", certainly, but old ties still die hard.

Democratic demands

The prosperity and optimism of the 1820s and early 1830s were shattered by events that shook Montreal a few years later. The 1837 rebellions in Toronto and Montreal indicated that not everyone was satisfied with the colonial gov-

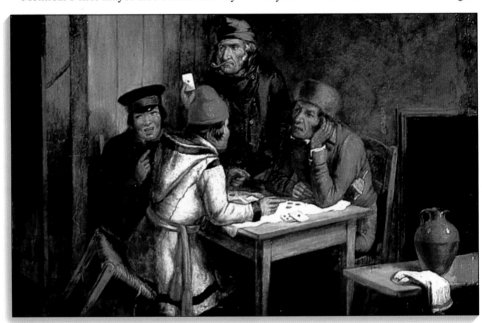

FIRST CAPITAL

Few Canadians or even Montrealers realize it, but for a brief shining moment the city served as the capital of an uneasy conjoining of Upper (Ontario) and Lower (Quebec) Canada. The feat was accomplished in 1843 when the British effected the Act of Union, thereby creating a unified Canada. Remarkably, each province received equal representation even though the English citizens of Canada by then far outnumbered the French.

The new Parliament began meeting in the conference rooms of Marché Ste-Anne, a trading hall on Place d'Youville. But in 1848 English rioters set the parliament buildings afire, burning them to the ground. The parliamentary meetings were moved, for a short time, to the elegant new Marché Bonsecours building just down the St Lawrence waterfront. But the ruling English had seen the writing on the wall and, only a short while later, the new nation's capital was moved from the distinctive silver-domed market to Toronto.

In 1857, Queen Victoria would move it again, to a surprising river town in the woods: Ottawa straddled the border between the provinces and was unknown enough not to inflame either side. The burning down of Marché Ste-Anne had ended Montreal's first and last taste of being in that particular political spotlight.

ernment and its encouragement for the rich to get richer. In Montreal, a group of reformers known as *les Patriotes*, led by, among others, Louis Joseph Papineau demanded the reform of a system that was to a large extent controlled by a clique of family interests. Representative government was a radical notion in these times, and the majority of people found the demands of the *Patriotes* unpalatable.

Britain refused to acknowledge the 92 resolutions drawn up by Papineau and his associates which demanded, among other things, the dissolution of the appointed governing Council of Lower Canada, known as the *Château Clique*

ravaged the population, and political clubs and duelling societies fomented the unrest by meeting publicly to argue and fight. On November 6, 1837, a fierce riot broke out on peaceful rue St-Jacques and spilled into Place d'Armes. After dark, the house of Papineau and the offices of the *Vindicator*, a newspaper supporting him, were wrecked. Two weeks of uneasy silence were broken by the imposition of martial law when Sir John Colborne, the commander-in-chief, set up his headquarters in the Château Ramezay and dispatched troops to hunt down the *Patriotes*. Many, including Papineau, fled to the United States.

(the reference is to Château St-Louis, Quebec's Government House). Papineau called for a council of elected representatives to replace the inbred and self-serving clique, which, like the Family Compacts controlling Upper Canada, doled out privilege and contracts with the arrogant disdain of absolute monarchs.

Violent riot

The atmosphere in Montreal was ripe for violence: cholera epidemics in 1832 and 1834 had

Tough justice

Others were not so resourceful. Twelve captured *Patriotes*, most of them young men who had worn, with a jaunty tilt, the white "O'Connell" top hat, a recognized badge of the radical, were publicly hanged by the authorities. Sixty or 70 more were banished, and Montreal's last sight of the rebellion was a chain gang of forlorn prisoners being marched down to the Bonsecours landing stage, there to embark on their long journey to New South Wales or Tasmania.

The sentences may seem harsh, but despite its new metropolitan status, Montreal was still a frontier town, and magistrates felt obliged to

LEFT: although forbidden by the Catholic church, 19th-century *habitants* enjoyed a game of cards.
ABOVE: a *habitant* urges his horse over the ice.

judge stiffly. In 1817, the crimes of sacrilege and shoplifting were still punishable by execution, as was the even more serious crime of horse-stealing.

Petty crimes were typically punished with humiliation in the stocks or the pillory, but judges were also in the habit of having small-time criminals branded on the palm of the hand with a heated iron. The brand, in the shape of a crown, was held to the flesh for as long as it took the convicted criminal to repeat "*Vive le roi!*" three times.

It was more likely to be "God save the King!" however, since the session lists from

Canada (today Ontario and Quebec) were joined in an Act of Union that was the beginning of modern Canada. In 1843 Montreal was made capital of the new united Province of Canada, but it enjoyed that honour for all too short a time – just five years *(see page 44)*.

Political setback

In 1848, while revolution was sweeping Europe, the reactionary element of Montreal sacked the Parliament Building and burned it to the ground after the legislators approved a bill to compensate *Patriotes* punished in 1837. The members of the house fled, leaving the building

these times show that the vast majority of tried criminals in Montreal were British or itinerant Loyalist Americans, and not francophone Québécois.

Modern beginnings

Britain's reaction to the trouble in the colonies was to dispatch the Earl of Durham to survey the state of public affairs there. Lord Durham's famous *Report on the Affairs of British North America* was the first document to isolate French–English tensions as a source of political worry in Canada.

In 1841, partly as a result of Durham's suggestions, the provinces of Upper and Lower

to be destroyed. The vandals, carrying the Speaker's ceremonial mace, ran through the streets and attacked the residences of the parliamentarians, including that of the governor general, Lord Elgin.

After this debacle, the Canadian parliament was moved to Toronto and alternated between that city and Quebec until a permanent site was chosen in Ottawa, on the banks of the Ottawa River.

A Boston newspaper gave a gloomy picture of the city in the 1840s: "Montreal wears a dismal aspect... the removal of the seat of government caused some 4,000 inhabitants to leave... every third store seems to want a occupant and empty houses groan for tenants." If that weren't enough, typhus brought to the city's harbour in 1847 killed more than 6,000 people; the Great Fire of 1852 – only the worst in a long series – lasted for 26 days, destroying 1,200 buildings and leaving 9,000 people homeless.

Commercial advances

Despite these setbacks, Montreal was well on its way to becoming what one contemporary called "the first city in magnitude

> ### HEALTHY WEATHER
>
> "The climate of Montreal, though severe in winter, is exceedingly conducive to health and longevity and the average mortality is much less than many other cities in North America."
>
> – Contemporary guidebook

building, based on Edinburgh's grand Bank of Scotland edifice, was erected in Place d'Armes by the Scot, David Rhind.

The railways came to Montreal in 1853 when the Grand Trunk Railway Co. began running a service to Portland, Maine, following it with a line to the still provincial city of Toronto in 1856.

A final event symbolizes this era of expansion and commercial vigour, when Montreal was the New York of Canada, its rue St-Jacques as important as

and commercial importance in British America". Although the fur trade was waning, the enterprising rich of Montreal had diversified their investments and Molson's steamship line was doing a good trade between Montreal and Quebec City.

The old harbour had been renovated by a number of energetic young builders, including Englishman John Ostwell, who at the tender age of 19 was given the job of designing the new Customs House. The Bank of Montreal

LEFT: Montreal's magnificent Notre-Dame Basilica was built in 1829, the towers being completed in the 1840s. **ABOVE:** sawing ice on the St Lawrence.

Wall Street. In 1860, Albert, the 19-year-old Prince of Wales (later King Edward VII), opened the magnificent Victoria Bridge.

Confederation

The stage was now set for Montreal to assume primacy of place in the new confederated Canada. In 1867, representatives of the colonies on the Atlantic coast decided to meet in Charlottetown, capital of Prince Edward Island, to discuss the prospects for a united Atlantic Colony. The leaders of Upper and Lower Canada, hearing of the conference to which they had not been invited, decided to crash the party and plead their own case. At the head of this group was John A. Macdonald, the wily, alcoholic Scotsman destined to be Canada's first prime minister. His slightly irresolute portrait now adorns Canada's $10 bill.

Macdonald and his cohorts chartered the *Queen Victoria* in Quebec City, loaded her with $13,000-worth of champagne, and steamed down the St Lawrence to Prince Edward Island. Despite a very modest reception – a single oyster boat – Macdonald was able, with the aid of his precious cargo, to persuade the Atlantic colonists that Canada should be part of any union. The rough terms for confederation were agreed upon at what one disgusted New

Brunswick editorialist described as "the great intercolonial drunk". They were later ratified at a conference in Quebec, and on July 1, 1867, the British North America Act created modern Canada by joining Nova Scotia, New Brunswick, Ontario and Quebec.

Scandalous deals

The new country was embroiled in scandal almost from the beginning. Macdonald quickly became involved in the Métis Rebellion scandal, an uprising that occurred when the government purchased Rupert's Land out west but neglected to take into account the indigenous population living there. The Métis were a mixture of French and Amerindian, and their leader, Louis Riel, won the sympathy of many Montrealers. When Macdonald decided to have Riel hanged, he was quoted as saying: "He shall hang though every dog in Quebec should bark in his favour."

Riel's death only served to entrench French–English hatred; he is still a hero today to legions of Quebec schoolchildren.

In addition, to hasten a railway link to western Canada and the Pacific, Macdonald and his colleague from Lower Canada, George-Etienne Cartier, had accepted party contributions from a group of Montreal businessmen who wanted the contract to build it.

The Canadian Pacific Railway (CPR) Bill was passed by Parliament in 1870 but the backroom dealing reached public attention soon afterwards. The focus of the scandal was Sir Hugh Allan, a prosperous Montreal shipper and owner of a massive estate called Ravenscrag. The estate's mansion is still standing. Today it houses the Neurological Institute of the Royal Victoria Hospital.

Incriminating telegram

With the CPR deal cut if not dried, Macdonald's ailing campaign was bolstered by "anonymous" gifts of money, first $60,000 and then $35,000. With his campaign in its final days, Macdonald foolishly wired Sir Hugh for more: "I must have another ten thousand. Will be the last time of calling. Do not fail me."

Sir Hugh considered the political financing simple tactics in good business, but the public did not see it that way. The office of Sir Hugh's solicitor in Montreal was ransacked late one night by a confidential clerk and, as a result, the incriminating telegram appeared on the front page of Montreal's newspapers. Macdonald and Cartier had to resign, and a despairing Cartier died the following year. Macdonald, a more accomplished political survivor, outlasted the public's short memory for wrongdoing and was back in office by 1878.

The railway was delayed, but not stopped. On June 28, 1886, with bands playing, the first passenger train steamed out of Montreal's old Dalhousie Station, bound for Port Moody, British Columbia. ❑

LEFT: Louis Riel, still a hero to legions of Quebec schoolchildren. **RIGHT:** the railway from Montreal to western Canada finally opened in 1886.

MODERN MONTREAL

As Canada's focus shifts towards Toronto, Montrealers still squabble over language and separatism – and try to forge a new economy

Montreal faced heady times. It was now indisputably the centre of the unified Canada, a Canada optimistic about its coast-to-coast railroad and its imminent entry into the 20th century. It was also arguably the most beautiful city in the country.

In 1868 an American visitor marvelled at the fine architecture of the town. "I am much struck," he said, "by the continued rapid growth of this now great northern city... The buildings everywhere in course of erection would dignify any city. There are none in the United States which present finer specimens of street architecture than are found, not isolated here and there, but in long blocks and throughout the city."

This aspect was most visible in the newly developed harbour, with a terrace of new buildings in the then-popular neoclassical style. Wealthy merchants from the old town moved their premises to larger lots on rue Ste-Catherine and rue Sherbrooke.

In 1891 Henry Morgan opened Canada's first department store, the Colonial House, later taken over by the Hudson's Bay Company.

Mixed blessings

But the glow of these golden years was dimmed by social inequity and industrial hardship. Montreal had several desperate, disease-ridden slums, of which Point St-Charles was the largest – a jumble of shacks housing the workers from Robert Griffin's soap factory and so known locally as Griffintown, a name it retained well into the 20th century.

Immigration was, from the late 19th century on, both blessing and curse. The cheap source of labour the immigrants provided for booming industry (now including huge grain elevators on the waterfront and heavier shipping) was welcome; but the population explosion posed serious difficulties for Montreal's housing and

sanitation resources. In 1825 the population of Montreal was 26,000; by 1850 it had doubled. By 1865 it had doubled again and the city passed the 100,000 mark. By 1910, Montreal's population was more than 500,000 and growing fast. The lot of many people was unremittingly hard: back-breaking factory work, tiny shacks

to live in, the constant threat of epidemics.

The new Montrealers came from everywhere: from Ireland fleeing famine, from eastern Europe, from China, from Greece, Italy and Portugal. And they followed the pattern being established in cities across North America. While the older inhabitants moved farther from harbour and train station – in the case of Montreal, farther up the hill – the new Montrealers put down their battered suitcases wherever, and as soon as, they could.

With this new diversification in Montreal, the old moneyed families increasingly began to shut their doors. In the 1890s Montreal was known as "the city of merchant princes", but

LEFT: the 20th century brought a building boom.
RIGHT: registering immigrants; they provided cheap labour but put a strain on Montreal's resources.

the princes were haughty. No longer did the aristocrats of Montreal walk the streets like James McGill, or even the garrulous Sir Hugh Allan.

Diverging cultures

Instead, they stayed in their Westmount estates, found others like themselves in exclusive new men's clubs like the Canadian and the Mount Royal, and moved around Canada's business counters from inside buildings that rose away from the downtown streets. Few bothered

> ### STRIATIC RECORD
>
> Today one can walk up boulevard St-Laurent, the fabled "Main" of Montreal, and map the waves of immigration: the Chinese on la Gauchetière, the European Jews near St-Urbain, the Greeks along avenue du Parc.

the national press and publicly decried as cowards. The same issue arose again during World War II. Whereas the war seemed to offer many English Canadians relief – and a job – the Québécois perceived themselves as once more bullied by imperial aggression overseas. Maurice Duplessis, premier at the time, argued that the federal government did not speak for French Canadians.

There was no easy solution. Jailing objectors was one option, but it risked creating martyrs.

to learn French as their grandfathers had, and the gap between rich and poor, and that between English and French, widened. The French still played the dominant role in Montreal's daily life, but the English minority controlled a disproportionate slice of the city's economy.

This animosity between French and English Montreal was then further exacerbated by the conscription controversy of World War I.

The Québécois men of Montreal had no particular quarrel with Britain's enemies, and many objected to being forcibly enlisted in the war effort. These so-called "zombies" became the scourge of Canada. They were vilified in

The federal government's inability to meet this crisis with effective measures became a symbol of its ongoing problem with the separatist sentiments among the Québécois.

The early English governors of Lower Canada had not faced the French fact squarely; now the easy mix of French and English that had marked Montreal's early history was gone. Economic disparity, the sense that control rested with a few privileged Westmount families, and the reality of Canada's growing anglophone population all contributed to a feeling among French-speaking Canadians that they were second-class citizens, considered a nuisance, and in danger of being assimilated.

Shifting focus

Moreover, by the 1950s, Montreal was no longer riding the strong wave of industrial and commercial success that had marked its entry into the new century. Canada's focus was shifting away from the river ports and towards the Great Lakes, especially Toronto. The historically strong bond that had existed between Montreal and New York – that had been present ever since John Jacob Astor had entered the fur trade in the 1820s by wooing ambitious Montrealers away from the Hudson's Bay and North-West companies – began to shift as well.

No longer did the wealthy of Montreal hire

dal Catholic society into a 20th-century democracy. Change, once slow to arrive, now worked its double-edged magic.

Emerging separatism

The church, no longer able to exert daily control, retreated in sulky seclusion. The descendants of Quebec's *habitants* were radicalized. Montreal and Quebec City, sites of the provincial government, became hotbeds of intellectual activity as the thinkers of Quebec society tried to find their footing in the shifting international terrain.

Separatism fomented in the seminar rooms

New York's celebrated architects to construct their massive monuments to themselves. Montreal was still a desirable place for a New Yorker to visit, but now for pleasure rather than business. If the high-rollers from New York wished to talk business, they now headed for dour, provincial Toronto and the gleaming towers of Bay Street.

Then, in the 1950s and 1960s the so-called "Quiet Revolution" *(see page 58)* began transforming the rural province from an almost feu-

LEFT: Canadian soldiers during World War I.
ABOVE: meteorologists call it an anomaly, Montrealers call it The Ice Storm, with capital letters to add impact.

THE ICE STORM

For five days in January 1998, a stationary trough of low pressure caused continuous rainfall over Quebec province. The temperature, just above freezing, sank at night, and the ice began to pile up. Thousands of trees and power lines snapped beneath the weight of the ice; city water mains burst; and several of the largest bridges onto Montreal Island were closed for safety.

As remarkable as the force of nature, however, was the way the people of this sometimes quixotic city pulled together to cope with their common fate. There was no violence or looting, no arguments over language. It was as if working together was the most natural thing.

of Université Laval and Université de Montréal, and in the cafés of the Grand Allée and rue Ste-Catherine. The prevailing feeling was that Quebec was culturally French, and always had been. Why, asked some, were the people of Quebec enduring a federalist government policy that failed to protect their culture and forced them, in effect, to become English?

Ottawa was conciliatory and threatening by turns, but matters did not come to a head until October 5, 1970, when the *Front de Libération du Québec* (FLQ) captured the British trade commissioner, James Cross. Five days later the FLQ kidnapped the Quebec labour minister,

Pierre Laporte, whose body was found two weeks later; Cross was eventually released. These acts of terrorism followed an extensive FLQ letter-bombing campaign and frequent calls for "Independence or Death!"

Waiting for the revolution

The Prime Minister, Pierre Trudeau *(see page 96)*, himself a Québécois and product of Laval's radical law faculty, but an ardent federalist, invoked the War Measures Act (Canada's equivalent of martial law) in this "October Crisis" for the first time during peacetime. The revolution, expected daily by the stu-

MUSICAL AIRPORTS

When are two airports not enough for a city? When they aren't used properly, according to Montrealers. Dorval was the city's original airport, constructed back in 1940 roughly 16 km (10 miles) west of downtown. To update its image for the coming Olympic Games and draw more business and tourist traffic, however, the powers that be decided to construct an elaborate new airport in the 1970s.

Mirabel began as one more of the city's grandiose projects of that decade – and, like many of its most visible public works, it has turned out to be an expensive failure. Built on a plain 56 km (35 miles) north of the city, near the foothills of the Laurentian Mountains, it opened in 1975 as

the largest passenger airport in the world, a good deal newer and more comfortable than its counterpart. But the city did not handle its abundance of runways well and, to this day, there is no direct rail link to downtown Montreal. Travellers must catch shuttle buses for an hour-long ride or else rent cars and fight the city traffic.

It came as no surprise, then, when in the mid-1990s the city announced it would be phasing out Mirabel as a passenger hub and using it almost exclusively for freight traffic. The latest plans concern $500 million-worth of improvements, mostly to aging Dorval – including, supposedly, the long-promised rail link to central Montreal.

dents on Montreal's streets, never came. Instead came the soldiers – 10,000 of them – ordered into Montreal on October 16.

But separatism was not quelled. The Parti Québécois (PQ), formed in 1968 by the dynamic journalist-turned-firebrand-politician René Lévesque, gained power in Quebec on November 15, 1976 and worked to bring the matter to a vote.

The PQ's 1980 referendum on "sovereignty-association" failed with the voters, but succeeded in driving many of the strong English minority from Montreal, where they had clustered for 300 years. Their companies quietly

International recognition

When, in 1967, French General Charles de Gaulle stood on a balcony of Montreal's City Hall and cried "*Vive le Québec libre!*" ("Long live free Quebec!"), it was heard not only across Canada but also around the globe.

Other, less controversial matters also brought the city world fame during this time. In 1967, to coincide with Canada's centennial celebration, the World's Fair was held in Montreal. Expo '67 brought millions of visitors, foreign and domestic, to Canada's most culturally diverse (if no longer most powerful) city. Aggressive politicking on the part of Montreal mayor Jean

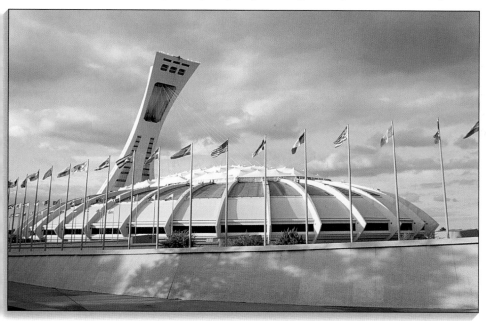

left Montreal during the 1970s and 1980s, setting up shop in Toronto instead, thus sealing Montreal's commercial fate: it had been demoted to the position of Canada's second city. Between 1976 and 1981, an estimated 100 head offices left Montreal, taking about 14,000 jobs with them. If Montreal business had been sputtering in the 1950s and 1960s, it was now in a tailspin. However, the separatism issue did bring Montreal and Quebec to the attention of the world.

Drapeau then brought the city the 1976 Summer Olympics. After the disaster of Munich in 1972, when terrorists murdered members of the Israeli team, the Montreal Games were a massive success and much-needed boost. Most of the Olympic visitors cared little that the city had overspent vastly on the facilities, or that the Olympic Stadium was – and is still – unfinished according to the original plans (*see page 209*).

Failed accords

With the defeat of the Parti Québécois in the 1980s, Quebec's political focus shifted away from strong separatism to demanding increased

LEFT: Ile Ste-Hélène was enlarged in the 1960s in preparation for Expo '67.
ABOVE: the stadium built for the 1976 Olympics.

participation in the Canadian confederation. The 1987 Meech Lake constitutional accord guaranteed Quebec's right to "a separate and distinct culture" – and its failure to be ratified in 1990 revived hostility between French and English Canadians. Under Quebec's newly restrictive language law, known as Bill 101, merchants were not allowed to display English signs in their windows. Unilingual doughnut bags were seized, Harris tweed imports were stopped until a French translation was supplied, and windows displaying "Wet Paint" signs were smashed.

Slowly, the elements of new constitutional amendments, including a modified version of

the Meech Lake demands, culminated in a second accord, in 1992 at Charlottetown, Prince Edward Island. The accord was submitted to a national referendum, requiring majority support in all provinces. Four provinces, including Quebec, rejected it soundly. In the wake of the defeat, Prime Minister Brian Mulroney resigned and in an election soon afterwards the Liberals, under Jean Chrétien, took over the reins of power, with the separatist Bloc Québécois becoming the second largest party.

This surprise result boosted the fortunes of Lucien Bouchard, formerly a Progressive Conservative environment minister who had quit over the failure of Meech Lake and founded

the Bloc Québécois. The son of a truck driver from the northern forestlands of Lac St-Jean, he became the most charismatic Canadian politician since Pierre Trudeau. The amputation of his left leg after he was attacked by a flesh-eating bacterium only served to enhance his charisma.

Until the next time...

Although himself a Quebecker, Jean Chrétien underestimated the strength of the separatist movement and was given a rude shock when, in a 1995 referendum, the proposal to grant Quebec independence was defeated by a wafer-thin margin of 1.12 percent. Quebec's separatist premier, Jacques Parizeau, resigned, but there was little for the "winners" to celebrate.

The high turnout of 93 percent of voters proved the strength of feeling on both sides, and the government in Ottawa had to face the fact that half of Quebec was seriously discontented. How long before the next referendum – and what would the result be? The answer from Lucien Bouchard (who became leader of the Parti Québécois in 1996) was unequivocal: "Keep hope," he told a dejected rally, "because the next time will be ours."

Politics in Quebec is not so simple, however. In April 1998 Daniel Johnston resigned as leader of the province's Liberal party and Jean Charest was persuaded to switch from leader of the federal Progressive Conservatives to leader of Quebec's Liberals. In November Bouchard called a sudden election. The Liberals' performance was less than inspiring, and pollsters unanimously predicted a massive defeat for the party. However, although the PQ won 75 seats compared to the Liberals' 48, the Liberals won the popular vote.

As a new millennium dawned and Quebeckers celebrated wildly in the streets of Montreal and elsewhere, they were prepared to give the PQ government yet another chance, perhaps, but their enthusiasm for another referendum seemed to have declined for the moment. They were looking forward with hope, together: to summer, to a new baseball season, to a new year. The squabbles of the past few decades seemed forgotten for an instant. ❑

LEFT: political signs are posted for the 1995 referendum. **RIGHT:** reflections of modern Montreal – the glass-sided BNP building.

The Quiet Revolution

Despite its many historic sites, Montreal will strike the visitor of today as a quintessentially modern place, a city of glass towers, busy streets, and cosmopolitan population. It was not always so.

In the years immediately following World War II, when most of North America was chugging happily towards the Space Age, the province of Quebec still resembled something like a medieval society. Montreal, its urban jewel, was run like an isolated city-state. Church interests dictated public policy

from back rooms, political corruption was rife, and the people lived in ignorance of a wider world.

The series of events that changed the face of modern Quebec, and made Montreal's reputation as Canada's most interesting city, are called in Canada "the Quiet Revolution" – an appropriate label in a country with little history of civil violence. Quebec's revolution was quiet, but it changed the province in profound ways.

If in today's Montreal you notice keen political debate in the newspapers and cafés and people taking advantage of the city's cultural opportunities, remember that it was not always possible. If you also notice that there are fewer black cassocks on the streets and more

churches sinking into disrepair – this, too, is the legacy of Quebec's social revolution.

Change, when it came, was swift. Quebec moved wholesale into the 20th century in just a few years (roughly 1960–65), with a handful of journalists, intellectuals and disaffected workers challenging the stagnation of the *ancien régime* with articles, debates and labour action. And what was the focus of these quiet revolutionaries of Quebec? The answer is not surprising. Reformist feeling on the streets of Montreal, as on the streets of Paris two centuries earlier, focused on two targets: the church and the state.

The Roman Catholic church, long a powerful force among Montreal's French Canadians and Irish, had found new strength in the mid-century influx of eastern European immigrants. It continued to play a role in Quebec life not significantly different from the days in the 18th century when prelates banned card playing and sacrilege was punishable by death. Rural and small-town inhabitants of Quebec lived in grinding poverty, deferring to the wisdom of parish priests and corrupt politicians, looking on Montreal and Quebec City as though they were foreign capitals instead of their own cities.

The church did little in those post-war years to dispel the ignorance and backwardness that held most of Quebec in thrall. The province's parish priests controlled most aspects of daily life, ruling rural Québécois with a combination of moral terrorism and personal authority.

Also, many of the province's most corrupt politicians learned their politics, as well as their theology, at the hands of Catholic educators, and were schooled early in the practice of annexing the moral high ground in debates on social policy.

Until the 1960s, political control of Quebec was lodged firmly in the hands of premier Maurice Duplessis (1890–1959) and his Union Nationale party. With a stranglehold on the provincial parliament – known as the National Assembly – Duplessis and his cronies were able to barter public works for votes, sell liquor and building licences for huge profits, and stretch their political tenure into a graft-ridden 16-year dynasty.

Duplessis had first been elected in 1937 and had guided disgruntled Québécois through the conscription crisis of World War II, articulating very well the isolationist stance most Québécois found persuasive. But from 1944 to 1960 the Union Nationale enjoyed absolute power in Quebec, and as a result allowed themselves the luxury of absolute corruption. A royal commission investigating the Union Nationale in 1961 estimated that more than $100 million-worth of graft had been paid out by companies doing business with the provincial government in these years.

Duplessis, a hysterical anti-communist, busted strikes with glee, enjoyed publicly humiliating his own ministers, and taunted his hapless opponents who could not promise the roads and hospitals he traded for votes.

Through all this, Quebec's powerful English minority remained unmoved; it was the journalist André Laurendeau who first suggested that they were actually supporting Duplessis as the province's *roi nègre*. The complicity of the English economic czars of Montreal suggested to Laurendeau, and to many others since, that Duplessis was a puppet – a "black king" allowed to rule a profitable colony by imperial interests jealous of their investments. While Duplessis was denouncing English businessmen in public, his tyrannical government was providing them with a very stable investment environment.

Still, the voters of Quebec have their own complicity to answer for; Duplessis did not stay in power because of the tacit approval of a few dozen powerful Montreal anglos. René Lévesque, who served in the Liberal government that overthrew the Union Nationale after Duplessis's death, called his reign *la grande noirceur* (the great darkness).

Duplessis's death in 1959 proved a catalyst to change beyond the walls of the provincial parliament. Rural Québécois discovered that ignorance and poverty were not divinely ordained conditions. The resentment building against the Duplessis government, in the universities and elsewhere, meshed a new liberal feeling that the moral totalitarianism of the church was outmoded and offensive. And the casual nexus between church and state was one of the first targets of this newly radicalized thinking, ending an era in which the parish priest would inform his parishioners of the "morally right choice" – the Union Nationale candidate – in provincial elections. Economic changes were also underway, and as Quebec's abundant natural resources (hydroelectric power, uranium and timber) became more valuable than ever in world markets, the Québécois began to experience fledgling fortune once again.

A kind of sexual revolution, related to the broad social changes happening across the United States and Europe, was also a driving force. The church could no longer exert unquestioned influence over previously devout Catholic young people who suddenly began living together without marrying, using contraception freely, and rarely attending church.

The nation, too, was changing. In 1965, to signal that the country had broken its firm ties with the British Empire tradition, the old Canadian flag, modelled on the Union Jack, was replaced by a Maple Leaf flag.

By the late 1960s, the new political feeling had gelled into strong Quebec separatism; the church

was either retreating into sullen isolationism or embracing the reforms of Vatican II; and the people of Quebec were enjoying a level of economic prosperity unimaginable a decade before.

As befits a quiet revolution – there were no barricades, no storming of prisons, no guillotines – Montreal today shows few tanglible signs of massive change.

But, seen in religious, political, social and economic terms, the revolution in Quebec's daily life was real enough: the *roi nègre* was dead. The *joie de vivre* that many Montrealers experience and express today has its roots in this "quiet" death of a quasi-theocracy that had dominated their culture for close to three centuries. ❑

LEFT: religion has exerted a powerful influence over Montreal and Quebec. **RIGHT:** signs of more liberal times – the annual Gay Parade on rue St-Denis.

A TALE OF TWO SOLITUDES

Montreal began as a divided city, and its two cultures developed along parallel fault lines. It resolved conflicts by mastering the art of compromise

Viewed from the south, Montreal reads like an open book. The left-hand page, spreading to the west, is in English. The right-hand page, opening to the east, is in French. But ethnic groups from all over the world populate the twin pages. Close the book, and the cover is in French. Yet the text is bilingual, with strong cosmopolitan accents.

Simple? Not really. Montreal is a city of obvious charm. It offers a gentle way of life exceptional in North America, and it is one of those rare cities with a lively downtown where an evening walk is perfectly safe. But Montreal is nonetheless a city of tensions – not racial but linguistic. They are resolved, day after day, in a lifestyle developed over the years by a population that has long since mastered the art of compromise.

Montreal is the second largest French-speaking city in the world (after Paris); the sidewalk cafés and the breakfast croissants are not considered at all exotic. It was built by Scottish merchants, whose Victorian homes remind you of London and Edinburgh. It is a city where, with French the official language, you can pass your whole life speaking nothing but English.

Diversified culture

Montreal is also an Italian, Greek, Vietnamese, Haitian, and Lebanese city; a city of the Ashkenazi Jews and the Sephardic Jews. You never have far to walk to find lemon grass or grape leaves, falafels or corned beef, saffron or marzipan, fresh pasta or Paris-style baguettes – not to mention the world's best bagels. (No, not in Manhattan, nor Brooklyn, will you find bagels more golden on the outside and more tender on the inside than those you buy fresh out of the old wood-stoked ovens in Montreal, whose recipe emanates from the *stetls* of Romania.)

In Montreal you can see French and Euro-

pean films while they're playing in Paris, and American films while they're playing in New York. This is a city where the newsstands bend under their stacks of dailies in French and English – from Montreal, from Paris, the *Times* of New York and the *Times* of London.

Here the TV offers several public and com-

mercial channels in French and English, plus the big US networks and another channel that re-broadcasts the best TV programs of France, Belgium and Switzerland.

The Montreal elite have always been unusually cosmopolitan. They read *Le Nouvel Observateur* and the *New Yorker*, Marguerite Yourcenar and Milan Kundera or Tom Wolfe, and they explore the universe with the open mind that comes from the practice of two languages and a long habit of life in a heterogeneous milieu.

With four universities (two French and two English), one English and three French daily newspapers, one French and two English

PRECEDING PAGES: Queen Victoria, symbol of British power and influence; re-enactment of traditional French military exercises. **LEFT:** café society. **RIGHT:** Scottish Highland Games at Douglas Hospital.

weekly newspapers; with a rich, challenging literature, serving up both the biting prose of Mordecai Richler and the lyricism of Réjean Ducharme; with its provocative avant-garde theatre and its vibrant motion picture industry that invariably pulls in the Canadian cinema prizes, Montreal can boast that it offers the most creative and most diversified cultural life in Canada.

Origins

The origins of Montreal lie in the St Lawrence River, from whose waters, in 1642, appeared the founders of the humble little French town

christened Ville Marie. The vestiges of Ville Marie are still to be seen, not far from the docks, in the beautiful stone buildings, humble chapels, and narrow paving-stoned streets of Old Montreal.

French Canadians are not a "minority" here as are the Puerto Ricans of New York, the Cubans of Miami, or the Asians of Los Angeles. The forebears of the *Montréalais* were the first European settlers in North America. Nor are French Canadians simply exiled French Europeans: from as early as the 17th century they established a society that was distinct from that of their European ancestors.

The city of Quebec, the only city in America

to be surrounded by ramparts like the fortified cities of Europe, was founded in 1608, when North America was a continent known only to the Amerindians and Inuit. This little cluster of colonists, trappers and adventurers dispatched the great *voyageurs* who discovered the Mississippi and the Rocky Mountains, and who founded the first colonies from which would issue the great cities of the northeastern USA.

In the United States, only Louisiana has retained some of the traits of the far-off days of French rule. In Canada, however, the descendants of the first French colonists have multiplied to form a mighty minority who live, learn and work in French – 6 million people, of whom 5 million are in the province of Quebec. With a total of more than 7 million inhabitants, Quebec is still the second most populous province in Canada, after Ontario.

Unique status

Canada is a federation, dividing its political power between the central government and the 10 provinces. Each province has its own parliament and relatively extensive powers, especially in education, health, and social affairs, as well as a goodly share of the economic ones.

Because the province of Quebec is the main home of the French Canadians and the only territory where they comprise the majority of the electorate, its successive governments have gradually acquired additional special powers, following upon accords with the federal government. Quebec is the only province that collects its own taxes, for example, and it maintains a network of delegations abroad functioning somewhat after the fashion of consulates. Quebec is likewise the only province whose official language is French.

One unintended result of all these special arrangements has been a sometimes impenetrable thicket of bureaucracy, which Quebec residents have come to take in their stride.

Sophistication and education

Montrealers today make up one of the most sophisticated populations on the continent. For the Québécois this has not always been the case, but in just a few years, beginning during the late 1950s, they decided to make up for lost time. They modernized their education system, took on more public responsibility, and shook off the tutelage of the church that had dominated them for so long. Once the "City of a Hundred Belfreys", Montreal became the cutting edge of this "Quiet Revolution" – appropriately named, since it was accomplished without civil violence *(see page 58)*.

Today, many of the city's old monasteries, convents and seminaries are condominiums, and its churches serve as recreation centres.

This period of intense intellectual and cultural ferment inevitably engendered a strong independence movement *(see page 53)* which, despite setbacks, continues to this day. Also, despite the adoption of language laws by various provincial governments – such as the controversial Bill 101, enacted in 1977 – requiring commercial signs to be written entirely in French, many francophones are still haunted by the fear of assimilation. This fear is all the greater now that demography is no longer on their side: the Québécois birth rate is among the lowest in the world.

Proud memories

Ironically though, it was the British who really developed Montreal. Under the French regime Montreal always played second fiddle to the city of Quebec. It was only with the English conquest of 1760 and the arrival of Scottish merchants that Montreal became the great metropolis of Canada – a position it retained up until the 1950s, when Toronto supplanted it as Canada's centre of commerce and finance.

The proud memory of this period remains in the beautiful Victorian buildings of the Golden Square Mile, that 19th-century fief of the first great Canadian businesses, and on the campus of McGill University *(see page 37)*, the first university of Canada, along rue Sherbrooke.

A great part of the architectural legacy of Montreal is of British inspiration. Indeed, Montrealers visiting London experience a sense of having been there before: a thousand-and-one details – in the architecture, the street map, and the statuary – remind them of their own city.

LEFT AND RIGHT: francophone social life centres around the sidewalk cafés, bistros, terraces and shops of rue St-Denis in the Latin Quarter.

Anglophones and francophones

In Montreal, the two great founding peoples of Canada live side by side. Of the 3 million inhabitants of the metropolitan area, some 70 percent are French-speaking, while 15 percent use English as their native tongue. The remainder of Montrealers are the more-or less recent immigrants who, with the passing of the years, have become integrated into one – and sometimes both – of the two great linguistic groups.

> **DIVIDED AFTER DARK**
>
> Montrealers even have parallel night lives. Anglophones frequent the pubs and clubs of Crescent and Bishop streets; francophone nightlife is in the cafés and bistros of rue St-Denis.

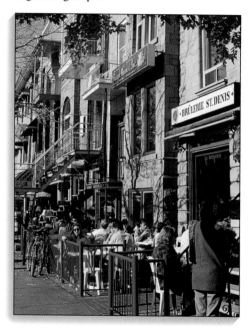

Coexistence has nearly always been peaceful. But the francophone and anglophone communities – the "two solitudes", as Canadian novelist Hugh MacLennan described them – have developed into parallel societies. They have emerged side by side without ever melding, each with its own schools, colleges and universities, hospitals, newspapers, novels, theatres, business communities and insurance companies. Each community has its own proletariat and bourgeoisie – the anglophone bourgeoisie is in Westmount, on the southwest slope of Mont Royal, while the francophone bourgeoisie is located in Outremont, on the northeast side of the same mountain.

However, these divisions are not cast in stone, and many Montrealers enjoy an occasional stroll on the "other side", becoming temporary tourists in their own home town. Francophones and anglophones meet at work, in business, or at Le Centre Molson, where they cheer with equal enthusiasm "their" hockey team, the Montreal Canadiens.

But Montreal resolutely remains a city of two solitudes; while there have been a number of intermarriages over the years, one language finally prevails in most partnerships, and the family is acculturated to one of the two language groups. This division obviously undermines the cultural potential of Montreal, and the misunderstandings engendered by mutual ignorance sharpen the linguistic tensions.

French, long considered to be the tongue of "peasants", has been the dominant language since the early 1970s, even in large private businesses. Francophones, who once found themselves relegated to second-class jobs, have vigorously asserted themselves in the business area, and now control a great proportion of Montreal's erstwhile anglophone institutions. Not all anglophones welcome this development, and not all francophones have forgotten the old vexations.

CIRQUE DU SOLEIL

To try to describe what Montreal's Cirque du Soleil (literally, "circus of the sun") does would be futile; it simply must be experienced. Each performance unfolds like a play, one act building upon the last, bringing home some theme – joy, life's fragility, impermanence, exuberance.

The circus began innocently enough, yet from small beginnings it has blossomed into one of the "greatest shows on Earth". It was 1982, in the streets of the artsy, scenic Quebec town of Baie-St-Paul, that a handful of performers formed a group of stilt walkers, jugglers and fire-eaters. Their impromptu street performances quickly blossomed into a travelling troupe performing intricately choreographed routines. The government of Quebec helped back the creation of a full-time, professional troupe based in a big top, and the Cirque was off and running, its high-flying theatrics winning many an international competition. Operations moved to Montreal in 1990, first occupying a structure on the extreme eastern end of the waterfront, near the enormous Molson Brewery.

Since then, the troupe has grown to 450 performers and nearly 2,000 employees, while taking up more or less permanent residence in Las Vegas, Orlando, Amsterdam and Singapore. Montreal is still the headquarters, though, out of a sleek new facility in the St-Michel district.

The basic problem is that each of the two communities perceives itself as a vulnerable minority. The anglophones, a majority in Canada but a minority in Quebec, see their numbers dwindling, and fear for the survival of their institutions. The francophones, a majority in Quebec but a minority in Canada, feel they are speaking an ever-threatened language. All this sparks endless political battles – battles which fortunately have remained verbal.

Don't be misled. Montreal is not Belfast. In daily living, Montrealers have developed the art of good-humoured coexistence. On St Patrick's Day, thousands of francophones don the green and descend to rue Ste-Catherine for the parade, celebrating with their anglophone fellow-citizens and cheering the floats that depict the history of the large Irish minority of Montreal, who have been a fixture here since the mid-19th century.

The French spoken in Montreal is shot through with English expressions, and Quebec English is laced with gallicisms. An anglophone Montrealer will speak of a manifestation instead of a demonstration, a cocktail for a cocktail party, a convention for a contract, and a *dépanneur* (or, even more briefly, a "dep") for a convenience store. And a Frenchman will speak of "le shock" of winter cold and planification to mean planning *(see page 132)*.

French lifestyle

The Protestant work ethic once fuelled Montreal's economic expansion; but it is the French influence that has especially marked its lifestyle. Montreal drinks to 3am and allows diners to bring their own bottles of wine into many of its restaurants. Local women have the reputation of being the most elegant and stylish in North America. Francophones – men and women – spend more on clothes, as well as on home furnishings, than any other community on the continent. Montreal probably possesses as many, if not more, importers of Milanese furniture than New York.

Montreal is also the only city in America where French cuisine is not reserved for a special outing, but is part of everyday life. When Montrealers entertain, the five-course dinner is

usually enhanced with wine imported from France. (Montrealers rarely drink Canadian wine, despite its much-improved quality.)

The ethnic mix

While Montreal has two main languages, it also has a throng of ethnic and cultural communities. The two most populous – Italian and Jewish – are also the oldest. The immigration of southern Italians and European Jews goes back to the 19th century, continuing through the first decades of the 20th century. Their respective contributions have melded into the city as a whole, like a powerful, fecund graft. Italian and

Yiddish are still heard, though less frequently, and these two communities – where the rate of French-English bilingualism is remarkably high – have long been integrated into the common life of Montreal.

Their family closeness, however, has enabled them to retain more of their own characteristics than other European immigrants. Germans, Hungarians, Slavs and Scandinavians, for example, have, in fewer than two generations, melted into the anglophone community.

There are also municipalities with a large Jewish majority, such as Côte-St-Luc and Hampstead. The Ashkenazi community of Montreal is especially noteworthy in that, of all

LEFT: Montreal's Cirque du Soleil has elevated circus to a new dimension. **RIGHT:** recent non-European immigration has changed the face of the city.

the Diaspora communities, it is home to the largest proportion of survivors from Nazi Germany. This makes the community very sensitive to Quebec nationalism, even in peaceful form. Characterized by an extremely high level of education, the Jewish community is distinguished in all domains, especially medicine, and it has left a deep mark on the intellectual life of Montreal.

The European immigration, which formed so many successive layers in so many quarters of Montreal, has given way in recent years to mighty waves of immigrants from Asia, the Antilles, and the Near East. These new groups

have transformed the face of the city. Haitians work the taxis, Chinese and Greeks the fast-food restaurants, and Moroccan Jews the garment district. Their children will be physicians, professors, and – why not? – prime ministers.

New communities

Boulevard St-Laurent, also known as the Main, is the best place to find the traces of these new communities. Running from the St Lawrence River all the way to the River of the Prairies, it divides the isle of Montreal in two – the francophone part to the east, the anglophone to the west. This street was the traditional path of the immigrants as they got off their boats and grad-

ually made their way "up" to the quarters of the lower middle class in the northern end of the city. They then streamed toward the middle-class neighbourhoods, eastward or westward, depending on the language of their adoption.

To the south you will still find Chinese grocery shops, little Jewish stalls, Portuguese fish stands, Greek tavernas, and creole bars, with each new layer of immigrants covering the last and pushing northward.

The most recent wave has been the yuppies. The old garment factories are "lofts" now, and the old thoroughfare, boulevard St-Laurent, is under accelerated gentrification. Sprinkled with avant-garde fashion shops and postmodern restaurants, it is now the place to go if you want to find youth of every extraction in an exciting mix of colours and tongues.

Changing times and lights

What does the future hold for the two solitudes of Montreal? Will they survive, or does the city's increasingly cosmopolitan aspect threaten to homogenize them into a linguistic and cultural blend? And how would that affect the character and future of the city? Perhaps linguistic and cultural exclusivity contradicts the very ethnic wealth of Montreal.

In these days of dissolving orthodoxies, as seen in Eastern Europe, and emerging polyglots such as a unified Europe, when nations are being virtually reinvented by their newest citizens, is the "two solitudes" approach itself a relic from the past? It seems that, while certain elements of the French and English communities may want their old solitude, it is doubtful that they can have it. Things are changing. And the old thinking may be destined to change, too, with the times.

Welcome to Montreal, then. But while you ponder its complexities, be careful crossing the street! Montrealers are always a little anarchic, and a stop light doesn't mean a thing. They have raised jaywalking to a high art, and they flaunt it. Drivers participate in this artistic display by slowing down only at the last second. If you survive this first contact with Montreal's street scene, the rest will be easy. ❏

LEFT: Montrealers come in all shapes and sizes.
RIGHT: shamrocks, fleurs-de-lys and British uniforms mingle on St Patrick's Day.

THE MONTREALER

Montreal's French and English counterparts lead
surprisingly similar – if often separate – lives of work and leisure

Who lives in Montreal? Well, the city has more than its fair share of luminaries. Anybody who's anybody in French Canadian politics and culture can be found here. Not, perhaps, in the phone book, but at theatres and cinemas, the chic St-Denis eateries and late-night cafés.

Pierre Trudeau sightings were a popular topic of conversation for decades until his death in September 2000. The former prime minister was one of the most famous downtown residents although the streets of Outremont, an exclusive inner-city neighbourhood, are packed with present and past political figures whom most Canadians would recognize, if not necessarily be able to put a name to immediately.

The French Canadian entertainment industry is also firmly ensconced in Montreal. Television and film stars frequent the restaurants around the Canadian Broadcasting Corporation (CBC) headquarters in the east end, while the more famous, such as comedian Michel Coté and director Denys Arcand, choose cafés nearer their residences. Rock stars Misou Misou and Robert Charlebois, plus the central figures in the Quebec literary scene, Michel Tremblay, Yves Beauchemin and Réjean Ducharme call Montreal home.

The English community, though much smaller, also boasts a few notables. Poet and songwriter Leonard Cohen is associated indelibly with the Plateau neighbourhood, while novelist Mordecai Richler has immortalized the former Jewish area along rue St-Urbain. The tycoon Bronfman family also live here. Other minority communities in the city, including Caribbean, African, European and Asian, all claim their own rich and famous; all have their venues in which to see and be seen, their newspapers and magazines where stars rise and fall. Montreal is not only a large centre but a cosmopolitan one. Diversity is its principal wealth.

LEFT: smiling young face of Montreal's future.
RIGHT: the laid-back, pragmatic approach of a more experienced citizen.

In fact, the city is so diverse that finding the "ordinary" Montrealer could be difficult. It is not always possible to say where he or she eats, or even shops. The "average" Montrealer doesn't exist, because this is a city of 3 million exceptions. Nevertheless, one can venture a few observations about the urban resident. People,

after all, *are* Montreal. Buildings and landmarks merely express the will and personality of a population.

The two people we shall choose to portray here reveal some of the distinctive individual traits – similar and dissimilar – that have evolved within two side-by-side cultures that frequently intersect, yet remain steadfastly apart from one other.

French style

Our fictional but typical French Montrealer is named Madeline. She lives with her husband in a condominium one street east of Outremont. The apartment is a second-storey walk-up with the standard exterior staircase. The building, located so near the classy neighbourhood, was recently renovated; prices went up, poorer people moved out, and Madeline moved in.

Buying a condominium makes sense in Montreal, a city where approximately 40 percent of the population live in apartments. Buying an apartment "almost" in Outremont makes dollars and sense; resale value is helped by location. The apartment is, by any standard, spacious – long corridors, high ceilings, with a balcony overlooking the street. The couple, both in their early thirties, are childless. They have space in abundance.

Madeline's husband works near the airport, she in a government office in Old Montreal. He takes the car; she rides the bus down to rue St-Antoine. Leaving at eight o'clock, she barely manages a cup of herbal tea and a piece of fruit. While waiting for the bus Madeline buys *La Presse* newspaper for light reading during the ride, but hopes her husband will pick up the more serious *Le Devoir*. In her heart, though, she suspects he will opt for the tabloid *Le Journal de Montréal* – there was a Canadiens hockey game last night and *Le Journal* has the best sports coverage.

At work, where she supervises a department,

PARIS ENVY

Montreal is uniquely Montreal, no doubt about it, but one can also – if one looks hard enough – occasionally see a trace of envy of a certain French-speaking capital to which it, perhaps, aspires more than it would ever let on.

Think about it. The city once put up notorious francophile Ben Franklin in an expensive home. It built an efficient subway system and then called it the Métro, designing a number of artistic, eye-catching stations and creating a striking "M" logo.

During the hullabaloo leading up to the 1976 Olympic Games, this city also paid absurd sums of money towards the design and construction of a prominent steel tower which would, they believed, print their skyline indelibly in the mind of the world. (It did, but for the wrong reasons.) The tower's designer, by the way, came from the capital of France, which we won't name here.

Montreal's got its own Latin Quarter, a largely student-occupied section of town centred around the bars, clubs, theatres and cafés at the intersection of rues Ontario and St-Denis. It's got a thriving fashion industry and club scene, both sometimes used as testing grounds for a certain European fashion capital's products before they are released to the general North American market. And they've even named a prominent Montreal park Champs de Mars.

Madeline spends a 15-minute break eating a muffin and reading the newspaper's entertainment listings. There are literally hundreds of things to do – music, theatre, night clubs – but she ends up making a reservation at a restaurant that is favourably reviewed. The restaurant is moderately priced and allows customers to bring their own wine. They need to be economical, what with the mortgage, taxes and payments on the car.

Because it is Friday – pay day – Madeline and two colleagues have lunch in a restaurant. The waiter, who is an anglophone, addresses them in French, but Madeline often answers in English, or English *and* French, just as she and her friends, one of whom is Italian, switch easily from language to language among themselves. She orders a salad. What do they talk about? Work. Husbands. The figure skating competitions on television. One colleague, who is reading a Michel Tremblay novel, offers to get tickets for his new play, opening in Montreal next week. They agree in principle to attend a Sunday performance. All three women smoke and order decaffeinated coffee.

Croissants and Chablis

Later in the afternoon Madeline gets off the bus at avenue Laurier to shop. She spends 15 minutes in a bookstore admiring Milan Kundera's new novel and a collection of Québécois fiction, but decides just to pick up a few magazines for the weekend. Besides, she has work from the office in her briefcase: who has time to read? At the bakery she buys croissants for breakfast and delectable cakes for a late-night snack. At the *Société des Alcools* (SAQ) liquor store, she lingers over the wines, finally selecting a three-year-old Chablis for dinner. A bit of window shopping follows. But it is still too cold, even in April, and she walks quickly home. The car is nowhere to be seen along the street.

Her husband returns shortly afterwards with a copy of *Le Journal* rolled under his arm. Traffic on the Metropolitan was even worse than usual, he complains, and he stopped to rent a video – *Batman*, dubbed into French – for midnight viewing. After changing, chatting with Madeline's mother on the phone – her parents

live in Chicoutimi, where she grew up – the couple slip the wine into a paper bag and look again at the address of the restaurant. Her husband, on learning that the cuisine is a mix of Thai and Chinese, hopes it won't be too spicy.

Over a dinner of grilled meats, egg rolls and good wine, impeccably presented, they discuss vacation plans for the spring. Madeline wants to return to Africa – the couple has been once before – but her husband vetoes it as too expensive and says he is leaning towards a Caribbean trip. They talk for a while about going to inexpensive Cuba, where many of their friends have been, but finally decide that they would prefer

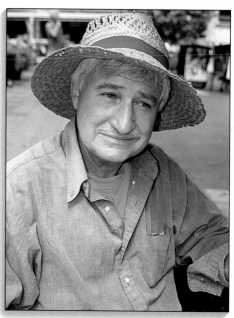

Martinique, which they know quite well. (Friends from the island come to visit nearly every summer.) They agree to phone a travel agent the following week to price a package including air tickets and a week in a beachfront condominium.

Later that evening they eat the cakes and sip cognac while watching the last 20 minutes of the CBC news. Then they go to bed, too tired to watch the video.

Anglo fun

Our English Montrealer is named John. He is a bachelor who lives in NDG (Notre-Dame-de-Grâce), a predominantly English-speaking

LEFT: many holidays are planned and decisions made on restaurant terraces in Montreal. **RIGHT:** trader on Place Jacques Cartier.

neighbourhood north of Westmount. His apartment is a "3½," meaning one bedroom with a kitchen and living room, and is rent-controlled – the only reason he still lives there. John drives a five-year-old Honda that he finally paid off six months ago, exactly two weeks before a garage bill left him $600 poorer. Commuting from NDG to the Sherbrooke architectural firm where he works takes 15 minutes, traffic permitting. This morning the traffic does not permit, however, and he arrives at the office a little late.

The firm is composed of French and English speakers. Fifteen years ago, when John first started working there, most business was con-

ducted in English. Today, French predominates. John, who was raised in Westmount and NDG, is fluent, though some of the older anglophone employees speak French only haltingly.

At lunch John hops onto a subway and rides to Place des Arts. He hopes to buy tickets for that night's concert at The Spectrum, but he arrives to find that it is sold out. Instead he picks up *The Gazette* and spends his hour in the record shops along rue Ste-Catherine. He buys two compact discs for his system and a cassette for the car stereo. Montreal is a great city for music. Listings for the weekend alone include classical concerts, jazz in bars, lots of rock bands, a Senegalese singer at Concordia

University, and a group of Pakistani musicians in a converted church in Côte-St-Luc.

Back at the office John returns a phone call from his friend Marc, a francophone friend from his McGill University days nearly 20 years before. Most of his friends are anglophones. Although a few have left Montreal – including his parents, who relocated to Toronto in 1978 – most of them continue to live in Westmount, NDG, or Pointe Claire, and still to work for downtown firms and companies. At parties his friends often talk about the political situation and about moving away, but only rarely do they turn their words into action and uproot themselves. Montreal is, after all, their home.

Marc has great news: tickets for the Canadiens game the next night. It is April, and April in Montreal traditionally means hockey playoffs. Recent years, however, have been lean, and this year's team only made it to the playoff round after a string of final-week victories. In any case, tickets for Montreal playoff games are impossible to get without connections. How did Marc manage it? John doesn't ask.

To celebrate he invites his friend to dinner. They meet at 7pm to enjoy a fiery Indian meal at a tiny restaurant on a downtown side street. The restaurant owner conducts business in English, which Marc speaks flawlessly. Afterwards the two men go for a few beers in an old college haunt near U de M (Université de Montréal). John orders, and begins to tell his friend about work, a woman friend, his plans to buy a fancy new convertible sports car with all the accoutrements. His friend laughs, knowing he will probably wind up getting something a little more sensible. But they both agree that John's summer vacation — a week in Vegas, followed by a week in New York City – will be absolutely spectacular.

Similar but separate

Different worlds? Hardly. Same city? Clearly. The city can be home to anyone. Anyone can, likewise, call it home. But in our fictional Madeline and John we have found a little bit of the real Montreal, a city that has been pulled apart by French–English tension but ultimately learned how to have a peaceable good time. ❏

LEFT: if you can't get tickets for the hockey game, you'll want to find a good seat near a television.
RIGHT: there's plenty of choice for entertainment.

THE JEWS OF MONTREAL

One of the city's most visible ethnic groups, Jewish Montrealers have also been one of its most influential and steadying communities

It's difficult to find a level shelf in Nat Levine's grocery shop on avenue du Parc, just off rue St-Viateur. Cans lean at odd angles, boxes waver and teeter. But if you're looking for a second-hand kettle or a pair of old boots, Nat's the person to see. Walk past the old-fashioned scale, past the bins of vegetables and fruits. Worn paperbacks and salvaged toasters jostle for shelf space in a dusty, cluttered corner. Paintings hang on the wall, crooked and unframed and very affordable.

At one time, Nat's shop was down the street, on the corner of Jeanne Mance, just east of avenue du Parc, across from the bagel shop warmed by the wood-burning oven, and from the kosher butcher where Hassidic Jews carefully eye cuts of meat. A popular Greek restaurant expanded and Nat was forced to move. But he still provides home delivery – free of charge – to long-time customers such as the elderly woman on rue Hutchison who phones in her order because she's too frail to make the trip.

When Levine's grocery first opened for business almost 50 years ago, most of Montreal's Jews could have strolled to the shop in minutes. They lived around the Main, or boulevard St-Laurent, a Yiddish-speaking world framed by French street names like Cadieux, Esplanade and Marie-Anne.

Multilingual mix

Today, the city's Jewish community is no longer shaped by the alleys and winding staircases of one neighbourhood but by the textures of many. Yiddish swirls along the streets of French-speaking Outremont as Hassidim prepare for Friday night services. Elderly Jews shuffle through the streets of Côte-des-Neiges and Snowdon, stopping to catch their breath or exchange gossip. Their bilingual grandchildren (they speak both English and *French*, not Yid-

dish) play in distant, grassy suburbs such as Dollard des Ormeaux.

And still they come back to the old neighbourhood, the Main, the children of parents from Poland, Hungary and Lithuania. Their children, too, make a modern-day pilgrimage to the street described as "the funnel through which repeated

waves of Jewish immigrants entered Montreal".

Tucked between the fashionable boutiques and trendy cafés on the Main are bits and pieces of the old community, scattered fragments along St-Laurent.

The old community is there as you step onto the wooden floor at Schreter's dry goods store: walls clothed with suits and sweatshirts, shorts and shoes. Once there, it's only a few blocks south to Schwartz's deli: open the door and walk through a curtain of smoked meat that local gourmets claim is second to none. ("When I die," a framed tribute proclaims, "I want to go to Schwartz's.") And catering to those Jews who prefer a slice of heaven is

LEFT: catering for a demanding clientele that values traditional cuisine. **RIGHT:** some Jewish couples cling to age-old customs; others are more modern.

Berson's monuments just across the street. Granite tombstones, polished and blank, rest waiting to be carved.

Migrations and exodus

An epigraph for Montreal's Jewish community would be premature. At 96,000, the community is alive and well, rooted in a history committed to survival. By standing on the corner of rues Notre-Dame and St-Jacques, you can hear the echoes of the city's – and the country's – first synagogue, which was built in 1777 by the Sephardic community, descendants of the Jews expelled during the Spanish Inquisition.

Geography and history unravel in an inseparable knot; distant countries have shaped the city's Jewish community. Tensions in Russia altered the face of Montreal, particularly when the assassination of Tsar Alexander II in 1881 sparked a series of pogroms, the Russian word for devastation, a synonym for organized massacres. Jews were the targeted scapegoats and Canada was regarded as a hand filled with promise, Montreal being its palm.

The Russian pogroms triggered the first large wave of Yiddish-speaking immigrants. Until then, Montreal's Jewish community was small. In 1847, when Jews numbered fewer than 200, the first Jewish society was organized to provide relief to the community's poor and needy, particularly the newer immigrants. In the last two decades of the 19th century, some 13,000 Jews arrived in Canada. Owing to the circumstances which forced them to flee, they were aware of the very essance of Jewishness that had cost lives in Russia. Customs and a way of life that existed in the *shtetls* (small Jewish towns) of old Europe were adapted to the streets of Montreal.

Docks to sweatshops

Through the funnel of the Main the wanderers streamed. Poor and displaced, they relied on mutual aid societies such as the first Hebrew Sick Benefit Society, founded in 1892. The need for financial help and medical benefits was acute. For some, it was a short trip from the docks to the sweatshop. They worked under deplorable conditions in the garment industry, toiling in cramped sweatshops wedged into old buildings, with little air or light. Days were long, wages were low.

One testimony from this period recounts the following anecdote: "One cloakmaker turned his four rooms into a shop and supposedly kept the other three as a home for his wife and seven children. But the shop was all over the place… A woman was making bread on a table, upon which there was a baby's stocking, scraps of cloth, several old tin cans and a small pile of unfinished garments. In the next room was an old woman with a diseased face, walking the floor with a crying child in her arms. Such conditions were typical in all garment centres."

The poor working conditions proved to be fertile turf for Jews in a labour movement committed to social change. Ideologies developed in eastern Europe by such groups as the Bund, a Jewish socialist party founded in Russia in 1897, were renewed in cities like Montreal with the drive to educate and unionize exploited workers. The Workmen's Circle saw itself not simply as a mutual benefit society but also as part of the larger labour movement, which was struggling to end capitalist exploitation.

Sidewalks became stages for social change. Corner stores turned into political arenas. Bookshops were transformed into debating dens. "Elstein's bookshop on Ontario Street was more than a store," according to one account. "It was virtually a club where anyone who read books would meet to argue politics and orientations."

The expanding community

Politics stretched far beyond the Main itself in Montreal. Three-quarters of the federal riding of Montreal-Cartier, centred around the Main, was Jewish. In August 1943 they made history by electing the first communist, Fred Rose, to the Canadian House of Commons.

Amidst the dust of the depression, small cottages sprouted into prayer houses. Hebrew resounded through forgotten lofts and spare

fruit man. Outside staircases everywhere. Winding ones, wooden ones, rusty and risky ones. An endless repetition of precious peeling balconies and waste lots making the occasional gap here and there."

Row after row of winding staircases, of cold-water flats, nurtured a generation of Jews who went on to make significant contributions to the arts and sciences in Canada, from the poet A. M. Klein to David Lewis, one of Canada's most eloquent politicians, who learned English poring over Dickens. Others have made a quiet difference, like political activist Leah Roback, white-haired and tireless, a button declaring

rooms in industrial buildings. By 1940, 40 of Montreal's 50 synagogues were located within 1.5 km (1 mile) of each other. Rue St-Urbain alone – immortalized in the novels of Mordecai Richler – had six.

Richler writes of the Jewish district, that it was "an all but self-contained world made up of five streets; Clark, St-Urbain, Waverly, Esplanade and Jeanne-Mance, bounded by the Main on one side, and Park Avenue on the other... On each corner a cigar store, a grocery, and a

LEFT: Shaar Hashomayim Synagogue in Westmount.
ABOVE: going shopping – the Orthodox Jewish community is highly visible on the streets of Montreal.

"Bread Not Bombs" pinned to her coat.

As their lot improved, Montreal's Jews moved out of the streets around the Main and into better homes and neighbourhoods. A revitalized wartime and postwar economy created what one social critic called "the social and economic conversion of the Jews".

Jews left the old neighbourhood and built synagogues in the new ones. Few of the original synagogues around the Main are still there. Where there was once a synagogue there is now a church or a parking lot.

On avenue Fairmount, Hebrew letters arch across the sky and disappear into the facade of what has now become a French school.

Time stands still a few blocks away at the Hassidic prayer houses on Jeanne Mance, around the corner from Nat Levine's grocery shop. But for the signs outside, they look like any other house on the block. The similarities end at the door. Inside, the rituals of an 18th-century religious philosophy continue.

The everyday world

Daily life for the city's Hassidic community, Canada's largest, is wrapped in Yiddish. Cohesion is one of the distinguishing marks of Has-

ENIGMATIC LIFESTYLE

Insular by choice, the Hassidim are an enigma not only to the French Canadians of Outremont, but also to the many Jews who are unfamiliar with their ways.

sions flared when a newspaper article spoke thoughtlessly of the "Jewish Problem" in Outremont. For many of the city's Jews, especially Holocaust survivors, the phrase rekindled memories of Nazi Germany. Others recalled the anti-Semitism of Quebec in the 1930s. Insensitive descriptions about how the Hassidim dressed and fear-baiting references to their growing numbers only made matters worse. Both French and English Montrealers were quick to denounce the paper's careless journalism.

sidism, as is charismatic leadership of the various sects. The *zaddik* (leader) is seen as a healer, confessor, moral instructor and also a practical adviser. Central to Hassidism is a determination to persist in devotion to God and not be distracted by the secular world. The two most traditional men walk about in their *kapotes* (black silk coats) and *spodiks* (fur hats), locks of hair curled around their ears. Women dress discreetly in modest clothing, children in tow.

Hassidism and secularism clashed in 1988 in a zoning dispute. A sect that wanted to build a new synagogue was pitted against a town council that balked at making the re-zoning changes. Ten-

Immersed in their Yiddish world, the Hassidim are a minority within a minority. More than half of the Jews of Montreal claim English as their mother tongue. The immigrants who arrived in Montreal earlier in the century arrived in a society dominated by an English-speaking minority. By virtue of a provincial school system that was separated on religious grounds, Jewish children were forced to attend English Protestant schools. The doors to French-language schools were closed to them.

As members of the anglophone minority of Montreal, many Jews found themselves on the wrong side of history when Quebec nationalism arose with the Quiet Revolution in the

1960s *(see page 58)* – a period in which French Canadians, after enduring centuries of discrimination at the hands of an English minority, began to reclaim their past and their status as a majority.

A shifting political scene

Shifts in the Quebec political scene coincided with changes in the Jewish community. A new wave of Jewish immigrants arrived in Montreal, bypassing the Main. Political instability in North Africa led many French-speaking Sephardic Jews to seek a new home. The majority of Montreal's Sephardic community, the election of the Parti Québécois (PQ) in 1976 on a platform committed to a sovereign Quebec. In the aftermath of the PQ's victory, many of the city's younger Jews left for Toronto. But they still gather at reunions featuring slabs of Montreal's smoked meat, and they cart bags of bagels to Ontario after trips to their native city.

An ageing population

Today, more than 20 percent of the city's Jewish community is aged over 65. Many, particularly women, live below the poverty line. That there is a "Jewish poor" in Montreal would

which now numbers more than 20,000, come from Morocco.

Through the Sephardim, some of the city's Jews saw the "French fact" of Quebec. The Sephardic community's desire to preserve its particular culture and identity mirrored the goals of French nationalists. Yet many Jews found it difficult to adapt to the new politics, particularly the elderly, used to a time when French was not the official language. Anglophone Jewish concerns were heightened with

LEFT: snow-shovelling is a winter chore for all Montrealers, regardless of ethnic background.
ABOVE: being trained in the ways of the forefathers.

probably come as a surprise not only to those who accept stereotypes about Jewish wealth, but also to many in the community itself who associate poverty with Jewish life at the turn of the 19th century.

Yet, as in the past, the community has responded. Services have been created to meet the needs of the elderly and kosher meals are brought to homes where the infirm can't cook for themselves. In the heart of Côte-des-Neiges, a low-income neighbourhood where many elderly Jewish people still live, Project Genesis provides storefront services to clients flustered when confronted by a French document or frightened by a rent increase.

The Jewish Immigration Aid Service, created in the wake of World War I, continues to help new arrivals. Auberge Shalom is a shelter for battered women where even the most Orthodox Jewish woman can find refuge, as it is run according to Judaic laws. At the Golden Age Association, stooped seniors practise Tai Chi and sculpt stone.

The Jewish Public Library, now in its 75th year of community service, features exhibitions, films and concerts that celebrate the city's Jewish heritage and links to the modern state of Israel. Here, grey-haired men scour Yiddish news-papers next to racks of Hollywood videos.

Preserving language

Across the street, next to the YM-YWHA, Yiddish bounces off the stage at the Saidye Bronfman Centre. Dora Wasserman's Yiddish Theatre company has become an integral part of Jewish Montreal, helping to preserve a dying language. Internationally acclaimed, it performs before thousands of Montrealers annually, including works by Nobel laureate Isaac Bashevis Singer, who once wrote, "If the Yiddish language is dying, it should only keep dying for the next thousand years."

In a still room at the Montreal Holocaust Memorial Centre, candles cast solemn shadows on a wall inscribed with place names etched in the collective memory of Jews. Founded in 1979, it is Canada's first Jewish historical museum and Holocaust educational centre. The museum examines not only the destruction of Jewish life during the Holocaust, but also European Jewry as it existed before Nazism wreaked its havoc on the continent. Local Montrealers donated many of the artifacts displayed in the museum.

Between one-fifth and a quarter of the city's adult Jews are Holocaust survivors. Continuity is an important theme: many Jews preserve and continue their traditions and way of life from before and during the Holocaust, and they continue to link European Jewry with the community today. A permanent exhibition, *Splendour and Destruction: Jewish Life That Was, 1919–1945*, is just one effort to maintain this link.

Contemporary Jews

The Jewish life that used to be in Montreal is no more. But, although demographics and the political landscape have changed the complexion of the community, it still has a great deal of colour and warmth. The city is home to the archives and offices of the Canadian Jewish Congress, a Jewish "parliament" that is national in scope.

Fluently bilingual Jewish Montrealers sit as city councillors. They are leading academics in McGill and other universities, where they were once restricted.

Bonds with Israel are also strong, with many projects linking the city to the country. Each year Jews take to the streets in a fund-raising March in aid of Jerusalem. True to a history of diverse opinion within Jewish communities all over the world, others have quietly promoted a dialogue with the Palestinians.

What fate awaits the Jews of Montreal? Some speak of the writing on the wall and nervously point to the resurgence of Quebec nationalism. Others are committed to staying and adapting to a new Quebec as they maintain a religion thousands of years older than the city itself.

Meanwhile, back at Levine's grocery store, it's business as usual, as Nat takes another order over the telephone. ❏

LEFT: generations of Jews have been laid to rest in the soil of Montreal. **RIGHT:** boulevard St-Laurent, the famous "Main", heart of the early Jewish community.

LE MELTING POT: ETHNIC DIVERSITY IN MONTREAL

Fully 40 percent of Montrealers come from outside Canada, attracted by the promise of prosperity, racial tolerance and political stability

It might come as a shock to learn that in Montreal, a city so closely identified with French culture, French Canadians have now become almost a minority. The successive waves of immigration have many explanations: foreign wars, the labour required to build a national railroad, the country's reputation as a place with a high quality of life, racial tolerance and political stability. Today you can find neighbourhoods of Arab life, Chinese life, Polish life, Greek life, and many other slices as well. The multitude of ethnic festivals that fill the busy summer calendar also testify to this diversity.

The Jewish influence has been well documented, but it is far from the only flavour here. Some 90,000 people of Asian descent call the city home, and their proportion is rising. Half of the new immigrants to Quebec province in the past 15 years have come from Asia.

The city's African and African-American communities are quite spread out these days, having once ruled the roost in Montreal's bawdy, jazzed-out Little Burgundy neighbourhood. Today only the odd Baptist church in the area testifies to the size of black Montreal; most now live on the edge of the city, in places like Parc-Extension or Notre-Dame-de-Grace.

Fully one quarter of greater Montreal's population – half a million people – come from Europe: Polish and Hungarian Jews dominate the Main; Greeks remain a large, visible and unified community on outer Parc Avenue; the Plateau's parks are filled with Portuguese footballers; and Mile-End is a veritable crossroads of Euro-culture.

▷ **CARNIVAL TIME**
There are echoes of the Rio de Janeiro carnival at the colourful Caribbean fiesta, known as the Carifête, which takes place in the city every year in June.

△ **FESTIVE FLAIR**
The annual Carifête festival is a celebration of Caribbean music and dance. Montreal has a sizeable Afro-Caribbean population.

◁ **LOCAL COLOUR**
Peruvian Indian children at Canada Day festivities, on July 1. Canada's stability and tolerance have long attracted immigrants.

▷ **INDIGENOUS TRIBE**
Mohawk Amer-indians performing a pow-wow dance. Indians had settled in the area centuries before the French arrived.

THE CHARMS OF LITTLE ITALY

Of all Montreal's ethnic neighbourhoods, Little Italy – far from the tourist throngs – may be the most delightful to the eye and palate. The first Italians to arrive, in the late 19th century, were sailors, some of whom turned entrepreneurs and built lodgings along the river. Many of the next wave were construction labourers, living near the huge Molson Brewery and new bridge construction projects which employed them.

Prosperous Italian families soon began moving into what were then quiet areas on the outskirts of the city, and this area, around Jean-Talon, St-Laurent and Dante streets, is now the hub of the Italian community.

Walking around Little Italy, you'll notice *gelato* shops and cafés serving square-cut, cold, thin-crust pizza the authentic Italian way. In the north of the neighbourhood, Jean-Talon Market provides a colourful glimpse of the rest of ethnic Montreal. Westmount housewives mingle with brightly turbaned African and Indian families in the alleys of fruit and veg.

KOREAN PROCESSION
Korean migration to North America began in earnest in the early 20th century, and accelerated during and after the Korean War.

A DAY AT THE RACES
The Dragon Boat races on the St Lawrence river take place every summer. Other events in the Chinese calendar include the Moon Festival in October.

◁ **CHINATOWN**
Montreal's Chinese population numbers 40,000, and the Chinatown district with its restaurants and shops, buzzes at weekends.

▷ **WELCOME SIGN**
Little Italy is the hub of the Italian community – Montreal's largest minority, numbering almost 200,000.

POLITICS, LANGUAGE AND IDENTITY

"Je me souviens" – I remember – is much more than a slogan
on a licence plate to Quebeckers; it is a crusade to save their culture

Politics are politics and people are people. Contrary to popular opinion, the Québécois are not obsessed with the machinations of independence. Newspapers refrain from spouting invective against confederation, cafés fail to hatch midnight cabals, and every day is certainly not *jour de la révolution*. Lives may contain a heightened level of consciousness about the structures of government, but lives also remain private and voluntary. Politics can be variously a pastime, passion, or obsession; it need never be a birthmark, a chain around the neck. Though tensions surrounding language and culture exist, Montreal is neither Beirut nor Belfast. This is worth remembering.

The city streets are gouged with potholes, and the highways, designed for carriages, discourage obedience to laws inadequate to the challenges of surviving the commute home. The St Lawrence River is treated like a sewer, the police department maintains its headquarters in doughnut shops, and zoning laws permit free-for-alls in neighbourhoods whose preservation is in doubt.

These are the issues and players of city politics. The mayor, councillors, citizens' groups, the media, children in primary school who use art class to agitate for pollution control: ordinary people dealing with substantial, concrete issues – homelessness, taxes, recycling facilities – in the hope of improving the quality of life in Montreal. Their voices are modified, in proportion to the scale of both the problems and prosperity endemic to Canadian society.

However, for many Canadians, and most outside observers, politics in Montreal and Quebec means rampant fratricide and divisions in a nation unable to reconcile its linguistic and cultural duality. Politics means language laws, majority rights, Quebec's meandering towards some form of independence from confederation and shouting matches. Moreover, with a growing frustration in other provinces with both Quebec and the federal government, politics means being impatient, ill-tempered and wishing the mess would resolve itself, for better or worse, and leave people in peace.

How did the situation deteriorate so rapidly? How did the evolution of Quebec suddenly

become a source of implosion for the entire country? Answers to these questions are everywhere; explanations are elusive.

Size does matter

First, a word about Canada. To describe the country as "massive" is accurate but inadequate. If anything, Canada is *several* massive countries bookended by oceans to the east and west, a polar cap to the north and the United States to the south. These massive countries – provinces – are home to only 31 million people – who cluster near the extreme southern borders to benefit from milder weather and warming trade breezes.

LEFT: thousands of Canadians gather in Montreal's Place du Canada in October 1995 to vote against separation. **RIGHT:** putting out the flags.

The term "country" is not being used too loosely here. In 1867, the architects of Canada's political house proposed a "confederation" of the various regions to defend against American territorial ambitions and strengthen their economic potential. No one envisioned a unified nation-state grounded in ideology and chauvinism. How could they have? The pact was agreed when British Columbia wasn't even accessible to Ottawa by overland transportation. (Nor would it be until the cross-Canada railway was completed in 1885.)

If the distance separating Montreal from Vancouver seems huge in an age of jetliners, fax

discrimination against the Québécois and their language – was built into the infrastructures of business and government and lingered until barely a decade ago.

Quebec joined the confederation in 1867 because it hadn't much choice. It has remained a part of the country for far more diverse reasons. More than any other province, Quebec *is* unto itself; it is psychologically, if not literally, a nation, possibly even a nation in the American model. Those who would deny Quebec's exceptional status – an attitude implicitly dismissive of tremendous cultural and economic achievements – only coarsen the debate.

machines and email, imagine how isolated they seemed in 1867. Confederation was political moderation and realism. Canada could *not* be like the United States. But it still could function, and its individual members, granted considerable autonomy over their affairs, could be at once self-sustaining *and* loyal to the large "collective".

Quebec's position

How does Quebec fit into the picture? Uneasily. It is at once a founding province and a conquered state. Though the conquering predated the confederation by 100 years, the legacy – English domination of commerce,

Besides, Canada was designed to accommodate diversity. How much diversity, though, and at what cost to existing structures, was never resolved. Quebec's nationalist aspirations have highlighted this ambiguity in the design.

Representation by population

It should be mentioned that Canada's political system, based on representation by population, heavily favours the country's most populous provinces, Ontario and Quebec. Two-thirds of all voters reside in these two provinces. A federal party cannot win an election without the tacit support of Ontario and the full backing of Quebec, whose voters tend to cast their ballots *en masse.* As a result, most of Canada's prime ministers came from the central regions and many of the major leaders have been Québécois. These include prime minister Jean Chrétien and two other recent prime ministers, Pierre Trudeau and Brian Mulroney.

Ironic alternatives

Ironies abound. First, literally speaking, it is not Quebec that suffers from a lack of power and influence. Such a fate belongs to the smaller provinces, especially those in the west. Second, disagreements aside, the English-Canadian political establishment is obliged to

Canadians. Chrétien, Mulroney, Trudeau and Jean Charest, former leader of the Progressive Conservative Party and now leader of Quebec's Liberal Party, are but a few examples. The ranks are far from closed inside Quebec. There is still plenty of room for alternative voices. Trudeau, Quebec's philosopher-king, tellingly described French Canadians in 1956 as "a people vanquished, occupied, leaderless, kept aside from business life and away from the cities, gradually reduced to a minority role and deprived of influence in a country which, after all, it had discovered and explored, and settled".

Quebec elected its first separatist provincial

pay great attention to Quebec's demands. By voting in one direction and thereby offering a party the guarantee of a full quarter of the seats in the House of Parliament, the province has become the country's king-maker; governments are elected or rejected and policies – like the North American Free Trade Agreement – need the good will of the Québécois. In a democracy, this is genuine political power.

Finally, a number of Canada's leading proponents of federalis`m are themselves French

government in 1976. The Parti Québécois of René Lévesque was the culmination of a "Quiet Revolution" (*see page 58*), a period of ferment, marked by outrage at paternalistic English control of Montreal business, and by the intellectual and spiritual assertion of Quebec's "self-hood".

Lévesque fired the imagination of French Canadians when he cried: "We are nothing more than an internal colony which lives at the will of another people." The logical next step, argued the Parti Québécois, was independence. "*Sovereignty-association*" were the buzz words in those days, focusing on an abstract relationship between the new nation of Quebec and

LEFT: the Hôtel de Ville (City Hall) in Old Montreal.
ABOVE: verbal skirmishes have been fought over the languages used on public signs.

Brain vs Brawn: The Secession Question

Conventional wisdom sorts Quebec politicians into two types: the intellectual and the street-fighter. Pierre Elliott Trudeau, former professor of jurisprudence from Université Laval and prime minister from 1968–79 and 1980–84, was the former; his arch-foe René Lévesque, chain-smoking head of the Parti Québécois, was the latter.

The dichotomy is misleading, obscuring the fact

that the two flavours are invariably swirled together in Quebec's political figures. Pragmatic, even Machiavellian, arrogant but charismatic – these are the qualities of Quebec's most talented politicians. But, no matter how able, all have been hamstrung by the issue of language.

Trudeau, Quebec's philosopher-king, strongly supported constitutional reform and federal bilingualism, but in 1968 his elaborate courting of Ottawa seemed to many Québécois a collaboration with the enemy.

Lévesque, a journalist, foreign correspondent and broadcaster, entered the provincial scene as a Liberal MP in 1960.

He emphasized not federalism (in which power

rests with the national government), but sovereignty-association; not bilingualism, but preferential treatment for the Québécois tongue. The hard-talking Lévesque swept into power in 1976 and challenged Trudeau, then prime minister, on the destiny of Quebec.

Robert Bourassa, the former bureaucratic leader of Quebec's Liberal Party, was hoist several times on the petard of language. With his health failing, Bourassa stepped down as party leader, and was followed by Daniel Johnston, scion of a family long-ensconced in Quebec politics.

While the Liberals were clinging to power in Quebec, the federal votes swung over to Canada's Progressive Conservative Party and Brian Mulroney, an Irish Quebecker from Baie Comeau, was elected to a second term as prime minister in 1988.

But the Canadian electorate's love affair with Mulroney's Conservatives was not to last, and in 1993 Liberal Quebecker Jean Chrétien was elected Canada's prime minister.

Jean Chrétien was an old Trudeau man from Shawinigan, Quebec. Not so Daniel Johnston, whose quiet demeanour was no match for PQ leader Jacques Parizeau. In 1994, Quebec elected the PQ to provincial power, and Parizeau pledged a referendum on independence.

After the 1995 referendum, Parizeau resigned as leader (and premier) and Lucien Bouchard stepped in to take over the reins of the PQ. He had a tightrope to walk: to PQ hardliners separation as an independent Quebec was imminent. Bouchard's diplomacy would be sorely tested. In 1998, with the resignation of Daniel Johnston, Jean Charest took over as leader of Quebec's Liberal Party.

Towards year-end, a sudden provincial election was called. The liberals lost to the PQ (by a margin of 48 to 75 seats), but despite dire predictions of the party's annihilation, it won a larger percentage of the popular vote – 43.7 percent compared to the PQ's 42.7 percent.

In the federal election held in November 2000, Jean Chrétien won a third mandate as Canada's liberal prime minister, gaining several more seats in Quebec at the expense of the Bloc Québécois. Although sovereignty remains a heated issue, another referendum seems unlikely in the near future. ❑

LEFT: René Lévesque, leader of the separatist Parti Québécois, took Quebec into the 1980 referendum.

Canada that would make for an economically painless withdrawal from federal funding.

In 1980 Lévesque's provincial government held a referendum asking the Québécois to decide the matter. They did; 60 percent voted to remain in Canada. Ironically, the very middle class that the Quiet Revolution helped to create regarded independence as too extreme, an unnecessarily radical measure to protect their culture and language. The Parti Québécois, deflated by the defeat, failed to win the 1985 election and was replaced by Robert Bourassa's Liberal Party.

> ## ALL BEING EQUAL
> From Vancouver to Halifax and from Windsor to Yellowknife, Trudeau's Canada would be home to both languages, both cultures; a country where tolerance was automatic and no one group would need special protection.

Bilingualism
The deciding factor in the independence movement of the 1970s was Pierre Trudeau. As prime minister from 1968 to 1984 (excluding a brief interruption in 1979), Trudeau forged a Canada of his own imagination and intellect. René Lévesque met his equal in this prime minister. For Trudeau, Canada was the sum of its linguistic diversity. He set about recasting confederation through the introduction of a mandatory bilingualism at all levels of the federal government.

Trudeau was determined to twist the arms of Canadians until even a Calgarian who'd never met a French Canadian, or an inner-city Montrealer whose English consisted of pop-song lyrics, would have to acknowledge both the value *and* the necessity of bilingualism. He was also, of course, subtly undermining the Parti Québécois freedom cry.

Rights and freedoms
It worked well, after a fashion. When Trudeau introduced a Charter of Rights and Freedoms to Canada's patriated constitution in 1981, the charter steadfastly ignored any conciliatory gestures toward Quebec's "two nation" ideal, and Quebec steadfastly refused to sign the document. Combatants settled into their respective trenches, and for a few years animosities were left to simmer while the inevitable evolutions

RIGHT: caricature of the British queen – a humorous indication that much of the animosity between the Québécois and their English-speaking conquerors has yet to be worked out.

occurred: Trudeau retired from politics, Lévesque died, and the Conservative government of Brian Mulroney came to power in Ottawa.

However, those commentators who felt that the withdrawal of Trudeau and Lévesque from the scene would deflate tensions were, unfortunately, proved wrong. When the "Quebec Question" flared again in 1988 it was with a ferocity that took most Canadians by surprise, and which left the country reeling.

Meech Lake
The spark was the Meech Lake Accord, the Mulroney government's 1987 attempt at a conciliatory constitutional agreement. The accord, which increased the powers of all the provincial governments in relation to Canada's national capital Ottawa, also included a "distinct society" clause that would allow Quebec to opt out of many federal programs and override any supreme court decisions that threatened its security.

Meech Lake argued for a different vision of Canada, and though not especially popular west of Ontario, it appeased Quebec and the federal government and seemed a reasonable compromise. All of Canada's provincial leaders signed the preliminary agreement.

Bills 101 and 178

The fraternity was short-lived. Within a year Quebec's Bourassa government placed the accord in jeopardy by exercising its privilege and overriding a supreme court decision. Why such a grave matter? The controversy was linked to concerns over previous legislation, Bill 101, the polemical 1977 Charte de la Langue Française (Charter of the French Language) that gave the French language primacy in Quebec through several stringent measures,

Quebec, even those also in French. It was necessary, claimed the government, to preserve the "rights of the majority". English Canadians were, once again, furious.

Backlash

The result was a backlash against Quebec. Premiers withdrew support for Meech Lake, jeopardizing ratification. Cities and towns in Ontario began to declare themselves "English Only", and the resentment towards both the Quebec sign laws and Trudeau-sponsored bilingualism intensified. Some people began to question the "two languages" model. Canada,

including the barring of English-language schools to new immigrants.

Bill 101 is unquestionably unconstitutional under the terms of the BNA Act – it denies English Quebeckers any right to use English in commercial situations. The law has also been known to produce risible results, with the so-called "tongue troopers" (agents of the Commission de Surveillance de la Langue Française) changing long-standing Quebec place names or fining any merchants who put English "Merry Christmas" signs in their windows. English Canadians were enraged.

In 1989, Bill 178 replaced Bourassa's law and banned English from all outdoor signs in

they argued, was multicultural, not bilingual. Canada was also a society grounded in tolerance, a land of "live and let live". Quebec, on the other hand, was (they argued) becoming more and more an ideological nation-state: an enclave of tribalism that flouted a "become like us, or leave" mentality.

Linguistic skirmishes

The issue is all to do with language. Quebec is a society that thinks, reads and writes in French. Eighty percent of its citizens subscribe to magazines and watch television programs that are foreign to the rest of Canada. Group identity is bound up inherently with language. Defending the language, therefore, through means such as Bills 101 and 178 enforced French education is a defence of identity. Says writer André Belleau: "We do not need to speak French: we need French in order to speak."

"How can English Canadians understand this?" the Québécois argue. Security and power are birthrights for native English speakers. Privileges are assumed. Not so for French Canadians; they are obliged to create their own political, social, even historical space both

In 1989 the the Liberals returned to power, but in the 1994 provincial election, the Parti Québécois, led by Jacques Parizeau, won a resounding victory. Its failure to win the referendum held in 1995, however, led to the resignation of Parizeau and the succession of its current leader, Lucien Bouchard.

Individual choice

You need only wander Montreal for a few hours to realize that it is an ethnically diverse city. Besides English Canadians,

within the country and the North American continent as a whole.

How does all this affect Montreal? The city is the heart of Quebec. It is where the major linguistic skirmishes are being fought. Yet most of these frictions appear silly. Banning bilingual signs, changing street names, the "language police", Parti Québécois youth leagues that seek out offending merchants: this kind of behaviour flatters no one, and even some Québécois seem embarrassed by it.

LEFT: festivities celebrate Montreals traditions and identity. **ABOVE:** the writing on the wall – a mural with a message.

the "allophone" community includes Italians, Greeks, Jews, people from the Indian subcontinent, the Caribbean and Africa.

When they first arrive, members of each of these communities function first and foremost in their native tongues. But what will be their second language and the language of their sons and daughters – English or French?

According to the Trudeau model for Canada, the choice should be up to the individual: schools, social services and all government bodies must be available in both official languages, even in provinces where scarcely a word of French is heard; this is the Quebec influence on Canada. ❏

Pierre Trudeau

What was it about Pierre Trudeau that fired the enthusiasm of so many Canadians? What did this arrogant, balding law professor from the radical seminar rooms of Quebec tell Canadians about themselves? Whatever it was – perhaps the Canadian ability to be great – Canadians responded in a way no prime minister before or since has dared to dream of. Trudeau was, if only briefly, a genuine national hero in a country largely without them, a rock star of a politician who made crowds swoon and ran the country

on the sheer force of his personality.

And what a personality it was. Behind the inscrutable mask of the Jesuit-trained intellectual lay a consummate joker, given to sliding down banisters, playing with yo-yos and frisbees, and keeping the exhausted press corps constantly guessing about his next move.

His wife, Margaret, was almost 30 years his junior, a former flower child who embarrassed Canadians with her own unplanned exploits: running around in a bathrobe at the Rolling Stones' hotel after a Toronto concert, dancing at Manhattan's Studio 54, giving candid interviews in *People* and *Playgirl*. This was the prime minister's wife? But, despite their oddball aura, Pierre and Maggie

proved an irresistible pair for normally cautious Canadian voters. Trudeau exited the national political scene on his own terms in 1984: rather like a king taking leave of his subjects.

He remained on the social scene in Montreal for many years, until the death of his youngest son in a freak avalanche accident in 1999 turned him into a recluse at the end of his life.

Pierre Trudeau died on September 28, 2000, two weeks before his 81st birthday. His state funeral, at Basilique Notre-Dame in Old Montreal, was the largest in Canada's history.

In many ways, Trudeau reflected the uniqueness of Canada. He was born in 1919 to a Québécois father, Charles-Emile ("Charlie") Trudeau, and a Scottish mother, Grace Elliott. The first Trudeau had come to Canada in 1659, and Charlie was a scion of the family, a shrewd businessman who left all three of his children million-dollar legacies at his death in 1935. Grace was a quiet woman from whom Pierre learned deportment, reticence, and the keen regard for discipline he carried into office. A bachelor until his fifties, he lived with his mother in their old house in Montreal until he was nearly 40. She died in 1973 when her son was in his second term of office.

Trudeau came on the national stage abruptly, rising quickly from his professorship at the Université de Montréal law school to become, in 1967, minister of justice under the Liberal prime minister Lester B. Pearson. When Pearson retired, Trudeau – who was then a young, charismatic and attractive French intellectual – stepped smartly into the party's power vacuum, winning a stunning victory at the chaotic leadership conference.

That was perhaps his luck, being in the right place at the right time; his *skill* lay in holding onto power, acquired so effortlessly, for more than a decade. Through some of Canada's most exciting political years, Trudeau was a national fixture: the man the Toronto *Sun*, western Canadians, and Bay Street grey suits loved to hate; the man Canadian children, Québécois, and everybody else loved to love.

The media called it "Trudeaumania" and, while Trudeau never claimed (like John Lennon) to be more popular than Jesus, he could convincingly have done so.

The social exploits of Trudeau are legendary. Before his 1971 marriage, he was seen with a variety of "beautiful young things" on his arm. After the marriage, he had well-publicized arguments with the gallivanting Maggie, a free spirit who hung out with Andy Warhol and took photos of New York celebs. She even had a brand of designer jeans named after her. Despite the trouble brewing in their marriage, the Trudeaus were devoted parents, with an unusual talent for having children on Christmas Day – the first two of their three sons were born on December 25.

That little quirk of fate seemed to bode well for Trudeau. The gods were smiling on him. Even the media circus of the marriage breakup in 1977 did not scar Trudeau publicly, as Canadians – by then disposed to suspect the flashy political magician – gave him new credibility as a single father and a martyr to responsibility. But who knows how much he suffered behind the well-crafted public statements of separation?

Much of Trudeau's celebrated arrogance, his unwillingness to suffer fools, whether in the House of Commons or the press corps, stemmed from his own severe mental self-discipline. It was learned early, at the Collège de Brébeuf in Montreal, where Trudeau was known as a scrapper who never backed down in a fight, verbal or physical. He shone at the Université de Montréal, and success took him to Harvard, the Sorbonne, and the London School of Economics. He came to Ottawa in 1965 as one of Lester Pearson's "Three Wise Men" – a trio of Quebec intellectuals, of whom Trudeau swiftly proved himself the ablest. He was arguably Canada's most brilliant leader.

However, Trudeau's refreshing frankness in debate sometimes appeared merely wilful, as when he told a House of Commons colleague to "Fuck off", explaining later that he had actually said "Fuddle duddle".

Late in his series of terms as prime minister, Trudeau's celebrated arrogance took a decidedly peevish turn, and the mania that had fired his early campaign victories was far from fashionable any longer. Indeed, the fashionable thing through the late 1970s was to mock the naiveté that had found Trudeau such a compelling figure in 1968. The *Sun*, the reactionary Toronto tabloid long given to hate-filled attacks on anything smacking of reform, consistently called Trudeau "PET" and delighted in reporting on his sartorial fussiness: the flashy jackets, the fresh rose in his lapel, the disco-age leisure suits. For *Sun* readers, no clothes horse could be considered a serious leader.

But these dismissive second thoughts are not necessarily born of mature reflection. And they cannot be allowed to nullify Trudeau's early success and the value of the national vision on which it was based. The Jesuit-educated overachiever, a child of strict but loving parents, had risen to international fame. He hobnobbed with royalty, rock stars, and international political meteors.

Yet, unexpectedly, behind the facade of fashionable living and easy brilliance there lived a hardworking scholarship boy, a clever Québécois bookworm who deeply loved his country and his province (in that order). Richard Gwyn, author of *The Northern Magus*, said succinctly of Trudeau's character: "Ambiguity is the only consistency."

And Canadians loved Trudeau for being a national visionary long before they indulged in typical Canadian put-downs – the second-guessing of anyone who does well; the "Who does he think he is?" attitude they learned from the Scots. He showed them who they could be: influential and envied players on the international stage. He showed them what a true national leader, rather than a mediator of regional interests, looked like.

Briefly they followed the lead, relishing his notoriety and the international status that notoriety bestowed on them. But, in their ultimate reaction to Trudeau's vision, Canadians showed him – and themselves – that they were not yet ready to embrace greatness. ❏

LEFT: Pierre Elliott Trudeau was a visionary leader who inspired his fellow Canadians.
RIGHT: his wife, Margaret, embarrassed them.

MONTREAL CUISINE

It's indisputable that Montreal is rich beyond its size in restaurants, rivalling Paris, New York and other world capitals for variety and quality

Walk down any street in Montreal, and the first thing you might well notice is the restaurants: dozens of them, of every stripe, with colourful signs describing raw oysters, grilled steaks, Lyonnaise cuisine, *empanadas*, or whatever else happens to be cooking. It's enough to start the mouth watering at once.

City tourist officials claim their city possesses more restaurants per capita than any in the world. We'll leave that argument for others to sort out. But this is certainly a cuisine of the people: what the city lacks in four-star ratings, it more than makes up for with value.

There are very few places here that will bust the budget, and one can always dine splendidly for a modest sum.

So how did this happen? Actually, Montreal's cuisine has evolved throughout its history, starting with the hearty food of the *habitants*, then adding a classical French touch – when the fur-trade money began to roll in – and, most recently, enjoying the influence of successive waves of immigrant arrivals such as the Jews, the Italians, the Chinese and the Portuguese.

Caloric Catholics

The meals that Montreal's original settlers ate weren't exactly *haute cuisine*, but they certainly got residents through the long cold winters.

Typically, a local cook in those early days would use whatever materials a farmer or labourer kept at hand and make a long-simmering stew: *fèves au lard* (baked beans in lard, bacon or a poor piece of salted pork) was one early caloric favourite, and so was *ragoût de pattes et de boulottes* (meatballs and pig's feet). Meat pies (*tortières*) became very popular, as did homemade sausages, slow-cooking stews of onions, a form of creamy fish chowder, and deep-fried potato doughnuts – washed down with local apple cider and followed by maple

PRECEDING PAGES: Montreal has a plethora of bars and eateries. **LEFT:** *boulangeries* sell a wide variety of breads. **RIGHT:** food festival of gourmet delicacies.

candy, the making of which the original Montrealers learned from native peoples.

The topper, though, must have been the *poutine* (pronounced poot-seen) – a greasy mess of French fries cooked in lard and then covered with a heavy gravy, surely one of the most destructive snacks known to mankind. Rural

Quebeckers, of course, still eat it in vast quantities and sneer at the warning. You can find *poutine* – and most of these traditional foods, plus hot dogs (but they have to be called *chiens chauds*) – somewhere in the city today.

As Montreal grew steadily richer, however, it began to eat a more varied diet. That legacy is most evident in the preponderance of French restaurants, both lowbrow and highbrow. French bread, croissants and decadent pastries are also ubiquitous at the *pâtisseries* and *confisseries* scattered throughout the city.

A good typical lunch or dinner item at reasonable cost is the local *entrecôte* (rib steak), rubbed with a mixture of spices and crushed peppercorns and then grilled over charcoals; you can find it in lots of places, but locals claim **Moishe's**, on St-Laurent, does it best.

Moving up the scale, downtown establishments will pry open your wallet for steak tartare or seafood. A better bet might be the pocket of especially good French places located just west of rue St-Denis, in the rue Duluth area. Entrées might range from lamb to *choucroute* to game. Downtown, on Main or along St-Denis, Belgian-influenced entries such as steamed or

A TASTE OF ITALY

Italian food is well-represented in Montreal, and no wonder. Italians are the second-largest ethnic group in the city, and they've been here for more than a century.

location serves the best desserts; the upper St-Denis has the most authentic, 1960s-rustic-cool atmosphere; and the second-floor Ste-Catherine location is probably the one with the best view.

There are several other vegetarian choices as well, including the inventive **ChuChai** on St-Denis – which is famous for fashioning soy into meat-like substitutes – and the beloved neighbourhood **Santropol**, long the gathering place for legions of social-activist types near parc Jeanne-Mance.

fried *moules* (mussels) are becoming fast favourites among the trendy set.

A new generation

There is also a profusion of vegetarian restaurants in Montreal. This is a city where carnivore and herbivore happily coexist in the search for the perfect bite.

The flagship in this trend has been **Le Commensal**, which has pulled off a rare trick: developing a successful chain of vegetarian-only restaurants. There are at least five in the city now, plus several more in the suburbs, the lower Laurentians – even one in Toronto for homesick Montrealers. The lower St-Denis

Many influences

French food is only the most obvious face of the city's democratically broad appetite; however, there are many, many others.

Jewish food is without question one of the city's signatures, and the anchorpiece is the smoked (actually pickled or corned) meat, first brought here by a Hungarian immigrant, which stars in practically every Jewish delicatessen in Montreal. Get it at **Schwartz's** on the Main first, then decide for yourself whether any other purveyor can possibly compare to this high standard.

The city's delicious local bagels – so distinctive that they are known as Montreal-style bagels – are another treat brought by the Jews. They're created through a combination of boiling and roasting above an open, wood-fired grill. The cooking smells waft tantalizingly along rues Fairmount and St-Viateur, where one can also sometimes buy *matzoh* boards and Jewish desserts such as *rugelach*. Try Fairmount Bagel Bakery or St-Viateur Bagel Shop on St-Viateur for the top bagels in town.

There are plenty of well-heeled Italian restaurants on and around the Main, but for the real thing – elderly women baking almond cookies, square pizzas and the like – head for the residential blocks just south of the Jean-Talon market,

rapidly developing a strong collection of up-scale Asian places as well and may be the next spot to watch for local food lovers.

Portuguese, Spanish and Latin American influences have not been lost on the city's taste buds, either. The Main is increasingly home to restaurants specializing in the Portuguese-style grilling of sardines, chicken and meats on an open flame; these main dishes are then served with an order of delicious pickled and roasted peppers. In Mile-End and elsewhere you'll also find lots of tiny shops roasting whole spiced chickens on a spit, South American-style.

north of the city centre. Montreal's thriving Italian community is centred here.

Recent arrivals

A growing Asian influence in the city is most evident in Chinatown – where the quality is far too variable to be reliable – or, now, in the newly upscale avenue Mont-Royal and rue Rachel areas. Both are lined by daring fusion-style restaurants; many have added the attraction of outdoor patios that are perfect for summer evening dining. Outer St-Laurent is

Left: fresh produce and interesting characters at Atwater Market. **Above:** culinary showmanship.

Surprisingly, Mexican, Cuban and Brazilian joints are now a dime a dozen on the Plateau. All offer pretty much the same thing – heavy meat dishes accompanied by heavy vegetables, extra-strong coffee and super-sweet pastries – at the same low price.

Finally, given the eclectic mix of the population, food can be accompanied by a wide variety of liquids. Drinking, in fact, has long been one of this city's chief entertainments, and its distinctive drinks – local Quebec beer, good French wine, cherry soda from a Jewish deli, tea at a tea salon, or Canadian-made Brio Italian bitter soda – tell a lot about the city's makeup, history and character as well. ❏

THE NEEDLE TRADE

Such is the concentration of garment firms here that more than half
the apparel marked "Made in Canada" is fabricated on the island of Montreal

It has been estimated that fully 60 percent of the city of Montreal's manufacturing jobs are in the textile or clothing sector, and once you have found – after much fruitless wandering – the rows of factories and factory shops tucked in their working-class neighbourhoods, you can well believe it. At last count, some 850

Sweatshops and boom times

While early furriers sowed the seeds for Montreal's future as a garment capital, its heyday didn't occur until the Industrial Revolution provided the tools for rapid mechanization of the clothes-making process. During the late 19th century, as factory technology from England

distinct clothing manufacturers – employing 26,000 local residents – were toiling away.

The rag trade's rise to prominence here began long ago – very long ago. It began, really, when the first *voyageurs* tramped into the snowy woods of New France to trap furs and ship them back to Europe. And when the Montreal-based Hudson's Bay Company became the world's pre-eminent fur-trading post during the 17th century, the city's fate as a centre of fashion and apparel manufacture was sealed.

Ever since, it has been one of those places in the world where designers, stitchers and knitters combine their talents to shape each season's newest idea of *haute couture*.

and New England trickled northward – the American Civil War's interruption of normal production was a major reason for this – Montreal's working-class quarters saw an explosion of new manufacturing plants. Many of these were coat, shoe and shirt factories, and many were run by the stereotypical French, Jewish or Italian tailor presiding over a hot roomful of female or immigrant labourers.

The original garment district grew up downtown, along boulevard de Maisonneuve where it cuts across rue de Bleury and boulevard St-Laurent; rows of furriers and warehouses still testify to its original presence. At first only fabric cutting was done in these factories, while the actual sewing was done at home by women working for piece wages. That would soon change as production increased; but as larger textile firms pushed the limits of decency ever further – employing children, keeping wages low – the workers eventually struck back. There were a number of apparel-industry walkouts in the Montreal area during the years leading up to World War I, and they succeeded in bringing public attention to the poor working conditions.

The garment district began moving around, first to a compact district on the Plateau centred around rue de Gaspé and then, finally, to a more northerly district closer to motorways and the city airport. A few factories can still be found tucked away on de Gaspé, but the vast majority of the city's clothing manufacturers now work out of slightly more modern-looking, multi-storey facilities lined up along distant rue Chabanel.

Saturday mornings bring a special treat, when many of these shops open their doors to retail customers – who get both tremendous on-site bargains and an inside glimpse of the cutting, stitching and other handiwork that goes into the handsome garments they are purchasing. It's a bit surprising to learn that the rag trade is going stronger than ever along this busy little street. Yet it is.

A few statistics illustrate just how healthy the clothing business has been in recent years. The number of jobs in Montreal's garment industry has jumped by 40 percent since 1993; clothing shipments out of Quebec province have quintupled (that is, increased by 400 percent) during the past decade.

World-famous knickers

Change has come to the industry along with changing times. Working conditions here are certainly better than they were a century ago. And while most of the clothiers had traditionally been controlled by Jewish or Italian businesses and tailors, a growing French influence has begun to show itself, particularly in the lingerie trade, in recent decades; this product is one of the industry's more visible faces, often exported.

Most of the businesses are now small and locally owned, which has kept pricing fair and the quality of goods high. In fact, Montreal is now rather well-respected among the world's clothiers, not just for its lingerie but also for the cut and quality of its menswear and children's clothing; two annual fashion events in the city, Mode-Homme (a men's fashion show) and the North American Fur and Fashion Exposition (NAFFEM), drive home this point.

It won't take you long to find the pricey lingerie or menswear shops downtown. But now, each time you find the "Made in Canada" label on the rack of a clothes shop, you'll know a bit more of the story about how it got there. ❑

LEFT AND RIGHT: mannequins model glamorous wares designed on the drawing boards of Montreal's (and the world's) top fashion houses.

WHY ICE HOCKEY MATTERS

*Hockey is tantamount to religion in Canada, and nowhere is
its gospel preached like it is in Montreal*

To understand ice hockey is, in some sense, to understand Canada itself. Across a frozen expanse, enterprising individuals dodge or fight off vicious obstacles, searching for the narrow openings that will bring them glory. And yet the individual cannot succeed – only the team, working together, can consistently send the puck home.

Hockey (the "ice" goes without saying) is raucous but also rule-bound: when individuals flout the laws of the game, they are physically removed from their fellows, placed in the penalty box – the "sin bin" – and the team must struggle on. Fighting is part of the game, but only when it is fair and obvious; dirty play (provided the referee can see it) will draw the penalty every time. Hockey is wide-open and honest, at once rough and graceful, team-oriented and individual, a swirling mixture of bone-rattling hits and the poetry of swift skating. It is like nothing else on earth – and it is Canada's game. It *belongs* to Canadians, in a way that little else does, and they know this almost from birth.

Nowhere is this sense of propriety stronger than in Montreal and its province.

Hockey Night in Canada

Legend has it that Canadians are notoriously self-effacing, finding little to boast about in their own achievements. But when the talk comes round to hockey, Canadians can rightly claim the laurels.

Let the propositions be clear: Canadians are among the best hockey players in the world, and Canadian fans perhaps the most loyal and discerning. Come Saturday night – "Hockey Night in Canada", as the CBC broadcasters so accurately call it – Canadians of all ages are glued to their television sets, even their radios, dissecting plays and performances in joyous technical detail.

LEFT: hockey legend Frank Mahovlich, in 1973, holding the puck which he used to notch his 500th goal. **RIGHT:** time for a break.

While many Americans view hockey as a cross between all-star wrestling and a roller derby on ice, for Canadians the game is an expression of national aspiration. Our game, our league, our players. What Canadian child has not "skated" around the living room, dumping an imaginary puck into the corner? What

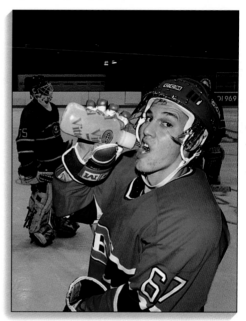

youth has not spent an eight-hour day chipping tennis balls into a foldable net in the back lane, playing until it was too dark to see, too cold to feel toes, and ignoring the call to dinner? For all of them, the hockey announcer's traditional cry, "He shoots... he *scores!*" is a dreamy mantra, a call to glory.

Desperate times

Of course there have been times – desperate times – when the Russians, Swedes, Czechs and even the Americans put Canada's hockey supremacy to the test.

Take 1972, the first Canada–Russia series. It was supposed to be a cake-walk, a mere workout, for Team Canada. But the Russians came to the Forum in Montreal, the Sistine Chapel of Hockey, and beat "our boys" seven goals to three.

Over the next few weeks, Canadians watched in stunned silence as this eight-game foregone conclusion suddenly became a live issue. Teachers wheeled clunky school TVs into classrooms so kids wouldn't miss the day games. The national team fought tooth and nail, and Canadians gaped until Paul Henderson's goal with 34 seconds left in Game 8 ensured victory and

> **UNPARALLELED POSITION**
>
> Montreal's place in the history of hockey is, like its place in the history of Canada, unparalleled.

Claim to fame

There is a lively dispute about the invention of hockey, with at least three cities – Kingston, Halifax, and Montreal – claiming to have witnessed the first game. In fact hockey closely resembles *kalv*, a stick-and-ball game played in the Netherlands as early as the 16th century.

Kingston claims to have been the site of the first North American hockey game on November 25, 1855, but the evidence is a little sketchy. Montreal's claim, though coming 20 years later, lies on firmer ground: on March 3, 1875, two

saved national pride. That goal is still replayed, decades later, on television commercials and sports programs as though it just happened a moment ago.

Still, a watershed had been passed. The novelist Mordecai Richler accurately expressed the feeling that swept from coast to coast after that first series. "We already knew that our politicians lied, that our bodies would be betrayed by age," he wrote. "But we had not suspected that our hockey players were anything but the very best... After the series, nothing was ever the same again in Canada. Beer didn't taste as good. The Rockies seemed smaller, the northern lights dimmer."

teams gathered to play on the city's Old Victoria Rink. The assembled hearties were mostly winter-idle rugby players, who muscled their way up and down the long rink using (according to one report) "a flat piece of board" as a puck. No record survives of the final score.

Hockey was not popular in Montreal at first, competing with the well-established rugby football, lacrosse and even cricket. Lacrosse, borrowed from the Indians, was by far the most popular sporting pastime in 19th-century Montreal. *Les toques bleus* – the blue-hatted members of the Montreal Amateur Athletic Association – were often to be seen playing the Indian game in the fields around Montreal. During the 1850s and 1860s regular clubs such as the Alma Mater and the Hochelagas took on the Shamrocks, the Montrealers or the Crescents.

Early games

The Canadians who played the first games of hockey probably borrowed many of the game's features from field lacrosse, as well as from the English game of field hockey. And like lacrosse as first played by Native Americans, early hockey had no official boundaries or rules: an indeterminate number of players could range far and wide to set up their goals. They had better be fit, however, since goals were often placed as far as 1.5 km (1 mile) apart. In this respect the early game also resembled primitive forms of English football, games of which often involved entire towns and ranged for several days over half a county.

The most common setting for a game was some shovelled patch of the frozen St Lawrence River. One reason for the game's early failure to fire the interest of Montrealers was the sheer effort involved in getting a game going. Imagine clearing a field every time you wanted to play lacrosse or soccer.

These difficulties were overcome during the 1880s when two enterprising undergraduates from McGill University, R. F. Smith and W. F. Robertson, codified the rules of hockey. They specified the approximate size of the playing surface, limited the skating players to eight a side (later six, and now five), and generally gave shape to the game as we know it today. Smith invented the puck by cutting down an India rubber ball that bounced too much for good play on the ice. Permanent winter skating rinks – usually uncovered – were built to make the business of finding suitable ice less hit-and-miss.

Writing the rulebook

Only in 1907 was the International Ice Hockey Federation formed to govern a game that was becoming more popular by the year. The National Hockey League (NHL) did not form until 1917 – six years after the Canadiens, the joy of Montreal, had been organized. There were seven teams in the early NHL: the Cana-

diens and Maroons of Montreal, the Toronto St Patricks (later the Maple Leafs), Chicago Blackhawks, New York Rangers, Boston Bruins, and Detroit Red Wings. From the beginning *les bons Canadiens* were a powerful force.

Le Club de Hockey de Canadiens (as it is officially known) has won more NHL titles than any other team, taking possession of Lord Stanley's Cup 23 times since the old Governor-General donated the trophy – at a cost to himself of $48.67 – in 1926. The Cup has grown, sprouting bottom layers like a tree grows rings, and *les Glorieux* has been there every step of the way. Its former Montreal temple, the

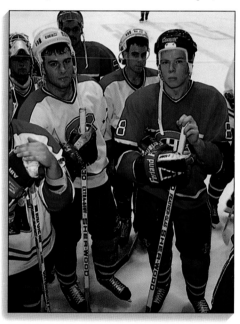

Forum, was so thickly festooned with NHL title banners that opposing players felt distinctly woozy at the sight of its crowded rafters.

New home, bad habits

Early in 1996, Le Centre Molson replaced the Forum as home for the Montreal Canadiens. A vast amphitheatre built on the platforms of the old Windsor Station, it can accommodate up to 21,247 people. When it opened on St Patrick's Day, more than 150,000 hockey fans waited in line to see their heroes' new base.

For purists, however, modern play has deteriorated as the NHL has grown and become more commercialized and money-

LEFT: players on the ice at the Forum, home of the Montreal Canadiens until 1996, when they moved to the Molson Centre. **RIGHT:** the future of the sport.

driven. Forwards are today as likely to dump the puck heedlessly into the corner, letting their linemen scramble, as they are to carry it into the enemy zone on the stick. There may be fewer fights than in the days of "beat 'em in the alley if you can't beat 'em on the ice", but dirty play – vicious hooking, cross checks, fines and suspensions – has become more common.

Les Habs

The Canadiens players have not exactly been above all this; they've produced their share of bad play, goon rookies, and the rest. But they

are still the example many fans turn to for peace of mind when all else in hockey seems tarnished. They represent what pro hockey was, and can be again.

Such widespread support cannot obscure the fact that the Canadiens are also very much a local product of Montreal, an 85-year family affair between city and club. Indeed, the "H" on their old-fashioned sweaters is popularly taken to initial "*Habitants*", the team's affectionate nickname, when it probably just means "hockey" (as in Club de Hockey).

Les Habs is the team that young Montrealers, indeed youngsters from across Quebec, dream of playing for. There is no other team, and the

hometown fans know it. A few of those wide-eyed French Canadian kids grow up to claim that birthright: donning the red and blue sweater, skating out onto the holy ice of Le Centre Molson and putting one away for *les Canadiens.* The rest just keep dreaming.

Power play

Many of the best players ever to lace up skates wore the Canadiens' sweater. First and best, perhaps, was Howie Morenz, the legendary "Stratford Streak". An Ontario boy, Morenz anchored the high-scoring 1920s line with two Québécois shooters, Billy Boucher and Aurel Joliat. In the inaugural game at the Forum, on November 29, 1924, the Morenz line pushed in six goals in a 7–1 defeat of the Toronto St Patricks. The stonewall in the Montreal goal was another legend, Georges Vezina (the Chicoutimi Cucumber), who rose to glory at the Forum from a small-town family of 22 children and gave his name to the trophy for goaltending excellence in the NHL.

In the 1940s, the power-play team captained by the great Maurice "The Rocket" Richard was so effective – it included Big Jean Beliveau, Dicky Moore, and Bernie "Boom Boom" Geoffrion – that the NHL was forced to change its rules. With Beliveau and Richard circling the net like angry hornets and Geoffrion unloading thundering slapshots from the point, the Canadiens were regularly scoring two or three goals in the course of a two-minute penalty. Finally, the League altered the rules so that any power-play goal would automatically end the penalty, putting opposing goalies out of their misery.

The Rocket was a fading blast when the Canadiens entered their greatest-ever period of glory, the epic five-year dominance of the Stanley Cup from 1956 to 1960. The team has won the Cup many times since then, including a hard-fought four-year streak in 1976–79, but the team of the late 1950s was probably the best ever assembled by the venerable old club. The roll call includes many of hockey's most illustrious names: Beliveau, Henri "Little (or Pocket) Rocket" Richard, Geoffrion, Jacques Plante – one of the best goalies ever and the first to standardize a face mask – and the coach a former player named Toe Blake.

There will be arguments about the merits of the brilliant late-1970s club that included

Ken Dryden, Jacques Lemaire, Serge Savard, Bob Gainey, and Yvon Cournoyer; but there was something elemental about that 1950s dynasty. It reigned before the World Hockey Association (WHA) expansion, before league-parity rules, before the Canadiens became just another business in the NHL, before *English* became the language of the dressing room. For five years this team, composed almost entirely of Quebec boys, could not be knocked off by the best hockey players in North America.

THE ROCKET

In the 1940s, Maurice "The Rocket" Richard, who skated like the wind with the puck seemingly glued to his blade, captained the Flying Frenchmen of the Forum.

The villain of the suspension was NHL president Clarence Campbell, just the latest example of a Scot shafting a Québécois. Sportswriter Tim Burke of the Montreal *Gazette* called the riot "the opening shot of the Quiet Revolution". However, by November 15, 1976, the revolution was over and won, and les Canadiens (many of them federalist, not separatist) skated through a game in which the election results dominated the scoreboard, proclaiming the Parti Québécois's stunning victory.

Hockey and politics

Something else was different in 1976, of course. The Parti Québécois had gained power in the province, deflating the powerful metaphor les Canadiens had always provided for downtrodden Québécois. Here was real, not symbolic, power. For many Montrealers, hockey became just a game, no longer a national placeholder capable of provoking the riots on rue Ste-Catherine that greeted the suspension of Maurice Richard in March 1955.

LEFT: Henri "Pocket Rocket" Richard, brother of the famed Maurice "The Rocket" Richard. ABOVE: hockey memorabilia at the McCord Museum in Montreal.

Dramatic interpretation

These events, dramatized in Rick Salutin's award-winning 1977 play *Les Canadiens*, show why the 1956–60 dynasty is a more potent symbol of what le Club de Hockey means to Montrealers – a source of fierce cultural pride when all else seems beyond reach.

Salutin's play, set in a miniature rink, reads Quebec's history through the lens of hockey. The musket that kills General Wolfe becomes the first hockey stick. Events are described by a commentator: "the shutout of the French Canadians at the Plains of Abraham... the sparkling teamwork of the Patriotes in 1867... the power play of 1867."

But the mythologizing of the Canadiens ends, in the second act of the play, when metaphors for power and Québécois aspiration are no longer necessary. Hockey is simply hockey; power is exercised in the National Assembly, not the Forum.

However, hockey is still a powerful element in Québécois culture, and the melding of hockey with drama continues.

A similar mini-arena setting, complete with commentator, organist and referee, is now used by the Ligue Nationale d'Improvisation (1718 Champlain, tel: 528-5430), which pits teams of uniformed actors against one another in the

competitive acting-out of improvised themes. (Penalties may be called for hamming it up.) Many of Quebec's best actors start their careers here, moving up from junior leagues to the televised national games, and then on to even bigger things.

The other great team of hockey's early years, the Toronto Maple Leafs, fell on some rocky times. For many years, the team did not weather expansion and the modern game as well as did Montreal. Only recently, sparked perhaps by the construction of a new hockey arena in downtown Toronto, has the team returned to the playoffs after a long stretch in the basement.

Sworn enemies

It is perhaps a little hard to imagine now, but there was a time when the Montreal–Toronto hockey rivalry was one of the most exciting in sport. If one were a Canadian, allegiance had to be pledged – Leaf or Hab, and no fence-sitters allowed. And hockey was clearly not the only thing at stake: there was civic pride, the least often examined undercurrent of racial and linguistic enmity.

The writer Roch Carrier distilled these issues in his short story *The Hockey Sweater*. A Quebec kid, a desperate Maurice Richard fan, needs a new hockey sweater and his mother writes away to Eaton's, the Canadian department store that sadly is no more. The resulting parcel holds a Maple Leafs sweater. *Quel désastre!* His mother will not send it back because it fits him. He is shunned by the other little Rocket Richards, a traitor to Mother Quebec, *Les Habitants*, and the Rocket himself. A young priest sends him to confession.

Torontonians have never been quite as hockey-mad as their counterparts to the east. Toronto hockey has produced its share of heroes – Francis "King" Clancy, Frank Mahovlich (who also played for the Canadiens), Red Kelly, Darryl Sittler, Dave Keon, Lanny Macdonald, coach Punch Imlach. but more recently it became known for a less glorious personage, the crotchety owner of the Leafs, ex-convict Harold Ballard.

Ballard, who went to jail in the 1970s for defrauding his own hockey club of $200,000, was so offensive to everyone that local sportswriters even started a tasteless Ballard-Watch pool when he was hospitalized for heart trouble, an ailment of which he eventually died. For years, Ballard's tight fist was widely believed to have kept the Maple Leafs from rightful place atop the NHL, as he fired coaches with abandon and paid sub-par salaries to his players. After a long legal battle over control of the immensely profitable club, Toronto businessman Steve Stavro became majority shareholder and chairman of the Maple Leafs' board in 1991.

National team

Anyway, the Canadiens, not the Leafs, are Canada's national team – or they ought to be,

LEFT: a statue commemorates Montreal's "Rocket".
RIGHT: diorama at "Rocket" Richard's museum.

though boorish western Canadians have occasionally been known to boo the French sections of the national anthem when the Canadiens are in town. "Some of the players were so angry they didn't want to go out on the ice," Serge Savard said on one such occasion in Vancouver in 1980. Fans in Winnipeg once demonstrated a better appreciation of what Les Habs represented, back when Winnipeg had an NHL club: the first time the Canadiens visited Winnipeg, most wore tuxedos and gowns to the arena.

Despite Winnipeg fans' loyalty, it was not enough to prevent the 1995 transfer of their Jets franchise to Phoenix, Arizona – a fate that also befell Quebec City's Nordiques (who now reside in Denver, Colorado). The Leafs and Habs, Canada's original NHL teams, have once again become Canada's last refuge.

So Les Canadiens deserve, at the very least, our respect. What if recent teams have been poor, have even – heaven forbid – missed the playoffs? They have persisted and succeeded. Those old-fashioned red and blue uniforms, as they glide across the ice, represent not just Canada's vision of hockey, but also a window on the tough and tireless teamwork that runs through Canadian history like a river. ❏

ICE DREAMS

Thousands of tourists make the annual tramp west to Olympic Park to see the Biodôme, stadium tower and Insectarium. Few, however, possess the insider knowledge – or, perhaps, the Montrealer's fanatic interest in hockey – to track down l'Universe Maurice-Richard (2800 rue Viau; open Tues–Sun, noon–8pm; free; tel: 251-9930) just across the way from the Biodôme. Located inside the Arena Maurice-Richard – itself dominated by the largest ice rink in Quebec – this tiny museum commemorates the hockey player who commands the highest place in Montreal's heart, no small task in this town.

Richard, a record-setting scorer who terrorized opposing goalies in the old Montreal Forum during the years from 1942 to 1960, was known as "The Rocket" for his blazing shots and rushes up and down the ice.

The museum contains some of the trophies Richard won, as well as his antiquated uniforms and skates. The man himself remained visible in the city's public eye even in advancing age, speaking frequently at sports and award functions before finally losing his battle to abdominal cancer in spring 2000 at the age of 78. Even though he's gone, however, fans will never forget how the intense Rocket lit up their hockey nights – and this little shrine ensures that even the young ones will know his story.

PLACES

A detailed guide to Montreal and Quebec City, with principal sites clearly cross-referenced by number to the maps

From its origins as a small French foothold on a vast and punishing land, to its present status as Canada's most urbane and exciting city, Montreal is a colourful swirl of people, politics, language and culture. It was here that faith and fur joined hands to transform irrevocably Canada's First Peoples. And it is here that Quebec's intellectual and artistic vigour has its most potent expression; where pride, politics and the past merge in a brilliant and ever-changing tapestry.

Montreal has been called a "phonic" city, with its mixture of francophones (French-speakers), anglophones (English-speakers) and allophones (those whose first language is other than French or English). While wires sometimes get crossed, and communication among these sundry cultures occasionally falters, the city has remained a cohesive, vital and peaceful social network.

To the surprise of many, London's influential *Sunday Times* reported at the beginning of the 1980s that, "Montreal now surpasses San Francisco as the most interesting North American city… There is a swagger about the city that one used to find in San Francisco before it went limp in the early '70s."

But, since then, has Montreal fulfilled that promise of excitement to come? To prove that it has, the Places section of this book guides you through the historic charm of Old Montreal, the dynamic modernity of downtown, the café society of the Latin Quarter and then through parks and islands, out into the surrounding countryside.

Comparisons are often made between Montreal and Quebec City. While the former is said to be more sophisticated, the latter is more historically intact and is considered the spiritual heart of the province. They aren't far apart (in Canadian terms) so it's not difficult to visit them both. Some of the trips in the Excursions chapter lead from Montreal towards Quebec City, and the last chapter in the Places section provides a fascinating insight into this, the capital of French Canada. ❑

PRECEDING PAGES: winter wonderland; autumn glory; expansive views from Mont-Royal. **LEFT:** architectural heritage in downtown Montreal.

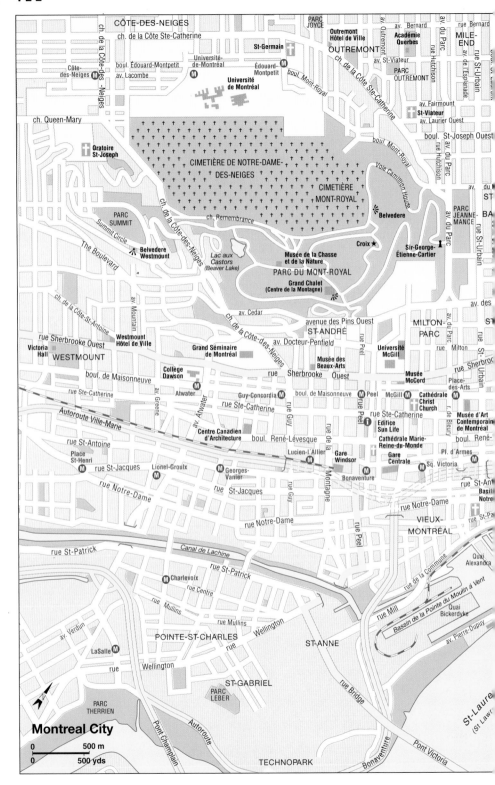

Montreal City

0 — 500 m
0 — 500 yds

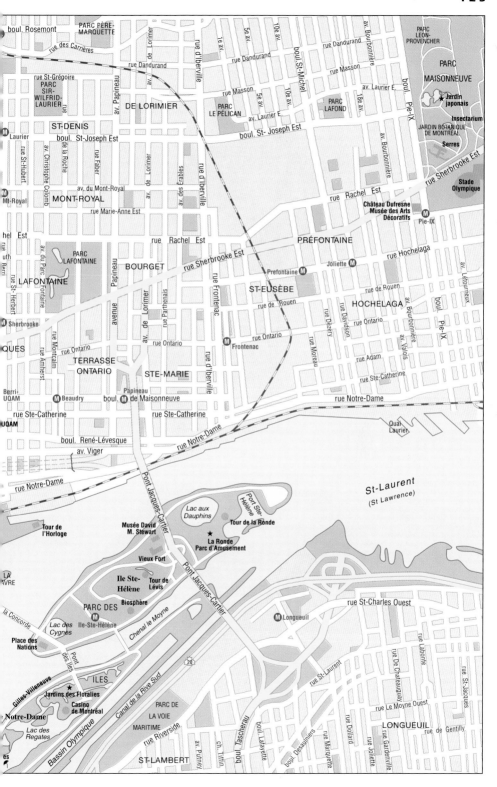

MAISONNEUVE
1643

OLD MONTREAL

Montreal's original French settlement is still its most beguiling historic district; a mixture of old homes, docks and churches, restaurants and squares, tiny alleys and grand public squares

Map on page 126

O ld Montreal is back. Once making up the entire city of Montreal, and its business centre until late in the 19th century, it is hard to imagine that in 1960 these streets were deserted, these buildings derelict and slated for demolition. Old Montreal came perilously close to extinction.

Then, in 1962, the Viger Commission declared the area historically invaluable. Houses were restored, buildings gutted and renovated, and restaurants, shops and pubs began to spring up to serve tourists and Montrealers. Every city inherits styles and traditions, heirlooms bequeathed to the next generation. Old Montreal is modern Montreal's inheritance and, thanks to foresight and initiative, it is very much a *living* inheritance.

The area is a provocative blend of commercialism and history. An 18th-century building houses a thoroughly modern business: banks of computers line a deep rubble wall, printers and fax machines operate inside stone vaults. Architects focus their creativity on pre-existing shapes and dimensions. Electricians wire rooms that smell faintly of paraffin. Painters strip and varnish narrow staircases with cross beams that force tall people to stoop. Old Montreal wants modern entrepreneurs to make history contemporary while making profits for themselves. Atmosphere is abundant, and the location can't be equalled. Why not set up shop in Old Montreal?

There is also another side to these restorations. Most Montrealers and tourists descend on the old city to sightsee during the day and dine in the evening. Afterwards they return to their homes or hotels, leaving the cobbled streets quiet and melancholy. But efforts to make the area a functioning neighbourhood are beginning to show results, with condominiums and apartments springing up. Old Montreal now has more than 2,500 permanent residents, and a burgeoning nightlife has begun to flourish in the eastern section.

LEFT: Paul de Chomedey, Sieur de Maisonneuve, stands proud in Place d'Armes. **BELOW:** Nelson's Monument.

The major squares

Old Montreal was once a neighbourhood of houses, shops and churches. It still is an area of public squares — four major squares in a nine-block radius that, until recently, served as community centres where people gathered to gossip and discuss the business of the day. What better way to explore Old Montreal than by using the squares as landmarks?

Stand in Place Jacques-Cartier and imagine yourself a citizen. The year could almost be 1790. The principal structures still stand, the churches and seminaries still function. The St Lawrence still borders to the south and the mountain to the northwest, and while the walls that protected Montrealers until the early 19th century are gone, the area remains distinct and

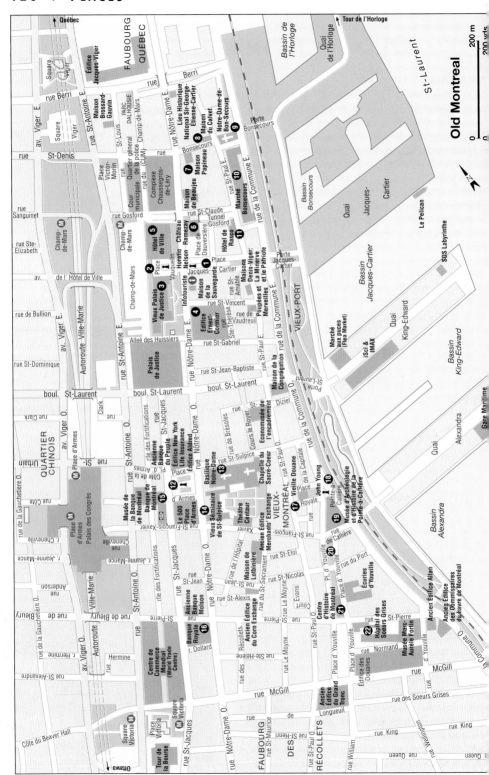

divisible. During the summer you can sit in a square for hours watching the merriment. In winter, though, a café seat has advantages.

Map on page 126

The heart of tourism

The obvious place to start a visit is **Place Jacques-Cartier ❶**. Rectangular in shape, lined with Victorian-style street lamps and cobblestones, the square has a grace and charm that conjures images of women strolling with parasols and men playing absently with pocket watches. The heart of tourist Montreal is here: restaurants and terrace cafés abound (plus a small tourism office). During the summer, sidewalks, already crowded, dissolve into hives of onlookers gathered around the jugglers, mimes and acrobats. Artists and *chansoniers* are also plentiful on narrow rue St-Amable, rue St-Vincent or any other sonorous alley.

The square slopes up from the St Lawrence River to rue Notre-Dame. There are excellent views of the port, the behemoth freighters being bunkered and provisioned, on any but the foggiest of days. In winter, though, Place Jacques-Cartier is subject to the quirky imagination of a city hall decorator who one year festooned the square with giant helium-inflated Christmas trees. Recent years have seen a return to more traditional Christmas displays. The features of the lovely old buildings around the square are pleasingly accented by abundant but tasteful lighting.

The square is also the launching point for Montreal's annual Fête des Neiges in late January, a brisk but lively winter festival that features ice sculptures in the **Vieux-Port** (Old Port) and ski and snowboard demonstrations in Place Jacques-Cartier.

At the top of the square, towering above the buildings, is **Nelson's monument**, an imposing if odd tribute to England's naval hero. Imposing because it stands 35 metres (115 ft) tall and dates from 1809. Odd both because the admiral faces *away* from the St Lawrence and, more to the point, that he is there at all. Little in public Montreal escapes political judgement: a memorial to the English conqueror of a French navy is lucky to have escaped intact.

Nelson squares off with a less grand **statue of Vauquelin**, an early French administrator, in tiny **Place Vauquelin ❷** at the crest of the incline. From this square, once the site of the town jail and the public flogging ground, "new" Montreal sprawls in all directions. Vauquelin, it should be noted, *is* facing the river, though his position may have more to do with keeping the bitter north wind to his back than anything else.

Nelson seems strangely out of place in Old Montreal.

BELOW: selling their wares in Place Jacques-Cartier.

New courts

Place Vauquelin is bookended by important buildings. To the west is Montreal's **Vieux Palais de Justice ❸** (155 rue Notre-Dame Est). This old court house, dating from 1856, was designed by John Ostell, the man responsible for the magnificent twin towers of the Notre-Dame Basilica on Place d'Armes. The style, known as classical revival, was extremely popular in Montreal at the time, particularly the thick columns and, when it was added in 1890, the cupola dome.

Re-enactments of military exercises make for colourful displays at City Hall.

The old court house is now occupied by government offices. Across the street at 100 rue Notre-Dame Est, is a later bastion of canon and code that was used until the 1970s for criminal cases. It was later converted into a conservatory and renamed **Edifice Ernest-Cormier** ❹ after its famous architect. It features massive columns fronting a lovely bronze door. Above the door are bas-reliefs detailing the history of criminal law. The Latin inscription over the cornice reads: "He who transgresses the law shall seek the help of the law in vain." Hardly comforting words for a defendant. The building currently showcases the talents of Quebec's finest young artists. It is home to both the art and drama conservatories, where aesthetic laws are transgressed daily.

The massive building at 1 rue Notre-Dame Est is the current **Palais de Justice**, inaugurated in 1971.

City Hall and Château Ramezay

East of Place Vauquelin stands Montreal's stately **Hôtel de Ville** ❺ (City Hall), a second-empire structure with slender columns and the mansard roof so common in Québécois architecture. The building, which dates from 1860, survived a major fire in 1922, and today it has an extra storey. During the holiday season tiny lights outline the building's striking architectural features in a dramatic seasonal silhouette. It was from a second-storey balcony here that Charles de Gaulle addressed a throng that crowded into Place Jacques-Cartier to see him in 1967. De Gaulle roused the Québécois with his cry *"Vive le Québec libre"* ("Long live free Quebec"). The crowd heeded his words.

Château Ramezay ❻ (280 rue Notre-Dame Est; open June–Sept: daily 10am–6pm; rest of the year: Tues–Sun, 10am–4.30pm; entrance fee; tel: 86

BELOW: Montreal's stately Hôtel de Ville.

708; fax: 871-8317), across from the city hall, is the most famous of the many restored houses around the square. Built in 1705, this low-lying fieldhouse has over the years served as offices and warehouses for the Companies des Indes, the official residence of British governors, a court house, school, seat of government, even a headquarters for the American army under Montgomery and Benedict Arnold when they briefly occupied Montreal in 1775.

Benjamin Franklin stayed in the house while on his mission to persuade Lower Canada to join the American revolution. The Château survived these incarnations nicely, and it still has the 1-metre (3-ft) walls and deep stone vaults ordered by its namesake, Claude de Ramezay, the 11th governor of Montreal. Today, it is a museum of life in 18th-century Montreal.

The rooms of Château Ramezay are worth exploring. Among the more curious artifacts are stern portraits of pioneer officials, religious icons, maps, a 1750 manuscript of liturgical chants translated into an Amerindian language, rugs, business ledgers, and a reproduction of the head offices of the Companie des Indes Occidentale in Nantes, France. The building was the North American headquarters of the French West India Company from 1745 to 1760.

A series of rooms recreates the interiors of diverse living quarters in New France. These include the offices of the governor, a dining room, kitchen and servants' quarters. All the rooms contain period furniture and some pieces are very fine, especially the cabinets. There are regular special exhibitions.

In the whitewashed vaults and narrow passages of Château Ramezay's basement is an attempt to do justice to the Amerindians who were displaced by Europeans. The predominant feature of the exhibit is a 19th-century photo collection showing "civilized" Indians smoking pipes and wearing suits and ties.

Map on page 126

TIP

There are 6,000 parking places in Old Montreal, but just one gas station. It's at 408 rue St-Antoine Est, corner of rue Bonsecours. Get there by following one-way St-Antoine behind City Hall.

BELOW: inside Château Ramezay.

Papineau and Calvet

Two other prominent examples of restoration include the **Maison Papineau** (1785) at 440 rue Bonsecours (not open to the public), known for its woo⸱ facade painted to look like limestone; and the **Maison du Calvet** (1770) a 401 rue Bonsecours (also not open to the public), with its distinctive high chim neys and steep roof to prevent snow from accumulating.

Both houses are well known for their historic namesakes, but Calvet is th more infamous of the pair. Pierre du Calvet was an administrator who betraye the French, first to the British in 1759 and then to the Americans in 1775, fc which he was duly imprisoned. Upon his release several years later Calve sought financial compensation from the Americans for his trouble, but wa refused. Next he sailed to England to protest his term in prison. Tragically, hi⸱ ship sank en route, and Calvet kept his traitorous status for perpetuity.

The Papineau family, in stark contrast, is among Quebec's most honoure⸱ Louis-Joseph Papineau, the leader of the 1837 rebellion in Lower Canada, wa born in this house, and six generations of the family, including many distir guished politicians and businessmen, have occupied it.

Maison Papineau was also the residence chosen by Eric McLean of the Vig⸱ Commission to begin the renewal of Old Montreal. In the early 1960s **rue Bor secours**, which holds both houses, was dreary and vaguely disreputable. Whe workers began to restore Maison Papineau, they eliminated two brick storey⸱ replaced all the windows and stripped the walls of 19 layers of wallpaper.

The refurbished Maison du Calvet is now a trendy bed and breakfast estal⸱ lishment – the Pierre du Calvet – complete with an excellent restaurant and quaint coffee shop.

TIP

Public washroom facilities in Old Montreal can be found at City Hall, the rear of Bonsecours Market or just across rue de la Commune from the Pointe-à-Caliière museum.

BELOW: flags are out on rue St-Paul.

While in this part of Old Montreal, you might also step into the **Lieu His-torique National Sir-George-Etienne-Cartier** (Sir George-Etienne-Cartier Historic Site) (458 rue Notre-Dame Est; open June–Aug: daily, 10am–6pm; rest of the year: Wed–Sun, 10am–noon, 1–5pm; closed Dec 19–April 7; entrance fee; tel: 283-2282), a series of exhibits highlighting the life of early explorer Cartier. There's a special Christmas exhibit each December.

Arguably the most charming street in Old Montreal is **rue St-Paul**. Cobble-stoned, the air smacking of the St Lawrence River 100 metres/yds to the south, and lined with 18th-century buildings that currently house restaurants, shops and government offices, the street is authentic without being precious, at once current and deeply historic. The three most prominent structures are Notre-Dame-de-Bon-Secours, Marché Bonsecours and the Hôtel de Rasco.

Sailors' solace

No symbol of Montreal's maritime heritage is more poignant than **Notre-Dame-de-Bon-Secours** ❾ (400 rue St-Paul Est; open May–Oct: Tues–Sun, 10am–5pm; Nov: Tues–Sun, 11am–3.30pm; free; tel: 282-8670). One must stand at the water's edge in the Vieux-Port to appreciate the church's impact. Rising above the clock tower is a statue of the Virgin Mary, her outstretched arms welcoming ships into port. For hundreds of years, seamen from Montreal made a pilgrimage to Notre-Dame-de-Bon-Secours to pray for safe passage.

Little wonder that the lively and busy interior of the "sailors' church" has a decidedly nautical look: there are votive lamps shaped like vessels, and carvings of ships – many donated by seamen – hang from the ceiling. *Secours* translates as "assistance" or "help", but the church's name in English – Our Lady of

Map on page 126

The symbol of Montreal is displayed outside government buildings.

BELOW: Notre-Dame-de-Bon-Secours.

A Living Language

The leading French dictionary, *Le Petit Robert*, defines linguistic purism this way: "The excessive concern for the purity of language, in accordance with an intangible and idealistic model." It is characterized by a desire to freeze a tongue at a certain stage of its evolution. Purism is autocratic. Worse, it is uninteresting.

Québécois, the French spoken in Montreal and throughout the province of Quebec, is anything but pure. Major French dictionaries published in Paris once took it upon themselves to denounce Québécois as a bastardization of the original tongue. They couldn't have been more misguided. Montreal French is a language crackling with vitality. Anglo-Canadians, Greeks, Africans, Asians, even the occasional transplanted US citizen seize the French tongue and contort, distort and otherwise twist it into new, unimagined shapes. Compound this with the ribald, earthy, but always original *joual* of the

Québécois themselves, a street-wise dialect bursting with word-puns and wit, and the linguistic stew is far from bland.

A major concern of linguistically sensitive francophones, however, is that the verbal climate is a bit too interesting. Québécois French, they sense, is fast becoming overrun by anglicism.

Yes, Montreal French is rife with English expressions. Many people are, after all, fluently bilingual; such a gift leads inevitably to a casual mingling of languages, especially with so much of the popular culture emanating from just across the border in the United States. A musician is super-cool if le mood that night is good. In the mornings people eat les corn-flakes, slip on their sportwear, and go faire du shopping. A rough and tough guy wears son tee-shirt and will spend evenings in a friend's living (living room) drinking les Ex (Molson's Export beer). At work, especially in an age of technology, one attends un briefing or un meeting to do some planning or perhaps engage in un autre brainstorming session. Later on the executive will relax with un coctail at un night-club. C'est OK to stay late to voir le show.

Quebec French is also characterized by certain expressions. Besides the accent, a Parisian will usually be able to identify a Québécois by phrases like *nous autres* (the rest of us), *j'ai-pas* (I don't know), the musical *binbin* (*bien, bien*: very, very good) plus the bookend greeting *salut!* (hi/bye) instead of the more formal *bonjour* and *au revoir*.

The Montreal accent is particularly noteworthy. Many visitors to the city, both French and those who've learned the language in school, are shocked at first by what they hear. More precisely, the shock is about what they don't understand. A thick Montreal accent is a marvel. It is skitterish, lightning-quick, and sounds initially as if the speaker is using his or her nose rather than mouth. Listen closely, extract the odd words of dialect, and what will emerge is a gregarious and engaging tongue almost totally lacking in the pretence of Parisian French. Québécois French doesn't sound like a textbook. It sounds like people! ❑

LEFT: newspapers are read avidly in Montreal, home of Canada's first paper.

Divine Assistance – lacks all the resonance of the original. The first church on he site was founded in 1671 by Marguerite Bourgeoys *(see page 27)*. Various ncarnations followed, and the current building dates from 1772. Typically Québécois features of Notre-Dame-de-Bon-Secours include the arched door, wooden belfry, and *oeil-de-boeuf* (a small round window in the gable). Interestingly, Saint Marguerite – who was canonized by Pope John Paul II in 1982 – returned from a visit to France in 1672 with a tiny wooden statue of the Virgin Mary. Against all odds, the statue has survived numerous fires and is now kept in a house on rue Sherbrooke.

Map on page 126

Marguerite Bourgeoys is a legend in Quebec. The **museum** (open same hours as the chapel; entrance fee; tel: 282-8670) in the basement of Notre-Dame-de-Bon-Secours, dedicated to her life, is a site of veneration for many Catholics, especially older residents who can recall an era when the Québécois Catholics were among the most devout and pious in Christendom. Her life is, naturally, shrouded in myth and folklore. The museum is modest, consisting largely of showcases that use miniature dolls to re-enact the key scenes of Saint Marguerite's long and active life. The dolls wear traditional costumes and smile sweetly. A more interesting activity, included in the price, is a climb up the creaky wooden staircase to the aerial chapel and observation tower.

The Habitat complex consists of 158 units hoisted into place like building blocks.

The view of the harbour from here is impressive. Visible to the south, astride the St Lawrence, are Expo '67's two most famous, or infamous, landmarks: Buckminster Fuller's 20-storey geodesic dome (previously the American pavilion and now the Biosphère – an intriguing interpretive centre on the ecosystems of the St Lawrence River and the Great Lakes) and architect Moshe Safdie's cubic apartment complex, Habitat, a startlingly ugly and awkward living space.

BELOW:
winter at Marché Bonsecours.

Stylish market

The **Marché Bonsecours**  (Bonsecours Market) (350 rue St-Paul Est; open daily mid-May–late Aug; free; tel: 872-7730) was once the most photographed edifice in Montreal. It has attractive facades, especially on the river side, and a Renaissance-style dome (1864) that was the first to be erected in the city. Remember that Montreal was, and still is, a port. Ships moving down the St Lawrence from Quebec would have spotted the dome and Notre Dame church before anything else. For a sailor, riding an autumn storm and fatigued from months at sea, these markers became emblems of security and shelter, visible even in dreams.

The Marché was primarily a market and exhibition centre. The vagaries of history, however, forced it to function briefly as both house of parliament (1849) and, between 1852 and 1878, as city hall. From the mid-1960s it served as offices for civil servants, but in May 1996 it reopened as a **public market** complete with farmers' stands. This runs from mid-May to late August but there are interesting craft and furniture outlets open all year round, as well as a café and a deli.

> *Montreal is pleasantly situated on the margin of the St Lawrence, and is backed by some bold heights, about which there are charming rides and drives. The streets are generally narrow and irregular.*
>
> – CHARLES DICKENS

Historic hotel and waterfront

In its day, **Hôtel de Rasco**  at 295 rue St-Paul was considered among the finest hotels in North America. Named after an Italian, Francisco Rasco, who emigrated to North America in the early 1800s, it was constructed in 1836 and featured a lavish restaurant that was "the place to be" in 1840s Montreal. A ballroom and concert hall were available for the cultured and/or wealthy.

In 1842 Charles Dickens, on the visit that would eventually produce *American Notes*, stayed at the hotel with his wife. Rasco Hotel, abandoned for decades, was restored in 198_ and currently houses government offices. Look for the name between floors of a simple, almost spartan greystone building.

A tour of Place Jacques-Cartier would be incomplete without a walk along the sweeping arc of **rue de la Commune**, once Montreal's waterfront. Rue de la Commune used to be a bustling thoroughfare lined with carriages and transport wagons. It had a promenade where strollers could watch the ships unload onto railway cars as thickets of masts swayed in the swell like compass needles. It is quiet now, largely inactive. But history is painted on the facades of the warehouses: J. Alfred Ouimet – Importer; Borque Wholesale Grocer; Standard Paper Box. Condominiums are beginning to take root in some of the derelict buildings.

BELOW: the market at night.

Place d'Armes

The expansion westward from the historic building of Place Jacques-Cartier to the skyscrapers of **Place d'Armes**  represents, in broad terms, the transformation of Old Montreal from an 18th-century French colonial outpost to a 19th-century English business centre. Keep in mind that pre-1759 Montreal was a walled city, even though the hilly topography of the region left many of the taller buildings, including bo_ churches, fully exposed to cannon fire from the St Lawrence River. The ramparts had four main gates, including one off rue Notre-Dame. The walls were 5.5 metres (18 ft) high and 1.2 metres (4 ft) thick, but historians emphasize their flimsiness, and it is generally accepted that they wouldn't have slowed down the enemy for very long.

When the ramparts came down in the early 1800s, the symbolism was inescapable. No longer defensive, no longer insular, Montreal was now open for business with the rest of Canada and, thanks to the St Lawrence, the outside world. Place d'Armes was where the major transactions occurred.

But first a word about the streets between the two squares. For many tourists, and most locals, Old Montreal in summer means eating, drinking and music. These narrow lanes, barely wide enough for a car, are lined with restaurants and cafés, along with Quebec's beloved *boîtes à chanson* (traditional music clubs). Rue St-Paul, rue St-Vincent and, further west, rue St-Pierre are also good to wander.

Worthy of mention if only as an aside, is the McDonald's at the intersection of rue Notre-Dame and boulevard St-Laurent. A plaque outside the restaurant informs the reader that here lived Antoine Laumet de Lamonīe (1658–1730), founder of Detroit *and* governor of the state of Louisiana. Lamonīe was certainly a busy man.

Visiting a *boîte à chanson* is virtually mandatory on any trip to Montreal. Literally a "music box", these beer halls are boisterous, frothy, *joie-de-vivre* establishments where musicians, often solo guitarists, run through the current repertoire of Québécois folk songs, anthems and the latest chart hits. The packed houses sing along, applaud, proffer requests that are adopted, deferred, or

Map on page 126

TIP

Watch the crowds, see where they are heading. Then, knowing which spots are popular and which are not, decide either to follow fashion or to set it.

BELOW: window boxes and old stone buildings typify Old Montreal.

Come early to Les Deux Pierrots. There are often long line-ups even before the music begins.

BELOW:
clapping along to French folk songs.

rejected out of hand – all depending on the tone and direction of the night. *Boîtes* are authentically Québécois and impervious, by and large, to the encroachment of technology on music. A guitar, a microphone, pitchers of beer, a convivial audience: what more is needed? The quintessential *boîte* in Old Montreal is Les Deux Pierrots on rue St-Paul. The lively mix of *chansonniers* and rock sing-alongs is hugely popular.

Finally, don't forget about the Vieux-Port. Though largely unused as a port, the park by the St Lawrence offers long summer evenings of music and dance. With the Montreal skyline as a backdrop and the river, active with ships and sail-boats, flowing gently past, the setting alone makes the park worth a visit.

Montreal's historic growth

Back to Place d'Armes. To stand in the square is to witness in visual terms the historic growth of Montreal as a city. The casual mingling of commerce with religion is, at first, rather disconcerting. Notre-Dame Basilica and the adjoining seminary appear lost among the banks and, by modern standards, miniature office towers. But after a while the congruities among the buildings make the juxtaposition less jarring. Perhaps there is also, in Quebec, a resigned acceptance of the "business of faith", and vice versa.

Maisonneuve, whose statue adorns the square, would certainly not have blessed this marriage of God and Mammon. As the founder of Montreal, Paul de Chomedey, Sieur de Maisonneuve, definitely deserved a memorial in a prominent location. But why Place d'Armes, while Admiral Nelson gazes so incongruously upon the city hall in Place Jacques-Cartier? The statue depicts Maisonneuve holding the banner of France. He is surrounded by other pio

eers, including Jeanne Mance, Louis Hébert and Lambert Closse. All the fig-
res are, in turn, surrounded by the likes of the Bank of Montreal and the New
ork Insurance Company. Are Montreal's founding fathers (and mothers) at all
ncomfortable with the company? Though Maisonneuve's expression is dour,
ae limestone otherwise reveals little.

Parked along the southern rim of the square, rain or shine, snow or sand
orm, is Montreal's venerable fleet of *calèches* – horse-drawn carriages. They
re hard to miss. If the sound of wooden wheels rattling over cobblestones
oesn't prick up the ears, the bellow of the drivers certainly will. "*Un calèche,
fonsieur?*" they will shout across Place d'Armes. Or, sizing up the mark as a
aurist: "Ride through Old Montreal for you, Sir?" In high season the compe-
tion is fierce, and drivers fan out across the square like angry bees. In winter
ae men sit stoically inside their vehicles, watching their breath dissipate in the
igid air. Under these circumstances, the invitation to visitors is more matter-
f-fact, less convincing.

Touring Old Montreal in a carriage can be delightful. Try it during the win-
r, with a bear skin protecting the lower body and, ideally, a flask of something
arm tucked inside the pocket. During the busy months it is often best to wait
ntil evening to hire a carriage. Then the streets are full of moving shadows;
aafts of light seep between drawn curtains, water trapped between cobble-
ones glistens under the yellow street lamps. Use a ride to experience the
mosphere of Old Montreal at different times of the day and year – but *don't*
re one to sightsee. Always do that on foot.

Place d'Armes is also home to the ubiquitous tour buses dropping visitors off
r cursory tours of Notre-Dame and its environs. The traveller aboard one of

Map
on page
126

TIP

Always bargain when
hiring a calèche. The
rate quoted for a tour
(usually around $30
per half-hour) isn't
always their best deal,
especially off-season.

BELOW: trotting
out in rue St-Paul.

Notre-Dame's twin towers are magnificent, the mark of greatness in architect James O'Donnell's design.

these buses who aspires to jump ship couldn't choose a better place to do i than the square, a launching point for just about all the most interesting areas c Old Montreal. Mutinies of this kind are to be encouraged.

Notre-Dame Basilica

Basilique Notre-Dame ⓭ (110 rue Notre-Dame Ouest; open: daily, 7am–8pm entrance fee; tel: 842-2925) is quite simply Montreal's most famous churc and justly so. The first chapel, built within the fort in 1642, was covered wit bark. The current structure (1829) is a little more grand. A contemporary Mor treal poet describes the church in winter:

> *In laden February, on rue St-Jacques*
> *we are dreaming the breeding of lilacs*
> *and shuffling on ice toward Notre-Dame.*
> *Suddenly the cold bright square*
> *the two arms of her towers and the walk*
> *into the blue sunrise of her altar.*

Each of the twin towers measures 69 metres (227 ft), and they were complete only in the 1840s by John Ostell, who succeeded as architect after O'Donnell death. The plainness of the exterior was both aesthetic and practical: Quebe lacked the stoneworkers to do the work. The decision to leave the facad unadorned was, in context, a wise one.

The west tower of Notre-Dame houses a 12-tonne/ton bell that it took a doze men to ring. Even today, powered by electricity, the bell is rung sparingly, us ally when famous Quebeckers have just finished tying the knot inside. Th basilica, still considered among the finest examples of the Gothic Revival sty

BELOW: Montreal's International Fireworks Festival.

FESTIVAL CITY

Montrealers start the summer months with a bang: t International Fireworks Festival in June featur pyrotechnical wizardry accompanied by music, wi nations competing from all over the globe.

Then (in July) follows the International Jazz Festival, o of the main events of this type in the world. A sm organization only a decade ago, the Montreal Jazz Festi has become a 10-day extravaganza with up to 1,0 musicians playing to throngs of onlookers at indoor a outdoor concerts *(see page 187)*.

No sooner has the Jazz Festival come and gone th the Just for Laughs (*Juste pour Rire*) comedy festival tak over *(see feature page 185)*.

The dates of the delightful FrancoFolies, often overlook by anglophones, seem to change each year but if you cat the right week you're in for a treat of mostly free conce by an incredible range of French-influenced musicia from many different countries.

Summer finally winds down with the Film Festival, whe bleary-eyed film buffs rush from one showing to the next an effort to keep pace with 200-plus quality internatio films on offer *(see feature page 182)*.

And that's just a taster. See Travel Tips for a full listi

n North America, was visited by architects from other cities to learn from)'Donnell's mastery.

The interior of the basilica is majestic. Designed by Victor Bourgeau, who also vorked on the Mary Queen of the World Cathedral in Dorchester Square *(see age 162)*, it is at once massive and welcoming, a feat achieved by the original se of woodworking and carpentry. Bourgeau encouraged local artists to use tra- itional methods and tastes. The result is a glittering, and at times overwhelm- ng, use of paints – the aqua-blue nave, for example, is delicate and refined – and rnately carved wood statuary.

Note especially the main altar, which is perpetually bathed in flowers, and the igures of Jeremiah and Ezekiel at the bottom of the pulpit. The wraparound bal- onies are also splendid; they serve to narrow the distance between the wor- hipper and the sacristy. Also worth noting is the haunting presence of giant ipes in the organ loft. The effect, achieved by back-lighting the organ (also one with the "sunrise" behind the altar), is stunning: fingers of bluish light rc upward into the nave.

Notre-Dame keeps long hours to satisfy the tourists, admirers and worship- ers who wander the aisles. Services are held several times daily, and those /ho are lucky might hear the organ. The sound is sonorous and celestial.

Adjacent to the west wall of the basilica stands – miraculously, some say – Iontreal's oldest building. The **Vieux Séminaire de St-Sulpice** ⓮ (116 rue Iotre-Dame Ouest; not open to the public) dates from 1680. The Sulpicians, the rder that founded the seminary, at one time wielded enormous power in New rance. In 1663 the Société de St-Sulpice took over missionary duties from the ociété de Notre-Dame, becoming, in effect, the landlords of all the island of

Map on page 126

Pop singer Céline Dion was married in Notre-Dame Basilica in December 1994.

BELOW: Basilique Notre-Dame.

Montreal. Even Maurice Duplessis would have envied such power. Today, more than 300 years after arriving, the Sulpicians – no longer *seigneurs*, no longer even the moral arbiters of life in Montreal – still own and operate the field stone seminary.

The seminary clock, by the way, was installed in 1701. It is considered the first public clock in Canada. Though the works were replaced by electronic movements in 1966, it still functions only periodically. Setting one's watch by would be unwise.

Search for bargains in "Antique Alley" on rue Notre-Dame.

Bank of Montreal

If Notre-Dame asserted francophone values, the **Banque de Montréal** (Bank of Montreal) building across Place d'Armes was an anglophonic retort. The neoclassical design of this 1847 structure offers an ornate facade that boasts six Corinthian columns with pediment sculptures – discernible only through lenses of some sort – of a sailor, a colonialist, and two Amerindians, one a "noble savage" and the other a recalcitrant hell-bent on rejecting civilization. The facade was designed by local architect John Wells.

The interior of the bank is stunning. The lobby is spacious, the colours gentle and the light soft at all times of day. The atrium in particular, linking the older part of the building with a 1905 addition, is lovely, lined by eight Ionic columns of Vermont granite with marble bases. The walls of the atrium are made of pink marble from Tennessee. In the majestic front hall one discovers another 3 columns, also of granite, and counters of marble. Gold leaf covers everything, and elaborate chandeliers hang from the ceiling.

BELOW:
Vieux Séminaire
de St-Sulpice.

The interior takes its grace from both the simplicity of the design and the continuous presence of natural light streaming down from massive windows. The bank's architects worked directly from models of Italian churches: it is hard not to remark upon the "basilica" style of the structure. A provocative gesture? Artistic inspiration? Also worth a look is a fine sculpture, *Patria*, in the atrium. The marble statue is a memorial to Canadians who died in World War I.

The Bank of Montreal offers visitors a small **museum** (129 rue St-Jacques; open: Mon–Fri 10am–4pm; free; tel: 877-6810) off the main lobby devoted to numismatics – money, to the layman. Displays of banknotes, coins, a collection of elaborate 19th-century piggy banks and other interesting memorabilia are to be found here. Tours are available both official languages.

Wall Street of Canada

In both tone and proportion the Bank of Montreal headquarters sent out a message: on **rue St-Jacques**, the street crossing the north end of the square, business would be calm, orderly and efficient. The result was the "Wall Street of Canada", an appellation applied to "St James Street" as it was called by anglophone Montrealers.

Until the late 1970s, rue St-Jacques was Canada's financial centre, a street of busy Victorian buildings swathed to varying degrees in stucco, wrought-iron

Map on page 126

olumns and elaborate porticos. A trolley down the middle of the road serviced office workers.

Among the many stately edifices are the Molson Bank building at 288 St-Jacques and the Bank of Commerce across the street. The Molson Bank building was built in 1866 using brewery profits that today fuel, among other things, the Montreal Canadiens hockey team. The bank itself no longer exists but the building that still bears its name, like all the offices at the corner of St-Jacques and rue St-Pierre, is impressive. None, however, quite stacks up to the **Banque Royale** ⓰ (Royal Bank).

randiose and ostentatious

ike it or not – and many Montrealers consider the building an exercise in ostentation – the former head office of the Royal Bank at 360 St-Jacques is a must-see on any tour of the business district. Constructed in 1928, the Royal Bank was for a brief period the tallest structure not only in Canada but the entire British Empire.

The exterior is grand but austere, even sober. Not so the interior. The architects who designed the building were said to have had in mind the Medici Palace Florence, Italy. They certainly had grandiose ambitions. The main doors are framed in bronze replicas of coins and lead into a lobby noted for its coffered ceiling and the marble steps which ascend to the main hall. Arches are covered with reddish limestone and walls are decorated with the coats of arms of Canada's provinces. Again, the ceiling is ornately coffered. There are marble walls, bronze screens, and the mosaic tiles on the floor are inlaid with Canada's royal coat of arms.

On each 23 June, the night before St-Jean-Baptiste Day, a parade snakes through Old Montreal along rue Notre-Dame, capped by late-night fireworks.

BELOW: Banque de Montréal.

*Opened in 1992, the
World Trade Centre
revived the fortunes
of Place Victoria.*

BELOW: the
ostentatious
Banque Royale.

The effect is either dazzling or disheartening, depending on taste. Both size and decoration, the Royal Bank begs comparison with the Bank of Montre building. To the untrained eye, they are both formidable.

Place Victoria

In the 1880s many commercial businesses followed the fashion and move their offices further west to **Place Victoria** at rue St-Jacques and rue McGill. T square was for a brief period a prestigious residential address and one of Mo treal's prime shopping districts. Barely 20 years later, however, departme stores, lured by the rapidly growing English community along rue Sherbrook moved again to the current "mecca" of rue Ste-Catherine. Place Victoria fad rapidly, only to be revived again by the opening in 1992 of the **Centre de Con merce Mondial** (World Trade Centre) (747 Square Victoria; open dai 7am–7pm; tel: 982-9888). Its 19th-century facade fronts a stunning office con plex with a soaring sunlit atrium, the Hotel Inter-Continental, the Nordheim Building, and a restored music hall where Sarah Bernhardt performed in 188

The historical demographics of commercial life in Montreal are a study skittishness and insecurity. Only the stalwarts – the banks and loan compani – had the presence of mind to stay along St-Jacques; until, that is, recent pol ical developments precipitated a wholesale rethinking of location.

Place d'Armes features other prominent buildings, as well. Dozens of offic and banks, many of them still functioning, line the streets on and around t square. But the area is also the focal point for Montreal's considerable nev paper industry. Within a few blocks can be found the offices of nearly all t major newspapers, and one significant ghost.

The *Montreal Star*, once the city's largest English paper, resided at 245 St-Jacques in the heart of the business district. Though the *Star* ceased publication in 1979, the *Montreal Gazette*, the current flagbearer, has offices on rue St-Antoine and in the old *Star* building on St-Jacques. The *Gazette*, launched in 1778, is the city's oldest newspaper. *La Presse*, North America's best-selling French daily, has both its original and modern home at the corner of St-Jacques and St-Laurent. The old *La Presse* building is quite stately.

Also in Old Montreal, appropriately isolated from the larger community, are the old offices of the erudite and influential *Le Devoir*. If the other buildings look like the offices of large, busy, mass-appeal publications, then *Le Devoir*, roomed for a different class of reader, is appropriately solemn and demure. Its former digs are at 211 rue St-Sacrement.

Banks, business, newspapers: the markers of the new 19th-century industrial city as delineated by Dickens in England, Zola in France, James and Dreiser in the USA. Place d'Armes is the product of these modern realities but, among the soaring new and old edifices competing for the square, none is more impressive, more substantial, than the towers of Notre-Dame. Peaceful co-existence is the unspoken motto of Montreal, and even the old warrior Maisonneuve, also compromised by location, appears resigned to the fact.

Origins of the city

Montreal began in **Place Royale** ⓱ and **Place d'Youville**. These two squares intersect each other at the site of Pointe-à-Callière, where Samuel de Champlain landed in 1611 and declared the spot a "place royale". Thirty years later, Maisonneuve chose that same site to erect the fort that became Ville Marie. An obelisk

Map on page 126

Below:
echoes of the past.

Famous Montrealers

Despite its cultural riches, Montreal has not produced an outstanding number of world-famous artists. But a few have risen to the top of their respective fields.

Leonard Cohen began as a somewhat controversial poet and novelist of the 1960s, attracting a small loyal following – particularly in restless, flower-power-era America. But he really found his calling when he began making music. Cohen's smoky delivery and sultry songwriting defy categorization; elements of jazz, torch songs and the blues creep in, all stirred together by Cohen's gravelly voice. He still lives on the Plateau.

William Shatner was educated at McGill but left the city for good soon afterwards to seek his fortune in Hollywood. It took some time, but he eventually found the role of a lifetime: that of Captain James Tiberius Kirk of the *Starship Enterprise*. The role of Kirk, on a short-lived but long-syndicated television program and then in a raft of like-themed motion pictures, has kept him working for most of his adult life. He rarely returns home.

To try to list the famous hockey players from this city would require too much space. Maurice "The Rocket" Richard was a visible presence here for decades, right up until his death in the spring of 2000, and many other former Montreal Canadiens are active in team and community activities.

Then there's novelist Mordecai Richler, who has captured the intricate workings of Jewish Montreal – particularly certain stretches of St-Urbain and Fairmount streets – in novels and collections of essays such as *The Apprenticeship of Duddy Kravitz*, *Solomon Gursky Was Here*, *Barney's Version* and *Oh Canada! Oh Quebec!* Richler spends time in London, but he can also be found in certain Outremont and Mile-End haunts.

Jacques Villeneuve lived in St-Jean-sur-Richelieu while compiling a fine career as a racing driver; Jacques was tragically killed in a crash, but his son, Gilles, is among the world's dozen or so top Formula One drivers.

Oddly, few prominent pop musicians have come from Montreal (save one, and we'll get to her in a moment). About the best the city had managed were the one-hit wonder dance band Men Without Hats – which knew a moment of chart success during the 1980s – and local heartthrob Cory Hart, who scored not one but two hits before fading from the international eye. Hart still lives on the Plateau, and resurfaces occasionally to do packed Montreal gigs. No-one seems to know what happened to Men Without Hats.

However, Céline Dion became one of the most successful female singers of her time – and her fame extends far across the ocean. Dion was a high-school dropout from tiny Charlemagne, Quebec, just across the river from the island of Montreal's northern shore, before she and her manager (and, eventually, husband) planned her subsequent conquest of America's radio airwaves. Dion continues to keep a home in the city, and has become French Canada's proudest export since "ice" beer. ❑

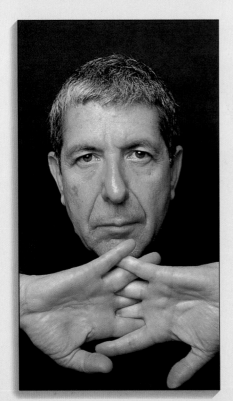

LEFT: Leonard Cohen, one of Montreal's famous sons, is still seen around town.

the eastern end of Place d'Youville commemorates the event. The inscription emphasizes that Maisonneuve ordered the simultaneous construction of a fort, chapel and a graveyard. Health, religion and death: the basics.

It is difficult to imagine how Ville Marie looked nearly 400 years ago. The St Lawrence has been pushed back for landfill, a small river that ran alongside the fort is now underground, and the dense forest that made reaching Mont Royal an arduous journey is today a forest of skyscrapers, the walk made tricky by rush-hour traffic. When Maisonneuve shifted the village to Place d'Armes – 100 metres (330 ft) north – it was a move inland, away from the dangers of the St Lawrence. Things have changed dramatically.

Birthplace

At **Pointe-à-Callière** remains the literal birthplace of Montreal, and the surrounding streets are its oldest neighbourhood. A plaque in Place Royale calls the site the "first public square of Montreal", affixing the date 1657 to its creation. In a sense the "community" of Montreal also dates from that year. Before 1657 Ville Marie was a wildly remote fort inhabited by a singular group of people: adventurers, traders, missionaries, soldiers and their officers.

Though it was where they lived, Ville Marie was not their home. Instead the fort was variously a potential market, potential mission, potential conquest. The stake these pioneers had in the colony, while considerable, was not likely to produce citizens and samaritans. That required settlers, ordinary people devoted to establishing a life for themselves and their children. Communities are the sum of citizens, not conquistadors. In European society the traditional symbol of a town was a public square. So, too, was this the case in Montreal.

Map on page 126

TIP

For orientation, remember that Place Royale runs north to south; Place d'Youville, east to west.

BELOW:
pumpkins decorate this restaurant courtyard in Place d'Youville.

TIP

Two lesser-known museums in Old Montreal are the Dolls and Treasures Museum at 105 rue St-Paul Est (tel: 866-0110) – just what it sounds like – and the Economusée de l'encadrement (Frame Museum) at 40 St-Paul Ouest (tel: 845-3368) – an ode to the art of framing artwork.

BELOW: "Artists Alley" in Old Montreal.

As part of the city's 350th anniversary celebrations in 1992, the **Musée d'Archéologie et d'Histoire de la Pointe-à-Callière**  (Museum of Archaeology and History) (350 Place de la Commune; open July–Aug: Tues–Fri 10am–6pm; rest of the year: Tues–Fri, 10am–5pm; entrance fee; tel: 872-9150) was opened on the site where Montreal was founded in 1642. State-of-the-art multimedia techniques in the modern Eperon building present the city's early history. The site is above a crypt, believed to date back to the first cemetery, where 17th- to 20th-century artifacts are on display. Visitors pass through this subterranean gallery on their way to the old **customs house**, now part of the museum.

Despite its importance, this was for many years the least known and least explored part of Old Montreal. Since the mid-18th century, attention had been drawn east to Place d'Armes and Place Jacques-Cartier. However, a transformation has been taking place here since the early 1990s, and both visitors and Montrealers are finding many reasons to acquaint themselves with the area once again.

At the southern end of Place Royale is a grandiose statue of John Young (1811–79), the harbour commissioner credited with making the city a world-class port. Young's gaze still encompasses rue de la Commune and the eastern docking facilities. Keep in mind that the river, which today appears distant from Old Montreal, once flowed precariously near the shops and warehouses along the Commune. Photos from the period tell the story: floods, especially in late winter, submerged the lower streets in 1 metre (3 ft) of water. Though landfill curbed the St Lawrence's reckless power, stinging winds and sleet remind the visitor of the seaway's proximity.

"Artists Alley" in Old Montreal.

eat of government

lace d'Youville ⓴, Old Montreal's largest square, commences at the statue and
ns west four blocks to rue McGill. Besides Pointe-à-Callière, the square's
her main attraction is the **Centre d'Histoire de Montréal ㉑** (Montreal His-
ry Centre, 335 Place d'Youville; open May–Sept; daily, 10am–5pm;
:pt–Dec: Tues–Sun, 10am–5pm; entrance fee; tel: 872-3207), formerly a styl-
h 1915 firehouse. Now a museum of Montreal history, it is worth a visit for
yone interested in studying the city's growth.

Place d'Youville was once the site of the parliament for both Upper and
)wer Canada. The market building here, erected after the 1837 rebellion,
sted only a dozen years before rioters, protesting an unpopular British bill,
urned it down *(see page 44)*.

Canada's pre-1867 legislature was housed briefly in the Marché Bonsecours,
en resumed its quixotic search for a home: Kingston, Quebec City, and finally
e current capital Ottawa.

rey nuns

ere are a number of restored buildings on the square, the most famous of
hich, the **Hôpital des Soeurs Grises ㉒**, runs off rue Normand. The old hos-
al traces its origins to 1693, the year François Charon de la Bare resolved to
gin a "house of charity" for Montreal's sick, poor and handicapped.

In 1753 Maria d'Youville, who founded the Sisters of Charity, extended the
oject into a hospital under the care of the sisters, known locally, because of
e colour of their habits, as the grey nuns *(soeurs grises)*. Though the hospi-
l moved to rue Dorchester in 1871, many of the original structures escaped

Map on page 126

The Centre d'Histoire de Montréal combines Dutch and English architectural styles.

BELOW: painting the perfect portrait.

demolition and were restored in the late 1970s. The restoration was superbl
done, and the hospital's west wing, including the remains of the original chape
are visible on rue St-Pierre.

The courtyard facing the square is also charming, and a delicate stained-gla:
window along rue St-Normand brightens an otherwise austere, function:
exterior. Both the Hôpital des Soeurs Grises and the adjoining **Ecurie d'Youvil**
(d'Youville Stables) are currently finding use as multi-purpose facilities. Th
courtyard of the stables, surrounded by 19th-century buildings, is a pleasa:
place for a cold drink in the summer.

Renewal

The bottom of St-Pierre, also off the square, is a heartening example of su
cessful urban renewal. Until recently empty, the block now houses luxury apa:
ments, law offices, architectural firms, even a fancy cheese and chocolate sh
It is also the location of a small museum devoted to Marc-Aurèle Fort
(1888–1970), an important Québécois painter. Fortin's watercolours of the
Lawrence in all its seasonal variety are famous throughout Canada. **Mus**
Marc-Aurèle Fortin (118 rue St-Pierre; open: Tues–Sun, 11am–5pm; entran
fee; tel: 845-6108), in the warren of streets one block south of Place d'Youvil
commemorates his works.

Further west, at the extreme edge of Old Montreal, are blocks of impressi
19th-century warehouses and customs houses. Rue McGill in particular h
several fine buildings, including the ornate former headquarters of the Gra:
Trunk Railway at number 360 and the Wilson Chambers Building at numb
474, near Place Victoria.

BELOW:
lots to discover at
iSci, the Interactive
Science Centre.

Map on page 126

The streets north of Place d'Youville were in limbo for many years, but gentrification is now taking place, particularly at the west end of rue St-Paul. However, some buildings remain derelict, awaiting an entrepreneur to restore them to life. Wandering along rue St-Pierre, rue St-Nicolas and rue St-François-Xavier, especially at night, can be an eerie but wonderful experience.

Change of use

The area is also home to the **Théâtre Centaur** at 453 St-François-Xavier (tel: 88-3161). The theatre, which hosts Montreal's leading English-language company, occupies a 1903 Beaux-Art structure that was the site of the city's stock exchange until 1966. Before the Centaur building, the stock exchange was located in the old *Le Devoir* offices just around the corner. Before *that*, well, Montreal's 19th-century wheelers and dealers carried out their business in a the St-Paul coffee shop.

Pedal power at the Old Port.

Buildings in Old Montreal change function far more quickly than they change facades. Why shouldn't they? Historic neighbourhoods often atrophy because they fail to meet modern needs, but a neighbourhood needn't lose its soul to remain vital. Old Montreal has been struggling to retain its shape – or, better, to find a new identity – for over 30 years. Though the struggle is not over, the future is bright. Both the Vieux-Port and Old Montreal have seen massive and ongoing restoration projects.

Three previously mentioned examples of the overhaul are the opening of the Museum of Archaeology and History in Place Royale, the Montreal History Centre in Place d'Youville, and the restoration of the Marché Bonsecours. The Vieux-Port de Montréal was also revamped for the city's 350th anniversary.

BELOW: Vieux-Port.

Map on page 126

Exhibit at the Interactive Science Centre.

RIGHT:
Quai King-Edward.
BELOW:
sailors' haunt.

The Old Port

Take time to admire the neoclassical old greystone warehouses along rue de ▮ Commune, overlooking the port. They are a rare example of waterfront plannin▮ in North America.

The port stretches over 2 km (1 mile) along the St Lawrence River and is ▮ hive of activity, virtually year-round. An attractive park runs alongside it, wit▮ a pedestrian walkway and a bicycle trail that goes to and even beyond th▮ Lachine Canal, a journey of at least 10 km (6 miles). Anyone with a sudden urg▮ to cycle after arriving at the Old Port can rent bicycles, or even skates, at th▮ Place Jacques-Cartier entrance to the port.

Besides a few remaining shipping activities within the port, there is a pop▮ lar **flea market** open from early May to early September; and the SC▮ **Labyrinthe** (end of Quai King-Edward; open May–Nov: daily; entrance fe▮ tel:1-800-971-7678), a 2-km (1¼-mile) maze of obstacle-filled foggy corridor▮

Also note the new **iSci Centre** (Montreal Interactive Science Centre) (Qu▮ King-Edward; open daily, 10am–6pm; entrance fee; tel: 496-4724, or 1-87▮ 496-4724 toll free; website: www.isci.ca) which opened in spring 2000 ▮ expand upon an existing IMAX theatre facility on a waterfront pier. This ne▮ complex's interactive offerings are divided into three exhibition halls coverin▮ the history of science: Life, Matter and Information. There are also two hig▮ tech theatres and three dining areas, including one on the St Lawrence.

If you're coming chiefly to sample the newly improved **IMAX theatre** (te▮ 596 IMAX, or 1-800-349 IMAX toll free; website: www.imaxoldport.com) tal▮ note that most of the showings are in French. (This being Montreal, it's alwa▮ possible the language police were involved in that decision.) An English versi▮ usually plays three times daily.

Changing times

Other attractions in the Old Port area include the **To▮ de l'Horloge** (Clock Tower) at the end of Quai ▮ l'Horloge. The tower was built in 1922 to comme▮ orate the merchant mariners who died in World War ▮ The climb of 192 steps to the observatory is reward▮ with a fine view of the city and river.

During winter months a large public ice rink is op▮ at Bassin Bonsecours, and in the summer, during t▮ Just for Laughs Festival, Quai Jacques-Carti▮ becomes a non-stop comedy routine.

A range of boat tours leaves from the Vieux-Po▮ including traditional harbour cruises with Croisiè▮ AML, glass-topped tours through the locks of t▮ Lachine Canal on a *Bateau Mouche*, exhilarating ra▮ ing tours with Les Descentes sur le St-Laurent. T▮ former control tower for barges on the Lachine Ca▮ now operates as a tourist information centre for ▮ Vieux-Port from mid-May to mid-September.

The revival of Old Montreal is ongoing, funded ▮ both the public and private sectors. Cobbled stre▮ continue to be restored, as do more and more of ▮ buildings along rue St-Jacques and rue McGill. C▮ Montreal is an integral part of any traveller's visit to ▮ city – and now it's also becoming a comfortable a▮ dynamic space for its own citizens and businesses.

MONTREAL'S ECLECTIC ARCHITECTURE

The city's architecture is a blend of all that the French, British and other Europeans brought with them – aspirations, memories and longings

▷ **ITALIAN JOB**
Atop the Cathedral of Mary Queen of the World on boulevard René-Lévesque, the marching tableau of saints is similar to that on St Peter's Basilica in Rome.

Montreal's French founders didn't come from Paris, but from Brittany and Normandy, seafaring men and pious women whose longing for status and recognition is sometimes sharply evident. Echoes of Parisian style can clearly be seen in such Second Empire constructions as the old Hôtel de Ville (City Hall) in the Old Port, with its slim columns and pitched roof, in the Maison du Calvet hotel's high chimneys, and on street after street of townhouses on the Plateau (around Square St-Louis, for example), often incorporating some sort of fleur-de-lys woodwork.

△ **EUROPEAN FLAVOUR**
Wrought-iron balconies are a feature of the older parts of Montreal which hark back to those found in the kinder climes of southern Europe.

The British influence is clearest along the Golden Mile (rue Sherbrooke), in Westmount's ivy-touched stone buildings and university, and in certain downtown banks (notably the Bank of Montreal in Place d'Armes). It's a look characterized by ruddy sandstones and Scottish crests.

There's no mistaking the hand of the city's considerable number of Italian immigrants, either. Have a look up at the Cathedral of Mary Queen of the World on boulevard René-Lévesque, and you'll see a marching tableau of saints very like that topping St Peter's Basilica in Rome.

Revival periods have come and gone in Montreal, leaving stone behemoths around Square Dorchester with grand but now little-viewed interiors well worth seeking out. A minimalist modern hand gripped the city during the 1960s and 1970s, leaving few interesting marks — but the World Trade Centre project is one very interesting exception. The architect in charge chose to wall off an entire *ruelle* (alleyway) beneath glass, preserving an interesting urban space.

▷ **BOURGEOIS ELEGANCE**
The Square St-Louis is lined with elegant 19th-century Second Empire style residences.

◁ **SIMPLE STYLE**
In contrast to most others in the city, the simple facade of Notre-Dame-de-Bon Secours is reminiscent of a rural French chapel.

THE NEED FOR SNOW FENCES

Some of the architectural flourishes that developed in Montreal were not the result of a longing for home, but simple practicality. Montreal's long, snowy winters meant that a considerable weight of snow and ice would accumulate on buildings, threatening leaks or even collapse. Steeply pitched roofs were an obvious solution, although it was still often necessary for owners to scale wooden ladders and stand precariously on high, shovelling off the snow-pack before it could cause damage. Snow fences were a way of preventing mishap. A shovel-wielding owner might easily slip, and if he did, a little iron fence was the only thing standing between him and an icy street far below.

Even today, on structures where they're no longer necessary, the small, delicate fences are still added as a reverent homage to days past; this is most obvious on the business district's so-called "Batman" building.

CITY LANDMARK
Montreal's superb Hôtel de Ville (City Hall) is perhaps the best example of French Second Empire architectural indulgence in the city.

▷ QUEBEC CITY
Founded by Champlain in 1611, Quebec City is three decades older than Montreal and retains a more distinctly French look in its residential and commercial architecture.

◁ OLD MONTREAL
Winding wrought-iron staircases and red brick in Old Montreal give the area a thoroughly Old World flavour.

▷ STUDY CENTRE
The Canadian Centre for Architecture is both a museum and study centre, with collections of plans, books and models.

Map on page 156

DOWNTOWN

Montreal's modern heart is a dazzling interplay of sleek modern architecture, lively nightlife and historic churches and buildings that speak of the grandeur of another era

The St Lawrence River is a confluence of seas and lakes, a brackish bridge between the Atlantic Ocean – Europe's border – and the Great Lakes that are the watery heart of North America. Montreal's downtown is also a meeting place, a concourse of commercial enterprises, businesses and residential neighbourhoods. North America and Europe mingle freely in every district to produce a lively jumble of restaurants, shops, churches, architectural styles and ethnic communities. Together, they create a vibrant picture that reflects the historical diversity of Montreal.

The first settlers built their homes snugly against the St Lawrence River in the area now called "Old Montreal". Though the river was an important source of livelihood, it was also what drove citizens to higher ground. Persistent flooding in the 19th century prompted city-dwellers to move north, where the views from the mountain and the beauty of the surroundings enticed them into permanent settlements.

The downtown has undergone three eras of expansion. The first came during the late 19th century when English and Scottish fur traders accumulated fortunes and the city centre shifted west from Place d'Armes to Dominion Square (now called Square Dorchester). During this period, waves of immigrants caused an expansion eastward, lengthening the parameters of the inner city. As a result, the area north of rue Sherbrooke was transformed from farmland into affluent urban neighbourhoods. The majority of Montreal's famous churches and illustrious buildings were built in this initial expansion.

Predictably, the subsequent period of growth began after World War II, extending through the building boom of the 1950s, whose architectural aesthetics have not worn well. This rapid development radically altered and in some cases destroyed certain downtown neighbourhoods. Under the prolonged leadership of autocratic Montreal mayor Jean Drapeau, the city underwent a third period of expansion during the 1960s and 1970s, a period marked by bold and often dazzling architectural experimentation. Many world-class projects such as the Métro, Expo '67, and the 1976 Olympic facilities were built during Mayor Drapeau's mayoral reign.

The Underground

Montreal's urban development, however, has produced not only a vibrant surface life, but also an intriguing subterranean world.

Begun in the 1960s and apparently based on an idea by Leonardo da Vinci, Montreal's **"Underground City"** includes railway and Métro stations, bus terminals, major hotels, offices, boutiques, restaurants,

LEFT: Montreal's architectural contrasts.
BELOW: Place Montréal Trust can be reached via the Underground City.

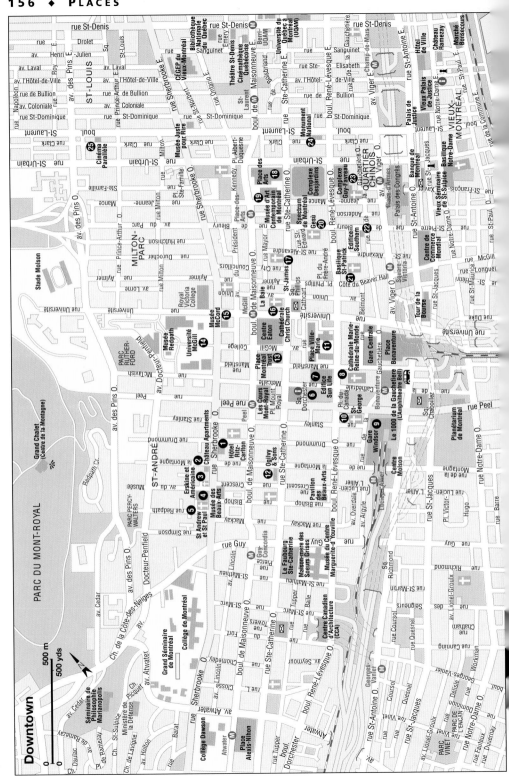

ank branches, department stores, cinemas, theatres, and numerous other out-
ts. In a city with dramatic temperature fluctuations, the underground down-
wn offers an environment that is warm and waterproof in winter and cool in
mmer. Glittering with chrome and smooth marble, it resembles a labyrinthine
ut opulent ant colony. Shops, businesses and services are linked by Mon-
eal's impressive and efficient transit system, the Métro – a network of 65
ations individually designed by prominent artists and architects. Entrances to
Iontreal's remarkable substratum are found throughout the downtown area,
d in all subway stations.

The downtown core is large, bordered roughly by **avenue Atwater**, **rue St-
enis**, **rue St-Antoine** and **rue Sherbrooke** *(see map opposite)*. Dividing it into
ve main areas makes for a relatively easy tour. These areas are: rue Sher-
rooke and Golden Square Mile; Dorchester Square; rue Ste-Catherine; Chi-
atown; and St-Laurent and the Main. Even in fine weather, you'll probably
ant to make use of Montreal's excellent Métro to access these areas. We'll
gin our tour at the northern edge of downtown – that is, at the foot of Mont
oyal along rue Sherbrooke.

xpansive era

he **Golden Square Mile** was the name bestowed upon the neighbourhood
closed by boulevard René Lévesque, rue Guy, rue Université and avenue des
ns. In 1900, the 25,000 residents of this square mile controlled a staggering
) percent of all the wealth in Canada. The buildings that remain from that
riod recall a grand and expansive era in Montreal's history. The most obvious
mbol of this golden age is the **Hôtel Ritz-Carlton** ❶ on Sherbrooke at rue
rummond *(see page 160).*

Imagine rue Sherbrooke nearly 100 years ago when
e Ritz-Carlton towered over the three-storey man-
ons and stately elm trees that lined the boulevard.
oday rue Sherbrooke is lined with many modern
otels, including the Westin Mont-Royal (formerly
own as the Four Seasons), office towers, art gal-
ries in converted turn-of-the-century houses, and
clusive shops such as the famous Cartier and
anada's own Holt-Renfrew.

erching gargoyles

here are also a few elegant apartment houses, includ-
g the imposing granite edifice just across the street
om the hotel. The **Château Apartments** ❷ were
ilt in 1925 for Senator Pamphile du Tremblay, a
rmer owner of the influential *La Presse* newspaper.
ne building is intended to resemble a castle on the
ire River in France, and it has some amusing
tails. The gargoyles perching on window ledges
ld onto coats of arms, and side turrets and crosses
rved from stone adorn the corners of the building. It
so has a lovely interior courtyard.

This château-style design, with its decorative tur-
ts, facades and porticos can also be seen in many
blic and private buildings throughout Quebec. It
presents the dominant architectural trend in the
ovince during the first half of the 20th century.

Map on page 156

Gargoyles perch on window ledges at the Château Apartments.

BELOW: parade on rue Sherbrooke.

Exquisite stained glass at the Erskine and American United Church.

Next door to the Château Apartments is the **Eglise Erskine et Américaine** ❻ (Erskine and American United Church) (corner rue Sherbrooke Ouest and avenue du Musée). Built in 1863, the church and its neighbour share a moody, almost medieval ambience. The severity of the rusticated stone exterior contrasts with the warm tones and circular floor plan of the interior. The exquisite stained glass windows are from the Tiffany Studio in New York.

Museum of Fine Arts

Next to the church on the north side of rue Sherbrooke is the **Musée des Beaux Arts** ❹ (Museum of Fine Arts) (1379 rue Sherbrooke Ouest; open Tues-Sun 11am-6pm; Wed until 9pm; entrance fee; tel: 285-1600; fax: 285-4070; website www.mmfa.qc.ca). Founded in 1860, this is Canada's oldest museum. The edifice, known as the Benaiah Gibb Pavilion, has a classical design and is faced in Vermont marble – a theme carried through to the lobby, which is dominated by an elegant marble staircase. The building was originally quite small and although an extension was completed in 1977, it was unfortunately not well matched to the original and suffered from a lack of natural light.

Happily, the matter was rectified in 1991 when the museum was expanded to the **Jean-Noël-Desmarais Pavilion**, just opposite on the south side of rue Sherbrooke. This new building is a stunning vision of white Vermont marble, designed by Moshe Safdie, and it is connected to the original building by an underground tunnel.

The museum's permanent collection consists of a wide range of paintings, sculptures and drawings from North America and Europe. There is a good sampling of European art from the 17th century onwards, including works by El Greco, Rodin, Dalí and Picasso.

Canadian Art is represented by Inuit woodcarving, soapstone sculpture and paintings by the Group of Seven – a seminal group of Ontario landscape painters – and contemporary artists like Paul-Emile Borduas, Jean-Paul Riopelle and Betty Goodwin. The museum also houses a fine collection of decorative arts from around the world.

On the north side of the road, west of the museum is the **Eglise St Andrew et St Paul** ❺ (Church of St Andrew and St Paul) (corner rue Sherbrooke Ouest and rue Redpath; tel: 842-3431). This is one of the many examples of Gothic Revival architecture in Montreal, and it is best known for its stunning stained glass windows. Two windows, located in the rear (left) and donated by the Allan family, are believed to have been done by Sir Edward Burne-Jones, the famous Pre-Raphaelite painter.

The Golden Square Mile

Adjacent to the Museum of Fine Arts is **avenue du Musée**, probably one of the best preserved streets in the area. It has little traffic and modern construction has made only a modest impact. The pleasures of residential architecture are subtle enough, and a stroll through this neighbourhood can transport you back to a different, slower-paced age. The status and wealth of these homes sets the imagination to wondering

BELOW: Musée des Beaux-Arts.

what life must have been like during the area's zenith in the first decades of the 20th century. One exhibit of paintings at the Museum of Fine Arts, born out of a similar curiosity, discovered works by Cézanne, Toulouse-Lautrec, Degas and Gaugin among the private collections of Montreal's former elite. Men who had expanded their wealth as rapidly and haphazardly as had Canada itself – through railways, shipbuilding and natural resources – built extravagant homes for their families and furnished them expensively.

Remember that in those days the neighbourhood would have been appropriately removed from the hustle and bustle of the downtown. With the slope of Mont Royal affording stunning vistas, trees providing the requisite privacy, the Ritz-Carlton only minutes away on rue Sherbrooke and Ogilvy's Department Store three blocks further south on rue Ste-Catherine, life would have been both tranquil and convenient for the residents.

The southern face of the mountain or the forests tucked into its plateau would have been ideal for a summer promenade. Hospitals and social clubs were close by, and excellent schools – such as the Trafalgar Girls' School on Docteur-Penfield and McGill University on rue Sherbrooke – absorbed the progeny of Montreal's affluent. Jobs could always be found for sons of the right kind of people, and neighbours on the Golden Square Mile were, naturally, the right kind of people – other business tycoons, bankers, various Anglo politicians, possibly foreign dignitaries from the consulates; even the rare wealthy French Montrealer who had been lured into the area by a beautiful home.

Elegant living, propriety, and social networks: along these steep narrow lanes life was, for a while, perfect. This was where all the newly gentrified Canadians wanted to live.

Map on page 156

The Golden Square Mile's favoured sons prospered in the business community that centred around Dominion Square (now Square Dorchester) and rue St-Jacques in Old Montreal.

BELOW:
Eglise Erskine et Américaine.

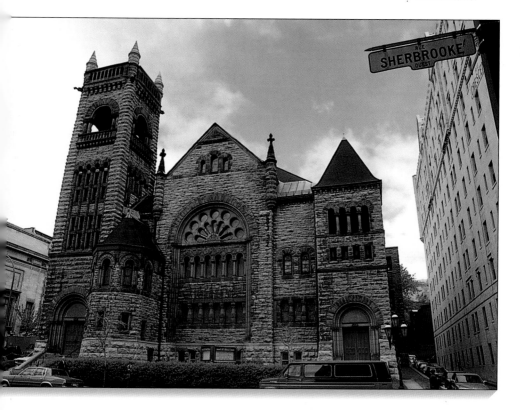

Grande Dame of Sherbrooke Street

Every major city deserves a Ritz-Carlton Hotel, but few are lucky enough to have one. Since its construction in 1911, Montreal's Ritz-Carlton has been a measuring stick for elegance and civility. The hotel is a symbol of old-world gentility in pleasant contrast to the sterile, hermetically sealed towers that pass for gracious accommodations today. The fact that the Ritz-Carlton Hotel has changed little in almost a century is precisely why it is such a special place.

In the early 1900s, Charles Ritz was thought to be the owner of the best hotel in all of Europe. The Ritz in Paris was rivalled only by the Carlton of London. It was Charles Hosmer, president of the Canadian Pacific Telegram, who thought Montreal could be well served by bringing together the rich traditions of these two great hotels.

Charles Ritz was finally convinced, but not without making stipulations unheard of at the time. He demanded that every room in the hotel have a private adjoining bathroom and a telephone. He also insisted that every floor be equipped with its own kitchen and that the concierge be available at all hours to fulfil the needs of the guests – no matter how ludicrous.

His instincts proved to be sound; the Ritz-Carlton became synonymous with top-quality service and the hotel assumed the status of a North American landmark.

During those early years the hotel played host to world-class luminaries such as the Prince of Wales, Queen Mary of Romania, and Hollywood stars Douglas Fairbanks and Mary Pickford. Though the hotel's bright lights were dimmed during two world wars, its status among the city's English-speaking elite picked up again in the 1950s and early 1960s.

While out-of-town guests were enjoying the fine service of the Ritz-Carlton, the hotel also established itself as an "unadvertised" private club for Montreal's anglophone business moguls. It became so closely associated with Montreal's business community that Canadian novelist Mordecai Richler immortalized the hotel in his novel *Joshua Then and Now*. His characters, attracted to the cosy charm of the Ritz, mourn its passing as a covert club in a humorous send-up: "The incomparable Ritz where once impeccably schooled brokers could conspire over malt whiskies and dishes of smoked almonds to send dubious mining stock soaring..."

A lot has changed since then but the Ritz still stands strong. The lobby is small, the bar is crowded, it has no gym and no pool, but what was good enough for guests 60 years ago, the hotel believes, is, with few modifications, good enough today. Size does not equal status; excellence is not demonstrated by gurgling fountains in a lobby. Qualities of status and elegance are, the Ritz-Carlton suggests, more subtle and elusive than we may believe. Others must agree, judging from the line-up of Rolls-Royces and custom-built Lincolns out in front of the hotel's doors. ❏

LEFT: The venerable Ritz Carlton Hotel is a symbol of elegance in the city.

Dorchester Square

A gradual shift of commercial enterprises from Old Montreal to areas further north allowed **Square Dorchester**  (formerly Dominion Square) to assume a predominant position in the downtown plan by the late 19th century: the presence of corporate headquarters, a large hotel and a centre of transportation helped secure its place. Though today many large office towers line boulevard René-Lévesque, and the southern portion of the square was renamed **Place du Canada**, Dorchester Square retains a symbolic importance.

It is one of the few green spaces left in a forest of brick and concrete and is always quite busy, especially during the summer. Office workers take their lunches under the tall elms while commuters stream across the square to Windsor Terminus. The stateliness of an older Dorchester Square remains, redefined by the number of glass and concrete skyscrapers that vie for attention.

The square, once a Catholic cemetery, was officially made a public park in 1869. For years it was the site of Montreal's immense "ice palaces" and the centre of the city's elaborate winter carnivals. Today there are a number of statues on the green, including those of the Scottish poet Robert Burns, Sir Wilfred Laurier, Prime Minister of Canada between 1896–1911, and a particularly well-executed monument commemorating the soldiers who fell in the Boer War. There is also a fountain that was dedicated at the time of Queen Victoria's diamond jubilee in 1897.

The highlight of the square is the justly famous **Edifice Sun Life** ❼ (Sun Life Building). It was begun in 1914, but its present form did not fully emerge until the completion of the two wings in the late 1920s. Variously described as an immense temple or a wedding cake, the building was once Canada's

Square Dorchester, or Dorchester Square, is also still known as Dominion Square.

BELOW: war memorial in Square Dorchester.

TIP

If you're interested in architecture, head west along René-Lévesque to find the Canadian Centre for Architecture (tel: 939-7026). Its collection of plans, models, books and photos is said to be the best of its kind in the world.

BELOW:
Cathédrale Marie-Reine-du-Monde.

largest, and it helped to establish the former Dominion Square as Montreal' new downtown centre.

The Windsor Hotel deserves some attention, albeit brief. Once among Mon treal's finest hostelries, the Windsor spanned an entire city block and had sumptuously decorated interior. A series of fires resulted in the hotel's demoli tion, and today only a late addition to the original remains. Designed in a 19th century Parisian style, the Windsor Building now houses offices. On the site o the old hotel is the Bank of Commerce, a tall 1962 glass tower with an extra ordinary narrow base.

On the southeast side of the square stands the **Cathédrale Marie-Reine-du Monde ❽** (Mary Queen of the World Cathedral) (1085 rue de la Cathédrale a René-Lévesque; tel: 866-1661). Its dome, once considered imposing, is nov adrift in a sea of skyscrapers. If the cathedral's exterior looks familiar, that because it was modelled after St Peter's in Rome – note the similar line of stat ues on the portico and the Greek columns. Mary Queen of the World Cathedra is only a quarter of the size of its Roman model and lacks, perhaps, a significan measure of grandeur.

There was strong opposition to the plan to replicate St Peter's, particularly b the church's primary architect, Victor Bourgeau, the man also responsible for th interior of Notre-Dame Basilica. Bourgeau lost the argument and the aestheti value of the church is still just a matter of opinion.

The cathedral, which took 20 years to build, was completed in 1884 an quickly became the centre of worship for downtown Catholic residents. Its inte rior is bright and airy. The altar canopy, a reproduction of Bernini's Baldacchin in Rome, is the most notable aspect in an otherwise unexceptional design.

At the far end of the square, at the corner of Peel and de la Gauchetière
streets, stands the architecturally uninspiring **Marriott Château Champlain
Hotel**. A rather lifeless concrete tower, the hotel is known locally as the
"cheese grater" building.

Saved from the wrecking ball by a group of concerned Montreal citizens,
Gare Windsor ❾ (Windsor Station) dominates the southwest corner of Place
du Canada. The site for the station was chosen for its elevation, away from the
St Lawrence's menacing spring floods. From a distance, the station looks like
a fortress fitted out with arched windows and rusticated stone.

Designed by New York architect Bruce Price, the building is a celebration of
strength and solidity. Its quasi-Gothic style and castle-like design are reminiscent of other structures built for the Canadian Pacific Railway by Price. A number of wings were added as the railway company grew, with the final wing
completed in the 1950s.

Windsor Station's imposing exterior is not, however, matched by its interior.
Renovations left the waiting area cold and uninteresting, and now it is utterly
empty: when the Molson Centre was built during the 1990s, the actual train
terminus was moved to a new complex just west of the new hockey rink. Known
as Windsor Terminus, that building now handles passengers and commuter
trains bound for or arriving from Dorval airport and the northern suburbs of
Pointe-Claire, Dorion and Rigaud.

Next is **Eglise St-George** ❿ (St George's Anglican Church), which was built
to accommodate Montreal's west-end Protestant population. The church was
completed in 1870 and is the square's oldest remaining building. It is certainly
worth venturing inside simply to admire the carved woodwork covering the

Map
on page
156

*Opening doors at
the Marriott Hotel.*

BELOW: times
have changed
at Gare Windsor.

TIP

You can change Métro lines at the following transfer stations: Berri-UQAM, Jean-Talon, Lionel-Groulx and Snowdon.

interior. The entire ceiling is also exquisitely carved and has managed to survive the years gracefully.

St George's illustrates the immense wealth of the Anglican community in Montreal, and it merits comparison with the lovely cathedral on Ste-Catherine. From its steps the view of Dorchester Square is magnificent: the dome of the cathedral is best appreciated from this angle – which was, perhaps, what the Catholic bishop had in mind.

One can also gain a fuller appreciation of the **Dominion Square Building**, located to the north, between Metcalfe and Peel streets. Its distinctive design is actually Florentine. Though the facade has been renovated to match the commercial storefronts on rue Ste-Catherine, from the steps of St George's one can still appreciate the gracefully arched upper windows that look over the green.

Place Ville-Marie

If Dominion Square serves as a symbol of 19th-century Montreal, **Place Ville-Marie** represents the city's modern face. The complex, located just east of the square on boulevard René-Lévesque, looms up behind the Sun Life Building. Place Ville-Marie's cruciform shape – unabashedly symbolic in an overwhelmingly Catholic city – figures in many travel brochure photos. The project was one of the first by the now world-famous architect I. M. Pei, who later caused a stir with his glass pyramid addition to the Louvre Museum in Paris.

The feature making Place Ville-Marie particularly distinctive is the vast underground city beneath, which links the complex with other plazas and the subway system. Place Ville-Marie is, in a sense, the prototype for this radical urban development.

BELOW: Christmas in Place Ville-Marie.

Place Ville-Marie is a complex of four buildings, dominated by the 45-floor Banque Royale Tower. These structures are connected by walkways and open-air plazas that host numerous outdoor cafés during the summer.

Map on page 156

Rue Ste-Catherine

At any time of the day or night, it seems the heartbeat of Montreal originates from somewhere along **rue Ste-Catherine**. Especially for Montreal anglophones, Ste-Catherine has been the main shopping district of the city since the latter years of the 19th century. The electric tram that formerly ran along the street enabled the many customers to shop in comfort – from Ogilvy's all the way to The Bay.

Today, commercial businesses have spilled onto the stately greystones and row houses – once private residences – on Crescent, Bishop and de la Montagne streets. Even a brief walk will reveal noteworthy architecture, elegant shops, massive department stores – and a newer patina of bookstores, coffee shops, fast-food purveyors and, like it or not, some of the seedier aspects of downtown Montreal.

Until recently, most Montrealers would have argued that rue Ste-Catherine begins further west with Le Forum, the former home of the beloved Montreal Canadiens. However, the street is relatively quiet until it intersects with rue de la Montagne. Located at the corner is **Ogilvy and Sons** , one of the city's best known department stores. The original granite structure still stands on the northeast corner, but the store has moved to the 1910 building on the west side of rue de la Montagne. A plaque on the newer building states that Ogilvy and Sons was established in 1866, making it one year older than Canadian Confederation.

Creating a carnival atmosphere.

At the corner of Drummond and Ste-Catherine is the classically styled Bank of Montreal, built in 1921. Architecture buffs can walk north on Drummond, where they will encounter a number of buildings that, though erected at the beginning of the 20th century, are still in excellent condition.

Another famous department store that once thrived on Ste-Catherine was Simpsons, located at rue Metcalfe. Simpsons was a mainstay of Canadian commerce. It was a classic family department store selling everything from shoes to furs to Inuit sculptures, with cafés and restaurants for the weary but insatiated shopper. In the early 1990s La Baie (The Bay – a modern-day, department store descendant of the original Hudson's Bay Company) bought out Simpsons, a long-time rival, and the magnificent Art Deco building is now occupied by a chic fashion store and a movie theatre complex with 14 cinemas and an IMAX theatre.

BELOW: Place Montréal Trust.

Next door is **Place Montréal Trust** (1500 Avenue McGill College; tel: 843-3000), an example of the most recent thinking on urban architecture in the downtown area. This shopping complex, an alternative to the labyrinthine underground city model of the 1960s, attempts to maintain a street presence – an active blend of shoppers, pedestrians, onlookers, commuters, even the proverbial "hanging out" crowd – and still allow for the ease of indoor shopping. It

Statues grace the McGill campus, the oldest of Montreal's four universities.

represents the city's continuing struggle to temper its harsh climate through experimentation in "living spaces". The food court isn't exactly gourmet, but there are fine clothes, lingerie and other treats to be found here.

The intersection of **avenue McGill College** is next. Take a moment to admire the view of **Université McGill** as it ascends the steepening slope of Mont Royal. At the foot of avenue McGill College is the underground entrance to Place Ville-Marie. This wide boulevard has recently been revitalized by a number of large building projects. New skyscrapers have helped shift the city's business district in a more easterly direction. Decorated with rows of lights in the winter, avenue McGill College has an expansive, rather grand feel. Watch for some amusing outdoor sculpture on the sidewalks and in the plazas.

A worthwhile detour up avenue McGill College, and east on rue Sherbrooke brings you to the **Musée McCord** (McCord Museum) (690 rue Sherbrooke Ouest; open 10am–5pm, closed Mon; entrance fee except Sat; tel: 398 7100; fax 398 5045; website: www.musee-mccord.qc.ca). One of the most important history museums in Canada, the McCord owns impressive collections of paintings, prints, drawings, textiles, decorative arts and photographic archives dating from the 18th century to the present day.

Phillips Square

Back down rue Université brings you to **Square Phillips**, the closest thing Ste Catherine's has to a centre. From the small green, Canada's two largest department stores are in plain view. The Eatons building is a two-block-long structure. Like its once-thriving rival Simpsons, Eatons was an all-purpose department store best known for its grand 9th-floor café, a lovely spot for afternoon tea.

However, this long-time Canadian fixture suddenly closed its doors during the summer of 1999 with a rush of going-out-of-business sales, leaving a void in the hearts of Anglo Montrealer shoppers – and in the complex that still bears the well-known name. The future of the store is uncertain. La Baie (The Bay) is housed in a smaller red sandstone building nearby, with a large modern addition attached, happily serving former customers of Eatons.

On Phillips Square stands a rather large, even grandiloquent **statue of King Edward VII**. The original Edwardian gentleman is an appropriate spiritual mentor for the area. Sharing the square with The Bay is **Birks**, one of Canada's oldest jewellers, and the **Canada Cement Company**. Housed in well-preserved structures, they are, like the Anglican Cathedral, reminders of the old English money that built so much of the city.

Map on page 156

Graceful and dignified

Though a sense of proportion on Phillips Square – befitting a classic downtown green – has been diminished by ungainly buildings and tacky billboards, the nearby older edifices and, in particular, **Cathédrale Christ Church** ⓰ (1440 avenue Union; tel: 288-6421), still offer a measure of grace and dignity. The church stands out prominently against the modern structures around it.

Designed by Frank Wills of Salisbury, England, in 1857, Christ Church is considered one of the finest examples of Gothic architecture in Canada. The building is cross-shaped, like many 14th-century English churches, and its exterior design reflects a careful and graceful balance in design. The lovely narrow spire is made of treated aluminium, the original stone having been removed because of its weight. Grace and balance are also evident in the church's interior, primarily of stone except for the ceiling. There are carved heads of saints above the doors and the arcades of the nave are capped by leaves representing indigenous trees.

BELOW: blending the old and the new.

Maison des Coopérants, the elegant modern glass tower behind Christ Church, ingeniously incorporates the lines of the church's apses and windows in its design. During the day the spire is reflected in its tinted glass; at night Christ Church is a shock of black outlined in the grey tones of the city.

Tucked between the church and Maison des Coopérants is the exclusive French restaurant **Le Parchemin**, a Parisian-style home done in the same speckled granite as Christ Church. One needs a thick wallet, or a slim and flexible credit card, to enjoy Le Parchemin's cuisine.

Further east

Continuing east on Ste-Catherine, the shops become less interesting and certainly less grand. You might even notice a few unpleasant parvenus – pornographic movie houses and sex shops – that settled in the area during the boom of underground shopping in Montreal and haven't yet been driven away. These blocks are best walked through to reach Place des Arts.

A worthwhile stop, though, would be **Eglise St-James** ⓱ (St James' United Church) at the corner of rue St-Alexandre. Unfortunately the facade of St

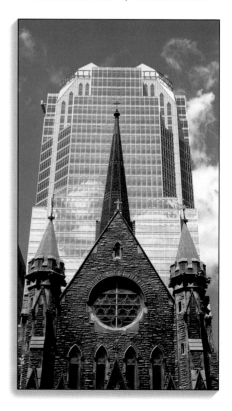

Contemporary art has its own museum in Montreal.

James' was inauspiciously covered over in an attempt to "integrate" it with the commercial face of the rest of the street. The best view of the church, from St-Alexandre, reveals a modest-sized Gothic edifice set in a quiet tree-lined green.

The architect, Alexandre Dunlop, decided on a rather unusual design for the interior. He chose a horseshoe arrangement, a design known as "Akron" in honour of a city in Ohio where it was first used. The style is also very much like the 18th-century convocation halls at Oxford and Cambridge universities in England. The curved wooden balcony and central chandelier are striking and the general effect is very pleasing.

Public place for art and festivals

The final stopping point on Ste-Catherine is **Place des Arts** ⓲. The complex, famous for the sweeping curves of its design, is actually composed of two buildings that contain a total of three concert halls. The larger of the two, Salle Wilfrid-Pelletier, is home to the Montreal Symphony Orchestra. Completed in 1963, Place des Arts is an example of the innovative architectural atmosphere that ruled in Montreal under mayor Jean Drapeau. It is the main stage for the summer festivals, and the hall has a permanent collection of works by modern Canadian artists including Robert La Palme and Micheline Beauchemin.

There are two more theatres in the smaller pyramid-shaped building, officially opened in 1966. Through an unusual design technique, the floors and ceilings of both theatres are suspended from thousands of springs, enabling the halls to be used simultaneously without fear of sound interference.

Adjacent to Place des Arts is the **Musée d'Art Contemporain** ⓳ (Museum of Contemporary Art) (185 rue Ste-Catherine Ouest; open Tues–Sun,

BELOW:
Place des Arts, the main venue for summer festivals.

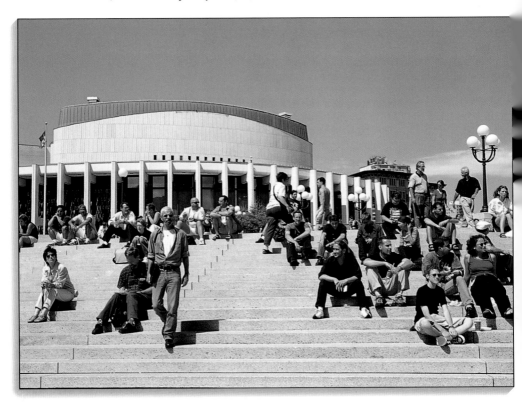

1am–6pm; Wed until 9pm; entrance fee; tel: 847-6226; fax: 847-6290). It has had a peripatetic history, with three homes since its founding in 1964 before finally moving to this 4,088-sq metre (44,000-sq ft) space above the Place des Arts parking garage. Post-1940 works of art from both Quebec and elsewhere are attractively displayed throughout the museum's eight rooms.

Directly across the street stands **Complexe Desjardins**. Grouped around a central atrium, the complex contains three office towers and a hotel, along with the ubiquitous floors of shops and restaurants. A three-dimensional wood sculpture by the Québécois artist, Pierre Granche, serves as a centrepiece in a brown concrete interior. The atmosphere is either serene or sterile, depending, perhaps, on your perspective.

Little Dublin

Historic Chinatown differs dramatically from the present-day neighbourhood. **Rue de la Gauchetière**, **St-Laurent**, and the small streets radiating from them were once home to the thousands of Chinese who began emigrating to Canada in the late 1800s. By law, the first immigrants were men only. Social and economic discrimination forced the community to band tightly together, creating a self-reliant ghetto that tended to attract some less than wholesome enterprises, including brothels and gambling dens.

The proximity of Chinatown to the downtown area, combined with the ramshackle condition of many of the residential buildings, made it a prime target for development. During the last two decades of the 20th century a number of the more interesting older edifices have been demolished. In their place today stand large government office buildings, multi-use indoor complexes, and barren parking lots. Old meets new in Chinatown, but not quite as harmoniously as in other parts of the city.

For the sake of our tour through downtown, it is easiest to call this neighbourhood Chinatown. Historically, however, the area belonged to another immigrant group, the Irish, and once even went by the name of "Little Dublin".

Interestingly enough, the two churches in "Little Dublin" have completely different histories. **Eglise du Gesù** ⑳, at 1202 rue de Bleury between Ste-Catherine and René-Lévesque, was an important site for Montreal's francophone community. For many years a Jesuit university, the College Saint-Marie, was located just south of the church.

Its reputation as a centre of rigorous intellectual activity, in the Jesuit tradition, was widely known throughout Canada. Many members of the French Canadian elite were educated there during the early part of the 20th century, including poet Emilé Nelligan. The school, eventually taken over by the University of Quebec at Montreal, was demolished in 1977.

Eglise du Gesù, modelled after its namesake in Rome, was built in the Italian baroque style. It was designed by an Irish architect, Patrick Keeley, and completed in 1865. The interior was renovated in 1983–84, and the murals and frescoes decorating the walls were repainted and restored. The original parquet floor at the front of the church is striking, as are

Map on page 156

A variety of shows can be seen in the atrium of Complexe Desjardins, which is also used for television recordings.

BELOW: the bustling streets of Chinatown.

Lions guard the entrance gates to Chinatown.

the imposing oil paintings of saints on either side of the altar, done by the Gagliardi brothers of Rome. The other church, **Basilique St-Patrick ㉑**, stands as a monument to the faith and building skills of the Irish community.

Across the street from St Patrick's, at 454 de la Gauchetière, is the **Unity Building**, an excellent example of the Chicago School of architecture (typified by the designs of Louis Sullivan) and the only one of its kind in Montreal. Though the building is in a state of disrepair, its uniquely projecting cornice is quite distinguishable despite layers of dirt.

Chinatown

To begin a tour of Chinatown proper, begin at the corner of de la Gauchetière and rue de Bleury. Standing on the northwest corner is the lovely **Edifice Southam ㉒** (Southam Building). Constructed in 1912 by the Southam Company – owners of many of Canada's largest newspapers, including the *Montreal Gazette* – it was sold in 1960 to a number of small businesses. Luckily, this delightful edifice remains intact.

There is a wealth of stone sculpture decorating the brick facade. Above the front entrance stand four women carrying coats of arms, each figure with different features and a different coat of arms. Two of the women are supported by full-bodied Cupids reclining in amusing positions. Myriad naturalistic carvings elsewhere – such as animals and leaf motifs – are certain to delight.

After another block, de la Gauchetière turns into a bricked pedestrian walkway opening onto a large plaza, **Complexe Guy-Favreau ㉓**. The massive buildings on either side of the plaza act as barriers: in the absence of any large trees or shrubs, the square looks rather barren, even in the summer. At one end

stands the **Chinese Catholic Church**, saved from demolition because of its status as a historical monument. Though the original church dates from 1835, it has undergone many reincarnations.

At the other end of the plaza stands the **House of Wing**, believed to be the oldest building in Chinatown. It truly speaks of another era: erected in 1825, its exterior looks its age. House of Wing, once the British and Canadian School, is now a noodle and cookie factory.

Rue de la Gauchetière from rue Côté to boulevard St-Laurent is adorned with two brightly coloured **ceremonial gates**. Note the pair of marble lions framing the entrance on St-Laurent, a recent gift to the city from the Chinese government. Anyone who is familiar with traditional Chinese architecture will recognize the gates (vestiges of pre-Communist China) as markers announcing the entrance to an important avenue, one that the emperor might travel. In China, the gates were meant to ward off evil spirits; in Montreal's Chinatown, however, they signal the beginning of a pedestrian mall lined with many restaurants and other commercial enterprises.

Try to come to Chinatown at the weekend. On Saturday and Sunday afternoons the streets teem with families. Chinese and Westerners alike eat sweets, gaze in display windows and search for those hard-to-find Chinese delicacies in shops and bakeries. The best way to explore this area is with chopsticks. Restaurants are thick on the ground, and they permit the curious epicurean to sample everything from Cantonese dim sum to spicy Szechuan beef. You can also snack on fried dough and moon cakes while you go shopping for Chinese herbs or cotton clothing. Most restaurants hang their menus in the window and advertise daily specials.

From the eastern gate of Chinatown on St-Laurent, you are just one block away from the **Monument National ❷**, a building worth examining for its handsome facade. Since it was built in 1894, the Monument National has always functioned as a theatre and was once the site of important cultural and political activity. This solid, grey granite edifice now houses the National Theatre School. Its students' performances, often of high quality, are presented in the Nouveau Palais de Justice in Old Montreal.

A few blocks up St-Laurent brings the traveller to "The Main", the final leg of the downtown tour. If, by this time, you are also on your last leg, pay attention to the many signs advertising cafés, bars and smoked meat houses.

Microcosm of Montreal

The essence of what makes Montreal unique in North America is to be found on **boulevard St-Laurent**. The street is a microcosm of the city itself, a neighbourhood bursting with ethnicity, old-world charm and the daily comings and goings of immigrants and their children. More and more, St-Laurent is also becoming the chic place to shop and eat; still, the street remains indomitably without pretence and has an energy all its own.

St-Laurent has always symbolized both division and unity in the downtown. It is still the east/west dividing line of the city's addresses while also being the

Map on page 156

TIP

It's cheaper to buy transit tickets (valid on any bus or Métro line) by the book if you're in town for a few days. Ask for a *carnet* of six tickets which costs $8 – nearly a 40 percent saving over individual tickets.

BELOW: summer street scene on St-Laurent.

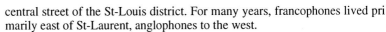

Map on page 156

Schwartz's deli first opened in 1927.

BELOW: a colourful corner on rue Ste-Catherine.

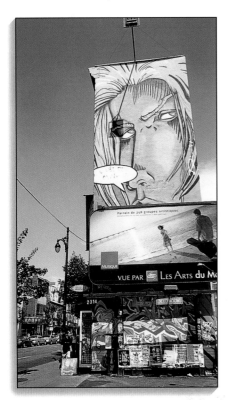

central street of the St-Louis district. For many years, francophones lived primarily east of St-Laurent, anglophones to the west.

Succeeding waves of immigrants changed the nature of that division and expanded the street into a thriving commercial district. The street became known as "The Main" when Russian Jews settled in droves during the 1920s. When much of the Jewish community moved out, Greeks, Hungarians, Portuguese and, most recently, Latin Americans moved in.

In the winter, the boulevard is decorated with giant, red-striped candy canes. In the summer, however, crowds are its decor, especially during the annual food fairs and ethnic festivals. One reason the street has managed to retain its charm is that many of the older facades have been utilized rather than torn down.

There is a mix of high and low, chic and oh-so-normal here that keeps the area both unpretentious and unpredictable. Discount shoe stores stand next door to hip cafés, while Greek bakeries and art galleries share old warehouse space. Come to St-Laurent to walk, browse and, most importantly, to eat.

The Main is known for its smoked meat delis, and delis are known for lots of honest food at honest prices. Try **Schwartz's Delicatessen** (officially the Charcuterie Hébraïque de Montréal) at number 3895, said to be the only restaurant that still makes its own smoked meat; Rubin Schwartz brought the curing recipe with him when he emigrated from Romania. **Moishe's Steakhouse** at number 3961 opened in 1938 on the site of the restaurant where Moishe himself had been a busboy, and it's still Montreal's best address for backroom power steak lunches or dinners.

A good place to admire the old buildings of St-Laurent is along the block between numbers 3640 and 3712, once called the **Baxter Block**. The attached buildings have impressively large arched windows and still retain the original central heating system. Also worth checking out is **Cinéma Parallèle** ㉕ at number 3684, which houses a café and arts cinema. At number 3950 are the Shubert Baths. Built in 1931, the baths were a necessity for the many people without bathrooms in their homes. The swimming pool is still open today.

Finally, one block over from St-Laurent on **rue St-Urbain**, is one of the city's most beloved cafés, **Santropol**. Its quirky interior, vegetarian menu, good heart – the proceeds go toward social programs and a meal wagon for the poor and elderly – and lovely outdoor garden have secured it a place in the hearts of many Montrealers.

It is worth remembering that, unlike other city neighbourhoods, a downtown area is likely to be a haphazard mix of the residential, the commercial, the old and the new, the interesting and the mundane. Montreal is no exception. While Dorchester Square, the Golden Square Mile and The Main are the most vibrant areas, especially historically, along virtually every downtown street and alley a curious traveller will find something that surprises, astonishes, pleases.

Such discoveries can be as exciting as learning about famous monuments or exploring churches. Even amid a sea of office towers, you never know what treasures may lie in the shadows. ❑

Art's Desire

Montreal loves the arts like it loves its food – which is to say, quite a lot. You'll rarely see both a public and a local government so vigorously supporting the efforts of the writers, painters, cellists, and dancers who inhabit a metropolis. After all, how many other cities can boast a Place des Arts – an open public square in the heart of its downtown district that is exclusively dedicated to festivals, sculpture, orchestral performances and theatre?

As usual, the twin arteries of boulevard St-Laurent and rue St-Denis are the major streets to keep in mind as you begin tracking this dense arts community. It can even be traced back to a single origin point, to one particularly nondescript building rising above The Main's craziest stretch. Behind its bland exterior, number 3575 St-Laurent serves as the de facto headquarters for the city's most significant arts organizations and for the art, dance and music studios of some of the city's top stars, folks who are better known in Paris and Vienna, perhaps, than at home.

Move east to the middle section of St-Denis, and you'll suddenly find theatres to be thick on the ground. Montreal is particularly strong in its dance and theatre offerings: several of Canada's top ballet companies – such as Les Grands Ballets Canadiens and the Les Ballets Jazz de Montreal – make their homes here, and so do a range of acting companies, including (but certainly not limited to) the Théâtre Centaur and the Théâtre du Rideau Vert (Green Curtain Theatre). Some of these companies perform along St-Denis.

On lower St-Denis (down the hill below Sherbrooke), film abruptly becomes the predominant medium. Here are the National Film Board of Canada, the Cinémathèque Québécoise and a number of other theatres within a rather short stretch. Several jazz and comedy clubs are located in the area.

Downtown, as one would expect, the arts really come into their own – especially the visual arts. One can visit an excellent Museum of Fine Arts, another of Contemporary Art, and still another showcasing Canadian Architecture, all less than a mile from the tallest skyscrapers. Other organizations are scattered in pockets around town, areas such as Outremont – which has the award-winning La La La Human Steps dance company and the Yiddish Theatre Company, to take just a few examples.

Montreal's acclaimed Symphony Orchestra performs in a specially designed building right on Place des Arts, itself the home to festival after festival. The city's profusion of festivals has already been noted elsewhere in these pages, but take note of this: most are squarely centred around some form of the arts. Film, jazz, dance, world music, comedy, more film: one after another they come, in waves, as the short summer deepens and then draws to a reluctant close.

Even the less-appreciated arts get their due here: Halifax may have its buskers' festival, but Montreal's got the annual International Mime Festival – though we haven't heard a word about it. ❑

RIGHT: musicians of all disciplines have a place in Montreal's rich art scene.

BOHEMIAN MONTREAL

Map
on page
178

*The vibrant heart of the city beats in a series of café- and
restaurant-lined streets between St-Denis and St-Laurent. Night or
day, this is where you'll find the essential Montreal*

few blocks east of the business district and north of Old Montreal lies an
elegant street of Victorian townhouses with a mixture of businesses: cafés,
croissanteries, boutiques, fine restaurants, French and English bookstores,
atres and cinemas. There are many streets in Montreal with a similar mix, but
ne have the easy charm of **rue St-Denis ❶**. It is the place where Montrealers
m to feel most at home, and casual observation gives the impression that the
é crowd has indeed made a second home here.

ne is tempted to say that nowhere else in Montreal has so Parisian or
ropean a flavour, but the truth is that nowhere is more essentially Montreal.
is is the focal point of many of the festivals that now fill the summer months
l the area where, traditionally, Québécois separatists gather whenever
ionalist feeling runs high. Recently the provincial government has begun to
mote it as a place for visitors as well, but fortunately it has been saved from
dreadful fate of turning touristy. With the local university such a dominant
sence in the area, and laws in place that restrict changes to the historic 19th-
tury facades, it seems doubtful that St-Denis will become tacky any time in
near future. Residents simply wouldn't stand for it.

PRECEDING PAGES:
marks of
distinction.
LEFT: rue St-Denis.
BELOW:
local colour.

ople-watching

AM ❷ (pronounced *Ooh-kwam*) stands for l'Uni-
sité du Québec à Montréal, which occupies the
king building at the corner of rue Ste-Catherine.
e architect, Dimitri Dimakopoulos, incorporated
steeple and south transept of the old Eglise St-
ques (1859) into his modernist design, to preserve
nething of the district's Victorian past in a
lding that otherwise embodies the modern hip
nosphere of the street.

JQAM enrolls about 22,000 students a year and, as
of the five campuses of Quebec's youngest
versity (founded in 1968), it has always been a
eral, progressive influence. English-speaking
olars spill into the area from a McGill University
ex which lies a few blocks west. With the constant
ronage of academics, the local cafés, theatres,
aurants, and book and music stores flourish.

rom UQAM come the intellectuals and the
dents, but the artistic crowd also makes rue St-
nis its turf. One of Canada's three major ballet
npanies, Les Grands Ballets Canadiens, and the
ébécois dramatic company Théâtre du Rideau Vert
een Curtain Theatre) have their home here.

or film-makers there is a permanent facility just
St-Denis at the **Cinémathèque Québécoise ❸** at
boulevard de Maisonneuve Est. Besides a
ertory cinema and a large reference library, the

Latin Quarter and Plateau

uilding houses a museum documenting the history of film-making equipment. The **Théâtre St-Denis ❹**, just north of de Maisonneuve, belies its ordinary xterior with a seating capacity of 2,500, making it the largest playhouse in e city after Salle Wilfrid-Pelletier at nearby Place des Arts.

Heaven knows where all the other people come from, but they all seem qually to belong here, whiling away hours in endless conversation over wine a sidewalk café; sitting on the front steps of a duplex flat, watching the orld go by on a warm summer evening; sifting through *La Presse* over ffee and croissants on a Saturday morning. The natives are obviously xtremely comfortable here.

Many guidebooks still refer to the rue St-Denis district – roughly the sec- on that runs from rue Ste-Catherine to rue Sherbrooke – as the Latin Quar- r, a name borrowed from the Quartier Latin in Paris between the Sorbonne d the Seine, a district renowned for its bohemian atmosphere. Both franco- hone and anglophone Montrealers have adopted this nickname, as it evokes e right connotations: Rue St-Denis has a Gallic flair, and a youthful, gently ohemian personality that attracts personalities – or anyone else who loves fé society and *la dolce vita*.

The cafés are not cafés at all in the traditional sense, as they pour far greater uantities of beer and wine than coffee. Tables are usually placed very close gether, decors are attractive but secondary, prices are reasonable, and the noke is inevitably thick; a good thing many cafés possess sliding windows that en to admit fresh air during summer. A few even offer a complete menu. lthough there are many cafés which provide music, for the most part conver- tion and people-watching constitute the entertainment along St-Denis.

As pleasant as it is simply to stroll the sidewalks, 's often rewarding to explore further. If the weather fine, the garden terrace at the rear of the Café St- ulpice can be magical, when furry white flakes of ollen swirl about in drifts so thick that it seems to snowing. Water splashes into a rock pool from a untain at the far end of the terrace. Empty in the te afternoon after the lunch crowd leaves, the vacant airs await a crowd that will arrive late in the ening and stay until 2 or 3am. *(For other cafés and teries in the area check out the Travel Tips, starting page 257.)*

he making of St-Denis

he particular spirit of the St-Denis district is the oduct of a fate that drove the street from riches to gs – and then back towards riches. The street was iginally carved out of the estates of two leaders of e 1837 rebellion against British rule, Denis-Ben- min Viger and Louis-Joseph Papineau. St-Denis came the main street of a posh residential district med the Faubourg St-Laurent, one of Montreal's st suburbs when the city overflowed its old defen- ve walls. Once home to the premier of the province d the elite of the business class, most of the original ildings were destroyed by the Great Fire that dev- tated Montreal in 1852. Some of the wealthy moved rth and west, but the district remained fashionable

Map on page 178

This glassworks boutique is one of many fashionable home-décor stores on St-Denis.

BELOW: tattoo you.

The Young and the Restless

One of the most important features of Quebec's recent social history has been the "Quiet Revolution" (see page 58) that broke the Catholic church's iron grip on its residents. Church attendance abruptly took a back seat to political discourse, the arts and public action instead of reaction; Montreal became a part of the broader world for perhaps the first time in its history.

But the single most visible manifestation of the province's recent – and remarkably rapid – changes might well be the explosion of youth culture that has taken downtown Montreal by storm.

Look around: comic shops, bookstores, used-CD purveyors and newsstands squeeze into every available crevasse. Montreal has four weekly newspapers, all full of articles about love, sex music and fashion. Sure, there have always been students here, but

they have never before been so forward, so visible, so in charge of the cultural moment.

For starters, the nightclub scene here is second to few in North America. Entire work weeks are counted off in anticipation of the weekend DJ. Friday and Saturday nights don't begin until at least midnight; they don't end – if they end at all – until a late-morning breakfast of eggs and coffee the next day at a diner. It's not unusual, either, for a high-profile DJ to be flown over from London or Stockholm for the occasion.

Quieter types hang out in one of the city's countless coffee shops or bars, taking a quick shot of espresso or lingering over a beer and a pack of Craven A cigarettes.

If anything further should develop with a potential partner, well, condom shops are ubiquitous and hip; imagine that a generation ago in this outpost of Catholicism.

It's not just the Montrealers, either. Youngsters come here from other places, particularly from rural Quebec and from the adjoining United States. Any weekend night, you'll find hordes of American college kids tramping up and down Ste-Catherine taking in the endless neon strip of nightclubs, bars, lounges, arcades and fast-food emporiums.

At last count, the city sported a half-dozen youth hostels and there's even a prominently placed youth tourism office (literally, "Tourisme de Jeunesse") on St-Denis near Square St-Louis. Young travellers from all over the city flock here to book bargain tickets, load up on travel supplies and books (alas, English speakers, nearly all of them are in French) and to post notes on a handy bulletin board.

Some of them have come for the jobs. Montreal may be second city to Toronto now in most matters, but a recent boom in high-tech business has appeared – and it's partly because there's such a ready supply of well-educated, multilingual, young workers constantly filtering into the city. The same people programming codes and filling phone orders in that cool Old Montreal stone-firehouse-turned-loft-office are the ones dressing in 1970s garage-sale clothing and dancing at all-night raves beneath the lava lamps. ❑

LEFT: dancing and music at the African Nights festival – fun for the young and young-at-heart.

ntil well into the 20th century. The Victorian elegance of some of the town-
ouses can be discerned in neoclassical and Art Nouveau embellishments on
ome upper storeys (particularly the Mendelson Apartments at boulevard de
Maisonneuve.)

In 1897, the Université Laval opened a centre next to the Eglise St-Jacques,
hich was then Montreal's cathedral, and so first drew academic life to the
ea. The **Bibliothèque Nationale du Québec ❺**, which maintains the offi-
al archives of the province, was erected in 1915 and still resides behind its
ately Beaux-Arts facade on the west side of St-Denis, sandwiched between
usy cafés. The Laval centre gained independence as the Université de Montréal,
ut it abandoned the area in the 1940s for its opulent new campus in Outremont.
Meanwhile, many large residences had been converted into rooming houses,
nd the clergy had opened homes for the growing numbers of the ill and desti-
te. Lacking the academy, St-Denis fell victim to the same urban decay that
ost of east Montreal began suffering as families with money moved out to, and
ttled down in, the suburbs.

In the 1960s, city planners made brave attempts to revitalize the area by
aking it a transportation crossroads. But the construction of the Voyageur bus
rminus on rue Berri only congested the roads. In 1966, the Berri-de-Mon-
gny Métro station (now Berri-UQAM) opened at the corner of rue Ste-Cather-
e. It was the central transfer station in the slick new subway system, but for
e most part easy access to underground shops left commuters without any
ecial reason to venture upstairs to the streets to patronize local business.
Money, if not respectability, returned to the district during the late 1960s and
70s as St-Denis cafés gained notoriety as a hotbed of separatism and radicalism.

Map on page 178

The way to Montreal's heart is through its stomach.

BELOW: learning the steps.

The National Film Board of Canada is, appropriately, located in the Latin Quarter.

Enterprising restaurateurs began to move in and renovate. Among the first wa Le Faubourg St-Denis.

There was no lack of vitality, as the street would explode with celebrations an demonstrations every year on the Québécois feast day: Fête Jean-Baptiste (Jun 24, now the Fête Nationale). The scene looked much the same whenever th Montreal Canadiens hockey club won the Stanley Cup, a pretty regular ever during the 1970s. Among the intellectual and artistic community that gathere here, the youth of Montreal defined themselves no longer as "French Canad ans" but as "Québécois".

The opening of UQAM in 1979, and a slow but steady effort to push the hea of downtown east toward St-Laurent, has had a positive effect. Today the are flourishes, with a steady influx of visitors from far and near supplementing th local clientele. All summer long, one international arts festival after anothe keeps the street busy and interesting.

Seedy... upscale... something for everyone

Still, the traces of a less prosperous past are visible in the less savoury flavour c some businesses; along "la Catherine" strip clubs and off-colour bookstores st pepper the busy central artery. The clubs seem to be able to resist the consta efforts of politicians to get rid of them. Legislators are eager to clear away th more lurid street signs but, ironically, the very laws that so carefully guard free dom of expression under Canada's charter of rights also make it almost impo sible to draft legislation that would eradicate the smutty language on storefront

Fortunately, however, the pleasant atmosphere of rue St-Denis is very differer In fact, the part north of rue Sherbrooke to avenue du Mont-Royal is increasing

BELOW: film crew on rue Sherbrooke.

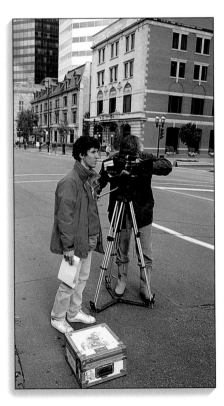

THE FILM SCENE

It's appropriate that Canada's National Film Board offic are located in Montreal, in a rather unusual facility the Latin Quarter, with the offices of Cinémathèq Québécoise just down the street. The city harbours surprisingly large film and studio community, bolstered its bilingual labour pool and good local training progran

Any time of year, walking through the Plateau or dow town, you're likely to see barricades and parking notic If you do, keep your eyes peeled: filming is probab going on, and it's often a major Hollywood motion pictu in the works. That could be Wesley Snipes or Den. Washington or Paul Newman tucking into dinner in th chic St-Laurent restaurant, glad (for once) to be just a tle bit incognito.

In summer, a raft of film festivals – Asian, B-movie, a film, and Québécois are just a few of them – para through the city, culminating in the grand Montr International Film Festival.

In 1999 ExCentris – a huge new multi-screen art-fi complex – opened its doors on the Main to mi> architectural reviews. Too drab and post-industrial, s some. Others were too busy sipping designer coffee a working on their screenplay in the café inside to compl

ecoming a fashionable, upscale shopping area. Antique stores and boutiques
ell fine Québécois tapestries, woodcarvings and handicrafts in pewter and pot-
ry, as well as more pricey European imports such as Tiffany lamps, African
arvings and Art Deco furniture.

Map on page 178

Other boutiques specialize in contemporary and futuristic designs in fur-
ishings. Trendy clothing stores and some excellent new and rare bookstores
nostly but not exclusively selling books in French) are sprinkled along the
whole length of the street.

Rue St-Denis is most alive during the summer festivals, of which there seem
o be no end. Among these events, the most important is the Montreal Interna-
onal Jazz Festival *(see page 187)* held every year in the first two weeks of July.
or much of the festival, the street is closed to traffic and becomes a carnival
rcade with tens of thousands milling along the street. It seems the whole city
omes out to hear the free concerts on temporary stages set up at the intersec-
ons, and to watch unofficial street performers juggle, mime and eat fire. With
,000 musicians from five continents, and up to 50 concerts daily, the festival
as helped to make avid jazz enthusiasts out of many a Montrealer.

But St-Denis is also a focus for the Just for Laughs comedy festival, the Fes-
val International de Nouvelle Danse, held every two years, the World Film Fes-
val and the International Mime Festival. Each of these is among the largest in
s medium and draws performers and fans from around the globe.

rince Arthur restaurants

estivals brighten up a city wonderfully, of course, but on **rue Prince-
rthur ⑥** there is an ongoing celebration of basic human pleasures: people

BELOW: catering for all tastes on rue Ste-Catherine.

It's all in the cards.

BELOW: a comedy
school in Montreal
ensures a supply of
festival talent.

and food. Citizens of Montreal claim to excel at enjoying life together, an
they have tried to resist the tendency of other modern cities to bury the huma
scale under megaliths and speedways. The restaurant district on Prince-Arthu
though a bit more contrived than St-Denis, represents a small triumph for th
pursuit of simple pleasures in the heart of the big city.

Just north of the bistros of St-Denis, the restaurant mall runs west from Squar
St-Louis to boulevard St-Laurent. In 1981, the city closed these five short block
to vehicles, paved them with brick, and spruced them up with trees, poster-pi
lars and a small fountain. It also encouraged new restaurants to forgo thei
liquor licences and allow customers to bring their own bottles of wine wit
them. The opportunity to dine well for less money held obvious appeal for thi
city full of epicures, and the street has flourished.

Restaurants offering a wide range of ethnic menus, especially Greek, Vie
namese and Italian, line the mall, interspersed by a few small boutiques. Québé
cois cuisine is harder to find. Most of the big Greek restaurants that dominat
this stretch have a similar atmosphere, price and menu, serving kebabs, stuffe
vine leaves, grilled chicken, swordfish and shellfish from the Maritim
provinces or the tiny Iles-de-la-Madeleine.

On weekend nights the mall fills with a meandering crowd of diners, often di
tracted by jugglers, musicians and sketch artists who find here an ideal foru
to show off their skills. Diners at second-storey windows get a view of th
whole parade of life below. Tables arranged out on the mall itself let custome
eat under the sun or the stars, or in the shade of a parasol.

Many restaurants here and elsewhere in Montreal no longer bother to di
play a sign that says *"Apportez votre vin"* (Bring your own wine). But it

worthwhile checking with the staff, since most Greek restaurants – and many others – encourage patrons to run into a liquor store or the local *dépanneur* (corner grocery) and pick up a bottle of something to bring inside.

There the waiter will gladly uncork and serve it as though the wine had been ordered from the menu. There is a handy *dépanneur* on the north side of Prince-Arthur, and around the corner on the main street, boulevard St-Laurent, there is a well-stocked provincial liquor store.

Daytime square

Access to the mall from St-Denis is through **Square St-Louis ❼**, a block north of rue Sherbrooke *(see also page 188)*. This small, pretty park with lots of benches around a broad Victorian fountain provides a treasured spot for locals to while away the summer hours, or in winter to skate on the paths that the city floods over.

It is an unmissable spot on any itinerary. Well-preserved and ornate 19th-century townhouses border three sides of the square, and you might glimpse the occasional celebrity here. Originally homes for the more well-to-do of French society, a number of these houses have more recently been bought by Portuguese families. The small front gardens are undoubtedly more lush and colourful than they were under their original ownership. At night, however, the beautiful park they face has unfortunately become a bit unsavoury in recent years; take care.

Nevertheless, the easy charm of St-Denis and Prince-Arthur gives the impression that Montrealers are "at home" in these wandering streets, bohemian retreats and quiet, beguiling cafés. And so they are; one could do worse than to

Map on page 178

TIP

If it's locals-only restaurants you're looking for, head north from the Prince-Arthur area to rues Duluth and Rachel – you'll find plenty there.

BELOW: big laughs.

COMEDY CENTRAL

This is a city that enjoys a laugh. Comedians have so pervaded everyday life here that they often star in television commercials.

Montreal is chock-full of festivals in summer, but the annual Festival Juste pour Rire (literally, Just for Laughs) in late July might be the most-anticipated one of all by locals. It's the last of the great comedy festivals in North America – a 10-day romp of out-on-the-street pantomime, magic, jokes, juggling, and a whole lot more – when an appreciative city turns out in force to laugh it up along several closed-to-traffic blocks of boulevard St-Denis in the Latin Quarter. At the same time, inside the historic Théâtre St-Denis, famous and soon-to-be famous standup comedians such as a young Jerry Seinfeld and an annual parade of talented Québécois jokesters.

And the laughs don't end when the festival does. The Musée Juste pour Rire at 2111 boulevard St-Laurent (open daily 11am–8pm; entrance fee; tel: 845-4000), said to be the only such museum in the world, uses a variety of exhibits and audiovisual presentations to convey the brightest lights of the regional comedy scene. It's just one more sign that, no matter how cold the winter gets, Montrealers will do anything for a laugh.

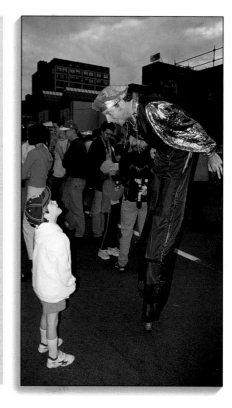

Map on page 178

The face of the "Diverse City".

BELOW:
taking a break.

join them for a day here in the heart of bohemian Montreal, where tourists are few and locals are abundant – and abundantly satisfied.

The Village

The blocks just east of the Latin Quarter, mainly row houses built for molasses factory workers, are today the vibrant heart of Montreal's gay community. It is known as The Village and is well worth exploring. Stretching east to west along rue Ste-Catherine Est, mainly between rue St-Hubert and avenue Papineau, it can be accessed from Berri-UQAM or Beaudry Métro stations. This area has had a somewhat mixed history, but is now one of the largest gay neighbourhoods in the world, known for its nightlife and lively events. The Divers Cité (Diverse City) gay pride parade in August, and the Black and Blue Party in October both draw huge crowds of participants, But the best way to really get a feel for the place is to stroll along the north–south side streets between rue Sherbrooke and boulevard René-Lévesque. Lovingly restored old homes, shady back gardens and colourful window boxes characterize this newly revitalized area of town. Around rue Amherst and boulevard de Maisonneuve is an ever increasing range of antique and speciality shops that are interesting to browse, as well as bars and nightclubs catering to the gay and lesbian community.

From the southern end of rue Amherst there is a striking view of the Clock Tower in the Old Port and from a bit further east along René-Lévesque, towards rue de la Visitation, you can see the modern Radio Canada building soaring up in front of the Jacques-Cartier Bridge. The fortress-like walls of the 200-year-old Molson Brewery building are visible near the port.

The beautiful **Eglise St-Pierre Apôtre** (Church of St Peter the Apostle), a major example of Quebec Gothic Revival architecture, was built in 1853 at the corner of boulevard René-Lévesque Est and rue de la Visitation. Designed by, architect Victor Bourgeau, it features flying buttresses and a 70-metre (230-ft) spire. In the finely decorated interior, the Chapel of Hope is now dedicated to victims of Aids.

Two other churches – **Ste-Brigide** (Romanesque Revival style containing some lovely 19th-century lamps) and **St-Pierre-et-St-Paul** (Montreal's Russian Orthodox cathedral) are both just a few blocks east of St-Pierre-Apôtre along boulevard René-Lévesque.

Rue Ste-Rose, behind these churches, is a pretty steet lined with restored old houses with mansard roofs and wrought-iron carriage gates.

In the northern part of The Village on rue Amherst between rue Ontario and rue Sherbrooke is the **Eco-musée du Fier Monde** ❾ (2050 rue Amherst; open Tues, 11am–8pm; Thur–Sun, 10.30am–5pm; entrance fee; tel: 528-8444). The old Art Deco bath-house is home to an award-winning museum dedicated to the period in the social and economic history of this neighbourhood when it was one of the birthplaces of Canada's industrial revolution. From here, return to rue St-Denis and take it easy in a café for a while before heading north to explore another fascinating area: the Plateau *(see page 188)*. ❑

The Jazz Scene

For 10 days in early July, the Montreal International Jazz Festival books 1,000 performers from around the globe into venues all over the city. What makes this festival extraordinary is that these venues include not only pricey clubs and concert halls but also whole streets, blocked off to let thousands hear free concerts at stages erected at major intersections on rue St-Denis and rue Ste-Catherine. These nightly block parties lend the city a euphoric jazz atmosphere that makes the festival the highlight of Montreal's summer – and one of the best jazz events anywhere. With an attendance exceeding 1,500,000, the festival now rivals Montreux and Monterey. One concert alone attracts 400,000 fans each year.

Ever since the days when Montreal was the only major city on the continent not subject to Prohibition, nightlife has flourished here. But jazz has held an insecure foothold in a town that has generally preferred dance music like swing or rock 'n' roll. Still, great jazz was heard in a handful of clubs throughout the 1930s and 1940s. The heart of the jazz scene throbbed away at "the Corner" where St-Antoine crosses de la Montagne, in a series of smoky jazz bars such as the oddly named *Rockhead's Paradise* (which unfortunately closed during the 1980s).

The most renowned performer to emerge from this era is the pianist Oscar Peterson, a Montreal native who began his career at 17 playing swing in the Johnny Holmes Orchestra at Victoria Hall in Westmount. He created his own sound in a trio that performed in the Alberta Lounge opposite Windsor Station, and he later found fame in the USA. Trumpet player Maynard Ferguson also started with Johnny Holmes, and he likewise found success in the States after forming his own band.

Sixty years ago, in the days of gang wars and rampant vice, there were hundreds of nightclubs open 24 hours a day. Jazz prospered with a small audience through the passionate devotion of its performers. They sustained the energy of Montreal's jazz until about 1954, when Mayor Jean Drapeau started to clean up the city. The heavy pressure on nightlife, and competition from television and rock'n'roll, smothered the jazz scene for a while, until the "Quiet Revolution" of the 1960s when the *Jazz Libre* quartet pushed free jazz to its limits.

The jazz audience in Montreal has been expanding ever since Alain Simard, then aged 29, presented the first jazz festival in 1979. The vibrancy of the festival does not represent the state of things during the other 11 months of the year, but unmistakably there is new life in today's jazz picture, including a local jazz label and a degree program in jazz studies at McGill University.

Finally, *Les Ballets Jazz de Montréal* adds another dimension altogether to the portrait of jazz in the city. To music ranging from Gershwin to Pat Metheny, sometimes exploring social themes such as gender relations and nuclear holocaust, it has presented numerous exuberant and accessible ballets to audiences worldwide. ❑

RIGHT: blowing down the house at the Montreal International Jazz Festival, held each year in July.

Map
on page
178

ANATOMY OF THE PLATEAU

*This is where you'll find some of the most interesting
neighbourhoods, people, bars, art galleries and restaurants,
some little-known to many Montrealers*

*The extent of the
entire Plateau area
(the core plus its
many extensions) is
fairly undefined, but
is bounded roughly
by the mountain to
the west, the
Canadian Pacific
Railway tracks to the
north and east, and
rue Sherbrooke to the
south.*

BELOW: a pleasant
park for strolling
and relaxing.

Montreal's most vital heart does not lie in its Old Port, or high in the
gleaming skyscrapers of downtown – not even in the fine museums,
homes and hotels lining rue Sherbrooke or that green park surrounding prominent Mont-Royal.

No, the place you should go to get off the beaten tourist track is a flat, rectangular section known rather simply as the Plateau. It's a deceptively plain
name for such an interesting place. The heart of the Plateau is bounded approximately by Sherbrooke to the south, Laurier to the north, St-Denis to the east and
St-Laurent to the west but with its many important extensions it covers an area
much larger than that. Go elsewhere for history; come to the Plateau for 90,000
living, breathing Montrealers.

It was, for a long time, woodlands and fields. When a railway line was
built through the Mile-End area during the late 19th century, however,
waves of immigrants arrived and built homes and established businesses.
A city hall and a number of fine churches swiftly followed. Today the
Plateau is divided into three or four sections by locals, but we'll go one better and make some finer distinctions (that will overlap each other in places)
as we begin our tour near the base of Mont-Royal.

Milton-Parc

Adjoining McGill University, **Milton-Parc** ❿ is populated almost entirely by American and Ontarian students, English-speaking professors, and Asian visitors
who have come to learn English. There are tall townhouses but few cafés or restaurants. Several interesting museums occupy its buildings, however, and the
McGill campus makes for a pleasant picnic spot,

St-Louis

The compact **St-Louis** ⓫ area centres around beautiful Square St-Louis and the cobbled pedestrian way
known as rue Prince-Arthur. This street is famous for
the dozens of "bring-your-own-wine" restaurants
elbowing each other for tourist business. The surrounding side streets contain some fine houses.

St-Jean-Baptiste

A small, largely residential quarter occupying the
middle stretch of St-Laurent, **St-Jean-Baptiste** ⓬
roughly covers the area between Parc Jeanne-Mance
in the west to rue St-Denis in the east, and from rue
Rachel in the south to avenue du Mont-Royal in the
north. In the past decade, it has become very Portuguese in character – you can't walk far without finding another Portuguese grocer, baker, restaurant or
travel agency. This lends it a friendliness remarkable

:ven for Montreal. A pronounced Latin American tilt is now becoming evident
around the fringes too – a blend of South American and Spanish arrivals mak-
ng their own toehold.

Mont-Royal

At one time, the **Mont-Royal** ⓭ area of the Plateau (not to be confused with the
'mountain" itself) was the home of an enormous tannery. Now, this once-fading
neighbourhood (along and off avenue du Mont-Royal between St-Laurent and
Papineau) is a hotbed of bistros, bakeries and new condominiums.

Mile-End

One of the city's most interesting little pockets, **Mile-End** ⓮ is so named
because it's exactly a mile from the city's unofficial crossroads (the corner of
Sherbrooke and St-Laurent). One of the important extensions to the Plateau, it
is bounded in the south by Laurier, north by Bernard, west by avenue du Parc
and east by St-Laurent. This was once part of the heart of Jewish Montreal;
now, however, it's that rare neighbourhood where Anglos and Francos live in the
same apartment buildings. There's a mixture here of families and young couples,
busy streets and green yards. The blend of bagel shops, French boutiques, Portuguese coffee shop terraces and Italian greengrocers is absolutely vital to sample at least once. You'll be amazed by the sight of Africans, Arabs and Jewish
kids paddling bagels into a wood-fired oven together while a Frenchman counts
out your change. The homes here are particularly fine as well, and many residents are keen gardeners; some even cultivate fruit trees.

*Come here to enjoy
an almost exclusively
French area.*

BELOW: Mile-End
garden on avenue
de l'Esplanade.

Laurier

A mostly French area with superb local character –
corner stores, butchers, bakers and so on – **Laurier** ⓯,
stretches along avenue Laurier from St-Denis east to
Papineau and from St-Laurent west to the Outremont
neighbourhood. Parc Sir-Wilfrid-Laurier is one of the
city's most pleasant for an afternoon stroll despite the
overhanging smokestacks of industry; they remind
the traveller that this was once a very working-class
district. The park, in fact, is built upon the remains of
several exhausted limestone quarries.

Petit-Plateau

An area roughly occupying the blocks east of St-Denis
to Papineau (and beyond) and from Sherbrooke north
to St-Grégoire, the **Petit-Plateau** ⓰ forms an extension that is considerably larger than the heart of the
Plateau itself. It includes part of the Laurier area, and
is almost exclusively French in character, having been
settled by generations of rural Quebeckers who came
to Montreal to find work and who still speak a rough
patois. English is rarely heard, cigarettes frequently
smoked, dogs freely walked, cars driven with wild
abandon and gesticulation. The cats sport leonine hair-
cuts, tiny corner bistros pack in the customers for long
lunches, and everyone owns a bicycle. This is
probably the place that most resembles the original
Montreal of a few centuries ago. ❑

WESTMOUNT AND OUTREMONT

*Montreal's historic enclaves of English and French wealth share
several traits: old money, beautiful buildings and a desire to
separate themselves from the city of Montreal*

Map
on page
194

A Montrealer would probably scoff at the idea that Outremont and Westmount share any physical or, worse, historical affinities. They might point out that Westmount is where well-to-do anglophones (English Canadians) have always lived and been the majority voice in the community. Outremont, on the other hand, has always been home to monied French Canadians (francophones). These neighbourhoods, in many ways, are considered to be the "two solitudes" of Canada.

On the surface, it appears that Westmount and Outremont are worlds apart. And yet a look into the origins of these cities within the city – neither of which is part of the city of Montreal, but separate municipalities – reveals common ground. Both communities were born out of the impulse to escape from the more crowded and sometimes dirty conditions of 19th-century city living. Both began as farming communities that developed at a slow pace around the sloping inclines of the mountain. Leaders of each community defended their power to control construction, landscaping, architectural styles and zoning. Most of all, they sought to preserve the privileged relationship each had with the mountain and the unique landscape they lived in.

Westmount is built on the western slope of Mont-Royal, known as the *petit montagne*. Though the area is surrounded on all sides by the city of Montreal, it is a significant parcel of land, covering nearly 405 hectares (995 acres). **Outremont**, on the other side of Mont-Royal, is the incorporated city to the north. Though smaller in area, to the eye it shares much in common with Westmount: gracious residences, leafy parks and lively commercial districts.

PRECEDING PAGES:
enjoying the winter.
LEFT:
Mont-Royal view.
BELOW:
feathered friends.

Westmount's beginnings

In the 1670s, the Sulpician Order established an outpost on what is now rue Sherbrooke Ouest, today considered the dividing line between the city of Montreal and Westmount. Two circular defence towers stand on the north side of the street in front of the Grand Séminaire as reminders of this early settlement. Eventually, the order began to cede lands on the *petit montagne* to farmers. Old Indian trails and horse tracks connected these farmers to the city but, by any standard, they were isolated, and it wasn't until the mid-1800s that the community on the *petit montagne* grew in size.

As transportation gradually became more efficient, Scottish and English fur traders, much taken with the splendid views, clean air and lower rates of taxation, began to settle in the area. In 1869 the first English school was established in what was then called the village of Côte St-Antoine.

Flowers abound in Montreal's wealthy neighbourhoods.

As more people settled in and around the village, a movement developed to preserve the residential, non-industrial character of the community. In 1890, the Côte St-Antoine Improvement Committee was formed and, composed of mainly anglophone residents, created a city plan for municipal buildings and parks. The committee was successful at regulating commercial development, and for many years it banned the "gathering of families under one roof" in apartment houses.

Its enthusiasm was fuelled by a desire for a peaceful residential community and a deep distrust of the Montreal city government. In a vote that was very nearly defeated, the city council changed the name of the village to Westmount in 1895, and the city of Westmount received its charter in 1908. As the population became more homogeneous, a distinct enclave of middle-class anglophone Montrealers became established.

Westmount residents appear to have been strict teetotallers and avid sportsmen at the turn of the century. In fact, they seem to have been absolutely wild about sport. Westmount established a golf course, a Toboggan and Snow Shoe Club, and a Cricket Club. The town hosted the 1894 Canadian Speed Skating Championships. It was the site of what is thought to be the first lacrosse match ever played under lights and, as every Canadian nationalist knows, lacrosse, not hockey, is Canada's national sport. Today, the city is renowned for its parks; a reflection, no doubt, of this long tradition of outdoor pursuits.

Outremont's beginnings

It was also the Sulpician Order that was the original owner of much of the land which is today the city of Outremont. The Order began to yield large portions

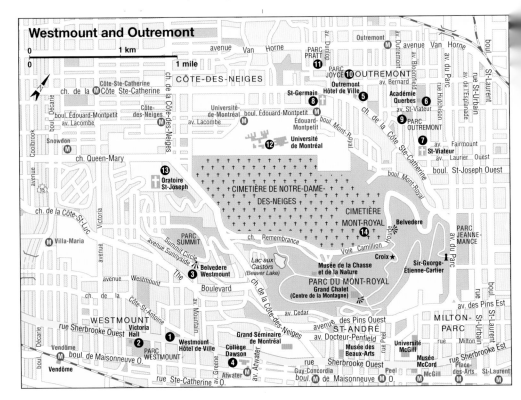

of its land in the early 1700s, but population growth was very slow owing to its distance from the crowded fortress of Montreal by the St Lawrence River. For many years the farms of the Outremont produced "Montreal melons" and prospered by selling them to hotels in New York.

In the mid-1800s the two largest landowners, besides the St Viateur religious order, were two farming families by the names of Bouthillier and Beaubien. The Beaubien family's power quickly translated into political influence when a son became mayor of Outremont.

Outremont's population quadrupled between 1900 and 1911. While the first settlers were primarily Scottish and English, newcomers included some French Canadians attracted to the less expensive homes as well as the proximity of Catholic churches. Jewish families also moved in and many set up shops along avenue Van Horne.

Like Westmount citizens, Outremont residents, fuelled by the fears of overdevelopment, formed a "beautification committee". They were successful in obtaining more park land and regulating the size of apartment buildings. In its greatest coup, the committee persuaded the utility companies in 1914 to bury their telephone and electrical wires underground, thus eliminating unsightly poles and wires on the streets.

Today, Westmount and Outremont are still fairly homogeneous compared with the rest of the city. For inner city neighbourhoods, they are both exceptionally lovely, full of green spaces, elegant architecture and plenty of personality. Their cultural identities have not been compromised and, for the residents of each, a wonderful balance has been struck between urban living and an appreciation of nature's beauty.

Westmount's heart

Cutting a large swathe from north to south, Westmount comprises two districts. The central portion shares more in common with the atmosphere of Montreal's downtown, while upper Westmount hangs precipitously, hugging the sides of the *petit montagne*. In a recent survey by the city designed to track historical buildings, it was revealed that a remarkable number of 19th-century structures have survived in Westmount. Little demolition has taken place except at the southerly edge of the city around the boulevard de Maisonneuve.

The municipal centre of Westmount is loosely arranged on the English "green" model. The City Hall sits on a triangular site at the apex of two streets: chemin de la Côte St-Antoine and rue Sherbrooke. Across the street is the beautifully landscaped Westmount Park, the municipal library, conservatory and meeting hall.

Westmount Hotel de Ville ❶ (Westmount City Hall), located at 4333 Côte St-Antoine, is an imposing Tudor-style structure surrounded by colourful beds of flowers. One of its architects, Robert Findley, was also responsible for the design of Westmount's other municipal buildings.

Nearby at 4574 Sherbrooke is the library, **Victoria Hall ❷** (tel: 989-5300), which opened in 1899, when

Map on page 194

About 19 percent of Outremont's population is anglophone, while the percentage of francophones in Westmount is roughly the same.

BELOW: traditional Westmount staircase.

Parc du Mont-Royal

Yuu can see it from just about anywhere in Montreal: buying a newspaper at the local stand, gazing idly out from a kitchen window, taking the dog for its nightly walk. Mont-Royal – or, as Montrealers call it, *la montagne* (the mountain) – looms up in the middle of the city like a natural obelisk proclaiming Montreal's presence.

For Montrealers, the mountain embodies a kind of grandeur, a place where nature's sublime and wild moods play freely across a landscape untouched by the heavy hand of urban development. Mont-Royal is more than a park. It is like an unmistakable family trait, a cherished reminder of a rich and vibrant history.

It was here in 1535 that explorer Jacques Cartier was led by Indians through wooded hills and up rocky crests to the summit. And it is here, today, that all of Montreal's ethnic groups can be found sunning, sledding, strolling, folk-dancing and picnicking.

That Mont-Royal is not covered by a network of roads, walks, cafés, electric cable cars and vast amphitheatres is largely owing to the aesthetic sensibilities of Frederick Law Olmsted, the man hired by the City of Montreal in 1874 to design the park. Olmsted, who also designed Manhattan's charming Riverside Drive and the elegant Morningside and Central parks, firmly believed that nature was a source of spiritual sustenance and that parks, properly designed, could provide urban dwellers with relief from the oppressive routines of metropolitan life.

Olmsted urged Montreal to preserve its gracious mountain and warned-off voracious developers. So far, he has been heeded.

Most of Mont-Royal's pleasures can be enjoyed in any season: a stroll through its 200 hectares (495 acres) along winding trails, a walk to the summit for a look at the 30-metre (100-ft) cross. The cross is now electrified, but the original was raised in 1643 by Paul de Chomedey, Sieur de Maisonneuve, when the fledging colony of Ville Marie was saved from a flood. You can also take a jaunt to one of the park's two lookouts for a spectacular view of central Montreal, the St Lawrence, and the Montérégian mountains.

Near the chalet in the centre are monuments to the explorer Jacques Cartier and to King George VI, as well as carvings entitled *La Sentinelle* and *Les Sans-Abris* (to the homeless). Visit the Musée de la Chasse et de la Nature for exhibits on local fauna and flora. Horse-drawn carriages (*calèches*) are a relaxing way to traverse the park and, in warmer months, free nature walks are conducted in French and English. In winter, skaters take to Beaver Lake (an artificially made pond) and cross-country skiers travel along tranquil tracks. Toboggan runs attract shoals of enthusiastic children.

Like Highgate and Brompton, the grand cemeteries of London, the Catholic and Protestant cemeteries of Mont-Royal contain ornate mausoleums, sinuous trails and almost suffocatingly lush vegetation. Covering half the mountain, these resting places are an eloquent, if rambling, statement on the subject of French Canadian genealogy. ❑

LEFT: winter pleasures – a *calèche* ride through parc du Mont-Royal.

free libraries were still a new idea. The building is distinguished by an unusual Romanesque style, with leaded-glass windows and delightful bas-reliefs which glorify "knowledge". The attached conservatory, also built in the 19th century, still functions, and it beautifies Westmount's parks and streets with its winter-grown plants. Victoria Jubilee Hall, although echoing the design of the city hall, is intended to resemble English medieval buildings and is used for a variety of public functions.

Going up the mountain

West of the municipal area is the oldest building in Westmount, located at 563 Côte St-Antoine. Because this street cuts across the lower half of the mountain, it made early construction on the steeper inclines extremely difficult.

Maison Hurtubise was built in 1688 by Pierre Hurtubise on land granted to his father by Maisonneuve. The house, the last remaining farmhouse from the 17th century in Westmount, reflects the style typical of residential architecture of the time, recognizable by its steeply gabled roof, fieldstone walls, small panes of glass and dormer windows. Because the house was built so far from Montreal (Ville Marie), early inhabitants named it *la haute folie*.

The Boulevard is a particularly lovely street, lined with imposing homes of every shape and size. These homes mirror not only the eclectic tastes of their original owners, but also more recent technical advancements in construction. Wreathing the top of the mountain are **avenue Sunnyside** and **Summit Circle**. Number 14 avenue Sunnyside, built in 1911 for Charles A. Smart, a member of the Quebec Parliament, is thought to be one of the most impressive residences in all of Westmount.

Map on page 194

Each Sunday evening in summer, and other evenings when the mood strikes, drummers congregate beside the Sir-George-Etienne-Cartier monument at the base of Parc du Mont-Royal to drum in a collective "tam-tam jam". Dreadlocks are prevalent – but not required.

BELOW: summer on the mountain.

Elegant architecture; the hallmark of Westmount and Outremont.

On Summit Circle is the **Belvedere Westmount ❸**, or Westmount Lookout, a small park and viewing area. It affords a breathtaking panorama to the west of the flat river valley and the volcanic upthrusts of a few mountains. The houses around the lookout seem precarious but sturdy; the dramatic views from their living rooms wouldn't appeal to anyone afraid of heights. Above lies the wooded peak of the *petit montagne*. In 1928 McGill University sold the land, once site of a botany laboratory, to Westmount, stipulating that it could never be developed. It is now a sanctuary for hundreds of species of birds.

Avenue Greene and Lower Westmount

Commercial enterprises in Westmount are clustered along avenue Greene and rue Sherbrooke. Here there is a mixture of convenience stores, banks and restaurants, all catering to the needs of the community. There are some upscale antique and clothing shops, but Westmount residents tend to prefer to spend big money downtown. Avenue Greene was refurbished with brick sidewalks and flower pots in the early 1970s and retains an unpretentious charm.

Sometimes referred to as Lower Westmount, the streets below Sherbrooke are full of interesting row houses. While obviously less grand than the residences on the mountain, these display everything from the fortress style to mansard roofs, with numerous examples of stone and wood designs.

Of particular note are the towers at numbers 4130–40 Dorchester (Westmount's first terrace), and those at numbers 41–47 Holton (which show the classic Montreal pattern of alternating units).

BELOW: tam-tam jam at the Sir-George-Etienne-Cartier monument.

Towards Montreal's downtown via rue Sherbrooke is **The Mother House of the Sisters of Notre-Dame**. Now the campus of **Dawson College ❹** (3040 rue Sherbrooke Ouest), Quebec's largest anglophone *cejep* (junior college), it is impossible to miss. An awe-inspiring edifice designed by J. Omer Marchand in 1904, its distinctiveness is derived, in part, from the well-judged use of pale-coloured stone and a flamboyant Beaux-Arts style. At one time the building was used simultaneously as a hospital, retirement home, school and headquarters for the religious order.

Outremont

Outremont's boundaries are roughly defined by the commercial **avenue Van Horne** and **avenue Laurier** and the residential **chemin de la Côte Ste-Catherine** and **rue Hutchison**. These boundaries are not strict, however, and the neighbourhoods which stretch beyond them are deemed, at least in the classifieds, to be "adjacent" or "outer" Outremont. Today, being on the edges of this chic section of Montreal is good enough to secure a higher rent from prospective tenants or better sale of a home. An address in Outremont tells people a lot about you: it means that you are most likely a francophone, most likely a dyed-in-the-wool urbanite, and wealthy enough to be able to afford this great in-town location.

It wasn't always this way. Before the gentrification that took place in the 1960s and 1970s, Outremont's streets, such as Laurier and Bernard, and especially avenue Van Horne, were common, ordinary car lanes.

They were even considered to be on the shabby side. The area around Van Horne was once semi-industrial and is still referred to as Lower Outremont.

Older residents remark that avenue Van Horne, the district's northern boundary, still has the original character of the neighbourhood. There you will find a modest array of shops and restaurants, row houses built more closely together, fewer parks and smaller gardens.

Map on page 194

Outremont's attractions

Outremont's municipal centre is rather understated. **Outremont Hôtel de Ville ❺** (Town Hall) and public library are located off Côte Ste-Catherine. Ironically, the city hall is housed in a stately private residence thought to have once been a trading post of the British-owned Hudson's Bay Company. It is one of the oldest buildings in Outremont, constructed around 1800. The library is also located in an old private home behind city hall.

The finest architecture in Outremont is found in its public buildings: churches, cinemas and schools. One of the most striking is **Académie Querbes ❻** at 215 rue Bloomfield. Designed by J.A. Godin in the Beaux-Arts style and completed in 1915, the building lends a distinctly European atmosphere to the otherwise typical North American residential architecture which surrounds it. Today, it houses a primary school.

Residents had to fight hard to save the Outremont Théâtre at 1234 rue Bernard. Plans to convert it into a multi-use complex were blocked by a public awareness campaign and a determined petition drive. The bas-reliefs on the outside of the building are remarkable, despite the considerable damage they've suffered because of the harsh weather. The interior is abundantly

TIP

Put on a good pair of walking shoes to explore the francophone version of "the elite". The sights listed here just provide a taste of Outremont's attractions.

BELOW: a leafy street in Outremont.

Map
on page
194

*There are restaurants
and cafés to suit all
tastes.*

BELOW:
Eglise St-Germain.

grand and reminiscent of Montreal's old theatres, including the Strand, Loews and the Capitol.

At the corner of avenues Laurier and Bloomfield is the imposing **Eglise St-Viateur ❼**, which was completed in 1913. Its Gothic Revival style is strongly represented in the church's facade which towers above the modest apartment buildings surrounding it. Interestingly, the sides of the church aren't as well constructed as the front – a frequent feature of buildings where the architect concentrated on the facade.

At Côte-Ste-Catherine and avenue d'Indy are two other interesting public buildings. **Eglise St-Germain ❽**, which stands at the intersection of these two roads, was built in 1931 and has a magnificently large bell tower as its centre-piece. The other building, facing out on Côte Ste-Catherine, was once the **Pensionnat du St-Nom-de-Marie**. Designed in 1903, its most striking feature is the classically designed portico which incorporates a remarkable number of other architectural styles.

The residential areas of Outremont are generally organized around a number of parks. The houses around **Parc Outremont ❾** are beautiful simply because of the fine construction techniques and the regularity of their design. The unique detailing makes them interesting to look at: one can see a variety of stained-glass designs, wood and iron trims and stone bas-reliefs inserted into the brick facades. These houses around Parc Outremont have the best view s of the changing seasons on the mountain. **Parc Joyce ❿** and **Parc Pratt ⓫**, which take their names from the farmers who once owned the land, also afford views of the mountain and the campus of the **Université de Montréal ⓬** and **Oratoire St-Joseph ⓭** (St Joseph's Oratory, *see page 203*), which rest on its northern face.

Also on the mountain, on the edge of Outremont, is the Protestant **Cimetière Mont-Royal ⓮** (Mount Royal Cemetery). Its sylvan landscape attracts species of birds found nowhere else in Quebec.

In these idyllic settings many famous French Canadians have lived and some still do. The leader of the Parti Québécois, Lucien Bouchard, lives in Outremont, and the late prime minister Pierre Trudeau grew up on rue McCullough. The popular Québécois writer Maurice Tremblay also lived in Outremont.

Lively contrasts

Finally, there is a lively contrast between the quiet, tree-lined residential streets of Outremont and its commercial areas which hum with activity day and night. Along avenues Laurier and Bernard you'll find a wealth of clothing shops, cafés *(see page 201)* and mouth-watering bakeries. A kind of architectural recycling goes on here. Many buildings on these two streets have been transformed from parking facilities into multi-use centres, or from garages into galleries. Here you can take your cat to a "postmodern" veterinary clinic or buy the latest in light fixtures or kitchen utensils. On avenue Laurier in particular, one will also find some fine French-language bookshops.

And what of the contrasts between Westmount and Outremont? Two solitudes? Perhaps. But polar opposites? Hardly. Those days are long gone. ❑

Outremont Cafés

When the word "café" is mentioned, images of smoky Parisian brasseries, sun-dappled terraces, and the smell of good strong coffee come to mind. This tableau can certainly be found in the cafés along avenues Bernard and Laurier in Outremont. For a taste of Europe, step into one of these cultural enclaves, most of which hum day and night. Experience the "café culture" of Outremont and savour a *café au lait* and a pastry.

The cafés on the busy thoroughfares of Bernard and Laurier range from the refined to the humble. From the exquisitely decorated to the unadorned, each has a distinctive ambience and a devoted clientele. What they all share, besides delicious coffee, is their neighbourhood role as meeting places.

Café Romolo, located at Jeanne-Mance and Bernard, is just outside the official limits of Outremont but its unique character and fine coffee draw a steady crowd. At small tables with plain wooden chairs people read newspapers or converse in small groups, their heads ringed in a haze of smoke, the smell of which mingles with the potent fragrance of fresh coffee. Smooth, frothy *café-au-lait* is served in tall glasses as in Italy and Spain; sugar and cinnamon sit on the tables. The café also serves *espresso*, alcoholic beverages, and pastries which the owner "imports" from the Greek bakery next door.

Le Bilboquet, at 1311 Bernard, is renowned for its ice cream, sorbet and frozen yogurt. The café is closed for a portion of the winter, but is kept busy all summer long. Its breezy interior is accentuated by an Art Deco green-pink-and-black tiled floor.

Another memorable café – forgive the pun – is the **Café Souvenir** at 1261 Bernard. Huge maps of European cities adorn the walls of this popular little restaurant, with a strong French ambience, where locals drop by for coffee or a simple meal.

A little further down the street, locals head for the **Café République** at 1051 Bernard when they feel like sampling something from the array of desserts that is always on offer.

La Croissanterie at 5200 rue Hutchison, nestles within a residential area and the café's daytime customers are generally neighbourhood regulars. They stop in for a sandwich, homemade pastry or a *cappuccino* made strong with a frothy mound of hot milk and a generous dash of cinnamon on top.

While there are a few cafés on avenue Laurier, **La Petite Ardoise** appears to be many people's favourite. Local artists display paintings and collages for sale, while a bulletin board at the back announces gallery openings and other cultural events. In the summer, a small back garden is transformed into an outdoor terrace.

Cafés in Montreal play an important role in promoting social cohesion. While they are an essential part of a francophone's cultural identity, many of the city's newer immigrants – Greeks, Italians and Africans – are increasingly drawn to them. And for anglophones, cafés are a special treat, serving as reminders of how "un-American" this North American city truly is. ❑

RIGHT: cafés in Outremont, and other areas of Montreal, are part of the fabric of society.

ST JOSEPH'S ORATORY

Celebrated as one of Christendom's outstanding monuments of faith, this is the Grand Central Station of devotional Catholicism in Montreal

Map on page 194

The word "oratory" means house of prayer – and St Joseph's Oratory is just that, albeit a very big one. St Joseph's cupola, rising 263 metres (864 ft) above sea level, is a vast, imposing, but familiar sight towering above Montreal's rooftops. Built in honour of Canada's patron saint, the shrine draws more than 3 million visitors a year, rivals devotions to the Lourdes and Fatima shrines and has a dome larger than any except St Peter's in Rome. St Joseph's is able to accommodate up to 12,000 people at one time, standing room only.

From the foot of the 278 stairs which lead up to the entrance, the **Oratoire St-Joseph** (St Joseph's Oratory) (3800 chemin Queen-Mary; open mid May–mid Sept: daily, 7am–9pm; rest of the year: daily, 7am–5.30pm; free; tel: 733-8211) is an overpowering presence. A giant, it exudes an unselfconscious resignation to its own enormity; an architectural arrogance characterizes the oratory, whose cumbersome haunches make the other edifices in Montreal seem like side dishes. For the devotional Catholic, St Joseph's is a religious event, a holy place, a sacred duty. For the casual visitor, it offers an intriguing glimpse into a Catholic culture that, at one time, permeated almost every aspect of French-Canadian life.

LEFT: the mighty dome of Oratoire St-Joseph.
BELOW: pilgrim paying homage.

Devotional acts

Whether religious inspiration or anthropological curiosity propels you to the site, a visit inevitably means an encounter with stairs – plenty of them: 99 from street level to the entrance of the crypt-church, and then an additional 179 up to the basilica proper. Pilgrimage groups usually gather around the bronze and granite monument to St Joseph located inside the main gate and, drawing a few deep breaths, prepare for a steep ascent towards the celestial structure.

Some pilgrims, as an act of penance and reverence, will make an edifying and excruciating climb on their knees up to the crypt-church. The stairs at St Joseph's are not properly *scalae santae* or holy stairs which, when ascended on the knees, are a way in which Catholics can obtain indulgences (divine pardon) for past, present or future sins. This rather painful practice, however, is still carried out by those seeking a devotional act to purify the soul for an encounter with the saintly patriarch.

First stop

The crypt-church, the first stop on the way up, was completed in 1917. It derives its name from its vault-like appearance and, one is tempted to add, its vault-like feel: the ponderous stone walls create the sensation of being sealed underground. The stained-

Many visitors choose to follow Louis Parent's famous Way of the Cross.

glass windows depict episodes from the Bible in which St Joseph features prominently: the Birth of Christ, the Circumcision, Life at Nazareth, and so on.

Illuminated chapel

Adjoining the crypt-church is what is called a votive chapel, designed for private devotions. St Joseph's importance for the Catholic church is reflected in the eight plaques which display the saint's titles: Guardian of Virgins, Terror of Demons, Protector of the Church, Hope of the Sick, Patron of the Dying, Comfort of the Afflicted, Mainstay of Families and Model of Workmen. (A busy saint!) In addition to preserving virgins and deflecting devils, St Joseph heals through miracles. The crutches and braces scattered throughout the chapel are "testimonies" left by pilgrims cured by the oil found in a basin beneath the statue of St Joseph. (The oil is also on sale in the gift shop.)

Illuminating the centre of the votive chapel is the flickering of more than 3,500 vigil lights, candles lit either in memory of the dead or as a request for blessing. The wrought-iron railing contains a holy relic, a tiny particle of St Joseph's clothing, allegedly authenticated and venerated for its miraculous healing powers. Behind the main lamp rack is the resting place of Brother André, the founder of the oratory who died at the age of 91 and was finally beatified by Rome – one step below Roman Catholic sainthood or canonization.

Founder of St Joseph's

Brother André was the lowly door keeper at Notre-Dame College, a boys' school across the street from the Oratory, before he became the celebrated founder of St Joseph's. A museum (open daily, 10am–5pm; donations; tel: 733-8211

isplaying artifacts related to his origins, childhood and service in the oratory located two storeys below the basilica. The exhibits include a peculiar "exact" eplica of the austere cell Brother André occupied while a doorkeeper and a thoroughly authentic" reproduction of the hospital room in which he died on anuary 6, 1937.

Map on page 194

Basilica and gardens

Heading upwards again, visitors climb towards solid Canadian granite, staunchly efending the oratory against time and the elements. A brief pause here under the Renaissance-style facade affords a bird's-eye view of Montreal before you nter the somewhat barren and charmless interior of the basilica proper and the sanctuary. Return, then, to the outside, where secluded gardens ranging beyond the basilica and out into the mountainside encourage meditative meanderings.

... the world's capital of devotion to Saint Joseph.

– CARDINAL TISSERANT

The 15 stone tableaux of Louis Parent's famous Way of the Cross, represent the stages of Christ's death and resurrection. Each station's foliage was carefully chosen to reflect a mood. At the third tableau, where Christ is shown falling on the way to crucifixion, the predominant colour is red to denote the flow of blood. Where Veronica wipes the face of Christ, the colours are delicate pastels to suggest tenderness. And at the 13th station, where Christ is taken down from the cross, the colours are bland and austere, conveying grief and desolation.

Endearing shrine

Although almost grotesquely huge, St Joseph's exterior is nevertheless stately. Endearingly simple, however, is the tiny shrine to Brother André, dwarfed beside the looming Oratory. Inside, cracked walls stand behind the faded paint of once-garish religious statues, and the floors groan as bended knees approach them. Simple, humble and worn out, the chapel is a welcome contrast, in a dusty sort of way, to the pomposity of its grandiose cousin next door. Here too are weathered plaques thanking St Joseph for his intercessions, some dating from the chapel's earliest days.

BELOW: bath time for Brother André.

Commercial aspect

Finally, a trip to St Joseph's wouldn't be complete without a visit to the gift shop back at the bottom of the hill. Here almost every kind of Catholic religious paraphernalia can be found, from statues of St Joseph, whose heart (assuming the statue is plugged in) will glow an ethereal rose, to miniature versions of the saint that are specially designed for the dashboard or refrigerator.

There are almost 100 varieties of rosary to choose from. Those made of expensive red crystal have beads shaped like hearts, while an economy model is made of lightweight plastic.

Here, with people pawing through bins of plastic medallions, glow-in-the-dark rosaries and laminated holy cards, St Joseph's commercial side is brazenly exposed. While celebrating the transcendent human soul, the shrine is also a monument to a culture capable of generating a commodity from even its most immaterial aspects. ❑

STADIUMS, GARDENS AND ISLANDS

Map on page 210

Olympic Park, with its associated museums and gardens, makes an intriguing day-trip. And on the city's playground islands it sometimes seems as if Expo '67 never ended

ravel east along rue Sherbrooke and the **Stade Olympique ❶** (Olympic Stadium) (4141 avenue Pierre-de-Coubertin; English tours daily at 12.40pm and 3.40pm; entrance fee; tel: 252-8687) looms up suddenly mid rows of unassuming duplexes, as though a mollusc-shaped starship from nother galaxy had settled down in the suburbs. Futuristic, grandiose, impractcal and incredibly expensive, controversy still surrounds the "Big O" long fter the memory of the 1976 Olympic Games has faded.

Roger Taillibert, the French architect who designed the stadium, claimed that ports arenas are the cathedrals of our age. The metaphor appealed to a city ith a history of building magnificent churches but the plan for the new sports ome – designed to assert the city's modern, cosmopolitan flair rather than its oman Catholic history – was far more ambitious, and ultimately it demanded ven more financial sacrifice. And just as the slow construction of St Joseph's ratory had depended upon the personal charisma of Brother André, so the idden realization of the Big O was only possible through the force of one pernality: the irrepressible Jean Drapeau, Montreal's mayor from 1954 to 1986. Drapeau gets credit for sheer visionary ambition.

he Olympic Stadium's revolutionary design boasts e **Tour Olympique ❷**, a leaning tower 55 storeys igh, from which a flexible Kevlar roof descends ong cables over the playing field. Tower and staium alike are imaginatively modelled in fluent irves that soar at beautiful and seemingly impossible igles from the rather drab working-class neighbourod surrounding it.

PRECEDING PAGES:
aerial view of Ile St-Hélène.
LEFT: the Biosphère.
BELOW:
Olympic Tower.

regnant man

ut Mayor Drapeau must also shoulder a large part of e blame for the Big O's other unofficial nicknames: he Big Owe" and the "the Big Uh-Oh". Montreal's adium just may be the most spectacular sports arena the world – but there is no question that it is the ost expensive. The price tag of $1.2 billion gives it e distinction of being one of the most costly buildigs ever constructed, and the bill is still far from eing paid off now, more than a quarter-century later. he price tag means that each of its 70,000 seats cost ore than $17,000. In 1984, an accounting firm deterined that the Big O had cost only slightly less than l the other domed stadiums in North America put gether – and that was before it had a roof!

Yet Drapeau had promised Montreal "modest mes" that would pay for themselves through revues from tickets and souvenirs. He remains notorious

Located conveniently close together, these facilities are well-signposted and easy to find.

for his assurance that the Olympics could no more run a deficit than a man could have a baby. Predictably, local cartoonists enjoyed depicting the former mayor heavy with child.

The reasons for the exorbitant price tag are easy enough to find in hindsight. The concept of a retractable canopy roof suspended from a tower leaning at 45° had never before been attempted on this scale. Since the top of the tower had to be centred over the stadium's roof, the circular opening in the centre of the stadium slants slightly towards the tower, so that the end of the ellipse near the tower's base is lower than the far end. The pleasing asymmetry of this design made the task of casting the huge, irregular concrete ribs of the stadium extremely tricky and delicate – and, of course, expensive.

But the real construction headaches were caused by the rigid deadline that Olympic Games always impose upon the host city. The clock ticked away as the builders waited for detailed plans from the architect. In the end, they built most of the complex in just two years, between 1974 and 1976. At the opening ceremonies, Montreal had a magnificent stadium, but there was still no tower and no roof. Nevertheless, in the giddy flush (and relief) of the moment, the city gave Drapeau a standing ovation. The tower would take another decade: it was not completed until 1987.

Did the city's professional baseball team, the Montreal Expos, need so extravagant a home? Defenders of the Olympic Stadium ask: does anybody worry about how much the Pyramids cost? Or the Roman Coliseum (which, as it happens, would fit onto the Big O's playing field)? Drapeau once reminded his critics that the ancient Athenians had rebuked Pericles for building the Parthenon instead of warships.

BELOW:
Olympic Stadium.

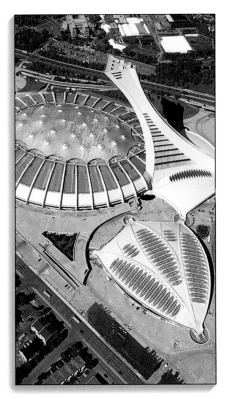

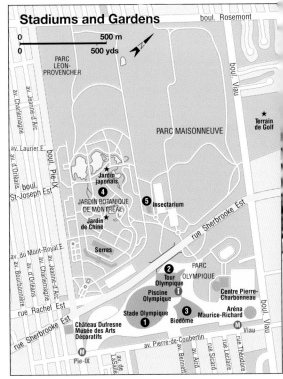

However, history has had the last laugh. The city's Canadian Football League team, the Alouettes, abandoned the stadium first. The Expos followed suit after the completion of a new downtown stadium for them in 2001. And for all its nifty engineering, the Olympic Stadium's retractable roof did not entirely eliminate rain delays and, due to ongoing problems, is now kept tightly closed.

Map on page 210

Unobstructed view

A visitor need only ride the funicular **cable car** that runs up the spine of the tower to the observatory deck to appreciate the architect's imagination. One might say that the tower combines the grace of the Eiffel Tower with the eccentricity of the Leaning Tower of Pisa. While the top of this concrete tripod overhangs the roof of the stadium, the hollow base forms the roof of the Olympic pools, with wing-like lobes that spread out on either side.

Thirteen storeys of office space fill up about two-thirds of the tower's neck, with a three-floor observatory at the summit where the tower broadens as its three corners begin to sweep apart. The exterior double-decker cable car carries up to 90 passengers and, emerging into the open air about a third of the way along its path, offers an increasingly spectacular view of the eastern horizon.

From the observation deck at the summit, the view extends about 80 km (50 miles) and includes an unobstructed westward view of Mont Royal and the city skyline, with the St Lawrence River winding around from the left. There is also a vertiginous view into the stadium.

The cables that suspend the roof pass down from a niche only a short distance below the deck, affording a unique perspective on the operations that once raised and lowered the 65 tonnes/tons of fabric. Forty-six winches had to oper-

TIP

Come equipped for a dip as the Olympic pools are open to the public year-round.

BELOW: inside the stadium.

ate in precise synchronicity in order to unfurl the roof over an area that measure more than 18,500 sq. metres (200,000 sq. ft). Now permanently lowered, th canopy stretches over the playing field as a tent-like cupola.

Problems and criticisms

For all this nifty engineering, the retractable roof did not entirely eliminate rai delays even when it worked. If an unexpected shower occurred in high winds the game had to wait until the winds let up before the roof could be unfurled. The roof could not be lowered if winds were stronger than 25 kph (15 mph), whil the roof of Toronto's SkyDome can operate in winds up to 65 kph (40 mph). A: it took almost 45 minutes to drop the roof into place, stadium officials nor mally let weather predictions determine whether the roof should be lowered for an event, rather than waiting for the rain.

Baseball fans who made the trek out to the stadium had long criticized the sight-lines at the Big O, which was designed more with track and field in mind. Perhaps this is one reason why the team has annually carried the lowest atten- dance figures in pro baseball. In any case, the stadium plays host to other sorts of events now that the roof allows the stadium to be used year-round. Trade shows and rock concerts attract crowds to the stands nowadays. Special events, such as the visit of Pope John Paul II or the spectacular production of Verdi's *Aïda* that came complete with a 12-metre (40-ft) sphinx, live elephants and over 1,000 singers, occasionally convert even die-hard pragmatists to Drapeau's grand point of view. Locals often grumble about the archaic seating and astro- nomical cost. Being Montrealers and wedded to tradition, though, they would never suggest closing or demolishing the structure now.

BELOW:
a brighter future
for the Expos.

LES EXPOS

The years 1979 and 1981 are stamped indelibly on the minds of local baseball fans. Why? Those were the last two years that Montreal's professional baseball club, the Expos, seriously contended for anything besides last place. The game has changed since then, but times have not been kind to les Expos.

Increasing television revenues led to a sharp upward spike in players' salaries during the 1980s, and that – combined with the strong American dollar – caught the Expos (as well as Toronto's Blue Jays) in a difficult bind. Ticket revenues are earned in Canadian dollars, while players are paid on an American scale; the 40 percent difference began to add up to a huge loss on the balance sheet. Talent was sold off, and fans all but disappeared, a situation exacerbated by the problem of drawing fans to the ageing Olympic Stadium.

But in late 1999, a Philadelphia art dealer suddenly purchased the team, inked a deal to break ground on a new downtown baseball stadium, and began emptying his wallet for decent talent. Murmurs began about baseball glory in Montreal for the first time in decades – alongside grumbles that the American might transfer the team south of the border. Yet another twist in the saga of les Expos.

Biodôme

Spreading out from the base of the Olympic Pools, the **Vélodrome** was built to accommodate the cycling events at the 1976 Olympic Games. However, another celebratory spin-off from the city's 350th anniversary resulted in the conversion of the space into an unusual life-sciences museum called the **Biodôme** ❸ (4777 avenue Pierre-du-Coubertin; open June–Aug: daily, 9am–7pm; rest of the year: daily, 9am–5pm; entrance fee; tel: 868-3000; fax: 868-3065). City botanists, biologists and zoologists have created four different ecosystems under one roof: a tropical jungle, a polar environment, a northern forest and the habitat along the St Lawrence River. Characteristic plants, animals and birds have been installed within each miniature world. Thanks to cleverly sited underwater cameras, visitors can even observe beavers hard at work inside their elaborate lodges.

Map on page 210

Botanical Garden

The Biodôme complements the glories of nature already on display across rue Sherbrooke. As sports fans roar inside their concrete cathedral, 26,000 species of plants repose in tranquillity at the **Jardin Botanique** ❹ (Botanical Garden) 4101 rue Sherbrooke Est; open May–Sept: daily, 9am–7pm; rest of the year: daily, 9am–5pm; entrance fee; tel: 872-1400). If Montreal, with its harsh winters, seems an unlikely setting for one of the world's largest botanical gardens, consider the pleasure of sitting in the warmth of the tropical greenhouse, among pineapple plants and orchids, during a December blizzard. However, most of the two million people who visit every year are more interested in houseplants and exotic gardens than they are in a chance to come in from the cold. Located on a 73-hectare (180-acre) rectangle across the street from the Olympic Park, the

Trees of all sizes are on show at the Botanical Garden.

BELOW: tea house at the Botanical Garden.

All kinds of visitors are attracted to the Botanical Garden.

garden complex has been steadily evolving since Brother Marie-Victori_ founded the project in 1931. A modest statue of the monk stands to the right, jus beyond the main gate.

Although a total of nine greenhouses protect the tropical flora from the ele_ ments, spring and the fall are still the best seasons for a visit, since the vas_ majority of plants are divided among the various outdoor gardens. Differen_ plant groups bloom each month between April and October.

Even those visitors who can't tell a begonia from a rhododendron ca_ enjoy a stroll among the blooms, but those who prefer a chauffeur can tak_ a 45-minute guided tour on the mini-train (runs May–Oct: daily, every 1_ mins from 9.30am–5pm). With about 30 plots in which the plants are groupe_ according to particular themes, a trip through the gardens is a little like mov_ ing through a series of stage or films sets. Some gardens are as much edu_ cational as sensory experiences.

The **Monastery Garden** has displays of medicinal herbs in an arrangemen_ that recreates the quiet enclaves of medieval monks in the age of Charlemagne_ Information panels offer useful trivia about such topics as the aphrodisiac powe_ of absinthe and the laxative properties of licorice. The poisonous plant section is only a short distance away. These plots are located just beyond the neatly arranged perennials and test gardens, to the left after the entrance.

Winding paths, ponds thick with lilies, rock gardens, and a "flowery brook" make a poetic setting at the centre of the gardens. An assortment of birds live among the aquatic plants in the ponds. In the **Alpinum**, flora from the world's mountain ranges are gathered together beside a quaint waterfall. When the flow_ ers bloom, choruses from *The Sound of Music* pop into mind. Beyond the ponds

BELOW: the Japanese house.

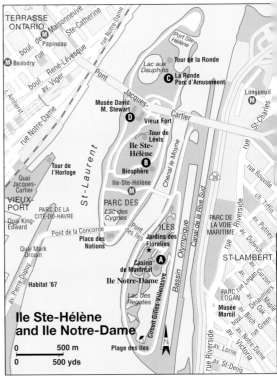

TERRASSE ONTARIO

Ile Ste-Hélène and Ile Notre-Dame

0 ___ 500 m
0 ___ 500 yds

Maps on page 210

hat lie behind the Alpinum, the **Arboretum** is more like an open park, with its rim heaths, dwarf spruces, shade trees and chestnuts. In the fall the maples begin to turn a splendid colour, and the dense assembly here provides a convenient way to go "foliage peeking".

The **Chinese Garden** is the largest outside Asia, with seven pavilions built in the Ming Dynasty style around a central lake; the Botanical Garden staff worked closely with the City of Shanghai on this project. The **Japanese Garden** is all serenity, with bubbling streams full of carp, and a tea room. Next to the **Rose Garden**, another interesting section collects forest specimens from a series of six villages called Montreal located in various parts of France.

The **greenhouses** recreate the climates of the warmer parts of the globe: an equatorial rain forest has the musty bouquet of orchids; then a hot, dry desert with human-sized cacti; and a Mexican villa with a popular collection of carnivorous plants including the famous Venus fly-traps.

Several permanent and temporary exhibitions are housed under glass here, as well; a computer controls the climate of each of the ecosystems. There are trivia-quiz computer games for the kids to play, and audio-guides in French and English. The rhododendrons, by the way, are planted in a specialized garden and they bloom in June, while the 100-plus species of begonias are gathered with the gesneriads in the tropical greenhouse.

More than any other single event in Montreal's history, Expo changed the way the city felt about itself, awakening it to its potential as a centre for international gatherings of all kinds.

New perspective

The small but intriguing **Insectarium** ❺ (4101 rue Sherbrooke Est; open May–Sept: daily, 9am–7pm; rest of the year: daily, 9am–5pm; entrance fee; tel: 872-1400) was opened in 1990 following the initiative of an enthusiastic collector named Georges Brossard. Part museum and part zoo, the project was designed to educate children and adults about creatures that usually get only negative attention from humans. Inside this pavilion, which is itself shaped like an insect, kids and grown-ups alike can peer into display cases and absorb their minds in games and puzzles that shed a whole new light on the world of bugs.

An extraordinary variety of perfectly preserved insects, from butterflies to golden scarab beetles, is mounted on the walls, while an assortment of living insects is housed behind glass walls. Some of these creatures seem to be a little shy of the spotlight, but they are easy enough to find with a little patience. All together, there are about 130,000 specimens here.

Expo islands

For another entertaining day-trip, visit the two islands in the St Lawrence River, opposite Old Montreal, that function as the city's fairgrounds.

Until the 1960s, there was only one island here, **Ile Ste-Hélène**, which was about half its present size. However, the earth excavated from the freshly dug Métro tunnels was used to expand the island and to create a whole new one next door: **Ile Notre-Dame**.

This park became the site of Expo '67, the great exposition that drew 50 million visitors during the summer of Canada's centennial year, 1967. The plans

BELOW: the world of bugs.

Map on page 214

Re-enactments of 18th-century parades take place at the old fort on Ile Ste-Hélène.

RIGHT:
fiery welcome
at La Ronde.
BELOW:
roller-coaster fun.

called for temporary structures that would stand for the summer of the exhibition and then disappear, but many of the 83 pavilions were so sturdy and impressive that it made no sense to demolish them. So Expo survived for 14 years as *Terre des Hommes* (Man and His World).

Playground for the city

Today, the site has taken on a whole new persona. On Ile Notre-Dame, the old French pavilion was converted in 1993 into the **Casino de Montréal** Ⓐ (tel: 1-800-361-4595). In 1995 the casino expanded into a neighbouring building, the Pavilion du Québec, connected by a futuristic walkway. Casino authorities claim it is one of the world's largest gaming places, and Montrealers do indeed come out in droves to enjoy a game of chance.

On Ile Ste-Hélène, the famous **geodesic dome** designed by Buckminster Fuller has gone through a dramatic transformation. Despite a fire burning away its outer skin in 1978, the former American pavilion still stands 20 storeys high. With no internal supports, it encloses 198,240 cu. metres (7 million cu. ft) of air. In 1995, with the opening of **Biosphère** Ⓑ, the pavilion became both an interpretive centre and a hub for the vast network of eco-watchers along the St Lawrence River and the Great Lakes' water systems. Through satellites and sophisticated computer technology, visitors exploring the four interactive exhibition halls receive a graphic lesson on the importance of water.

La Ronde Ⓒ (open June–Sept: daily, 10am–9pm, mid-May–June: Sat–Sun only, 10am–9pm; entrance fee; tel: 872-6222), the amusement park built for Expo, is still going strong on Ile Ste-Hélène. The original Mini-Rail and cable-car SkyRide still seem novel ways to get around the park. Montrealers with children make an annual pilgrimage to La Ronde to experience the thrills of rides such as Le Monstre, one of the world's tallest roller-coaster rides at 46 metres (150 ft), and a popular complex called Aqua-Parc, with a waterslide for everyone from toddlers to daredevils. During two weeks in the early summer, admission to La Ronde includes a ringside seat from which to view the annual **International Fireworks Competition**. Each night for two weeks a different national team attempts to put on the most spectacular pyrotechnics display over the river and the city skyline.

In mid-June the roar of Formula One racing cars from the Air Canada Grand Prix can be heard on the **Circuit Gilles-Villeneuve**, the race track on Ile Notre-Dame. A refuge from all this noisy excitement is not far away: a chunk of Ile Ste-Hélène is still green, wooded and quiet, except for the traffic on the Jacques Cartier-Bridge.

The past can be visited on Ile Ste-Hélène at the 1822 fort near the bridge. At the **Musée David M. Stewart** Ⓓ (Stewart Museum; 20 chemin Tour-de-l'Ile; open mid-May–mid-Oct: daily, 10am–5pm, Thur until 9pm; rest of the year: daily, except Tues, 10am–5pm; entrance fee; tel: 861-6701), as well as naval and other military paraphernalia, during the summer visitors can see the Compagnie Franche de la Marine and the 78th Fraser Highlanders re-enact parades dressed in 18th-century costumes. ❑

THE ST LAWRENCE: RIVER OF HISTORY

The St Lawrence River has long been a lifeline for Canada's vast hinterland, a highway between the Great Lakes and the Atlantic Ocean

The reason Montreal came to be established where it was is simple – it sits beside a very large river that connects the Atlantic Ocean (and thus Europe) with Canada's vast inland lakes and forests. The St Lawrence was essentially the highway to the West, and is the true mother of Montreal, Quebec City and modern Canada.

As the interior of Canada was gradually opened up, a parade of steamships sailed up and down the river, carrying furs and wheat to France. Between 1830 and 1850, the short line of stone piers along the waterfront was extended again and again until it stretched more than 6 km (4 miles), and the total freight handled in the port increased more than thirty-fold. A system of grain elevators and silos was constructed to process the wheat coming downstream from the Midwest; sugar cane from the Caribbean and oil from Texas and South America would also soon come to this waterfront for processing. By World War I, Montreal would become the second-most important port in North America after New York City.

In 1959, Queen Elizabeth II and President Eisenhower presided over the official opening of the St Lawrence Seaway – a parallel series of channels which diverted freighters around the various rapids and navigational obstacles along the river's course. Montreal didn't know it at the time, but the opening of the Seaway would mean that the port was soon overshadowed by those at Toronto and Chicago.

▷ **PORTAGE MONUMENT**
The Portage Monument recalls the days when canoes had to be transported overland to avoid treacherous rapids along the river.

MONTREAL'S HIDDEN RIVIERA

△ **INDUSTRIAL SKYLINE**
Having seen many incarnations, and been given several face-lifts, the port still remains a part of Montreal's cityscape.

▽ **WINTER SPORTS**
Sportsmen drag and paddle 22-kg (50-lb) canoes across the frozen river in the ice-canoe races at La Fête des Neiges, held in January.

▽ **PLACE YOUR BETS**
Picturesquely located on Notre-Dame island, Montreal's casino has become an outstanding success story, with over 15,000 visitors a day.

▽ **MARITIME HIGHWAY**
St Lambert lock on the St Lawrence River, which continues to be one of the world's busiest shipping channels, linking the Great Lakes with the Atlantic.

EDUCED ROLE
ntreal's Old Port is still a king port, despite the ning of the St Lawrence way, which meant that s could reach the Great es without stopping here.

ISTORIC CANAL
Lachine Canal was npleted in 1821, allowing s to bypass a cherous set of rapids. banks are now popular cyclists and joggers.

In spite of its diminished importance today, what remains of Montreal's Old Port is certainly still impressive. The city's younger set seems finally to have accepted the river at its feet and have even begun to play with it a bit.

Riverside attractions such as an IMAX movie theatre and a new science centre are the obvious nods to tourism, but the city's real homage to its home river becomes clearer down the back streets.

Walking north along the river from near the base of the Bonaventure highway connector, you soon come to the former barge control tower on the canal; it now houses a summer tourist information centre. Events such as a large beer festival take place on the adjacent docks throughout the summer.

River cruises depart throughout the day from the docks around the river, the best way to see it in its entirety. Alternatively you can take the lovely and popular path upriver beginning in the Old Port.

EXCURSIONS

Excursions from Montreal include everything from frothing rivers to classical music, flashy ski lodges to peaceful monasteries, French resorts to English farm towns

Map on pages 224–5

Montreal is ideally situated for quick getaways to an astonishing variety of four-season adventures: river rafting on the Rouge; ice-fishing on Ile Perrot; climbing frozen waterfalls in Estrie; hiking, skiing and mountain biking; craft fairs and pleasure boat cruises; gondola rides and aqua slides; historic forts and ports; maple sugar feasting and sleigh rides at *cabanes à sucre* (sugar shacks); manors and museums; bushwhacking and moose tracking. Disappear with a tent into the wilds of a *réserve faunique* (wildlife reserve), rent a chalet, or sleep in a log castle with room service.

Points of the compass

To the north lie the deep silent woods, glacial lakes and alpine villages of the Laurentians, resting on the oldest rock formation on the planet – the Canadian Shield. To the south lie the rolling pastures, brightly painted barns and white-steepled towns of the Estrie, a French version of New England. To the east are five of the Montérégian hills, carved by the ancient Champlain Sea, arcing across the St Lawrence plain; and the historic Richelieu Valley. This is the battleground of the Iroquois, French, English and Americans, and the scene of the 1837 Patriots' Rebellion against the British regime. To the west lies the Outaouais, land of big logging lakes and rivers and the great fighting muskie.

PRECEDING PAGES: autumn splendour. **LEFT:** Festival des Montgolfières. **BELOW:** horseback riding and trekking.

The **Laurentians**, Quebec's *pays d'en haut* (highlands) and the **Estrie** (the Eastern Townships) are the two main playgrounds for Montrealers. North America's first alpine ski rope-tows were erected at Prévost in 1930 and at St-Sauveur-des-Monts in 1934. Montrealers soon flocked to the Laurentians to try the newfangled sport, and the glamour of ski and après-ski began to saturate the region.

Today, acrobatic skiing, torchlight parades, and tobogganing are all popular on Quebec slopes. The Laurentians have the largest concentration of alpine ski centres and lighted runs in North America, and the Estrie runs a close second. But summer brings another medley of pleasures – canoeing, sailing, horseback riding, camping, fishing, swimming, water-skiing, or cappucino-sipping on a well-situated café terrace; antiquing, boutiquing, gallery browsing, summer theatre and *boîtes à chansons* which keep going till dawn.

Like the Laurentians, the Estrie (from *est* for east and *patrie*) is ski and sailboat country, sprinkled with chic auberges and inns, artisan boutiques and impeccable restaurants. But the farm culture tempers the elegance of resort towns like Lac Brome, Eastman, North Hatley, Sutton and Magog with an earthy charm. The milder microclimate and proximity to the US border give the region an adventurous spirit.

The following excursions are divided into four categories: Laurentians, Estrie, Montérégie, and Coeur-du-Québec, with the trips arranged in order of importance. They provide a focus for day or weekend trips, but try taking the scenic routes – No. 117 through the Laurentians, No. 138 (known as the Chemin du Roy), No. 132, No. 342, No. 344 and No. 223. Exploring the back roads, called "rangs", will lead you to chance encounters, roadside curiosities and other unmapped treasures.

Laurentians

1. Heart of the Laurentians

Route: Laurentians Autoroute 15 North to Ste-Adèle, or take the more scenic local 117 North; from Ste-Adèle, take 117 North to Val-David and Ste-Agathe-des-Monts.

Ste-Adèle ❶ is a lively ski resort and a thriving writers' and artisans' colony by the shores of Lac Rond and the slopes of Mont Ste-Adèle. Visit the **Village de Séraphin** (297 Montée à Séraphin; open mid-June–Sept: daily, 10am–5pm; early–mid-June and early–late Sept: Sat–Sun only, 10am–5pm; entrance fee; tel: 450-229-4777), a reconstruction of a mid-1800s Laurentian settlement, inspired by Québécois Claude-Henri Grignon's 1933 novel *Un homme et son péché* (A Man and his Sin). Each house in the village is based on a Grignon character or illustrates an episode in the life of Séraphin Poudrier, the novel's miser protagonist. The village of 20 buildings includes a post office, general store, doctor's office and school, with a miniature train running through the grounds.

Val-David ❷ is known for its abundance of traditional Québécois houses with mansard roofs, attractive inns and fine cuisine and also its talented painters and artisans. Quebec's first *boîte à chanson* (folk-song club) was built here in 1959, and now the rustic structure houses the **Théâtre-de-la-Butte** (tel: 819-322-2295), a café-theatre that features French-Canadian plays.

Rock climbers flock to Val-David to scale **Mont-Condor**, 38 metres (125 ft) high, halfway between Val-Morin and

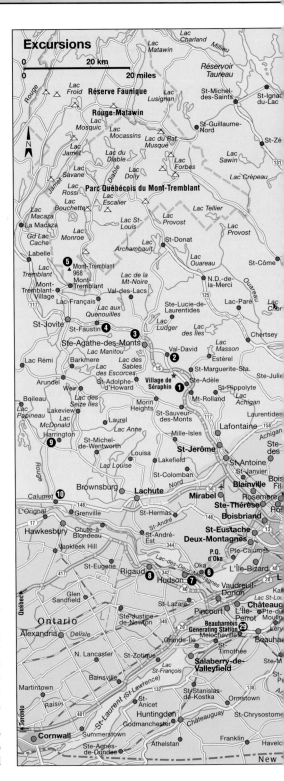

Excursions

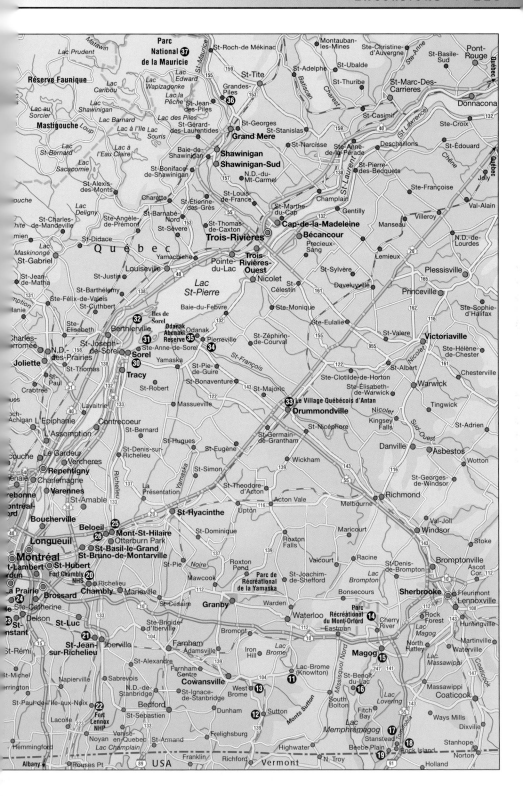

The Laurentians are among the oldest mountain ranges in the world, and over time erosion has softened most of the peaks into gently rounded hills.

Val-David, and the awesome 22-metre (72-ft) **Condor Needle**, one of the few rock needles in Eastern Canada.

Ste-Agathe-des-Monts ❸ is the metropolis of the Laurentians, and a hot spot for Québécois and international celebrities, especially during the Festival des Arts Hiawatha, a dance festival held each July. With three public beaches and a gorgeous lake, the traffic of bikinis, sailboats and sailboarders is something fierce. To get an idea of the Laurentians' old-guard wealth, take a quick cruise around **Lac des Sables** on the *Bâteau Alouette*. You'll see such baubles as the estate built by Twentieth Century-Fox tycoon William B. Fox and the 42-room "summer cottage" built by a millionaire who kept his own orchestra to play for him day and night, and a greenhouse in which he cultivated only roses.

2. Mont-Tremblant

*Route: Laurentians Autoroute 15 North, exit 83; to 117 North to Ste-Agathe-des-Monts; Chemin Tour du Lac to Chemin du Lac-Caribou to **St-Faustin Education Centre**; from St-Faustin exit on 117, towards Lake Superior and **Mont-Tremblant** park entrance.*

The **Forest Education Centre of the Laurentians** (Chemin du Lac-Caribou, St-Fausti; tel: 819-326-1606) in **St-Faustin** ❹ exhibits a fiery blaze in autumn. Two hiking trails and six interpretation trails wind around Lac du Cordon, over rustic boardwalks and footbridges. Quebec's eight Forest Education Centres are there to inform the public about the anatomy and ecology of a forest. This centre has animations, videos and free pamphlets on autumn colouration, conifers and Quebec forests, richly illustrated and well written. Naturalists will gladly show you the insides of a jack pine cone or let you sniff some oil extract

BELOW: Lac des Sables, Ste-Agathe-des-Monts.

of white pine, and the exhibits at the Interpretation Pavilion will tell you everything you always wanted to know about trees.

Algonquin sorcerers called their mountain Manitonga Soutana (Devil's Mountain) because it roared and rumbled whenever the tranquillity of its forested slopes was disturbed. To protect this wilderness, **Mont-Tremblant ❺**, the highest of the Laurentian peaks (968 metres/3,176 ft) was established as the first of Quebec's **provincial parks** (22.5 km/14 miles east of Highway 117 North; free; tel: 819-688-2281) in 1894. The mountain is thick with maple and pine forests, and it shelters black bears and Virginia stags, beavers, lynx and hundreds of bird species. The park's 400 lakes and three major rivers – the Rouge, Matawin and du Diable – all provide great swimming, canoe camping, and fishing for trout or jumping landlocked salmon.

You can take a cruise on Lac-Tremblant, go hiking and horseback riding, or take the chair lift up to the top of the mountain from the Station Mont-Tremblant Lodge. You can camp here in winter as well as summer. As for skiing, Mont-Tremblant is the highest skiable peak in Eastern Canada, with a vertical drop of 650 metres (2,132 ft), and the longest trail in Quebec at 5 km (3¼ miles) long. However, the development of a large and very popular ski resort by an American firm has recently blighted this landscape somewhat for the purist, bringing lodges, condominiums and the unmistakable whiff of big money.

3. Lac-des-Deux-Montagnes and Oka Park
*Route: Laurentians Autoroute 15 North, exit 21 to 640 West, which leads to the park's eastern reception centre; from Paul Sauvé Park, Route 344 West to **Oka**; ferry to **Hudson**; 342 west to **Rigaud**.*

Map on pages 224–5

Help is at hand for swimmers at Mont-Tremblant provincial park.

BELOW: summer pleasures at Mont-Tremblant.

Cheese has been made by the monks at Oka since 1893.

Colourful sailboards float like confetti off the silvery 7-km (4-mile) long beach of the **Parc d'Oka** (2020 chemin Oka; tel: 450-479-8337), on the **Lac-des-Deux-Montagnes**. The lake's shallow waters are ideal for trying out the sport, and rental facilities are close by. But the most exotic recreation here is a canoe excursion through the marsh around Grand Bay. You'll paddle through a floating garden walled by rushes and cattails, carpeted with flowering lily pads and delicate duckweed, with marsh ducks, muskrats and Great Blue Herons in your wake, and possibly arouse the curiosity of beavers at work. Call the park for information on excursions led by park naturalists.

Parc de Récréation Paul-Sauvé's summer activities feature geological excursions, forest nature walks, bicycle trips to explore the dunes and effects of glaciation, and evening talks on Oka's native American legends. The park's flat wooded terrain is popular with cyclists and cross-country skiers.

Oka ❻ and **Hudson ❼** are two charming lakeshore villages linked by an old ferry across Lac-des-Deux-Montagnes. French-Canadian Sunday-school songs describe pilgrimages to Oka to buy cheese made by monks at **l'Abbaye Cistercienne d'Oka** (1600 chemin d'Oka; open Mon–Sat, 4–5pm), one of the oldest monasteries in North America. Oka's Trappist monks came from the Bellefontaine Abbey in France, and you can see the humble miller's home where they first settled, stroll the gardens that surround the monastery, and buy the world-famous Oka cheese.

A climb to the top of the **Oka Calvary**, east of the village and across from Parc Paul-Sauvé, is loveliest in autumn. The stations of the cross up here were built between 1739 and 1742 to inspire the local Amerindians, and three of the seven original chapels have been preserved. Since 1870, Amerindians and

BELOW: paddling in Parc d'Oka.

pilgrims from all over Quebec have come to Oka to celebrate the Feast of the Holy Cross on September 14 and to enjoy the magnificent view of the Lac-des-Deux-Montagnes from the summit.

From Oka you can take the tiny car ferry across to **Hudson** to go antique hunting. The seasonal ferry leaves from the dock on rue des Anges next to the Argenteuil Manor. From Hudson, you can drive on to **Rigaud ❽**, a charming spot, and from mid-March to late April, gorge yourself on maple syrup dishes at the **Sucrerie de la Montagne** (300 Rang St Georges; tel: 450-451-5204).

4. Rouge River rafting
Route: Highway 15 North to 148 West; from April to September only.

The Rouge River has some of the best whitewater rafting in North America on the 25-km (15-mile) course between **Harrington ❾** and **Calumet ❿**, in Quebec. "Steep Throat", a ledge drop of 3.7 metres (12 ft), has been called "the Everest of rafting in Canada", and other Rouge River rapids are known by such names as Confusion, Turbo in the Morning, Avalanche, Washing Machine, Slice 'n' Dice and The Monster.

Don't be daunted. Experienced river guides will brief you on "body surfing", "hydraulic action" and "ledge drops" and be there to yank you back into the raft in less than 30 seconds should you inadvertently bail out. Most day packages provide 5–6 hours of rafting (about 18 km/11 miles) and include a lunch break, along with all equipment, one experienced river guide per raft, shuttle service from the base camp, and a post-dinner video show of the day's adventures.

Estrie or Cantons-de-l'Est (Eastern Townships)
1. Knowlton/Lac-Brome/Sutton
Route: Eastern Townships Autoroute 10 East to exit 90, to 243 South to Lac-Brome; 104 West to 215 South to Sutton; 139 North to West Brome; 139 North to Eastern Townships Autoroute West.

Lac-Brome (Knowlton) ⓫: A mill pond cuts through the heart of this Victorian village, and colourful boutiques in 19th-century houses give it a festive air. Lac-Brome is a pleasant spot for lunch, brunch, coffee with wickedly rich desserts, antiquing, or just strolling beside the pond and lake. Flocks of wild ducks are omnipresent: they are Lac-Brome's gastronomic speciality, and Lac-Brome is surrounded by splendid (not necessarily flat) cycling country. Interestingly, the majority of the residents of this town are English-speaking, and they head up the festivities during the annual fall festival called Townshippers' Day – a scrap of anglo culture in a sea of franco countryside.

In stagecoach days Lac-Brome (Knowlton) was a stop on the Boston to Montreal run, and this story is told in the **Pettes Memorial Library**, established in 1894 as the first free library in Quebec, as well as in the **Brome County Historical Museum** (130 Lakeside Road; open mid-May–mid-Sept: Mon–Sat, 10am–4.30pm; Sun, 11am–4.30pm; entrance fee, tel: 450-243-6782).

The museum's buildings house Abenaki artifacts,

Map on pages 224–5

Oka achieved national infamy in 1990 when local native peoples took up arms to protest the town's decision to build a golf course over their ancestral burial grounds.

BELOW: the mill pond at Knowlton.

pioneer bric-à-brac such as foot-warmers and pill-making machines, a local history archive (survey maps and old letters), a military collection, general store, blacksmith shop, fire tower and county courthouse. The white brick building was the original village school (1844) and contains a World War I Fokker biplane with the camouflage covering still intact: it was sent to Canada in 1919 as part of the war reparations. For hiking and bicycling maps and news of local happenings, contact the Lac-Brome Chamber of Commerce (tel: 450-242-2870) or drop by the village grocery store for a look at the bulletin board.

Sutton 12 bustles with hikers and skiers bound for the winding, wooded trails of Mont-Sutton, as well as shoppers bent on finding quilts and woven rugs, ceramics and pewter in the local artists' cooperatives. The main street of this ski resort at the base of Mont-Sutton is flanked with graceful old houses, auberges, craft shops, art galleries and tempting restaurants and outdoor cafés.

In summer the Saturday flea market on Curley Street (open mid-May–early Oct, 8am–3pm) is lively, and on Sunday the local tradition is brunch followed by a hike up Mont-Sutton. Star-gazing *soirées* are popular, as is summer mountain biking. Local topographical and cycling maps give the best routes for excursions on 10-speed or *tout-terrain* mountain bikes. For information and maps on all the cycling routes in the area, contact Sutton's Chamber of Commerce (tel: 450-538-8455 or 1-800-565-8455).

The **Sutton Heritage Museum** (30A rue Principale; open late June–Sept; entrance fee; tel: 450-538-2544) tells the history of communications in a collection of antique switchboard and telephones, phonographs and radios housed in an early post office, telegraph office, printing shop, fire alarm centre, telephone exchange and radio station.

BELOW: Brome annual fair.

Map
on pages
224-5

*The Orford Arts
Centre, home of the
renowned annual
Orford Festival.*

F.G. Edwards Country Store in **West Brome** ⑬ (at 12 McCurdy Road, just off Route 139) is worth a detour to visit, even if you don't buy a thing. A wheelbarrow and feed sacks deck the front porch, and locals hover around boxes of candy-coloured seeds that will sprout into sugar snap peas, pencil pod black wax beans and Kentucky Wonder green pole beans. This locally hallowed institution was founded in 1857 to serve the farmers of West Brome. As in horse and buggy days, it's still the place to swap yarns, post local news and buy everything from pitchforks, socks, boots, horse bridles, yoyos and udder wash, to baby chicks, penny candy, ant traps and bird feeders. A browse through this aromatic shop will give you a feeling for rural life in the Estrie.

2. Orford/Magog/St-Benoît

*Route: Eastern Townships Autoroute 10 to exit 115, to 141 North, to **Parc Récréational du Mont-Orford**; 141 South to **Magog**; from Magog, follow signs to rural road to **St-Benoît-du-Lac** along the west side of **Lac Memphrémagog**.*

Classical music rings into the woodland air during the Orford Festival, organized by the internationally renowned **Mont-Orford Arts Centre** (3165 chemin du Parc; concert season: July–mid-Aug; fee for some concerts; tel: 819-843-3981 or 1-800-567-6155; website: www.arts-orford.org). From early July to mid-August, this thriving arts centre in the heart of the Estrie's hills becomes the hub of a festival of concerts and art exhibitions held in studios, halls and churches throughout the area.

The **Parc Récréational du Mont-Orford** ⑭ (Route 141; entrance fee; tel: 819- 843-9855), is popular in all seasons. In winter there is skiing, skating and snowshoeing. In summer there is swimming in the two lakes, hiking, golf, chair-lifts to the summit, and hang-gliding over the Sutton Mountains and Lac-Brome, the Monteregian hills and St Lawrence plain.

BELOW:
bucolic views.

Magog ⑮ isn't a spectacularly pretty resort town, but its location at the northern tip of Lac Memphré-magog, the 48-km (30-mile) long narrow lake link-ing Quebec with Vermont, makes it handy for boating. Magog has a variety of restaurants, shops and art gal-leries, a public beach and a lakeside trail suitable for in-line skating, walking and biking. You can take a cruise, rent a sailboat with a private skipper, fish for *ouananiche* (landlocked salmon), test your balance on a sailboard, or see Lac Memphrémagog from a snorkelling mask or while dangling from a parachute 46 metres (150 ft) in the air.

As an exhilarating, effortless and rather goofy way to see the lake, para-sailing has caught on. Your harness is attached to a parachute, which is towed by a motor boat. For information on water-skiing and para-sailing on Lac Memphrémagog, contact Les Activités Nautiques Tribord, Magog's Federal Wharf, tel: 819-868-2222.

Gregorian chants echo over Lac Memphrémagog from the handsome pink granite towers of the Bene-dictine abbey of **St-Benoît-du-Lac** ⑯ (tel: 819-843-4080). Commanding the lake like a fairy castle, the monastery's octagonal towers, triangular gables and narrow pointed windows were designed by Dom Paul

Take a cruise in a vintage wooden boat.

BELOW: water sport on Lac Massawippi.

Bellot (1876–1944), a French monk who settled here in 1937 to become one of Quebec's major ecclesiastical architects. Then, in dramatic contrast to the rest of the monastery, a starkly beautiful new church by Montreal architect Dan S. Hanganu was consecrated in 1994.

The monks of the Benedictine order of Solesmes, France, are the only people inhabiting this independent municipality. You can tour the abbey's rich mosaic interior, participate in the vespers Gregorian chanting (Sun Mass; Mon, Tues, Wed, Fri, Sat, 5pm; Thur, 7pm), pick apples in the abbey's orchard, and buy cider and delicious cheeses (St-Benoît, Ricotta and L'Ermite), made by the monks. You can even stay here as a guest and wake up to dawn over Mont-Orford. The abbey reserves 40 rooms for men and 15 for women (tel: 819-843-2340), but none for couples.

3. Stanstead/Rock Island/Beebe Plain

Route: Eastern Townships Autoroute 10 to exit 121 to Highway 55 South to the ***Stanstead*** *exit; from* ***Rock Island***, *Route 247 West to* ***Beebe Plain***, *and 247 North to Magog.*

Estrie's border towns are hotbeds of intrigue and smugglers' tales. **Stanstead** ⑰ has many buildings of architectural interest – Stanstead College (1872), the Ursuline School (1884), the Christ Church Anglican Church (1858) and Butter House (1866). The Colby Curtis Museum on Dufferin Street features antiquarian toys, military artifacts and mementoes of 19th-century life.

Stanstead's main street leads directly into **Rock Island** ⑱ which straddles the Quebec–Vermont border. In some houses a meal is cooked in Canada and eaten in the United States; the bathtub is in Canada and the toilet in the USA – which makes for endless local jokes. Dilapidated factories, mills and river buildings give Rock Island an air of decay, but there are architectural gems, notably the Romanesque revival **Haskell Free Library and Opera House**, built on the boundary line in 1904 (Route 143 and rue Church). The ground floor is a feast of lustrous wood, marble and granite, gorgeously lit by stained-glass windows and chandeliers. The international boundary puts the circulation desk and stacks in Canada and the reading room in the USA. Upstairs the 450-seat opera house is a scale-model of the Boston Opera House. The performers sing on the stage in Quebec while the audience applauds in the United States.

The white line down Canusa Avenue, the main street of **Beebe Plain** ⑲, divides the USA from Canada. According to international law, Mrs Brown cannot cross the street to borrow a cup of sugar from Madame Blanche without first reporting the matter to customs. But in a spirit of community goodwill, local immigration officers ignore the fine print.

Montérégie

1. Fort Chambly/St-Jean-sur-Richelieu / Fort Lennox

Route: Autoroute 20 or Highway 112 East to 223 South to ***Chambly***; *223 South to* ***St-Jean-sur-Richelieu*** *and* ***St-Paul-de-l'Ile-aux-Noix***.

Fort Chambly's castle-like walls have been licked by the treacherous rapids of the "River of the Iroquois" for nearly three centuries, and **Fort Chambly National Historic Site** ❷⓿ (2 rue Richelieu, Chambly; open mid-May–mid-Oct: daily, 10am–5pm; Mar–mid-May and mid-Oct–Nov: Wed–Sun, 10am–5pm; entrance fee; tel: 450-658-1585) stands by the edge of the Richelieu Rapids, the names of the heroes of New France carved in stone at its gates. The first fort on this site was built of wood in 1665 by Captain Jacques Chambly and the soldiers of le Régiment de Carignan-Salières, to defend against Iroquois attack. And the first European settlement on the Richelieu grew up around its borders, becoming the town of Chambly. In 1709–11, the wooden fort was replaced by the massive structure with five-sided corner bastions that stands today.

It was occupied by the French until 1760, by the English until 1775, and by the Americans under General Montgomery until 1776. It later held American prisoners during the War of 1812 and Canadian patriots during the Patriot Rebellion of 1837–38.

After exploring Fort Chambly and its museum of weapons and artifacts, take a look at the **St Hubert House** (1760), **Maigneault House**, and the **Laureau House** (1775). You can see the operation of the Chambly canal's three locks, or go canoeing in the Chambly basin, just below the Richelieu Rapids.

On the way to Fort Lennox, stop at **St-Jean-sur-Richelieu** ❷❶ to stroll through the old section of this historic military town, along rues Jacques-Cartier, St-Charles, Longueuil and St-Georges, and also on the promenade along the Chambly Canal. St-Jean, with its graceful riverside setting, has a long history as a summer resort for Montrealers. A lively public market is held here on Wednesday and Saturday, and in August, during the 10-day Festival des

Map on pages 224–5

One of the many picture-postcard villages in the Cantons de l'Est (Eastern Townships), North Hatley is at the northern tip of Lac Massawippi, east of lacs Memphrémagog and Magog, northeast of Stanstead and Rock Island.

BELOW: the black line on the floor of Haskell's Free Library is the Canada/US border.

Montgolfières, outrageously colourful hot-air balloons float over its rooftops and steeples. Cruises on the Richelieu (tel: 450-346-2446 or 1-800-361-6420) leave from the wharf at the foot of rue St-Georges.

At its northern end, **l'Ile-aux-Noix** is an idyllic spot for picnicking and hikes along the marshy riverbank to observe painted turtles, muskrats, bullfrogs and diving kingfishers. And at the southern tip of this island, which is only 24 km (15 miles) from the US border, is the impressive star-shaped fort at **Fort Lennox National Historic Park** ❷ (open mid-May–early Sept: daily, 10am–6pm; early Sept–early Oct: Sat–Sun, 10am–6pm; entrance fee; tel: 450-291-5700), with a moat 18 metres wide by 4.5 metres deep (60 ft by 15 ft).

The French built the fort in 1759 to defend against a British advance, but they evacuated it the following year under British siege. In 1775, the Americans captured l'Ile-aux-Noix and used it as a base from which to launch attacks on Montreal and Quebec City, but only a year later a smallpox epidemic forced them to abandon the fort.

Lively animated tours of Fort Lennox take you through the guardhouse (dating from 1824), gunpowder magazine, officers' quarters, prison, barracks and commissary, and a museum exhibiting military equipment and documents. On special days actors perform re-enactments of 18th-century skirmishes, using replicas of period uniforms and weapons. Fort Lennox is accessible by the Crosières Richelieu ferry from St-Paul-de-l'Ile-aux-Noix, at the Reception Centre on 61st Avenue.

Rent a paddle boat for an hour.

BELOW: orchards along the Richelieu.

2. St-Constant/Ste-Catherine Locks

*Route: Highway 15 South to exit 42; 132 West to 209 South to **St-Constant**; from St-Constant, take 209 North to 132 West to **Côte Ste-Catherine Locks**.*

Depending on how enamoured you are of trains, you can spend a few hours or a day exploring the rolling stock which stand like old soldiers at the **Canadian Railway Museum** in **St-Constant** ❷ (120–122 rue St-Pierre; open May–Sept: daily, 9am–5pm; Sept–mid-Oct: Sat–Sun, 9am–5pm; entrance fee; tel: 450-632-2410) – the largest railway museum in Canada.

Exhibits here include antique locomotives, trolleys and trams, sleepers and street sweepers, snow-ploughs, boxcars and cabooses, parlour cars, diners and diesels, a one-car travelling schoolhouse and even some horse-drawn sleighs, spread over 6 hectares (15 acres) and housed in two giant hangars. An elaborate model electric train whistles through papier-mâché mountains and steams past tiny cows, using a variety of more than 200 locomotives and cars. It's the liveliest attraction in the Hayes Building, which houses Canadian Railway Historical Association archives, artifacts and memorabilia. At the authentic 19th-century railway station, you can board a diesel locomotive or a vintage Montreal streetcar for a short but dramatic mile.

Just down the road from St-Constant, another transport adventure takes place at **Ste-Catherine** ❷ as deep-sea oil tankers, long-lakers and grainers make their way through the **Côte-Ste-Catherine Locks** into the St Lawrence Seaway. The bridge lifts, the ship edges through the narrow canal; valves open and the water drains to lower the ship to seaway level; finally a horn blast signals the huge vessel to pass.

Cross the lifting-bridge to the far side of the lock for an eye-level view of the captain's deck and crew's quarters of ships from as far away as Panama and the former Soviet Union.

The bridge serves as the entrance to **Côte-Ste-Catherine Park**, which affords a stunning perspective of the thunderous Lachine Rapids, the Montreal cityscape and the Montérégian hills. The park has a swimming pond, a camping area and bicycle path running along the whitewater's edge, and close by is an island colony of herons.

3. Mont St-Hilaire/Vieux Beloeil

*Route: Autoroute 20 East to exit 113; 133 South to **Mont-St-Hilaire**; bridge over to **Beloeil**.*

When the wind is calm and the air balmy, you can lie for hours on "Sugar Loaf", the flat rocky summit of **Mont-St-Hilaire** ㉙, taking in the contours of the land below. The Montérégian hill is only 410 metres (1,345 ft) above sea level, but it rises abruptly from the St Lawrence plain, affording a dreamy view of its sister peak, Mont-Royal, in the heart of the metropolis, the Richelieu River and the sinewy St Lawrence, and Mont St-Bruno, St-Grégoire, Rougemont and Yamaska.

Mont St-Hilaire is an ecological marvel thriving only 35 km (22 miles) from Montreal – an environment so unspoiled that UNESCO designated it as the first

Map
on pages
224–5

The first Canadian railroad opened in 1836 to carry vacationers from the Montreal suburb of La Prairie to St-Jean-sur-Richelieu and back, a total distance of less than 80 km (50 miles). The line no longer operates.

BELOW: biked out.

Biosphere Reserve in Canada. This highest of the eight Montérégian hills shelters the last vestige of the dense woodland that once covered the St Lawrence Valley. In a lush hardwood forest with canopies of 30-metre (100-ft) red oaks and 250-year-old white pines, there are hundreds of mosses and ferns, 600 species of flowering plants, 32 of flowering trees and 187 species of birds.

Mont-St-Hilaire's hiking trails wind through an aquatic zone, a wildflower meadow, lush ferny areas, along Lac Hertel – a lake once humming with seven mills – and eventually up to an exposed windy summit with Arctic vegetation. The countryside around here is also ideal for bird-watching, cross-country skiing and snowshoeing.

In the Mohawk language, "Kahnawake" means "at the rapids", a reference to what is known today as the Lachine Rapids.

Just across the Richelieu River from Mont-St-Hilaire's apple orchards lies **Beloeil ㉖**, established in 1694. Its yacht harbour, boutiques, art galleries, artisan shops, restaurants and cultural centre attract Montrealers in all seasons. **Vieux Beloeil**'s magnificent old buildings include a presbytery built in 1772, the Près-Vert and Lanctôt houses, and the Rouville-Campbell Manor, now an art gallery.

The Quebec painter Ozias Leduc was born in the Correlieu House, and the local church contains one of his frescoes.

4. Kahnawake/Melocheville
*Route: Autoroute 20 West to **Lachine**; across the Mercier Bridge to **Kahnawake**; 132 West to **Melocheville**; follow Hébert Blvd (Route 132) to the **Beauharnois Hydro-Québec Generating Station** and **Emond Street**.*

At **Lachine ㉗** there are two museums worth visiting. The **Lachine Museum** (110 chemin de Lasalle; open: Wed–Sun, 11.30am–4.30pm; tel: 514-634-3471 ext. 346 or 332; fax: 514-637-6784) has furniture and artifacts from the early

BELOW: every line tells a story.

colonial period and features the commercial and industrial history of Lachine in the 19th century. The historic site called the **Fur Trade in Lachine** (1255 boulevard St-Joseph; tel: 514-637-7433) tells the fascinating story of the critical role of the fur trade in the development of Canada.

Cross the Mercier Bridge to the south shore of the St Lawrence River and the Mohawk reserve of **Kahnawake** ㉘ (tel: 450-638-9699; fax: 450-638-9843). It was here in 1990 that a major land dispute took place between the Mohawks and the Quebec and federal governments. It made international headlines and became a symbolic stand against the mistreatment of Native peoples across the country. Visitors are welcome to visit the reserve and its cultural centre, museum, art gallery, and the St Francis Xavier Mission Church, established in 1720. There are several craft and artifact shops; displays of traditional Mohawk songs, dances, art and food; plus a campsite overlooking Lac St-Louis where campers can rent a teepee or tent, or bring their own.

Enormous is the only way to describe **Beauharnois Generating Station** ㉙ (80 rue Edgar-Hébert, Melocheville; tours mid-May–early Sept; free; tel: 1-800-365-5229), one of the world's largest hydroelectric facilities. Sitting between lakes St-François and St-Louis, the plant makes full use of the 24-metre (79-ft) drop between the two lakes to power the water as it speeds through the adjacent lock at 8 million litres (2.1 million gallons) per second, producing an average of 11.7 billion kWh annually. In winter Quebec uses all the power produced, but come summer, its excess capacity is passed along to Ontario and the USA via 735,000-volt power lines.

Guided tours of the generating station take in the Beauharnois information and interpretation centre, the vast alternator hall – where staff use either electric

Summer pleasures in rural Quebec.

BELOW: whitewater kayaking.

Map on pages 224–5

A pollution-free way to travel through the pristine waters.

carts or tricycles to inspect the plant's 36 turbines (each weighing over 100 tonnes/tons), the control room, and a sensational rooftop view of power line extending in all directions, with Montreal and the St Lawrence in the distance

Archaeologists at **Pointe-du-Buisson Archaeological Park** (333 rue Emond Melocheville; tel: 450-429-7857) say it will take decades to interpret the masses of material unearthed on this 27-hectare (66-acre) woodland site by the St Lawrence River rapids. A remarkable Iroquois complex containing 7,965 objects, four fireplaces and the traces of 42 poles of longhouses was found during the month of April 1967 alone.

Tomahawks, stone utensils, pipes and harpoons dating from as long as 5,000 years ago indicate that this site was once the hunting, fishing and burial grounds of several Amerindian peoples and a stopping point for explorers, missionaries, soldiers and merchants en route to the Great Lakes.

Hundreds of artifacts are displayed in the two exposition centres. You can take a guided archaeological tour of five digging sites and on special days take part in activities related to Amerindian music and dance, Iroquois medicine, carving arrowheads, and making corn masks and dolls.

Coeur du Quebec

1. Sorel/Ste-Anne-de-Sorel

*Route: Eastern Townships Autoroute 10 to 30 North to **Sorel**; 132 East to **Ste-Anne-de-Sorel**.*

Canada's fourth oldest city, **Sorel** ❸ is known for its busy shipyards and its lively marina – the focus of nautical tourism in Quebec. The **Place du Marché** at the end of rue Roi near the port is a bustling marketplace, and the **Carré**

Royal is a magnificent 18th-century park curiously shaped like the Union Flag of the United Kingdom.

Sorel makes a very convenient base from which to explore the bewitching archipelago of islands off its shore.

Ste-Anne-de Sorel ❸ has come to be known as *Pays du Survenant* (Land of the Unexpected Visitor) because of Germaine Guèvremont's novel of that name. The rich flora and fauna of the **Iles de Sorel** ❷ can be seen from the motorized canoes of **Excursion dans le Marais** (3755 chemin du Chenal-du-Moine; open May–end Sept; reserve ahead; tel: 514-742-3113) which lead you through the marshes to see the world's largest heron-breeding grounds.

The chemin du Chenal-du-Moine leads across a steel bridge to **Ile aux Fantômes**, whose dwellings are set up high on pilings as a protection against flooding. From a dead-end road you can cross over to the **Ile d'Embarras** and its tiny fishing village strung with drying fish nets. Two old ice houses on the tip of the island are now restaurants featuring traditional regional cuisine – notably *gibelotte*, fish stew made from the locals' daily catches.

Croisières des Iles de Sorel Inc. operate cruises from mid-May to the end of the first week in September, from the quay at 1665 chemin du Chenal-du-Moine, tel: 450-743-7227.

2. Odanak Abenaki Reserve

Route: Autoroute 20, exit 181 to Le Village Québécois d'Antan; from Drummondville, Route 143 to Route 132 northwest to Pierreville/Odanak.

Le Village Québécois d'Antan ❸ (the Quebec Village of Yesteryear) (1425 rue Montplaisir; open early June–early Sept: daily, 10am–6pm; rest of Sept: daily 11am–4pm; entrance fee; tel: 819-478-1441 or 5412) in Drummondville is not as corny as it sounds. The 18th-century village that has been recreated on this pastoral site attracts serious historians, cultivated museum-goers, film-makers, and Québécois looking for their roots, as well as those eager for nostalgia.

The village's 50 historic buildings and 30 historic reproductions constructed by regional artisans portray the days of colonization between 1810 and 1910. Guides in period costume animate 25 traditional houses in nine different architectural styles, and 18 artisan workshops, including a saddlery, tinsmith, shoemaker and broom-maker, and cabinet-maker – *à la Québécois*.

The list goes on: an oddly stocked general store, apothecary, old post office, blacksmith forge, a sawmill, a telephone museum, an old style *caisse-populaire* (savings bank), a one-room schoolhouse, a *cabane à sucre* (sugar shack), a garage and gas station with antique cars, even a covered bridge (circa 1878) transported from Stanbridge. Farm animals have their own cattle shed, henhouse, and pighouse, a safe distance from the restaurant and picnic tables.

Around the corner from **Pierreville** ❸ the small town that is Canada's biggest producer of fire engines, is the **Odanak Abenaki Reserve** ❸ (open all year; entrance fee; tel: 819-294-1813) on the shores of the St Francis River. During the 17th century the

Map on pages 224–5

BELOW: country-style Halloween decorations.

Map
on pages
224–5

TIP

For an introduction to the region's dominant pulp and paper industry, visit the *Centre d'Exposition sur l'industrie des pâtes et papiers* on your way through Trois Rivières to Grandes-Piles.

RIGHT: Lac-des-Deux-Montagnes in Parc d'Oka.
BELOW: man's best friend.

Abenakis came from New England to settle in Odanak, and the Jesuit established a mission here to educate them.

In the heart of the reserve is a riverfront park graced with rustic gazebos, teepees, carved totem poles and contemporary Abenaki sculpture. The stone chapel built in 1828 is filled with Amerindian woodcarvings, and the red brick convent across the way from it has been transformed into a museum of Abenaki history and culture. On the rambling porch stand massive wooden sculptures of mythological figures, and inside are 14 rooms filled with Abenaki history, culture and crafts.

The **Musée des Abénaquis** (108 rue Waban-Aki/ Route 226, Odanak; open May–Oct: Mon–Fri, 10am–5pm; Sat–Sun 1–5pm; rest of the year: closed weekends; tel: 450-568-2600) contains displays on constructing birch-bark canoes, Abenaki cornhusk masks, ash-splint basket-weaving, and a model of a 17th-century Abenaki fort. Local shops sell sweetgrass baskets, buckskin jackets, native crafts, and smoked sturgeon, a local speciality. From Highway 20, take exits 175–85.

3. Mauricie National Park

Route: 40 East to 55 North (at Trois Rivières); 55 North to 155 North to Grandes-Piles; park entrance at St-Jean-des-Piles.

On a cliff overlooking the St-Maurice River is the lovely village of **Grandes-Piles** ㊱, once a transfer harbour for lumber boats, and the **Village du Bûcheron** (Lumberjack Village) (780 Fifth Avenue, Grandes-Piles; open mid-May–mid-Oct: daily, 10am–5pm; entrance fee; tel: 819-538-7895). The heyday of Mauricie's logging and lumberjacking (1850–1950) is celebrated in 25 log buildings containing hundreds of photos and more than 5,000 artifacts. The village has an art gallery and craft boutique, and on weekends you can see the sawmill in operation and have a typical lumberjack meal at the Cookerie.

Parc National de la Mauricie ㊲ (Mauricie National Park) (north of Shawinigan; open all year; entrance fee; tel: 819-536-2638) is a paradise for would-be Robinson Crusoes. This watery wilderness speckled with tree-covered islets has 34 lakes which are off-limits to motor boats.

From the Ile-aux-Pins lookout over **Lac Wapizagonke**, a peek through field glasses reveals a jaunty red canoe beside a camper dozing in blissful solitude on a white sandy islet beach.

The national park is a canoe camping and trout fishing heaven. All the lakes are accessible by well-bridged portage trails, but the most popular route is the 11-km (7-mile) stretch up Lake Wapizagonke's shoreline of cliffs and densely forested hills.

The park is wild enough for moose, black bear and coyote, wolf and lynx, yet tame enough for picnicking, swimming, camping in summer and winter, cycling, hiking and bird-watching. Some 200 species of birds have been sighted here, and more than half of them nest in the region. Cross-country ski trails in the park are open from December to March, depending on snow conditions. ❑

QUEBEC CITY

The political and spiritual heart of the province, Quebec City is rich in history, culture and beauty. The old part of the town is a UNESCO World Heritage Site and a living museum

Map on page 246

The spectacular geographical position – on a clifftop, at the neck of the mighty St Lawrence river – that made Quebec so appealing to the French colonists had actually been noted thousands of years earlier by Native Canadians. They had settled a small community here known as Stadacona, from which they ruled a small riverside territory known as "the village" ("Canada" in their language).

When Jacques Cartier sailed up the river to the village in 1535, his men were weary and sick. They managed three visits without serious incident, then sailed home to France carrying a load of what they thought was gold. It turned out to be fool's gold, and the French stayed away for a time, but the beaver pelts Cartier also brought home would eventually seal Quebec's fate as a colonial trading outpost. Legendary explorer Samuel de Champlain established the city in 1608 – he called the opportunity a "gift of God" – as the first permanent settlement in what would one day become Canada. He named it for what the natives called the spot: Kebec, or "narrowing of the river".

At first the colony remained small, though religious. (One estimate placed the population of clergy at 15 percent of the entire colony.) It was not until the fur trade began picking up steam in the early 18th century, largely fuelled by fashions in faraway Europe, that Quebec City began to grow by leaps and bounds.

PRECEDING PAGES: winter carnival in Quebec City. **LEFT:** Château Frontenac. **BELOW:** Old Man Winter.

Arrival of the British

However, the British also coveted the river city for its strategic position as a port town from which they could both explore Canada's vastness and control the restless American colonies to the south. General James Wolfe attacked the French troops outside the city in late 1759; after three months of cat-and-mouse, the decisive battle was fought on the so-called Plains of Abraham just above the Old Town – a place every Québécois knows by heart.

It was a terrible fight. The British had used a surprise manoeuvre, somehow climbing the undefended cliff walls that the Québécois believed would never be breached, to reach the Plains. Both generals, the French Montcalm and Wolfe, were killed – but the Québécois were routed. Soon the British would move up the river to take Montreal; the Union Jack was raised above that city on September 9, 1760. Papers had not yet been formally signed – that would not happen until three years later, in Paris. But it was, for a time, the end of French control of the city.

The French agitated continually, however, and the British were forced to make major concessions to them with the 1774 Quebec Act. But America was not pleased with the new cosiness between its two main

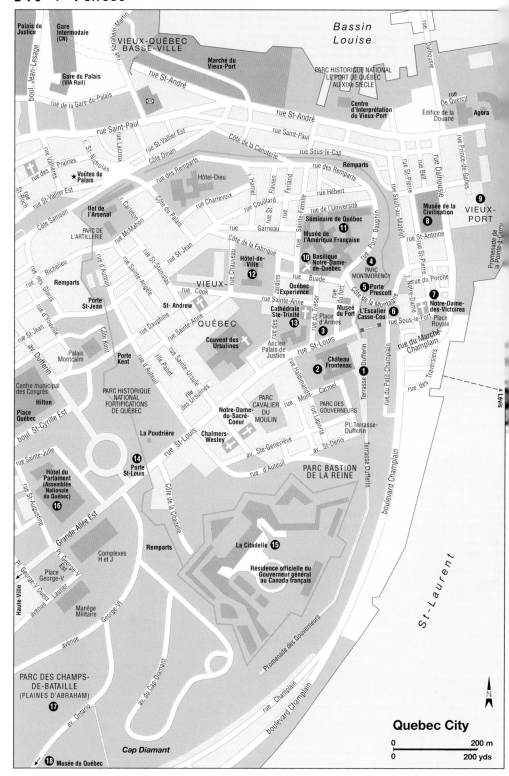

Quebec City

| 0 | | 200 m |
| 0 | | 200 yds |

nemies, and American armies marched through Maine to Quebec City in the harsh winter of 1775. However, the combined efforts of British and French forces swiftly repelled them. To ensure the incident would not be repeated, the city's distinctive walls were constructed. Today it is the only fortified city in North America north of Mexico.

The British divided Canada in half in 1791, naming Quebec City the capital of so-called Lower Canada; when Canada became a distinct nation, Quebec City remained the administrative capital of its province.

The early 19th century was a time of rapid change in the city as waves of immigrants poured in and shipping boomed. Soon Montreal began to capture more business, however, as Canada began trading more with the United States – using Montreal's extensive rail lines – and less by sea with Great Britain. Quebec became a second city, inhabited by government paper-pushers, but as the immigrants moved upriver it also reverted almost exclusively to its previous Frenchness.

Standing sentinel

"The impression made upon the visitor by this Gibraltar of North America: its giddy heights; its citadel suspended, as it were, in the air, its picturesque streets and frowning gateways; and the splendid views which burst upon the eye at every turn: is at once unique and everlasting."

Remarkably, Charles Dickens's comment on Quebec City is still appropriate more than a century and a half after his visit. It retains its 18th-century ambience with narrow, winding streets and horse-drawn carriages and fine French cooking behind charming facades. The only dramatic change in the old town is the construction at the turn of the century of a castle-like hotel that perches on its promontory overlooking the St Lawrence River: the Château Frontenac.

The province's cryptic motto, *Je me souviens* (I remember), insists upon the defence of Québécois tradition, language and culture. Here in the provincial capital, reminders are everywhere that this defence was once performed by soldiers with guns from turrets and bastions. Today, the politicians and civil servants of Quebec City have taken over the job, using the milder instruments of democracy, but are hardly less ardent in their purpose.

The walled city of Quebec still stands sentinel over the St Lawrence. The views are as lovely as ever: from the **Terrasse Dufferin** ❶ in front of the **Château Frontenac** ❷ one looks out at the blue Laurentian hills and Mont St-Anne, the rolling countryside and the boats passing on the shimmering St Lawrence 60 metres (195 ft) below.

To the Lower Town

Diagonally opposite **Place d'Armes** ❸, the former drill and parade ground, rue du Trésor runs down to rue Buade. **Rue du Trésor**, named after the building where colonists used to pay their dues to the Royal Treasury, is today the artists' row, hung with quite decent watercolours, etchings and silkscreens. **Rue Buade** winds downhill to **Parc Montmorency** ❹

Map on page 246

There are lots of small hotels within the city walls.

BELOW: music on Terrasse Dufferin.

Only the fittest take this shortcut to the Lower Town.

(usually tranquil however busy the rest of the old town becomes), opposite the grand **Ancien Bureau de Poste** (Old Post Office) with its rather pompous monument to Bishop François-Xavier de Laval-Montmorency, first bishop of Quebec and founder of its largest university.

Côte de la Montagne drops steeply down to the left, winding down into the Lower Town, following the ravine that Quebec's first settlers used to climb from the Lower Town to the Upper. Just beyond the **Porte Prescott ❺**, a recent reconstruction of the original erected here in 1797, is **L'Escalier Casse-Cou ❻**, the "Breakneck Stairway". This staircase, not quite as daunting as it sounds, leads to the narrow **rue du Petit-Champlain,** which is lined with craft shops.

From the foot of L'Escalier Casse-Cou, Place Royale is just around the corner. Thus one tumbles from the Château Frontenac into the cradle of French civilization in North America.

Place Royale, where the first settlement in America stood, was the business centre of Quebec City until about 1832. Its name derives from the bust of Louis XIV, the great Sun King of Versailles, that was erected here in 1686. Today, it is the scene of constant play and concert performances, usually re-creating the culture of the 17th and 18th centuries. **Eglise Notre-Dame-des-Victoires ❼**, dominating the square, was built in 1688 and reconstructed after Wolfe's devastation of the Lower Town in 1759. The church is named for two early victories against the Anglo-Americans – or rather, one victory and one lucky accident.

The victory was against a Bostonian, Sir William Phipps (knighted for discovering 32 tonnes/tons of ship-wrecked bullion), who sailed to Quebec with 34 boats and 2,000 men in October 1690, and demanded its surrender. Governor Frontenac promised to reply with his cannon, and during six days of fighting his

guns hammered the fleet. By land, snipers, fighting Indian-style against Phipps's troops drawn up in formal battle-order, killed 150 men with only one loss to their own party. Phipps withdrew on the sixth day, unaware that the French had just run out of ammunition.

The lucky accident – or to the French, Our Lady's victory – was the storm in the Gulf of St Lawrence that destroyed the enormous British fleet of Sir Hovendon Walker in 1711, saving Quebec from almost certain defeat. Both these events are depicted in little scenes above the odd, turretted altar.

Modern "old port"

Crossing the road that runs along the waterfront, **rue Dalhousie**, you leave the 18th century behind and encounter the more modern world of the port. On the right is the entrance to the government-operated ferry services to Lévis on the other side of the river, while straight ahead the *M. V. Louis Jolliet*, a colourful and popular cruise boat, docks.

Walking north beside the river leads to the award-winning modern **Musée de la Civilisation** ❽ on rue Dalhousie (open mid-June–early Sept: daily, 10am–7pm; early Sept–mid-June: closed Mon; entrance fee; free on Sun, Sept–June) which presents thematic exhibitions on such subjects as language, thought, the body and society. The museum is the centrepiece of the new commercial and community complex, called the **Vieux-Port** ❾ (Old Port) despite its thoroughly contemporary design: overhead walkways of red and silver tubing and plexiglass walls connect spacious, functional pavilions. The complex surrounds the Agora, a 6,000-seat amphitheatre set among flower-beds, waterfalls and fountains, used for cultural events, particularly evening concerts throughout the summer.

Map on page 246

The Musée de la Civilisation, designed by the contemporary Canadian architect Moshe Safdie, incorporates Maison Estèbe, a merchant's house dated circa 1752.

BELOW: the new complex known as the Old Port.

The Upper Town

The easiest way to get back to the Upper Town is by taking the little **funicular** at the head of rue Sous-le-Fort, which is worth the small charge to save wear and tear on the feet in this city-made-for-walking. It shinnies up the cliff (daily 7am–midnight) from the house of Louis Jolliet (the explorer of the Mississippi River) to the Terrasse Dufferin.

At the intersection of rue Buade and Côte de la Fabrique is the baroque cathedral of Quebec City, **Basilique Notre-Dame-de-Québec ⑩** (open daily, 7.30am–4.30pm). The city's main church has been here since 1633 when Samuel de Champlain built Notre-Dame-de-la-Recouvrance in gratitude for the recovery of New France from the British. As with the later victories, the French settlers considered this rescue from Protestant infidels an act of God. Next door stands the **Séminaire de Québec ⑪** (guided tours in summer; entrance fee) and the Université Laval. The Jesuits established a college here in 1635, a year before Harvard opened, but the seminary was officially founded only in 1663 by Bishop Laval.

The university still exists, though its modern campus is now in the suburb of Ste-Foy, and these buildings serve their original purpose as a seminary and high school. The seminary's **museum** (open June–early Sept: daily, 10am–5pm; Sept–June: closed Mon; entrance fee) is probably the city's finest general museum, with splendid modern facilities for the displays of baroque and Renaissance art and some of the finest of 19th-century Canadian art.

There is also a gruesome unwrapped mummy dating from the time of Tutankhamun, an oriental collection, and some intriguing old scientific contraptions. Across the street from the cathedral is the monument to Cardinal

BELOW: restaurants and shops on rue St-Louis.

Taschereau, looking formidable, as if ready to carry out his threat to excommunicate any worker who joined a union. Behind is the grey, ample **Hôtel-de-Ville ⑫**.

Around the corner stands the only rival to the Château Frontenac on the city's skyline: the Price Building. With 17 storeys, it just about qualifies as the old town's only skyscraper. One is enough, and fortunately the 1937 Art Deco style is not out of keeping with the neighbourhood.

Straight on, however, stands the **Cathédrale Ste-Trinité ⑬**, the first Anglican cathedral built outside the British Isles and thoroughly English from its design (on the model of St Martin-in-the-Fields in London) to its pews made of oak imported from the Royal Windsor Forest. There is also a throne in the apse called the King's Bench, but rather ironically, though it has been graced in its 200 years by queens, princes, princesses and governors-general, it has not, so far, been the seat of a king.

Lively rue St-Louis, with its snug little restaurants and pensions, slopes up from the end of rue des Jardins to the **Porte St-Louis ⑭**, rebuilt in a grand neo-Gothic style (complete with turret and crenellated gun-ports) to replace the 17th-century original. In the old **Poudrière** (Powder Building) beside the gate, an interpretive centre has been set up, providing information on the history of the city walls. The walls have been restored and are a protected historic site, but you can walk on top of them (for free) in a complete 4.6-km (2.8-mile) circuit around the Old City,

Back in front of the Porte St-Louis is the lane that leads to **La Citadelle ⑮**, the star-shaped bastion on the summit of Cap Diamant, 100 metres (330 ft) above the St Lawrence (tours Apr–Oct: daily; entrance fee).

They're changing the guard at the Citadel.

BELOW: artists on rue du Trésor.

Horse power provides a picturesque mode of transport.

The Citadel, with its Changing of the Guard ceremony (mid-June–Labour Day: daily, 10am) and Beating of the Retreat (July, Aug: Wed–Sat, 6pm), appeals to childhood notions of soldierly glory and adventure. But, however colourful, it continues to play a military role as the headquarters of Canada's French-only Royal 22e Régiment, known as the "Vandoos" (a rather crude rendering of *les vingt-deuxièmes*). There is a museum outlining their history, as well as a more general military museum. Built by the British in the early 1800s according to plans approved by the Duke of Wellington, with double granite walls and a magnificent position above a sheer cliff, the Citadel was considered one of the most impregnable strongholds in the Empire.

Outside the city walls

Beyond the wall's confines, the city becomes suddenly roomy, opening out onto the **Grande-Allée** and the lawns of the **Hôtel du Parlement ⑯**, the seat of the National Assembly, Quebec's provincial government. Though not old by the city's standards (building began in 1881), the elaborate French Renaissance design by Eugène-E. Taché does seem to embody Quebec's distant roots in the court of Louis XIII. Its symbols, however, are purely Québécois; the important figures of her history are all there, each trying to outdo the other's elegant pose in his alcove on the facade: Frontenac, Wolfe, Montcalm, Lévis, Talon… Below, Louis-Philippe Hébert's bronze works include dignified groups of Indians, the "noble savages" of the white man's imagination.

Outside, on the terraces of the Georgian houses that border the Grande-Allée west from the National Assembly, visitors and civil servants enjoy the cuisine, wines and serenading violins of some of Quebec's liveliest restaurants.

BELOW: cruising past the Ville Basse, or Lower Town.

Love and war

A block south, there is gentle peace. **Parc des Champs-de-Bataille** , or the Plains of Abraham, runs parallel to the Grande-Allée with spectacular views across the St Lawrence to the Appalachian foothills. Its rolling lawns and broad shade trees have known far more romance than fighting, many more wine-and-cheese picnics than violent deaths but, however incongruously, it commemorates a vicious 15-minute battle in 1759 where Louis-Joseph, Marquis de Montcalm, lost half of North America to the British. It wasn't quite that simple, but the fact remains that the Indian fighting style of the Canadians had won them success after success against the British until the Marquis de Montcalm, a traditionalist and a defeatist, became head of the land troops. Always ready to retreat even after a victory, and rarely pressing an advantage, Montcalm steadily reduced the territory that he had to defend.

General Wolfe, who sailed down the St Lawrence with half as many troops as Montcalm held in the fortress of Quebec City, never really hoped to succeed in taking it and so he destroyed 80 percent of the town with cannon fire.

Montcalm would not emerge to fight a pitched battle and, in a last-ditch, desperate attempt, Wolfe took 4,400 men up the cliff in silence by cover of night to the heights where there was no hope of turning back. Montcalm had been expecting Wolfe at Beauport, north of the city, and he rushed back to fight on the Plains. Throwing away every advantage, time, the possession of the city stronghold, and the sniping skills of his men, Montcalm fought the kind of European-style set battle that his troops were improperly trained for. Wolfe was killed, Montcalm mortally wounded and, though the British held only the Plains at the battle's conclusion, the French surrendered the city.

Map on page 246

Quebec is a city like no other in the country. It is the beating heart of what many believe might one day become its own distinct nation.

LEFT: a romantic city. **BELOW:** the Plains of Abraham.

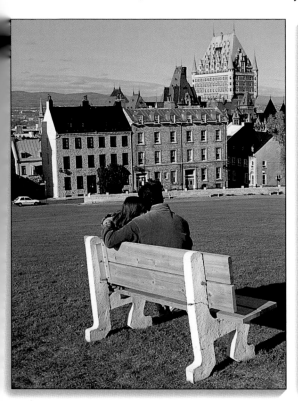

Map on page 246

Some of the villages on Ile d'Orléans are over 300 years old, with examples of Normandy-style wooden and stone dwellings.

RIGHT: ice-climbing at the winter carnival.
BELOW: Ste-Anne-de-Beaupré.

Two robust little Martello towers within the park were built as out-posts of the British defence system between 1804 and 1823. Their walls on the side facing the enemy are 4 metres (13 ft) thick, narrowing to a mere 2 metres (7 ft) on the side facing the town (open early June–early Sept: daily; free).

An interesting battlefield interpretive centre (tel: 648-4071/5641) which focuses on the dramatic military history of the park is housed in the **Musée du Québec ⑱** (Quebec Museum) (1 avenue Wolfe-Montcalm; open June–early Sept: daily, 10am–5.45pm, Wed till 9.45pm; early Sept–late May: closed Mon; entrance fee; tel: 643-2150). Standing at the far end of Parc des Champs-de-Bataille, just beyond the now vacant jail called the **Petit Bastille**, this imposing neoclassical building is also home to a large proportion of the best Quebec art. Painters such as Alfred Pellan, Marc-Aurèle Fortin and Jean-Paul Riopelle are not quite household names throughout the world, but the work of these modern artists has a wide range from expressionistic landscapes to frenetic abstracts.

East of the city

If you have an extra day in Quebec, pack your bathing suit and head east for 10 km (6 miles) either by the upper Route 360 or the lower road, Route 138, to **Parc de la Chûte-Montmorency** (open daily; free).

These falls at 83 metres (272 ft) are considerably higher than Niagara Falls, though less dramatic because they are so much narrower. Here, however, instead of looking at the falls from the top down, you approach the base, which means that the closer you get, the wetter you get from the spray. The province has thoughtfully built a large granite platform at the base of the falls so that visitors can actually stand inside the chilly cloud of spray. In winter, the spray forms a solid block which grows up from the bottom into a "sugarloaf" of ice and snow, providing a splendid slope for tobogganing.

Fertility and healing powers

South of the falls, the bridge to the **Ile d'Orléans** turns off the autoroute. In 1970, the provincial government declared the island a historic district to prevent the encroachment of the city and the tourist trade from destroying the milieu of one of Quebec's most picturesque and historic areas. The exceptionally fertile soil brought early prosperity to the island. In the 1600s there were as many inhabitants here as in Montreal or Quebec, and farming is still the vocation of most of the families, many working land that has been passed down since Quebec's earliest days. Few visitors can resist indulging themselves at the roadside stands that offer fat strawberries swimming in lakes of thick, fresh cream topped with maple sugar.

Back on the north shore of the St Lawrence, a little further east, the town of **Ste-Anne-de-Beaupré** houses a cathedral where a large annual pilgrimage takes place in late July. The fountain of St Anne, in front of the church, is said to have healing powers. The town exemplifies the gaudy tourism that is being avoided on the Ile d'Orléans, but the basilica itself, begun in the late 1920s to replace earlier chapels, is worth a visit. ❑

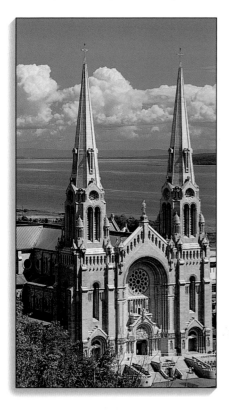

INSIGHT GUIDES

Travel Tips

Insight Guides Website
www.insightguides.com

Don't travel the planet alone. Keep in step with Insight Guides' walking eye, just a click away

New Insight Maps

Maps in Insight Guides are tailored to complement the text. But when you're on the road you sometimes need the big picture that only a large-scale map can provide. This new range of durable Insight Fleximaps has been designed to meet just that need.

Detailed, clear cartography
makes the comprehensive route and city maps easy to follow, highlights all the major tourist sites and provides valuable motoring information plus a full index.

Informative and easy to use
with additional text and photographs covering a destination's top 10 essential sites, plus useful addresses, facts about the destination and handy tips on getting around.

Laminated finish
allows you to mark your route on the map using a non-permanent marker pen, and wipe it off. It makes the maps more durable and easier to fold than traditional maps.

The first titles
cover many popular destinations. They include Algarve, Amsterdam, Bangkok, California, Cyprus, Dominican Republic, Florence, Hong Kong, Ireland, London, Mallorca, Paris, Prague, Rome, San Francisco, Sydney, Thailand, Tuscany, USA Southwest, Venice, and Vienna.

INSIGHT GUIDES

The world's largest collection of visual travel guides

CONTENTS

Getting Acquainted

The Place 258
Climate 258
Government & Economy 258

Planning the Trip

What to Wear 259
Entry Regulations 259
Health & Insurance 259
Money Matters 259
Animals 259
Tourist Offices 260
Getting There 260
Public Holidays 260

Practical Tips

Media 261
Postal Services 261
Telecoms 261
Local Tourist Offices 261
Internet Access 261
Travelling with Children 261
Consulates 262
Women Travellers 262
Travellers with Disabilities 262
Religious Services 263
Medical Services 263
Emergencies 263
Security & Crime 263
Gay Travellers 263
Extension of Stay 264
Business Hours 264
Tipping 264

Getting Around

On Arrival 264
Public Transport 264
On Foot 265
Car Hire 265
Bicycle Rental 265
Tours 266

Where to Stay

Montreal Hotels 267
Montreal B&Bs 268
Montreal Hostels 269
Quebec 269

Where to Eat

Montreal 270
Quebec Restaurants 274
Quebec Cafés & Nightspots ...274

Nightlife

Montreal 275

Culture

Museums 276
Art Galleries 276
Concerts & Operas 276
Movies 277
Ballet, Theatres 277
Public Libraries 277
Festivals 277

Shopping

Montreal 278
Quebec 279

Sports

Participant 280
Spectator 281

Language

Words and Phrases 282

Further Reading

General 287
Other Insight Guides 287

Getting Acquainted

The Place

Area: Located in the province of Quebec, at the confluence of the Ottawa River and the St Lawrence Seaway, Montreal is built on an island about 40 km (32 miles) long and 16 km (10 miles) wide. The central downtown area is compact and densely populated, the outlying areas less so. Away from the main island, the landscape tends to be predominantly rural.

Quebec City lies where the St Charles River meets the St Lawrence River. It is located on top of and around a cliff.

Situation: 45° 30' N, 73° 36' W (Montreal), 46° 52' N, 71° 23' W (Quebec City).

Population: Montreal itself, the second-largest city in Canada after Toronto, has approximately 1 million rsidents, while the larger metropolitan area – which includes 27 additional municipalities on the island of Montreal – contains about 3.2 million.

Quebec City's population is roughly 170,000; its larger metropolitan area contains approximately 600,000 people.

Language: Officially French; Montreal is the largest French-speaking city in the world after Paris. English is also widely spoken in Montreal, less so in Quebec City.

Religion: Catholicism predominates, but Protestant, Jewish and other faiths are also widely represented, particularly in Montreal.

Time Zones: Montreal and Quebec City are in the Eastern Standard Time Zone, along with New York City and Boston, one hour ahead of Chicago, and three hours ahead of San Francisco. On the last Sunday in April, the clocks are moved ahead one hour for Daylight Savings Time. On the last Sunday in October, the clocks are moved back to Standard Time. This follows the mnemonic "spring forward, fall back". At noon in Montreal and Quebec City it is:
11am in Chicago
9am in San Francisco
8am in Hawaii
5pm in London
2am (the next day) in Sydney.

Currency: The Canadian dollar is worth approximately $0.65 US and £0.45.

Weights and Measures: Canada uses the metric system. One kg is approximately equal to 2.2 lbs; one km is approximately equal to 0.62 miles.

Electricity: Canada uses the North American "standard" electricity of 110 volts. European appliances (220–240 volts) will require special adaptors, sold in travel shops. Some hotel bathrooms may be wired for use with European-style appliances.

International Dialling Code: 1.

Area Codes: Unless otherwise stated, the area code for telephone numbers is 514 for Montreal and 418 for Quebec City. Surrounding areas also carry 450 and 819 area codes, noted here wherever necessary.

Topography: Mont Royal is the dominant geographical feature of Montreal, while Cap Diamant, a rocky cliff overlooking the St Lawrence River, is Quebec City's.

Climate

Montreal has nearly five months of cold and snow. Montrealers, however, rarely hibernate. Skating, skiing and sledding are very popular. The Métro subway system is well heated, and the Underground City provides a haven from the cold. In summer, the city comes alive with the warm weather, and outdoor cafés and festivals bring people out on the streets. In July, the temperature can reach 32°C (90°F), yet average temperatures hover around 21°C (70°F) during the day. Quebec City, located some 250 km (150 miles) upriver and northeast of Montreal, is a bit colder and drier – in winter the difference in temperature can be quite noticeable.

Weather Information

In Montreal, tel: 283-4006. Channel 17 (Météomédia) is also a continuous weather channel, albeit in French. In Quebec City, tel: 648-7766.

Average Daily Highs

Month	(°C)	(°F)
January	-10	15
February	-10	15
March	-3	27
April	6	42
May	13	55
June	18	64
July	21	69
August	20	68
September	15	58
October	9	47
November	2	35
December	-7	20

Government and Economy

Montreal is governed by a mayor, a 56-member council elected for four years, and a six-member executive committee selected by the council. As in all Canadian municipalities, the city government is controlled by the provincial legislature.

In spite of a recent drain of business to Toronto and the USA, Montreal is still the headquarters for many of Canada's largest banks, railroad lines and insurance companies, and an important centre for shipping and industry.

Most jobs in Quebec City fall into one of two categories: government or tourism. As the capital of Quebec province, the town is full of administrators employed to work on Quebec's substantial government programs. Most of the rest of the working population are employed in the city's restaurants, gift shops, and inns.

Planning the Trip

What to Wear

In the cold winter months, travellers should bring warm clothing that can be worn in layers, hats, gloves and boots – especially for Quebec City in deep winter, when frostbite isn't unheard of. In summer, bring a sweater for the cool evenings but also bring light clothing for potentially warm, humid days. Pack sportswear and a bathing suit, since many Montreal hotels have health clubs and indoor pools.

Entry Regulations

VISAS AND PASSPORTS

US citizens do not need a visa or a passport to enter Canada, just proof of citizenship (birth certificate plus photo ID e.g. driver's licence). All other visitors need passports. People registered as aliens in the US should carry their US alien registration or green card. Visitors wishing to stay in Canada for more than three months may require a visa.

CUSTOMS

There are no restrictions on bringing in personal clothing but gifts must be declared and are liable to duty over the value of $60 each. Visitors aged 16 and over can bring in duty-free up to 200 cigarettes, 50 cigars and 200 g (7oz) of tobacco. Personal cars can be brought in (for up to six months), as can boats, canoes, rifles and shotguns (but no handguns or automatic weapons) and 200 rounds of ammunition, but all these items must be declared. If you are driving a rental car keep the contract with you. There are strict restrictions on bringing in vegetation and food. Regulations are subject to change, so if you have questions before you arrive, call Canada Customs on (514) 283-9900, fax: (514) 283-5757, website: www.ccra-adrc.gc.ca/customs/general/acis/menu-e.html

Health and Insurance

The usual city cautions – pollution, traffic, crime – apply, but on the whole Montreal and Quebec City are remarkably safe and comfortable places to visit. There are no poisonous plants, snakes or insects. Pollen is only copious during a brief spring period. Winter can bring ice to the streets, making walking or driving awkward.
For a free (donations accepted) list of English-speaking physicians contact the International Association for Medical Assistance to Travellers (IAMAT):
Canada: 1287 Clair Avenue West, Toronto, Ontario, M6E 1B8, tel: (416) 652-0137.
Europe: 57 Voirets, 1212 Grand-Lancy, Geneva, Switzerland.
US: 417 Center Street, Lewiston, NY 14092, tel: (716) 754-4883.
If your health insurance does not cover medical problems while travelling, the following companies may be of assistance:
Health Care Abroad, Wallach & Co, 107 West Federal Street, PO Box 480, Middleburg, VA 20118-0480, tel: 1-800-237-6615 or (540) 687-3166.
Travel Guard International, 1100 Centerpoint Drive, Stevens Point, WI 54481, tel: 1-800-782-5151, fax: 1-800-955-8785, website: www.noelgroup.com.
Hospital and medical services are excellent. Rates for care vary, but adult in-patient care starts at around $2,000 a day for non-Canadians.

Money Matters

Travellers' cheques and major credit cards are readily accepted, but cash may be needed for small restaurants and stores. Some establishments also accept US dollars, though at a less-than-fair exchange rate. In general, use ATMs to withdraw Canadian funds in amounts up to $500 Canadian – you will get the best rate this way (your home bank will automatically do the conversion on a no-comission basis). If you must buy Canadian dollars, do so before you leave home to avoid long lines at the airports or change bureaux. Travellers' cheques can also sometimes be purchased in Canadian dollars.
Banks in Montreal open 10am–3 or 4pm. For currency exchange downtown try Currencies International, 1250 rue Peel, tel: 392-9100, open Monday to Friday 8.30am–9pm.
In Quebec City, try Caisse Populaire Desjardins du Vieux-Québec, 19 rue des Jardins, tel: 694-1774, open daily 9am–6pm from mid-May to mid-October; during the rest of the year, open 9.30am–5pm weekdays only, but until 6pm Wednesdays and Thursdays.
Any other large bank or credit union (caisse populaire) in either city can also probably exchange major currencies at a pinch.

TAX

A 7.5 percent provincial sales tax (PST) plus a 7 percent federal goods and services tax (GST) apply to nearly all goods and services – this is charged in addition to an item's marked price. Hotels in Montreal (but not Quebec City) will also add on a 2 percent city lodging tax.

Animals

Dogs and cats coming into the country must be declared and accompanied by proof of vaccination against rabies. Livestock, horses and fowl must be accompanied by a permit, and they are subject to health inspection on arrival.

Books and foods are taxed at only 7 percent, however, and ready-made meals are not taxed at all. Keep all receipts, as refunds of some taxes can be obtained by submitting the original receipts and a government form (available from border officials and also some merchants).

For further information about the tax laws call Revenue Quebec, tel: 873-4692.

Tourist Offices

When you arrive, excellent maps of the city are available at all tourist information offices (see below, Practical Tips, Local Tourist Offices). For information beforehand, contact:

US: Call toll-free 1-800-BONJOUR (266-5687).
UK: Visit the Canada Centre, 62–65 Trafalgar Square, London W1
France: Call toll-free 0800-90-7777 from 15.00–23.00 (French time).

Getting There

BY AIR

Two airports serve Montreal. Dorval International is 22 km (14 miles) west of the city and handles domestic, US and international flights. Take the direct VIA train to downtown Montreal. Mirabel International, 55 km (34 miles) to the northwest of the city, handles charter flights from outside North America but little else. To reach the city, one must rent a car or catch a bus taking half an hour to the city centre.

Quebec City's Jean-Lesage Airport (640-2600) is located about 15km (10 miles) west of the city and almost exclusively handles shuttle flights from Montreal and other provincial points. The La Québécoise shuttle service (872-5525 or 520-2916 for reservations) carries passengers into town at a very reasonable cost; a one-way trip costs $9 per person. The taxi ride into the city costs approximately $30.

BY RAIL

Amtrak has a daily service from New York City in the US. To obtain information on fares, tel: 1-800-872-7245.

Montreal is connected to most major Canadian cities through VIA Rail, tel: 1-800-361-5390 or 989-2626. The terminus for both companies is at Gare Centrale at 895 rue de la Gauchetière Ouest (Métro: Bonaventure).

Regular VIA trains (1-800-361-5390 or 692-3940, www.viarail.ca) connect Quebec City to Montreal and the rest of Canada. There are three railway stations in the Quebec City area; for most practical purposes, travellers will be coming from the west (Montreal). This station is conveniently located near the historic Lower Town. Travellers coming from the east (Nova Scotia or New Brunswick) detrain at the suburb of Lévis, across the St Lawrence River, from where ferries and buses carry them to the city. The suburban station at Sainte-Foy will be of little use to most visitors.

BY CAR

Many highways lead to Canada. At the Canadian border be prepared to show proof of citizenship and your vehicle's ownership papers. On holidays and weekends, traffic backs up and travellers can expect a wait of half an hour or more at the crossing. From New York, take I-87 (the New York State Thruway), which becomes Highway 15 at the border 47 km (30 miles) from the outskirts of Montreal. From New England, take Route I-89 to Route 133, which becomes a two-lane road at the border. From Vermont, take I-91, which becomes Highway 55 in Canada, and follow this route to Highway 10 Ouest (West) to Montreal. From Toronto take Highway 401 directly to Montreal.

Quebec City is most easily reached from major Eastern US cities via I-91, which becomes Autoroute 55 in Canada; follow this route to Autoroute 20, then turn onto route 20 Est (East). Continue approximately 140 km (90 miles) to Route 73. Turn North and cross Pierre-Laporte Bridge into Quebec City, then exit onto Route 175 and follow signs for Vieux Québec.

Throughout the province of Quebec, the road signs are in French. The speed limit and distances are posted in kilometres. The speed limit is 100 kph (62 mph). Quebec has a mandatory seat-belt law.

BY BUS

Greyhound/Trailways connects Montreal with various cities in North America. Vermont Transit connects Boston, New York and other cities in New England with Montreal. Both lines use the bus terminal at 505 Maisonneuve Blvd Est, tel: 842-2281. You can walk downstairs from the terminal to Montreal's central Métro station.

Quebec City's bus station (525-3000) is located next to the Lower Town train station.

Public Holidays

Government agencies and many banks, businesses and schools close on many of the following holidays:

- **January** 1st – New Year's Day: Fireworks above Mont Royal 2nd
- **April** Good Friday, Easter Sunday, Easter Monday
- **May** 24th (or closest Monday) – Fête de Dollard/Victoria Day
- **June** 24th – Fête Nationale (Saint-Jean-Baptiste Day, Quebec Holiday)
- **July** 1st – Canada Day (only lightly celebrated in French Canada)
- **September** 1st Monday in September – Labour Day
- **October** 2nd Monday – Thanksgiving
- **November** 11th – Remembrance Day
- **December** 25th – Christmas, 26th – Boxing Day

Practical Tips

Media

There are French and English language newspapers, as well as radio and television stations in Montreal. For listings of television stations check the daily newspapers. Radio stations are listed in the Yellow Pages of the telephone book.

The two major daily newspapers in Montreal are *La Presse* (French) and *The Gazette* (English). Montreal also has four weekly newspapers with extensive arts and entertainment listings. *Mirror* and *Hour* (both English) and *Voir* and *Ici* (French) are available free of charge at various newsstands, restaurants and stores around the city. Many smaller newspapers, journals and special interest publications are also found in the city.

Montreal's English-language daily paper, the *Gazette*, is also sold in Quebec City. The city has its own two daily newspapers, *Le Soleil* and *Le Journal de Québec*, though both are French-only. There's also a local version of the Montreal alternative weekly newspaper *Voir*, again in French. Find the CBC at 104.7 FM and Radio Canada at 980 AM for English-language news. On the television, only channel 4 (CFCM) is in English.

Postal Services

The main Post Office (general delivery) in Montreal is at 1250 rue Université, tel: 395-4539, fax: 395-0325, open Monday to Friday 8am–7pm. There's another branch at 1695 rue Ste-Catherine Est near avenue Papineau, tel: 522-3220, fax: 522-5758, open Monday to Friday 9am–5.30pm. Some tobacco shops and pharmacies along

boulevard St-Laurent and other major streets also sell postage stamps – look for the red Poste Canada signs.

Stamps can also be bought at coin machines in airports, bus terminals, and hotel lobbies.

You can have mail addressed to you at Poste Restante, or general delivery at the Post Office at 1250 rue Université. The American Express office will also hold mail for its customers at 1141 boulevard de Maisonneuve Ouest.

Telegrams and cablegrams are handled by CNCP Telecomm-unications at 740 rue Notre-Dame Ouest, tel: 861-7311, fax: 395-5250. Open for inquiries by phone daily 8am–11.30pm or in person Monday to Friday 8am–4.30pm.

Quebec City's main Post Office is located at 300 rue St-Paul (tel: 694-6175) in the Lower Town. It is open Monday to Friday 8am–5.45pm. As in Montreal, a few tobacco shops and pharmacies also sell postage stamps.

Telecoms

Public pay-phones require 25¢. Long-distance calls may be dialled directly to all points in North America and most European countries. Travellers can buy a La Puce phone pass from any Espace Bell phone services shop. La Puce is a prepaid calling card in denominations of $10, $20 and $50.

In Montreal there is a central Espace Bell shop at 892 rue Ste-Catherine Ouest, tel: 866-6686. For more information, tel: 282-0619.

The area code for Montreal is 514, for Quebec City is 418, and 450 and 819 are used for surrounding areas.

Local Tourist Offices

These offices distribute a variety of information, and can also book accommodation, including B&Bs. In Montreal look for:

Infotouriste. The main office (Centre Infotouriste at 1001 Square Dorchester, tel: 873-2015) and the smaller branch in Old Montreal (on

Place Jacques-Cartier at rue Notre-Dame) are designated by street signs with a '?'.

Greater Convention and Tourist Bureau of Greater Montreal, 1010 rue Ste-Catherine Ouest, Suite 410, tel: 844-4056, fax: 844-7141.

Tourisme Québec, CP 979, Montreal H3C 2W3, tel: 1-800-363-7777, fax: 864-3838, www.bonjour-quebec.com.

Quebec City's main **tourist information kiosk** is located at 835 avenue Wilfred-Laurier (tel: 649-2608), near the Plains of Abraham. A **provincial tourism office** is located at 12 rue Ste-Anne in the Upper Town, near the Frontenac; it's open from 9am–5pm daily, longer hours in summer.

Internet Access

Internet access in Montreal is available at the second-floor Starbucks coffeeshop inside the Chapters bookstore at 1177 rue Ste-Catherine Ouest, tel: 843-4418.

In Quebec City, there is access at Café Internet du Palais Montcalm, 955 place d'Youville, tel: 692-4909, and Bar L'Étrange, 275 rue St-Jean, tel: 522-6504.

Travelling with Children

Montreal offers many entertaining possibilities for children, from zoos to theatre productions. Most of the major sightseeing spots have special programs for children. Check the listings later in Travel Tips or the local newspapers for more ideas. Quebec City has fewer offerings, but if you can reach the surrounding area with a car, the options expand.

MONTREAL

Angrignon Park and Farm. A large farm with over 100 animals, offering guided tours and special programs for children. The farm is open daily June to Labour Day 9am–5pm, admission free. The park is open year round and popular winter activities include ice skating, cross-country skiing and a winter fairyland landscaped and lit-up for kids. For more details, tel: 872-4689 or 872-3816.

Cirque du Soleil, tel: 1-800-678-2119, fax: 722-3692, website: www. cirquedusoleil.com. Inventive circus (no animals) that appeals to all ages.

Dow Planetarium, 1000 rue Saint Jacques Ouest, tel: 872-4530, fax: 872-3102, website: www. planetarium.montreal.qc.ca. A Zeiss projector and 100 auxiliaries project the sky onto a dome screen 20 metres (65 ft) in diameter. Shows are narrated in both French and English and change every few months. Many special seasonal events. Open 12.30–8.30pm. Special reservations are needed for people with disabilities.

Grands Ballets Canadiens, tel: 849-8681, fax: 849-0098. Performs *The Nutcracker Suite* every year around Christmas.

IMAX Theatre, Quai King-Edward, tel: 496-IMAX or 1-800-349-IMAX, web: www.imaxoldport.com

ISCI Centre, Quai King-Edward, tel: 496-ISCI or 1-877-496-ISCI,

website: www.isci.ca Interactive science centre where children (and adults) can run, click and read their way through numerous situations and problems.

La Ronde, Ile Ste-Hélène, tel: 872-4537. A 55-hectare (136-acre) amusement park with international shows and circus. Open seasonally.

Maison Théâtre, tel: 288-7211. Theatre devoted exclusively to children and teenagers. Closed in summer.

Montreal Museum of Fine Arts, tel: 285-1600, fax: 285-4070, website: www.mmfa.qc.ca Has several programs designed for children and includes family activities at weekends.

Musée d'Art Contemporain de Montréal, tel: 847-6226, fax: 847-6290. Children and family activities of all kinds involving current displays.

Parc Safari, Located 70 km (43 miles) from the city in Hemmingford, tel: 1-800-465-8724 or (450) 247-2727, fax: (450) 247-3118. Drive-in wild animal park. Open in summer and early fall.

Saint Leonard Cave Exploration, tel: 328-8511 or 252-3323. Investigate 500-million-year-old rock formations.

Consulates

Australia: 50 O'Connor Street, Suite 710, Ottawa, tel: (613) 236-0841. Open weekdays 8.30am–5pm (visa/immigration services 9am–1pm only).

France: 1 Place Ville-Marie, Montreal, tel: 878-4385.

South Africa: 1 Place Ville-Marie, Room 2615, Montreal, tel: 878-9217. Open weekdays 9am–12.30pm and 1.30pm–4.30pm

UK: 1000 rue de la Gauchetière Ouest #4200, Montreal, tel: 866-5863. Open weekdays 9am–5pm (no passport or visa services).

USA: 1155 rue St-Alexandre, Montreal, tel: 398-9695. Open weekdays 8.30am–noon, also 2pm–4pm Wednesdays.

QUEBEC CITY

Aquarium du Québec, 1675 ave des Hôtels, Ste-Foy, tel: 659-5264.

Chocomusée de la Chocolaterie Erico, 634 rue St-Jean, tel: 524-5122. Tiny chocolate museum with free admission and the assumption you'll cave in and buy some chocolate afterwards.

Glissades de la Terrasse (Snow Slide), Dufferin Terrasse next to Château Frontenac, tel: 692-2955. Illuminated sledding run with outstanding views; equipment can be rented. Open daily 11am–11pm in winter, weather permitting.

IMAX Theatre, 5401 blvd des Galeries, tel: 627-8222. Open daily until late hours.

Mégaparc des Galeries de la Capitale, 5401 blvd des Galeries, tel: 627-5800, fax: 627-5807.

Women Travellers

Women will want to take all the usual precautions, but Montreal and Quebec are relatively safe compared to other North American cities of similar size. Rape is uncommon. For more information, contact the **Montreal Women's Centre**, 3585 rue St-Urbain, tel: 842-4781. There is a local condom shop chain, **La Capotérie**, at 2061 rue St-Denis, tel: 845-0027 in Montreal.

Small entertainment park within a shopping mall, featuring rides, a skating rink, and miniature golf. **Musée de l'Abeille (Museum of the Bee)**, 8862 blvd Ste-Anne in Château-Richer, 27 km (17 miles) northeast of Quebec City, tel: 824-4411. Free museum explaining the industrious bee's life. Optional Bee Safari is free for young children, fee for adults and kids over 12.

Travellers with Disabilities

A brochure published by the Montreal Convention and Visitors Bureau, tel: 844-4056, fax: 844-7141, gives complete information about facilities accessible to disabled people. The following organisations offer services in Montreal:

Association Régionale pour le Loisir des Personnes Handicapées de l'Ile de Montréal, 525 Dominion, Suite 340, tel: 933-2739, fax: 933-9384, e-mail: arlphim@videotron. net. Special information on recreational activities.

Bell Canada offers a relay system for the deaf and mute. Special telephones may be obtained from the Raymond Dewar Institute, tel: 256-5757.

Canadian National Institute for the Blind, 2155 rue Guy, Suite. 750, tel: 934-4622.

Keroul, 4545 Avenue du Pierre de Coubertin, tel: 252-3104, fax: 254-0766, e-mail: keroul@

craph.org. Provides assistance to disabled people.
Raymond Dewar Institute, 3600 rue Berri, tel: 284-2581, TDS: 284-3747, fax: 284-5086. website: www.surdite.org. Library, viewing room and reference centre available for use by the deaf and mute.

In Quebec City, the regional association which campaigns for disabled rights can be reached on 529-6134.

Religious Services

MONTREAL

Buddhist: Montreal Buddhist Church, 5250 rue St-Urbain, tel: 273-7921.
Catholic: Mary Queen of the World Cathedral, 1085 rue Cathédrale, tel: 866-1661.
Greek Orthodox: St George Antiochian Orthodox Church, 555 rue Jean-Talon Est, tel: 276-8533.
Jewish: Poale Zedec Synagogue, 7161 rue St-Urbain, tel: 274-0148.
Muslim: Message of Islam Foundation, 8350 boulevard St-Laurent, tel: 385-3443.
Protestant: Christ Church Cathedral (Anglican), 1444 rue Union, tel: 843-6577.

QUEBEC CITY

Catholic: St. Patrick's, 1145 avenue de Salaberry, tel: 524-3544.
Greek Orthodox: Annuciation Greek Orthodox, 17 boulevard René-Lévesque Est, tel: 523-8564.
Jewish: Congregation of Beth Israel Ohev Shalom, 1251 Place de Mérici, tel: 688-3277.
Muslim: Islamic Centre of Quebec, 784 avenue Myrand, Ste-Foy, tel: 683-2193.
Protestant: Anglican Cathedral of the Holy Trinity, 31 rue des Jardins, tel: 692-2193; Quebec Baptist Church, 70 Grand Allée Ouest, tel: 872-8258; St. Andrew's Presbyterian, rues Ste-Anne and Cook, tel: 694-1347.

Medical Services

Health care is excellent in Montreal, but it can be expensive, especially for non-residents – a comprehensive package of health/travel insurance is strongly recommended for all travellers to Canada.

Most hospitals have emergency rooms with doctors on hand round the clock. For information on clinics and other health services consult the *Yellow Pages* of the telephone book.

Hospitals in Montreal
Catherine Booth Hospital, 4375 Montclair, tel: 481-0431.
Centre Hospitalier Jacques Viger, 1051 St-Hubert, tel: 842-7181.
Jewish General Hospital, 3755 chemin de la Côte, Ste-Catherine, tel: 340-8222.
Maisonneuve-Rosemont Hospital, 5415 de l'Assomption, tel: 252-3400.
Montreal Children's Hospital, 2300 Tupper, tel: 934-4400.
Montreal General Hospital, 1650 avenue du Cédar, tel: 937-6011.
Royal Victoria Hospital, 687 avenue des Pins Est, tel: 842-1231.
Saint-Luc Hospital, 1058 St-Denis, tel: 281-2121.
Villa Medica Hospital, 225 Sherbrooke Est, tel: 288-8201.

Pharmacies in Montreal
There are many full-service pharmacies throughout the city. The Jean Coutu Drug Store, 1370 avenue Mont-Royal Est, tel: 527-8827, provides a 24-hour service.

Dentists in Montreal
The **Dental Clinic**, 3546 rue Van-Horne, tel: 342-4444, fax: 342-0611, offers 24-hour service.

Quebec City
The city's largest hospital, **Hôtel-Dieu**, is at the foot of the cliff at 11 rue de la Palais (691-5151). Other emergency or out-of-hours **medical advice** can be obtained by phoning 648-2626, while **dentists** on-call can be reached on 653-5412.

Emergencies & Other Services

Dial **911** in Canada to connect to the police or other emergency assistance. No coins are needed.
Quebec Poison Control Centre, tel: 1-800-463-5060.

Security and Crime

As a rule, it is safe to walk around downtown **Montreal** in the day and evening. Areas to avoid at night include the X-rated movie houses along rue Ste-Catherine Est, Parc du Mont-Royal and Parc Lafontaine. Gay travellers may not wish to travel alone at night in the Latin Quarter or "Gay Village" areas. Whenever possible, travel with another person while sightseeing or shopping, particularly at night. Do not walk in deserted or run-down areas alone. If driving, lock your car and never leave luggage, cameras or other valuables in view; put them in the glove compartment or boot. Park under a street light.

Never leave your luggage unattended. While waiting for a room reservation, for example, keep your property in view. Never leave money or jewellery in your hotel room, even for a short time.

Carry only the cash you need. Use credit cards and traveller's cheques whenever possible, and avoid displaying large amounts of cash.

Quebec City is exceptionally safe within the central city. In quieter areas, the same cautions listed above apply.

Gay Travellers

A number of resources exist in Montreal, including **L'Androgyne**, a bookstore at 3636 St-Laurent, tel: 842-4765; the **Centre Communautaire des Gais et Lesbiennes** at 2075 Plessis (528-8424) and the organisation **Divers Cité** at 4067 boulevard St-Laurent (285-4011), which coordinates a huge annual parade and other events.

Extension of Stay

If you plan to extend your stay over the standard three-month limit, contact the Department of Employment and Immigration in Ottawa, Ontario. There is a $65 application fee for the extension.

Business Hours

Standard business hours are 9am–5pm. Banks are usually open weekdays 9am–5pm. Museums follow standard business hours, and shops are generally open Monday to Wednesday 10am–6pm, Thursday and Friday 10am–9pm, Saturday 10am–5pm. Many stores are now open on Sunday, though with shorter hours, usually 11am–5pm.

Tipping

It is customary to tip waiters and taxi drivers 10–15 percent of the bill or fare. Some restaurants add the tip to the bill, but this will be identified on the check. For porters, $1 per suitcase is expected. For hotel doormen who hail a cab or give other assistance, $1 should be given.

Getting Around

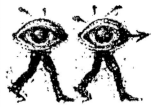

Montreal's central areas are each quite compact and walkable, but getting from one to another usually requires a car or some form of public transport. Driving can be nerve-wracking, but the city's excellent bus and Métro system make travelling around easy. Quebec City is smaller and is best explored on foot – parking is scarce and expensive.

On Arrival

MONTREAL

The **Aerobus** bus service, tel: 931-9002 is available from service counters at both Mirabel ($18.00) and Dorval ($15) airports. Several major **taxi companies** also provide service from the airports for roughly $25 from Dorval and $55 from Mirabel.

A **limousine service** is available from Dorval to downtown Montreal without a reservation for a flat rate of $40.50. From Mirabel, service can be arranged through **Montreal Limousine Inc.**, tel: 333-5466, fax: 333-1998. The trip from Mirabel to downtown will cost roughly $95. By cab or limousine, the trip from Mirabel takes 45–60 minutes, and from Dorval 20–30 minutes, depending on traffic conditions.

QUEBEC CITY

Taxis are available from the airport. In summer a cheaper alternative is the bus service operated by Maple Leaf-Dupont (tel: 649-9226) which makes four trips a day during the week with a reduced service at weekends.

Public Transport

Public transport in **Montreal** is very efficient, clean and comfortable. The Société de Transport de la Communauté de Montréal (STCUM) administers both the bus and Métro, and the tickets and transfers are good on either service. Exact change is required on the buses.

The rubber-wheeled Métro trains *(see map facing inside back cover)* operate from 5.30am–1am and run every three minutes on crowded lines. Routes of the Métro trains are indicated by the name of the last station on the line and by colour. The single fare for adults is $2.00, a strip of six tickets $8.25, daily passes $5, three-day passes $12.25, and monthly passes $47.00. All tickets are interchangeable on buses and subways.

Ask a driver or punch a button on a machine to get a transfer *(correspondance)* to continue your journey from bus to Métro without having to pay twice. Free maps of the Métro and bus system are available at ticket booths. For more information, tel: 280-5100.

The **Quebec City** area is served by the good STCUQ bus system (tel: 627-2511), which operates from 5.30am–1am. Single tickets cost $1.70, day passes $4.60; if you need to buy a ticket directly from the driver, bring exact change. The hub of most routes is at Place d'Youville on the near edge of the Upper Town, a short walk up avenue St-Jean. A *funiculaire* (elevator) with a small charge and a winding staircase (free) also connect the upper and lower towns.

TAXIS

The rate for all taxis in Montreal and Quebec City is $1 per kilometre with a $2.25 minimum charge. The orange or white plastic sign on a taxi roof is lit when the taxi is available. The major taxi companies in **Montreal** include: Champlain, tel: 273-2435; Co-op, tel: 725-9885; La Salle, tel: 277-2552;

Veterans, tel: 273-6351. In **Quebec City**, they include Taxis Co-op Québec, tel: 525-5191 and Taxis Québec, tel: 525-8123.

DRIVING

Driving is on the right side of the road. Unlike in the rest of North America, a right turn is not allowed at a red light. A blinking green light or a lit green arrow mean that a left turn is allowed; a solid green light means that it is only allowed if traffic is clear.

Drivers in Montreal and Quebec City can be rather reckless, and this especially true of the cities' cab drivers – always expect the unexpected. Take special care on both cities' bridges, where construction work often leads to sudden lane closures, lane changes and lane mergers at breakneck speed. Signage is also sometimes poor; if at all possible, map out your route in advance, including exit numbers.

In case of accident, contact the local police at once (dial 911 for emergency help in both cities). You will need to fill out an accident report and also contact your rental agency if applicable. If you are a member of the AAA (in the US) or AA (in the UK) driving associations, you may use the towing and repair services of the CAA. Call 861-1313 in Montreal or 624-0708 in Quebec City for assistance. There is also a CAA office in downtown Montreal at 1180 rue Drummond who can supply maps and help with other services.

Parking is tight in both cities and regulations are strictly enforced; fortunately, however, the enforcement usually means a ticket, not being clamped or towed

Walking in Montreal or Quebec City is very enjoyable and finding your way around is quite easy. Street names and directions are in French.

away. Note that all signage will be in French only – ask a merchant for guidance if you are confused.

In Montreal, residential parking in neighbourhoods is often restricted to residents who display stickers on car windows. The largest central parking facility is located on Square Dorchester, beside the Infotouriste building.

In Quebec City, try one of the private lots along rue St-Jean or a hotel lot. Note that many Quebec City downtown hotels reimburse the cost of parking.

CAR HIRE

Most car rental companies have branches at the airports, major hotels and their central offices. Rates vary by firm and by model and size of the car. Most companies offer unlimited mileage and special weekend rates as well as liability insurance. Petrol and collision insurance are extra, and there is a 15 percent sales tax.

Montreal
Avis, 1225 rue Metcalf, tel: 866-7906 or 1-800-321-3652, fax: 866-5214. Open Monday to Friday 7am–9pm, Saturday 7am–6pm, Sunday 8am–9pm.
Budget, 1240 rue Guy, tel: 937-9121 or 1-800-268-8900. Open Monday to Friday 7am–9.30pm, weekends 7am–9pm.
Thrifty/Viabec, 1076 rue de la Montagne, tel: 845-5954, fax: 845-9880. Open Monday to Friday 7.30am–8.30pm, weekends 8am–5pm.
Hertz, 1475 rue Aylmer, tel: 842-8537 or 1-800-263-0678. Open Monday to Friday 7am–9pm, Saturday 7am–7pm, Sunday 8am–9pm.
National, 1200 rue Stanley, tel: 878-2771 or 1-800-387-4747, fax: 874-1601, website: www.nationalcar.com. Open daily 7am–11pm.
Via Route, 1255 Mackay, tel: 871-1166, fax: 871-1232. Open Monday to Friday 7am–9pm, Saturday 7.30am–5pm, Sunday 9am–7pm.

Riding a bike is popular in Montreal and Quebec City, especially in the parks. A network of cycle paths covers 225 km (140 miles) of Montreal – you can buy maps from sporting goods stores. Favourite routes include: Lachine Canal, the Seaway, rues Christophe Colomb and Berri, rue Rachel, Parc Angrignon and Parc du Mont-Royal. There are few cycle paths in Quebec City, but it's possible to get around the Upper or Lower Town efficiently by bicycle. Below are a few companies that rent bikes.

Montreal
Bicycletterie J.R. Cyclery, 151 rue Rachel Est, tel: 843-6989. Open Monday to Wednesday 9am–6pm, Thursday to Friday 9am–9pm, Saturday 10am–5pm, Sunday 10am–3pm.
La Cordée Plain Air, 2159 rue Ste-Catherine Est, tel: 524-1515. Open Monday to Wednesday 9am–6pm, Thursday to Friday 9am–9pm, Saturday 9am–5pm, Sunday 10am–5pm. $300 deposit.
Velo Adventure, Promenade du Vieux-Port de Montréal, tel: 847-0666. Open Monday to Friday 11am–6pm, weekends 9am–6pm.
Vélo Québec, La Maison des Cyclistes, 1251 rue Rachel Est, tel: 521-8356, is an organization devoted to cycling. It provides brochures, guidebooks and information on paths.
Quadricycle International, blvd St-Laurent, tel: 849-9953. Open May to October, Monday to Friday 11am–8pm, weekends 10am–11pm.

Quebec City
Cyclo Services, adjacent to railway station, tel: 692-4052. Open year-round.
Vélo Passe-Sport Plein Air, 22 côte du Palais, tel: 692-3643, open mid-April to October.

Quebec City
Avis, tel: 872-2861 at the airport, tel: 523-1075 in town (located in the Hilton Hotel on boulevard René-Lévesque). Open Monday to Friday 7am–midnight, Saturday 8am–10pm and Sunday 8am–midnight at the airport; open Monday to Friday 7am–6.30pm, weekends 8am–5pm in town.
Hertz, tel: 871-1571 at the airport, tel: 694-1224 in town (44 côte du Palais, corner of St-Jean). Open Monday to Friday 7am–midnight, Saturday 8am–9pm and Sunday 8am–midnight at the airport; open Monday to Thursday 7.30am–5.30pm, Friday 7.30am–6pm, Saturday 8am–4pm and Sunday 8am–5pm in town.
National, tel: 871-1224 at the airport, tel: 694-1727 in town (295 rue St-Paul). Open Monday to Friday 7.30am–10.30pm, weekends 8am–11pm at the airport; open Monday to Friday 7.30am–6pm, weekends 8am–5pm in town.

CRUISES

Montreal
Amphi Tour. An interesting tour on an amphibious bus which explores the land and water of Old Montreal and the Old Port. Open 1 May to 31 October 10am–midnight, tel: 849-5181.
Croisières Bellevue. Open May to end-September, these cruises leave from Ste-Anne Locks daily except Mondays at 1.30pm, 3.30pm and 7.30pm; tel: (450) 457-5245.
Croisières de Port de Montréal. This company conducts guided cruises in the afternoon and dinner/dance cruises in the evening from May to October. Departures are from the Clock Tower Pier and the Jacques Cartier Pier. For reservations and information, tel: 842-3871 or 1-800-667-3131.
Lachine Rapid Tours, 105 rue de la Commune. A 90-minute jet-boat trip down the Lachine rapids. Open summer 10am–6pm. Costs $48 per person; group rates are also available. For reservations, tel: 284-9607.

Le Bateau-Mouche, 90 St-Paul Ouest, tel: 849-9952. Glass-topped boats offer a distinctive perspective of the city, from early May to early October. Daytime cruises last an hour, evening dinner cruises last 3 hours.

Quebec City
The ferry (for both foot-passengers and cars) between Quebec City and Lévis runs all day and for most of the night, providing excellent-value-for-money views of the river, cliffs and city. Board in Place Royale on the city side of the river or beside the VIA rail station in Lévis.
M.V. Louis-Jolliet, berthed at the port, offers daytime and evening cruises throughout the summer. Tel: 692-1159.

FLIGHTSEEING
Delco Aviation. Flights over Montreal in a sea-plane. The views are spectacular. The company also offers destinations outside of Montreal. The fee is $40 per person for the flight, which is available daily 8am–8pm, tel: (450) 663-4311.

BUS TOURS
Several companies offer narrated tours in buses, vans or limousines. Many offer walking tours as well. The length of tours varies, and many options are available. Check with the companies below for more information.

Montreal
Gray Line, 1001 rue du Square Dorchester at Infotouriste office, tel: 934-1222.
Hertz Tourist Guides, tel: 739-7454.
Visites de Montréal, tel: 933-6674.
Guidatour, tel: 844-4021 or 1-800-863-4021.
Taxi Lasalle, tel: 277-2552.

Quebec City
Old Quebec Tours, tel: 664-0460.

Tours
There are many sightseeing companies in **Montreal** – by foot, horse-drawn carriage, even seaplane. Some focus on standard tourist attractions, others on architecture and urban restoration, still others on culture. Numerous *calèches* (carriages) can be found lined up along rue Notre-Dame and rue de la Commune in the Old Port.
In **Quebec City**, there are fewer offerings but the *calèches* are once again a reliable (if pricey) option. Look in the Lower Town.

CARRIAGE RIDES

Montreal
Calèches Boisvert Inc. Departures from rue Notre-Dame, Square Dorchester, Parc du Mont Royal, Place d'Armes, and Place Jacques-Cartier. The fee is around $50 an hour, tel: (450) 653-0751.

Quebec City
Calèches de Vieux-Québec, tel: 683-9222.

WALKS

Montreal
Guidatour. Specializes in Old Montreal tours leaving from Notre-Dame Basilica; multilingual guides. Tel: 844-4021 or 1-800-363-4021.
Heritage Montreal. Tours of Montreal architecture, tel: 286-2662.
Step on Guides, 1302 St-Antoine. City tours lasting 3 hours; tours of Old Montreal and the Underground City, tel: 935-5131.
Tourism Plateau Mont-Royal, tel: 524-8767 or 1-888-449-9944. Guided tours of the Plateau, focussing on poets, writers and culture.

Quebec City
Maple Leaf Guide Services, tel: 622-3677 or 1-877-622-3637. They do it all – in your car, their car, their bus or on foot.

Where to Stay

Most hotels in Montreal fall in the expensive to deluxe range, especially downtown. Large hotels often offer weekend or family discounts. Prices can range from $300 a night for a double room in a deluxe hotel to $55–$75 a night in a moderate hotel. For a free accommodation booking service, call 878-1000.

Price Key

Prices are for one night in a double room in high season
$ = Less than $100
$$ = $100–$150
$$$ = $150–$300
$$$$ = More than $300

Montreal Hotels

Auberge de la Fontaine
1301 rue Rachel Est
Montreal, Quebec H2J 2K1
Tel: 597-0166 or 1-800-597-0597
Fax: 597-0496
E-mail: info@aubergedelafontaine.com
Relaxed hotel featuring outstandingly friendly service overlooking the trees and paths of Parc Lafontaine. Some rooms have terraces or balconies. **$$**
Auberge des Glycines Inc
819 blvd de Maisonneuve Est
Montreal, Quebec H2L 1Y7
Tel: 526-5511 or 1-800-361-6896
Fax: 523-0143
Convenient location in heart of Latin Quarter offsets a tired look. All rooms come with private bath, a bonus for the low price. **$**
Best Western Ville-Marie
3407 rue Peel
Montreal, Quebec H3A 1W7
Tel: 288-4141 or 1-800-361-7791
E-mail: information@
hotelvillemarie.com

Plain hotel in central downtown location with modern business conveniences. Also has health club, voicemail service, free local calls, hairdryers etc. **$$–$$$$**
Château de L'Argoat
524 rue Sherbrooke Est
Montreal, Quebec H2L 1K1
Tel: 842-2046
Fax: 286-2791
E-mail: chateauargoat@videotron.ca
A small European-style hotel located in the Latin Quarter. Complimentary continental breakfast. **$–$$**
Château Versailles Hotel and Tower
1659 and 1808 rue Sherbrooke Ouest, Montreal, Quebec H3H 1E3
Tel: 933-3611 or 1-800-361-3664
Fax: 933-8401
E-mail: versailles@montreal.net.ca
Converted from two Edwardian mansions in downtown. Special weekend rates October to May. **$$–$$$**
Courtyard by Marriott
410 rue Sherbrooke Ouest
Montreal, Quebec H3A 1B3
Tel: 844-8855 or 1-800-449-6654
Fax: 844-0912
Tastefully decorated lobby and large rooms – some with kitchenettes – plus superb views of the city. Also features a piano bar, health spa, masseuse and rooftop (indoor) pool. **$$–$$$**
Days Inn Downtown Montreal
215 blvd René-Lévesque Est
Tel: 393-3388 or 1-800-668-3872
Fax: 395-9999
New addition to downtown, with well-furnished rooms and a good Chinese restaurant upstairs (see Where to Eat) despite the drab location. **$$**
Days Inn Midtown Montreal
1005 rue Guy
Montreal, Quebec H3H 2K4
Tel: 938-4611
Fax: 938-8718
Two restaurants, bar and meeting facilities. **$$**
Four Points Sheraton
475 rue Sherbrooke Ouest
Montreal, Quebec H3A 2L9
Tel: 842-3961 or 1-800-842-3961
Fax: 842-0945
Sauna and exercise room. Central location, walking distance to Métro and the Underground City. **$$–$$$**

Holiday Inn Montreal Midtown
420 rue Sherbrooke Ouest
Montreal, Quebec H3A
Tel: 842-6111 or 1-800-HOLIDAY
Fax: 842-9381
website: www.holidayinn.com
Basic Holiday Inn style, two bars, café-restaurant, health club and indoor pool. Package rates available. **$$**
Hôtel de L'Institut
3535 rue St-Denis
Montreal, Quebec H2X 3P1
Tel: 282-5120 or 1-800-361-5111
Fax: 873-9893
website: www.ithq.qc.ca
Owned and operated by the Quebec Institute of Tourism and Hotels, this hotel is the training ground for future hotel and restaurant managers. Institutional exterior but as would be expected the service is excellent. **$$**
Hôtel de Paris
901 rue Sherbrooke Est
Montreal, Quebec H2L 1L3
Tel: 522-6861 or 1-800-567-7217
Fax: 522-1387
E-mail: hdeparis@microtec.net
Near the heart of the Latin Quarter. Reasonably priced, with a decent bistro-style restaurant downstairs. **$–$$**
Hôtel du Parc
3625 avenue du Parc
Montreal, Quebec H2X 3P8
Tel: 288-6666
Fax: 288-2469
E-mail: rooms@duparc.com
In the Mont-Royal district with squash and tennis courts, Nautilus equipment and an all-season indoor/outdoor pool. **$$$**
Hôtel Gouverneur Place Dupuis
1415 rue St-Hubert
Montreal, Quebec H2L 3Y9
Tel: 842-4881 or 1-888-910-1111
Fax: 842-1584
Attached to city's central Métro station by underground link. All rooms have views of Montreal, Mont-Royal or the St Lawrence River, and rooms are quite well-furnished with extended cable TV and more. Some suites. **$$–$$$**
Hôtel Le St-André
1285 rue St-André
Montreal, Quebec H2L 3T1
Tel: 849-7070 or 1-800-265-7071
Fax: 849-8167

Complimentary in-room continental breakfast. **$**

Hôtel Lord Berri
1199 rue Berri
Montreal, Quebec H2L 4C6
Tel: 845-9236 or 1-888-363-0363
Fax: 849-9855
E-mail: info@lordberri.com
Unattractive location, but at least it's near the bus terminal. Rooms are decent enough, equipped with alarm clocks and video games.
$–$$$

Hôtel Manoir des Alpes
1245 rue St-André
Montreal, Quebec H2L 3T1
Tel: 845-9803
Fax: 845-9886
E-mail: admin@hotelmanoirdes alpes.qc.ca
Victorian building with emphasis on quiet; included Continental breakfast served in nice breakfast room. Soom rooms have jacuzzis.
$–$$

Hôtel Maritime
1155 rue Guy
Montreal, Quebec H3H 2K5
Tel: 932-1411 or 1-800-363-6255
Fax: 932-0446
website: www.hotelmaritime.com
E-mail: info@hotelmaritime.com
Designed with the budget-conscious corporate traveller and private guests in mind, this hotel

also does special hockey packages. **$$–$$$**

Hôtel Omni Montreal
1050 rue Sherbrooke Ouest
Montreal, Quebec H3A 2R6
Tel: 284-1110 or 1-800-843-6664
Fax: 845-3025
Multilingual concierge, fitness centre, 24-hour room service, and sauna in an excellent location. Includes the superb Zen restaurant *(see Where to Eat)*.
$$$–$$$$

Hôtel Ruby Foo's
7655 blvd Decarie
Montreal, Quebec H4P 2H2
Tel: 731-7701 or 1-800-361-5419
Fax: 731-7158
website: www.hotelrubyfoos.com
E-mail: info@hotelrubyfoos.com
Oriental decor, outdoor swimming pool, health club, spa and beauty salon. **$$**

Hôtel Wyndham Montreal
4 Complexe Desjardins
1255 rue Jeanne-Mance
Montreal, Quebec H5B 1E5
Tel: 285-1450
Fax: 285-1243
E-mail: info@wyndham-mtl.com
Well-situated in downtown Montreal, near Chinatown and Place des Arts. Perfect for visiting the FrancoFolies and other open-air festivals downtown. **$$$**

Montreal B&Bs

B&Bs offer good value for money in Montreal, some providing excellent accommodation and good breakfasts for a reasonable price. There are too many to list here, but they can be booked through the agencies listed below. Alternatively, many can be contacted direct through the website: www.bbcanada.com.

A Bed and Breakfast – A Downtown Network
3458 avenue Laval
Montreal, Quebec H2X 3C8
Tel: 289-9749 or 1-800-267-5180
Fax: 287-2386
E-mail: bbdtown@cam.org
Discounts on tours, and family and extended rates are available. Multilingual hosts.

Bed and Breakfast Network
422 rue Cherrier
Montreal, Quebec H2L 1G9
Tel: 738-9410 or 1-800-738-4338
E-mail: bbmtlnet@total.net
Accommodation in French- or English-speaking homes in downtown locations at reasonable prices. Also short-term apartment rentals.

Hospitality Montreal Relais
3977 rue Laval
Montreal, Quebec H2W 2H9
Tel: 287-9635 or 1-800-363-9635
Fax: 287-1007
E-mail: pearson@videotron.ca
This company arranges accommodation in private homes, complete breakfasts are included in the prices.

Price Key
Prices are for one night in a double room in high season
$ = Less than $100
$$ = $100–$150
$$$ = $150–$300
$$$$ = More than $300

L'Abri du Voyageur
9 rue Ste-Catherine Ouest
Tel: 849-2922
Fax: 499-0151
Small, budget-traveller oriented facility isn't by any means luxurious, and the location is only middling at best. But it's one of the city's least expensive hotels. All rooms share toilets. **$**

La Reine Elizabeth
900 blvd René-Lévesque Ouest
Montreal, Quebec H3B 4A5
Tel: 861-3511 or 1-800-441-1414
Fax: 954-2256
website: www.cphotels.ca
Well-positioned downtown high-rise hotel, built by the Canadian Pacific railway empire and still well maintained. It connects to city rail station; some rooms have kitchenettes, while some are luxury suites. The Beaver Club restaurant *(see Where to Eat)* is on the premises. **$$–$$$$**

Le Centre Sheraton
1201 blvd René Lévesque Ouest
Montreal, Quebec H3B 2L7
Tel: 878-2000 or 1-800-325-3535
Fax: 878-3958
Gourmet restaurant, indoor pool, health club, shiatsu massage, and specialty boutiques all in a convenient location. **$$$**

L'Hôtel Montreal Crescent
1366 blvd René-Lévesque Ouest
Montreal, Quebec H3G 1T4
Tel/fax: 938-9797
Small intimate hotel, close to Molson Centre and nightlife. All rooms are air conditioned and come with television; there is also child care on the premises. **$–$$**

Montreal Bonaventure Hilton
1 Place Bonaventure
Montreal, Quebec H5A 1E4
Tel: 878-2332 or 1-800-878-3881
Fax: 878-3881
Situated in more than three quarters

of a hectare (2 acres) of gardens on top of Montreal's Underground City. Two restaurants, exercise room and rooftop swimming pool, 24-hour room service. **$$–$$$$**

Radisson Hotel Montreal Centre
777 rue Université
Montreal, Quebec H3C 3Z7
Tel: 879-1370 or 1-800-333-3333
Fax: 879-1760
This comfortable hotel boasts a revolving rooftop restaurant, complete spa facilities, a heated pool and aerobics classes.
$$–$$$$

Ritz-Carlton Hotel
1228 rue Sherbrooke Ouest
Montreal, Quebec H3G 1H6
Tel: 842-4212 or 1-800-363-0366
Fax: 842-3383
E-mail: ritz@citenet.net
This is perhaps the city's most distincitve and historic hotel *(see page 160)* catering to an elite clientele, even if the rooms are a bit smaller than one would expect for the money. It has lovely period decor and the Café de Paris restaurant is on the premises.
$$$–$$$$

Taj Mahal
1600 rue St-Hubert
Montreal, Quebec H2L 3Z3
Tel: 849-3214 or 1-800-613-3383
Fax: 849-9812
E-mail: tajmahal@videotron.net
Close to Montreal's bus station, this is a good value hotel, but has very plain rooms despite the new name (previously called the Thrift Lodge). Free local calls, free parking, restaurant on-premises. **$**

Travelodge Montreal Centre
50 blvd René-Lévesque Ouest
Montreal, Quebec H2Z 1A2
Tel: 874-9090 or 1-800-363-6535
Fax: 874-0907
This is a modern, European-style business hotel in downtown Montreal with small, well-maintained rooms and contemporary (if a bit sterile) furnishings. Voicemail services are also available. **$$**

Montreal Hostels and 'Y's

Auberge Internationale de Montréal
1030 rue Mackay
Montreal, Quebec H3G 2H1
Tel: 843-3317 or 1-800-663-3317
Fax: 934-3251
E-mail: info@hostellingmontreal.com
Smartly designed, fairly central hostel

is the city's best. Rents rooms year-round to hostel association members or non-members.

Vacances Canada Quatres Saisons
5155 rue de Gaspé
Montreal, Quebec H2T 2A1
Tel: 270-4459
Fax: 278-7508
Dormitory space near Mile-End and the former garment district. Rents spartan but affordable rooms all year-round.

YMCA
1450 rue Stanley
Montreal, Quebec H3A 2W6
Tel: 849-8393
Fax: 849-8017
Conveniently located and reasonably priced accommodation. Wide range of sports facilities and cafeteria for men, women and families.

YWCA
1355 blvd René-Lévesque Ouest
Montreal, Quebec H3G 1T3
Tel: 866-9941
As expected single and double rooms for women at reasonable rates. Longer-term residence (minimum eight weeks) is also available. The hostel offers convenient cafeteria, pool, sauna and whirlpool.

Quebec City Accommodation

Use the Montreal price key above to gauge the prices of the hotels listed below. Quebec City also has lots of small, family-run hotels and guesthouses that can be booked through the tourist office *(see Local Tourist Offices under Practical Tips above)*. As with Montreal, B&Bs can be contacted direct through the website: www.bbcanada.com.

Auberge St-Antoine
10 rue St-Antoine
Tel: 692-2211 or 1 (888) 692-2211
Fax: 692-1177
The central Old Port location and fantastic rooms make this a popular, classy choice for many travellers. Pleasant balconies and washrooms. **$$$**

Hôtel Dominion
126 rue St-Pierre
Tel: 692-2224 or 1 (888) 833-5253
Fax: 692-4403
Built in 1912 at the base of the city's cliffs, this was the first skyscraper in Quebec City. Now it's a set of tastefully appointed rooms at surprisingly affordable prices. **$$**

Hôtel La Maison Demers
68 rue Ste-Ursule
Tel: 692-2487
This unprepossessing little place, right on a small sidestreet near everything, has a great reputation for hospitality. But it's small, so call ahead in summer, and try to learn a bit of French before you do. Some rooms have shared washrooms. **$**

Hôtel Manoir d'Auteuil
49 rue d'Auteuil
Tel: 694-1173
Fax 694-0081.
An 1835 townhouse of more than a dozen rooms, each quite well done-up in Art Deco style, and fairly close to the city fortifications and other sights. **$$$**

Le Château Frontenac
1 rue des Carrières
Tel: 692-3861 or 1 (800) 441-1414
Fax: 692-1751
The top choice in town for atmosphere and views. The comfort level isn't completely modern at Canada's most famous hotel – it was built in 1893, after all, and has more than 600 rooms – but the wonderful bar and vistas more than make up for this. **$$$**

Where to Eat

The French passion for fine cuisine means dining out is a pleasure in Montreal and Quebec City.

Montreal's tradition for good food dates back to the 19th century, when Montrealers welcomed boats of food, drink and spices from China, India and Europe. And it expanded as waves of immigrants arrived and continued arriving. The original French fare was heavy indeed but has since been refined (mostly). For a closer look at some local specialties and the various ethnic influences see the chapter on Montreal Cuisine (page 101). There is no shortage of restaurants (5,000) or varieties of cuisine. Although wine with the meal can be expensive, the food is often great value – and some places, particularly in the rue Prince-Arthur area – allow you to bring your own wine to cut costs.

Quebec City is less cosmopolitan but still a gastronomic delight, and even fast food is a cut above the average. Service and atmosphere are valued, so only the best restaurants survive.

Montreal Restaurants

FRENCH

Alexandre
1454 rue Peel
Tel: 288-5105
Fax: 288-0932
French brasserie serving cassoulet (stew), blood pudding, sausage, roast beef and a dozen beers on tap. Open daily 11.30am–3am. **$$$**

Beaver Club
Hôtel Reine-Elizabeth
900 blvd René-Lévesque Ouest
Tel: 861-3511
Fax: 954-2256

Extremely upmarket French restaurant with a hunting-lodge atmosphere and wood panelling. Canadian, French and wild-game meals. Serves lunch Monday to Friday noon–3pm, dinner Tuesday to Saturday 6pm–11pm. **$$$$**

Café de Paris
Hôtel Ritz-Carlton
1228 rue Sherbrooke Ouest
Tel: 842-4212
Fax: 842-4907
Located in the Ritz-Carlton hotel, serving filet mignon, French food, excellent chocolate mousse. Afternoon high teas. Serves lunch daily noon–2.30pm, dinner daily 6pm–10pm. **$$$$**

Price Key

Average price for a three-course meal
$ = Less than $10 per person
$$ = $10–$20 per person
$$$ = $20–$30 per person
$$$$ = More than $30 per person

Chez Bernard
275 rue Notre-Dame Ouest
Tel: 288-4288
Fax: 288-5403
French restaurant serving filet mignon, Dijon-style lamb, seafood salads, chocolate profiteroles. Lunch daily 11am–3pm and dinner 5.30am–10pm. **$$$$**

Chez La Mère Michel
1209 rue Guy
Tel: 934-0473 or 934-0709
Colourful and innovative French cookery (steaks, breast of duck), great wine selection. Lunch Tuesday to Friday 11.30am–3pm, dinner Monday to Saturday 5.30pm–midnight. **$$$$**

Chez Queux
158 rue St-Paul Est
Tel: 866-5194
Fax: 866-7758
Truly French fare, emphasising game meats like rabbit and venison, and dishes such as double-cut pork chops with chèvre, sweetbreads and the like. Lunch weekdays 11.30am–2.30pm, dinner daily 5pm–10pm. Also Sunday brunches, 11.30am–3pm. **$$$**

Hélène de Champlaia
200 Tour de l'isle
Ile Ste-Héléne
Tel: 395-2424
One of the city's finest restaurants, attached to the casino on Ile Ste-Héléne and extremely pricey. Lunch weekdays 11.30am–2.30pm, dinner Sunday to Thursday 5.30pm–10pm, Friday & Saturday 5.30pm–11pm. **$$$–$$$$**

La Binerie Mont-Royal
367 ave Mont-Royal Est
Tel: 285-9078
Extremely lowbrow, habitant diner. Heavy food such as lard and beans, poutine. Open daily 6am–10pm. **$**

Le P'tit Plateau
330 rue Marie-Anne Est
Tel: 282-6342
Cosy little neighbourhood restaurant serving high-quality food. Locals line-up early to get in. Open Tuesday to Saturday 5.30pm–10pm. **$$–$$$**

Les Chenets
2075 rue Bishop
Tel: 844-1842
Fax: 844-0552
Country French cooking in rustic room of hanging copper pots and fresh flowers; also has a bistro (**$$**). Near Fine Arts Museum. Lunch weekdays 11.30am–3pm, dinner daily 5.30pm–11pm. **$$$**

Les Halles
1450 rue Crescent
Tel: 844-2328
Fax: 849-1294
Among the city's finest French restaurants, a place for splashing out while downtown. Dishes include rack of lamb, quail, duck etc. Lunch Tuesday to Friday 11.45am–2.30pm, dinner Monday to Saturday 6pm–11pm. **$$$–$$$$**

Pierre du Calvet
415 rue Bonsecours
Tel: 282-1725
Fax: 282-0456
Excellent yet affordable French meals served in a historic Old Port house which also functions as a superlative little hotel. Dinner daily 5pm–11pm. **$$$**

Ty-Breiz Crêperie Bretonne
933 rue Rachel Est
Tel: 521-1444
Fax: 527-6434
Smoky family place serving big

dinner and dessert *crêpes* in a friendly atmosphere. Extremely popular with the (Franco) locals. Open daily 11.30am–10pm. **$$$**

FUSION

Chez Desjardins
1175 rue Mackay
Tel: 866-9741
Downtown restaurant serving some of the city's best seafood meals in a refined atmosphere. Dinner only, daily 5pm–11pm. **$$$**

Italasia
4833 blvd St-Laurent
Tel: 281-8008
Fax: 281-5556
This new St-Laurent place mixes Italian and Asian cuisines with good results. One of the city's largest outdoor patios makes for peaceful outdoor dining. Open Monday to Friday 11am–3am, dinner only weekends 5pm–3am. **$$$**

L'Express
3927 rue St-Denis
Tel: 845-5333
Fax: 845-7576
Superlative, if expensive, bistro where the beautiful (or at least well-heeled) dine in St-Denis. Food is mostly French, with some experimentation. Open daily 8am–3am. **$$$**

Le Parchemin
505 rue Ste-Catherine
Tel: 845-5243
Expensive food served in an interesting location: a stone house wedged between an Anglican church and a skyscraper. Lunch weekdays 11.30am–3pm, dinner Monday to Saturday 5pm–11pm. **$$$–$$$$**

Publix Bar Resto Café
3554 blvd St-Laurent
Tel: 284-9233
Fax: 284-3670
Trendy bistro on the Main serving pizza, French food, pasta, and other light meals. Open Monday to Wednesday 11.30am–1am, Thursday to Saturday 11.30am–3am. **$$**

Resto-Bistro La Chronique
99 avenue Laurier Ouest
Tel: 271-3095
Fax: 271-4770

Fine seafood meals are served at this near-Outremont bistro decorated with sepia photographs. Lunch weekdays 11.30am–2.30pm, dinner Tuesday to Saturday 6pm–10pm. **$$$**

Toqué!
3842 rue St-Denis
Tel: 499-2084
Fax: 400-0292
Among the city's best restaurants, but dress up or you'll feel the eyes in the brightly painted room on you. A place to eat eclectically and be seen. Dinner daily 5.30pm–11pm. **$$$$**

GREEK & ITALIAN

La Piazzetta
4097 rue St-Denis
Tel: 847-0184
Fax: 847-0129
Serves pizza, as one would expect, plus other Italian dishes. Sunday to Thursday 11.30am–midnight, weekends 11.30am–1am. **$$$**

La Popessa
3801 rue St-Denis
Tel: 982-1717
Quick and friendly Italian restaurant where the chef cooks your pasta sauce before your eyes. Open 11am–11pm daily. **$$**

Mediterraneo Grill
3500 blvd St-Laurent
Tel: 844-0027
Fax: 844-9848
Youthful and trendy bistro-style place serving primarily grilled meats and seafood, plus chocolate crêpes for dessert. Good wine bar. Open daily 6pm–midnight. **$$$$**

Milos
5357 avenue du Parc
Tel: 272-3522
Undeniably Montreal's best Greek restaurant, pulling out all the stops with lamb, seafood and more. Not cheap, however. Lunch noon–3pm daily, dinner 6pm–midnight daily. **$$$$**

Pizzelli Restaurant Bar
4250 blvd St-Denis
Tel: 849-4646
Inexpensive pizza bar serving by the slice or pie. Open Sunday to Thursday 11am–midnight, weekends 11am–1am. **$**

JEWISH

Ben's Delicatessen
990 blvd de Maisonneuve Ouest
Tel: 844-1000
A tired Jewish deli that has seen better days, but go for the atmosphere and technicolour fountain drinks. Open Sunday to Wednesday 7am–2am, Thursday to Saturday 7.30am–4am. **$**

Brisket
1073 côte du Beaver Hall
Tel: 878-3641
Fax: 878-3843
Central deli serving burgers, sandwiches etc. Open weekdays only, 11am–8.30pm. **$$**

Fairmount Bagel Bakery
74 avenue Fairmount Ouest
Tel: 272-0667
The city's best fire-roasted bagels, individually or by the bag, and it's always open. **$**

Schwartz's
3895 blvd St-Laurent
Tel: 842-4813
A must-eat deli on any tourist itinerary. Superlative Jewish smoked-meat sandwiches, steaks, pickles and fries – plus cherry soda. Open Sunday to Thursday 9am–midnight, Saturday 9am–1am., Sunday 9am–2am. **$**

St-Viateur Bagel Shop
263 rue St-Viateur Ouest
Tel: 276-8044
Runner-up in the contest for best bagel, this is still a fine choice to sample the city's distinctive style. Always open. **$**

STEAKS, BURGERS & BBQ

Biddle's Jazz & Ribs
2060 rue Aylmer
Tel: 842-8656
Fax: 842-2665
Just what it says: good jazz, barbecued chicken and ribs in an Anglo section of the downtown district. Very enjoyable. Open Monday to Saturday 11am–midnight, Sunday dinner only 6pm–midnight. **$$$**

Brochetterie du Vieux-Port
39 rue St-Paul Est
Tel: 866-3175
Fax: 866-6171

Old-Port restaurant specializing in grilling of meats and fish, shish-kebab style. Open weekdays only, 11am–midnight. **$$**

L'Anecdote
801 rue Rachel Est
Tel: 526-7967
The city's best hamburgers, served regular or with a choice of gourmet cheeses and toppings. Open 7.30am–10pm weekdays, 9am–10pm weekends. **$**

L'Entrecôte St-Jean
2022 rue Peel
Tel: 281-6482
Excellent downtown steakhouse, serving grilled steaks in a house sauce, and chocolate dessert. Open Monday to Friday 11.30am–11pm, weekends 5am–11pm. **$$**

Le Bifthèque
6705 Côte de Liesse
Tel: 739-6336
Fax: 739-1173
Yet another Montreal steakhouse, but a good one if you happen to be over in this part of town. Open Sunday to Wednesday 11.30am–10pm, Thursday to Saturday 11am–11.30pm. **$$**

Le Keg
25 rue St-Paul Est
Tel: 871-9093
Fax: 871-9818
A fun Canadian chain serving burgers, steaks, beer etc. Lunch weekdays 11.30am–2pm, dinner Monday to Thursday 5pm–10pm, Friday 5pm–11.30pm, Saturday 4pm–11.30pm, Sunday 4pm–10.30pm. **$$**

Moishe's
3961 blvd St-Laurent
Tel: 845-3509
Fax: 845-9504
The city's top steaks, grilled to perfection and seasoned just right. Bring your wallet and dress nicely. Open daily 5.30pm–11pm. **$$$$**

Restaurant Mike Bossy
1175 Place du Frère André
Tel: 866-5525
Fax: 871-1896
Now run by the former NHL hockey star, this multi-level restaurant still features steaks and fish on its uncomplicated menu. Lunch daily in the Rotisserie Bistro (**$$**) 11.30am–2.30pm; dinner daily in

the bistro (**$$**) and in Les Grands Salons dining room (**$$$$**) 4.30pm–10pm. **$$–$$$$**

LATIN-AMERICAN

Bayou Brasil
4552 rue St-Denis
Tel: 847-0088
Fax: 445-8764
Serves a mixture of Brazilian (grilled meats) and Cajun (such as alligator!) food. Also has a bar. Dinner only, Sunday to Thursday 5pm–11pm, weekends 5pm–midnight. **$$$**

Jano
3883 blvd St-Laurent
Tel: 849-0646
Grilled Portuguese-style meals of fish and meat plus superb side dishes, right on the Main. Dinner only, daily 5pm–12midnight. **$$–$$$**

La Bodega
3456 avenue du Parc
Tel: 849-2030
Fax: 849-2946
Serves *paella*, seafood, grilled meats and other Spanish dishes. Open daily noon–midnight. **$$$**

Solmar
111 rue St-Paul Est
Tel: 861-4562
Fax: 878-4764
Old-Port restaurant serving Portuguese food, such as grilled chicken, inside or out on a terrace; or you can order from the French menu next door. Open daily noon–11pm. **$$**

EASTERN EUROPEAN

Café Mozart
361 rue St-Paul Est
Tel: 871-0717
Outstanding Eastern European cuisine in a central Old-Port location. Choose from placky, Hungarian goulash, strudel, schnitzel and the rest. Lunch weekdays 11.30am–3pm, dinner weekdays 6pm–11pm; open continuously noon–11pm weekends. **$–$$**

Café Sarejevo
2080 rue Clark
Tel: 284-5629

Fun place serving Bosnian fare such as spicy meatballs, plus the bonus of nightly music and dancing. Dinner only, Tuesday to Wednesday 5pm–1am, Thurday to Saturday until 3am. **$$**

Stash Café Bazaar
200 rue St-Paul Ouest
Tel: 845-6611
Polish cuisine in the heart of the Old Port. Open Monday to Saturday 11.30am–9pm, until midnight Fridays and Saturdays, open Sunday noon–10pm. **$$**

Troika
2171 rue Crescent
Tel: 849-9333
Fax: 849-9334
Upscale Russian dining (chicken Kiev, beef stroganoff, caviar) with vodka, in a room of heavy dark furnishings. Live accordion music. Dinner daily 5pm–11pm. **$$$$**

ASIAN

Furama
215 blvd René-Lévesque Est
Tel: 393-3388
Tucked above a nondescript hotel in a nondescript downtown location, this good dim-sum restaurant is surprisingly affordable. Open 11.30am–9.30pm daily. **$–$$**

Katsura
2170 rue de la Montagne
Tel: 849-1172
Fax: 849-1705
One of the city's better-known and more central sushi restaurants, plus *yakitori* noodles and other choices. Lunch weekdays 11.30am–2.30pm, dinner Monday to Thursday 5.30pm–10pm, later weekends. **$$$**

L'Etoile des Indes (Star of India)
1806 rue Ste-Catherine Ouest
Tel: 932-8330
Montreal is not known for good Indian cooking, but this restaurant is a decent enough choice for korma, tikka masala and such like. Lunch Monday to Saturday 11.30am–2.30pm, dinner daily 5pm–11pm. **$$**

Nantha's Kitchen
9 rue Duluth Est
Tel: 845-4717

Among the city's most inventive and best Asian restaurants, it features Malaysian cooking incorporating elements of Thai and Vietnamese cuisine. Dinner only, daily 5.30pm–11pm. **$$**

Thai Grill
5101 blvd St-Laurent
Tel: 270-5566
Fax: 270-5048
Lunchtime buffets, great satay and other Thai meals for dinner. Reservations often necessary at weekends, as it's very popular with locals. Lunch and dinner daily. **$$–$$$**

Zen
1050 rue Sherbrooke Ouest
Tel: 499-0801
One of the city's most inventive Asian restaurants, downstairs in the Westin Mont-Royal Hotel. Open daily 11.30am–2pm and 5.30pm–9pm. **$$$**

OTHER

Alpenhaus
1279 rue St-Marc
Tel: 935-2285
Fax: 935-7272
Swiss and other dishes such as beef bourguignonne, fondues, wienerschnitzel, and rack of lamb. Open weekdays noon–11pm, dinner Saturday 4.30pm–11pm, Sunday 5.30pm–11pm. **$$**

Byblos Le Petit Café
1499 ave Laurier Est
Tel: 523-9396
An interesting litle Iranian café which opens its terrace in summertime. Pittas, meats, soups and so on. Open 9am–11pm daily. **$–$$**

Frites Alors!
5235 avenue du Parc
Tel: 948-2219
Local chain serving up quick meals of Belgian-style fries and sausage in a surprisingly classy environment. Other locations around town. Open Monday to Saturday 11.30am–10pm, Sunday noon–9.30pm. **$**

La Louisiane
5850 rue Sherbrooke Ouest
Tel: 369-3073
Fax: 369-3702
Cajun food such as crawfish etouffée and jambalaya, decorated with photos of the Big Easy jazz scene. Dinner Tuesday to Wednesday 5.45pm–9.30pm, Thursday to Sunday 5.45pm–10.30pm. **$$$**

Marché Mövenpick
Place Ville-Marie
Tel: 861-8181
Fun Swiss-styled restaurant where you choose your meal and watch a chef cook it before your eyes. Montreal steaks, Swiss raclette, Asian stir-fry, single-malt Scotch, smoothies, French desserts – they're all there. Open 7.30am–2am daily. **$–$$**

Price Key

Average price for a three-course meal
$ = Less than $10 per person
$$ = $10–$20 per person
$$$ = $20–$30 per person
$$$$ = More than $30 per person

Nil Bleu Restaurant
3706 rue St-Denis
Tel: 285-4628
Fax: 285-2304
Ethiopian meals of sauces, meats and vegetables to be scooped up with bread. Lunch Tuesday to Saturday noon–2.30pm, dinner daily 6pm–11pm. **$$**

Restaurant des Gouverneurs
458 Place Jacques-Cartier
Tel: 861-0188
Old-Port tourist attraction on Place Jacques-Cartier serving international selection of meats and seafood. Open daily 11am–midnight. **$$$**

Restaurant Witloof
3619 rue St-Denis
Tel: 281-0100
Fax: 281-6789
Belgian cuisine (tartare, mussels) plus – of course – a wide selection of those great Belgian beers. Lunch Monday to Saturday 11am–3pm, dinner Monday to Wednesday 5pm–10pm, Thursday to Saturday until midnight, Sunday 5pm–10pm. **$$**

VEGETARIAN

Café Santropol
3990 rue St-Urbain
Tel: 842-3110
Not completely vegetarian, but the sometimes-crazy menu leans that way; a counterculture favourite. The terrific back patio lets you eat your sandwich or salad among more greenery. Open Monday to Thursday 11.30am–midnight, weekends noon–2am, Sunday noon–midnight. **$**

ChuChai
4088 rue St-Denis
Tel: 843-4194
Astonishingly creative *faux*-meat prepared from soy, wheat and seitan products in a handsome St-Denis establishment. Lunch daily noon–3pm, dinner daily 5pm–10pm, later weekends. **$$**

Le Commensal
1720 rue St-Denis
Tel: 845-2627
Very popular and good local chain of buffet vegetarian restaurants, open daily 11am–11pm. Other locations at 5043 rue St-Denis (on the Plateau) and 2170 Ste-Catherine Ouest (downtown). **$**

Wrapps
5124A rue Sherbrooke Ouest
Tel: 482-8542
Sandwich and light-meal eatery near the Golden Mile, catering to a McGill College and business crowd. Open daily 11.30am–8pm. **$$**

CAFES AND COFFEEHOUSES

Montreal's café scene is widely famous. For classic Parisian-style cafés, head either for the Outremont district – around avenues Laurier and Bernard – or rue St-Denis. Even the chains here roast and brew a good cup. Most of these places are open late hours.

Café Republique
1051 avenue Bernard Ouest, Outremont
Tel: 277-0502
Typical Outremont café, especially known for its tasty selection of desserts.

Café Rico
969 rue Rachel Est
Tel: 529-1321
Non-smoking neighbourhood coffeehouse serving fair-trade coffees to a largely counterculture crowd.

Café Romolo
272 avenue Bernard Ouest, Outremont
Tel: 272-5035
Coffee served in tall glasses, as you'd find it in Spain or Italy, along with Greek pastries and other treats. Big windows give an airy feel; open late, until 3am, and serves meals too.

Café Souvenir
1261 avenue Bernard Ouest, Outremont
Tel: 948-5259
Parisian-style café serving breakfasts, simple meals and good coffee beneath maps of European cities.

La Brûlerie St-Denis
3967 rue St-Denis
Tel: 286-9159
This small, local chain roasts what is reputedly the city's best cup of coffee, and lets you linger over it as long as you like. Several other locations around town as well.

La Croissanterie
5300 rue Hutchison, Outremont
Tel: 278-6567
Neighbourhood café serving rich coffees, light sandwiches and croissants. Interestingly decorated.

La Petite Ardoise
222 avenue Laurier Ouest, Outremont
Tel: 495-4961
Refined place to sip café au lait,

consume homemade pastries, or eat fish meals (**$$**). Local art featured on the walls.

Le Bilboquet
1311 avenue Bernard Ouest, Outremont
Tel: 276-0414
Original home of Montreal's finest locally made ice cream and frozen yogurt. Bright interior, summer terrace.

Second Cup
3965 blvd St-Laurent
Tel: 844-0347
Popular Ontario-based chain serves decent coffee drinks and desserts, but its real value is as a stronghold of Anglo culture – come here to hear English. Other branches on avenue du Parc, rue Ste-Catherine, and ave Mont-Royal.

Quebec City Restaurants

Aux Anciennes Canadiens
34 rue St-Louis
Tel: 692-1627
Serving heavy multi-course meals of *habitant* food such as pork, peas, beans and maple sugar, this restaurant tends to attract crowds of both locals and tourists. You'll wait in line. Open daily noon–10pm. **$$$**

Café de la Terrasse
1 rue des Carrières
Tel: 692-3861
Very close to the looming Frontenac, its terrace has spectacular views. The French food is great, too. Breakfast daily, 7am–11.30am, lunch daily noon–2.30pm, dinner daily 5.30pm–10.30pm Also Sunday brunch. **$$$**

Café d'Europe
27 rue Ste-Angele
Tel: 692-3835
Fine French food, once again – think flaming desserts and rich sauces – and as usual here, it won't come inexpensively. Lunch Monday to Saturday 11.30am–2.30pm, dinner daily 5pm–10.30pm. **$$$–$$$$**

Casse-Crêpe Breton
1136 rue St-Jean
In a city full of crêpe places, this is the best one – and right on one of Quebec City's main people-watching streets. Don't forget a dessert crêpe. Open weekdays 8am–11pm, weekends 7.30am–midnight. **$**

Gambrinus
15 rue du Fort
Tel: 692-5144
French food served in a gentle environment, typical of Quebec City upscale dining. A minstrel works the room in summer, and the *terrasse* offers a great view. Lunch weekdays 11.30am–2.30pm, dinner Monday to Saturday 5pm–11pm, Sunday 5pm–10.30pm. **$$$–$$$$**

L'Astral
Hôtel Lowes Le Concorde
1225 Place Montcalm
Tel: 647-2222
This restaurant features the double benefits of a fantastic view – it rotates once per hour – and excellent French gourmet meals. Open Monday to Saturday, 11.45am–midnight, Sunday 10am–midnight. **$$$**

L'Échaudé
73 rue du Sault-au-Matelot
Tel: 692-1299
A typical French gourmet restaurant serving moderately priced but good food in a stylish Art Deco room.

Quebec City's Cafés and Nightspots

Café Krieghoff
1089 avenue Cartier. Tel: 522-3711
Finest coffeehouse in Quebec City, a haunt of artists and musicians. Good inexpensive meals as well.

Chez son Père
24 rue St-Stanislaus
If you want to hear true Quebec traditional music – the kind you'll clap your hands along to – come to this Old Quebec songhouse.

Le Ballon Rouge
811 rue St-Jean
One of the city's most popular gay nightclubs.

La Fourmi Atomik
33 rue d'Auteuil
A widely known alternative music bar in the basement beneath another club housed in a former chapel. Techno, punk and world beat are among the genres.

Le Dagobert
600 Grand-Allée Est
Popular dance club spread out over three storeys of the building. Lots of dancing and, in summer, a terrace.

Le Saint-Alexandre
1087 rue St-Jean
An English pub in the heart of French territory, featuring loads of beer selections.

Lunch weekdays 11.30am–2.30pm, dinner daily 5.30pm–10pm. Also Sunday brunch, 10am–2.30pm. **$$**

La Caravelle
68 1/2 rue St-Louis
Tel: 694-9022
Terrific French meals in a coolly chic location right in the action. Nightly performances by a singer add to the atmosphere. Open daily 11.30am–11.30pm. **$$$**

Le Cochon Dinge
46 boulevard René-Lévesque Ouest
Tel: 523-2013
Inexpensive meals (burgers, fish, pasta) that offer few of the surprises or prices of the French places in town. Several other locations in town as well. Open Monday to Thursday 7am–midnight, Friday 7am–1am, Saturday 8am–1am, Sunday 8am–midnight. **$**

Price Key

Average price for a three-course meal
$ = Less than $10 per person
$$ = $10–$20 per person
$$$ = $20–$30 per person
$$$$ = More than $30 per person

Le Commensal
860 rue St-Jean
Tel: 647-3733
All-vegetarian restaurant featuring a good buffet, juices and desserts. A place to find Quebec City's counterculture. Open Monday to Wednesday 11am–9.30pm, Thursday to Sunday 11am–10.30pm. **$**

La Grande Table de Serge Bruyère
1200 rue St-Jean
Tel: 694-0618
Perhaps the city's top restaurant, serving Bruyère's brand of nouvelle cuisine. Reserve ahead. Open daily for dinner only, 6pm–10pm. **$$$**

Le Paris-Brest
590 Grand Allée
Tel: 529-2243
This place, set along the glitzy Grand Allée, serves up French cooking below street level. Closed Saturdays. Lunch weekdays 11.30am–2.30pm, dinner Monday to Saturday 5.30pm–11.30pm, Sundays 5.30pm–9.30pm. **$$**

Nightlife

Montreal Nightlife

It's worth strolling round Montreal at night as the streets are a buzz of activity. Clubs and bars provide varied avenues for entertainment. Check listings in the newspapers for up-to-date happenings. Cocktail lounges are open until 2am, bars and cabarets until 3am. Major hotels have nightclubs with discos, comic shows and other entertainment.

CASINOS

Casino de Montréal
1 avenue de Casino
Ile Notre Dame
Tel: 392-2746
The French pavilion for Expo 67 now houses an enormous Las Vegas-style casino. The four floors contain over 2,500 slot machines and numerous electronic games, as well as blackjack, roulette and baccarat tables. No jeans and trainers. Many hotels offer special casino packages. Open daily 11am–3am.

NIGHTCLUBS/DISCOS

Balattou
4372 blvd St-Laurent
Tel: 845-5447
Tropical mix of soca, salsa, rai, reggae and dancehall.

Bar Minuit
115 avenue Laurier Ouest
Tel: 271-2110

Le Belmont
4423 blvd St-Laurent
Tel: 845-8443

Salsatheque
1220 rue Peel
Tel: 845-0016
Latin dance.

Sky
1474 rue Ste-Catherine Est
Tel: 529-6969
Gay dance club.

JAZZ CLUBS

Biddle's
2060 rue Aylmer
Tel: 842-8656

Café Sarajev
2080 rue Clark
Tel: 284-5629

Café Thélème
311rue Ontario Est
Tel: 845-7932

L'Air du Temps
191 rue St-Paul Ouest
Tel: 842-2003
Local and international talent. Opens at 5pm.

Upstairs
1254 rue Mackay
Tel: 931-6808

BARS

The legal drinking age in the province of Quebec is 18. Microbrewery beers, produced by small, independent breweries, are very popular among Montrealers. Brands to try include: Boréale (Blond, Rousse, Noir and Fort), Brasal, La Maudite, La Fin du Monde, Blanche de Chablis, Cheval Blanc. A wide selection of bars lines the St-Laurent strip between Sherbrooke and Mont-Royal – some of which come with attitudes, dress codes and ridiculously pompous doormen. Also try out the bars along rue St-Denis (a slightly more refined crowd) or along rue Crescent, where you'll hear a lot more English and find ale on tap.

Altitude 717
Place Ville Marie, 44th floor
Tel: 397-0737
Chic top-floor bar with panoramic views of Montreal; dress smartly. Dance club one storey higher gets going late-hours at weekends. Expensive restaurant (**$$$–$$$$**) also on premises.

Bar St-Sulpice
1680 rue St-Denis
Tel: 844-9458
Old house in the Latin Quarter. Popular front terrace facing street and back patio surrounding fountain in summer.

Deux Pierrots
104 rue St-Paul Est
Tel: 861-1270
Situated right in the Old Port, this is probably the city's most famous *Boîte à Chanson* (Québécois song club).

Else's
156 rue Roy Est
Tel: 286-6689
Well-decorated Plateau neighbourhood hangout for Anglos, featuring a distinctive look and English and Irish beer on tap. Yes, it's owned by Else.

Jello Bar
151 rue Ontario Est
Tel: 285-2621
This retro cocktail lounge in a slightly dodgy area of the student quarter specializes in fixing martinis.

La Cervoise
4457 blvd St-Laurent
Tel: 843-6586
Bar right on the busy main street serving beer brewed on the premises; happy-hour specials.

Pub Quartier Latin
318 rue Ontario Est
Tel: 845-3301
Very popular student bar serving beer on tap to an acid jazz and dance music background.

Shed Café
3515 blvd St-Laurent
Tel: 842-0220
A fixture on the Main, with patio seating in summer.

Sofa
451 rue Rachel Est
Tel: 285-1011
Dimly lit, laid-back bar with sofas scattered about the room. Frequent jazz acts on a small stage.

Whisky Café
5800 blvd St-Laurent
Tel: 278-2646
High-class, elegant bar with Montreal's most astonishing bathroom fixtures. A bit far out of the centre, but quieter than downtown bars.

Culture

Museums

The major museums in Montreal and Quebec City are described in the main text. Listed below are additional museums of interest. As well as their permanent collections, many of the museums have changing exhibits. Call for details of special exhibits and events, or check the arts section in the newspapers.

Montreal Museum of Decorative Arts, 2200 rue Crescent, Montreal, tel: 284-1252, fax: 284-0123, website: www.madm.org. Houses the Liliane and David M. Stewart collection of international design dating from 1940. Also regular exhibitions on furniture, glassware, textiles and ceramics. Open Tuesday to Sunday 11am–6pm (Wednesday until 9pm).

Musée des Soeurs Grises, 1185 rue St-Mathieu, Montreal, tel: 932-7724, fax: 937-0533. Features the tomb, religious objects and death chamber of Mother d'Youville. Open Wednesday to Sunday 1.30–4pm. Admission free.

Redpath Museum, 859 rue Sherbrooke Ouest, Montreal, tel: 398-4086, fax: 398-3185, website: www.mcgill.ca/redpath. Houses a fossil exhibition with dinosaur bones and an anthropological collection including two Egyptian mummies. Open Monday to Friday 9am–5pm, Sunday 1–5pm, closed Friday from Fête National to Labour Day. Admission free.

Saint-Laurent Art Museum, 615 blvd Ste-Croix, Montreal, tel: 747-7367, fax: 747-8892, e-mail: mas101@ globetrotter.qc.ca. In the former chapel of Collège Saint-Laurent. A permanent collection of Quebec art and handicrafts from wood sculpture to textiles and Amerindian art. Concerts frequently held on Sundays. Open Thursday to Sunday 1–5pm, Wednesday 1–9pm. Closed Monday and Tuesday.

Ursuline Museum, 12 rue Donnacona, Quebec City, tel: 694-0694. One of the buildings on the estate of the Ursuline Convent, the oldest girls'school on the continent. The museum deals with the Ursulines and their lives in the 1600s and 1700s, with displays of belongings of the early French settlers. Open Tuesday to Saturday 9.30–noon and 1.30–4.45pm, Sunday afternoons only.

Art Galleries

Articule, 4001 rue Berri, Montreal, tel: 842-9686. Canadian contemporary art and media installations.

Canadian Guild of Crafts Quebec, 2025 rue Peel, Montreal, tel: 849-6091. Inuit art and Canadian crafts such as blown glass, porcelain and ceramics.

Galerie-Boutique Métiers d'Art, 29 rue Notre-Dame, Place Royale, Quebec City, tel: 694-0267. Quebec-made crafts.

Galerie Dominion, 1438 rue Sherbrooke Ouest, Montreal, tel: 845-7471. Canadian and international painting and sculpture from the 19th and 20th centuries.

Galerie Simon Blais, 4521 Clark, Montreal, tel: 849-1165. Canadian contemporary art.

Concerts and Operas

Montreal offers music from western classical to various world music groups. For events on a particular day, consult the arts sections of the city's newspapers. The web site – www.infoarts.net – also has listings of all current arts events, spectacles and performances. In Quebec City the French-language magazine *Voir* is distributed free and provides information on the main events in the city.

McGill Chamber Orchestra is one of Montreal's oldest chamber groups, and it plays in the Place des Arts and the Eglise Saint-Jean-Baptiste, tel: 398-4547.

Metropolitan Orchestra of Montreal, young musicians perform at the Théâtre Maisonneuve, tel: 598-0870.

Montreal Symphony Orchestra has an international reputation, and performs at Place des Arts and in the city's parks during summertime, tel: 842-3402.

L'Orchestre Symphonique de Québec (Quebec Symphony Orchestra) is Canada's oldest symphony orchestra. It performs at Louis-Frechette Hall in the Grand Théâatre de Québec, 269 blvd René-Lévesque Est, Quebec City, tel: 643-8131, where you can also see the **Opéra de Québec**.

Opéra de Montréal was founded in 1980 and stages four or five operas a year. Considered one of the 10 best companies in North America, tel: 985-2258.

Movies

As the host of major film festivals, Montreal's selection of films is noteworthy. There are close to 100 movie theatres in the city, so check the newspapers for showings and locations. Some of the specialized cinemas in Montreal include:

Cinéma du Parc, 3575 avenue du Parc, tel: 281-1900.

Cinémathèque Québécoise, 335 blvd de Maisonneuve Est, tel: 842-9763, fax: 842-1816, website: www.cinematheque.qc.ca.

Ex-Centris, 3536 blvd St-Laurent, tel: 847-3536. Hot new alternative-film showcase theatre on the main street in a slab-like building. Now home to Montreal's famous annual international film festival.

IMAX Theatre, Quai King-Edward, Old Montreal, tel: 496-IMAX (4629).

Ballet

The **Grands Ballets Canadiens** has been performing in Montreal for more than 30 years. Their repertoire includes classical and modern pieces and work by new Canadian composers and choreographers. Tel: 790-2787 or 849-0264.

Theatres

Montreal offers at least 10 major French theatre companies and many smaller theatres (see *Yellow Pages* of telephone book for full listing). Quebec City also has several theatres, with most productions in French (check in *Voir*).

English

Centaur Theatre, 453 rue St-François Xavier, Montreal, tel: 288-3161.

Saidye Bronfman Centre, 5170 chemin de la Côte Ste-Catherine, Montreal, tel: 739-2301.

French

Théâtre Saint-Denis, 1594 rue St-Denis, Montreal, tel: 849-4211 or 790-1111.

Théâtre D'Aujourd'hui, 3888 rue St-Denis, Montreal, tel: 282-3900.

Théâtre la Chappelle, 3700 rue St-Dominique, Montreal, tel: 843-7738, fax: 987-9754, e-mail: tlc@cam.org.

Théâtre du Nouveau Monde, 84 rue Ste-Catherine Ouest, Montreal, tel: 866-8668.

Théâtre du Rideau Vert, 4664 rue St-Denis, Montreal, tel: 845-0267 or 844-1793.

Théâtre Périscope, 2 rue Crémazie Est, Quebec City, tel: 529-2183. Includes performances for children.

Théâtre Quat' Sous, 100 avenue des Pins Est, Montreal, tel: 845-7277. Box office open Monday to Friday noon–5pm.

Public Libraries

There are a number of public libraries in Montreal. The Montreal Central Library is located at 1210 rue Sherbrooke Est, tel: 872-5923. Other resource libraries include:

Bibliothèque Nationale du Québec in three locations (tel: 873-1100 for all buildings): Saint-Sulpice Building, 1700 rue St-Denis; Conservation et Siège Social, 2275 rue Holt; Aegidius Fauteux Building, 4499 avenue de L'Esplanade.

Collections spéciales et Archives privées, 125 rue Sherbrooke Ouest, tel: 873-1100.

Festivals

Calendar of Events

January–February

Carnaval de Québec (Winter Carnival): late January to early February in Quebec City. Huge winter party, the continent's largest and most lively winter festival, taking over most of downtown Quebec City.

La Fête des Neiges: from mid-January to early February: this features snow sculptures, cross-country skiing competitions, barrel-jumping, dog-sled races, ice-canoe races, folk dancing, strolling makeup artists and clowns. This is Montreal's answer to Quebec City's Carnaval.

Information

Festivals of all kind abound in Montreal – including art, music, film, theatre, sports and traditional dance – demonstrating the city's truly international character. The main season for celebration is May to September. The Calendar of Events, available at information centres in the city, is a detailed list of all festivals and celebrations. The main information office is located at 1010 rue Ste-Catherine Ouest, tel: 844-4056. Quebec City also has a good selection of festivals. Some of these, marked Quebec City, are included in the list below. The Société de Fêtes et Festivals de Québec publishes an extensive list of festivals in both places, tel: 252-3037, website: www.festivals.qc.ca

March
St Patrick's Day Parade held in Old Montreal

April
Théâtre du Monde

May
International Children's Theatre Festival of Quebec
International Festival of Young Cinema
La Super Enfant-Fête
La Tour des Enfants
Montreal Air Show
Montreal International Chinese Film Festival
Montreal International Mime Festival
Museum Day: open house at 16 of Montreal's museums
Sun Carnival
Super Motorcross Laurentide
Theatre Festival of the Americas

June
Air Canada Grand Prix: part of the Formula One world circuit
Antiques Bonaventure: the dealers descend
Beer Mondial: taste over 250 brands of beer from 25 countries
Benson & Hedges International Fireworks Competition
Carifête: festival of dance and music from the Caribbean
Festival du Nouveau Cinéma de Montréal: film buff's heaven
Festival Orford: music festival through August, Parc du Mont-Orford
Fringe Festival: theatre festival presenting new works by young artists from around the world
Jour de St-Jean-Baptiste: Quebec Province holiday on 24 June
Lachine Folklore Festival
La Classique Cycliste de Montréal
Le Tour de L'Ile de Montréal
Montreal Chamber Music Festival
Montreal International Music Competition
Worldwide Kite Rendez-vous

July
Drummondville World Folklore Festival
Festival d'été (Summer Festival), Quebec City
Festival Juste Pour Rire/Just for Laughs Festival

International Dragon Boat Race Festival
Lachine International Folklore Festival
Lanaudière International Festival: lots of classical music
Montreal International Jazz Festival: big names in concert halls plus free outdoor concerts and carnival atmosphere in the streets
Nuits d'Afrique

August
Du Maurier Open: international tennis competition
Lasalle Car Festival
Les Fêtes Gourmandes Internationales de Montréal
Les FrancoFolies de Montréal: a celebration of francophone songs
Les Medievales de Québec: Medieval costume festival every other year in Quebec City
Montreal World Film Festival
Rock Sans Frontières
Hot Air Balloon Festival, St-Jean-sur-Richelieu
World Footbag Championship: the "Hacky sack" competition

September
Festival Internationale de Nouvelle Dance: in odd-numbered years only
Marathon de L'Ile de Montréal
Montreal International Marathon: 42-km (26-mile) run for both professionals and amateurs
Montreal International Rock Festival
Montreal International Music Festival: classical music gets its turn
Festival des couleurs (Autumn Festival), Mont Ste-Anne

October
Autumn Moon Festival: in Chinatown near the beginning of month
Black and Blue Weekend
International Festival of New Cinema and Media
International Scientific Film Festival
Montreal New Music Festival

November/December
As the cold weather sets in, social activities grow fewer, except for a brief flurry of festivities around Christmastime.

Shopping

Montreal, Canada's fashion capital, offers a vast number of boutiques and department stores selling fashionable clothes, gourmet food, handicraft objects, Inuit art, antiques and collectibles. With its weekly auctions, antique dealers and fur salons, Montreal is a place where you really can shop 'till you drop.

Montreal Shopping Areas

Avenue Laurier. Located in Outremont, a posh French district on the northern slope of Mont-Royal, the merchants here have a reputation for importing and selling the very latest European trends in clothes, food (world renowned *pâtissier* Lenôtre of France opened its first North American store on Rue Laurier) and home fashions.
Boulevard St-Laurent. Also known as The Main, this artery between the mostly French districts of Eastern Montreal and the anglophone sectors of the west-end provides a sensory assault. From rue Viger northward, Chinese, Eastern Europeans, Greeks, Portuguese and Italians have carved niches. You'll find Polish grocers, high-fashion houses, Portuguese bakeries and furniture stores, all within a few blocks of each other. Not to be missed are institutions like the Montreal Pool Room with its steamés, and Schwartz's smoked meat sandwiches. Only a few Greek signs remain on blvd St-Laurent, the Greek community having since made its way to avenue du Parc and rue Jean-Talon. The Greeks have been replaced by Portuguese immigrants with their clothing and ceramics stores.

Montreal Department Stores

Holt Renfrew: 1300 rue Sherbrooke Ouest, tel: 842-5111. Fine fashion for men and women and designer clothes from Europe, Canada and the US.

La Baie: 585 rue Ste-Catherine Ouest, tel: 281-4422. The oldest "store" in Canada, a direct descendant of the Hudson's Bay Company – though today you'll find fancy clothing instead of furs.

Ogilvy: 1307 rue Ste-Catherine Ouest, tel: 842-7711. Elite merchandise ranging from home fashions to high fashion.

Little Italy. With its espresso cafés, *gelateria* (ice cream parlours) and *pasticeria* (pastry shops), this area huddles round Marché Jean-Talon, one of the lesser known attractions of Montreal, where saris, chadors and Mao shirts form a delightful tapestry. Wherever you hail from, you will have compatriots in Montreal.

Old Montreal. Handicrafts by Quebec artisans are for sale in the rue St-Paul boutiques of Old Montreal, in Le Rouet stores, at the Canadian Guild of Crafts on rue Peel and in Bonsecours Market. Rue Notre-Dame, east of rue Atwater, boasts antique dealers specializing in wondrous Victorian furniture and European goods. On Sunday, while others recover from Saturday night, bargain hunters flock to the clothes discounters along rue Notre-Dame east of rue McGill.

Place Ville-Marie. Right in the heart of downtown, this cruciform office tower contains a variety range of trendy boutiques on its bottom floors plus the excellent Movenpick restaurant.

Plaza St-Hubert. This slightly downtrodden area, stocked with inexpensive clothing and houshold items, is a favourite among the neighbouring Greek, Italian and Middle-Eastern families. It comes alive in the spring, when preparations are under way for the famous weddings these communities celebrate.

Rue Chabanel. If it's bargains you're looking for, shop right off the factory rack here west of outer St-Laurent. A row of six-storey buildings packed with everything you can imagine: jeans, bathing suits, lingerie, sweaters, and more! On Saturday morning, regulars (often the women who work in these modern-day sweatshops) go through these floors like nobody's business. Newcomers just gawk and zigzag through this unique shopping experience.

Rue de la Gauchetière. Chinese and Asian markets are concentrated here, among bright red and yellow signs. It's a pleasure to see whole families buying their weekly groceries on Sunday after the traditional Cantonese Dim Sum buffet in one of the local eateries.

Rue St-Denis. With cafés and restaurant terraces spilling on to the sidewalk, the lower section of this street is known as the Quartier Latin for its student population. But upper St-Denis has gone from late granola to early avant-garde, and is now venturing into design and decoration, offering shoppers beautiful things for the home. Not to be missed is Arthur Quentin and, for coffee lovers, La Brûlerie. This is where the city's French middle- and upper-class come to buy their beautiful clothes and outfit their handsome apartments.

Rue Ste-Catherine. Montrealers and tourists alike window-hop with characteristic verve here, where musing and browsing extends way past store hours and into the wee hours of the night. Watch for the up-and-coming fashions of the moment in the dramatic store windows here.

Rue Sherbrooke. There are scores of art galleries in the Victorian row houses of what used to be called the Golden Square Mile, an exclusive area on the south slope of Mont Royal where the business tycoons of the Victorian era built expansive villas, many of which still stand.

Montreal's Markets and Malls

Atwater Market: 138 rue Atwater, tel: 937-7754. Very lively on weekends, this market features specialty foods. Over 60 farm producers sell fresh fruit and vegetables.

Bonsecours Market: 350 rue St-Paul Est, tel: 872-7330. Bustling market, boutiques and temporary exhibitions. Good café and deli in the basement.

Complexe Desjardins: 4 Complexe Desjardins, tel: 281-1870. Offering a huge number of boutiques, bars, and cinemas, this underground shopping centre is decorated with fountains, trees and waterfalls.

Faubourg Ste-Catherine: 1610 rue Ste-Catherine Ouest, tel: 939-3663. Reminiscent of New York's Fulton Market and Boston's Quincy Market, this shopping spot features fruit, vegetable and import stands, *pâtisseries*, *charcuteries* and an

Quebec City Shopping Areas

Lower Town (Vieux-Québec): a mixture of souvenir shops and interesting galleries. Head for rue St-Paul for antiques, and the Quartier Petit-Champlain (just off Place Royale) for boutiques.

Grand Allée: This, the main artery that brings you into the Upper Old Town, is well known for two things: chic shopping and very French cafés.

Rue St-Jean: Just west of the Upper Town, this is the largely undiscovered area where rows of *chocolatiers*, gourmet food shops and clothing shops compete for the attention of locals. As tourists don't know of it, prices are fairer.

array of restaurants and snack bars.

Jean-Talon Market: 7075 rue Casgrain, tel: 937-7754. In "Little Italy" and bordered by cheese counters, fishmongers and butchers shops. Has 100-plus farm producers.

Maisonneuve Market: 4445 rue Ontario Est, tel: 937-7754. Outdoor market open May to October.

Place Bonaventure, 900 rue de la Gauchetière, tel: 397-2222. Includes 135 shops with merchandise from all over the world. Restaurants, cinemas, banks, a Post Office and a supermarket are all located within this downtown shopping concourse.

Place Montreal Trust: avenue McGill College /rue Ste-Catherine, tel: 843-8000. Five levels of boutiques and services. plus direct access to the Métro. This is one of downtown's most poular indoor shopping malls, with its own food court.

St-Jacques Market: rue Amherst and rue Ontario, tel: 937-7754. Open year-round, it offers fruit and vegetable stands in spring and summer and flowers and plants in the fall and winter.

Sport

Participant

Outdoor sports of every kind are very popular in every season and there are many excellent facilities on offer. Information about all local facilities on offer in the Montreal area can be obtained from Access Montreal, tel: 872-1111 or 872-2237 (24 hours).

For Quebec City contact the Tourist Information Office (tel: 649-2608) or the Bureau of Parks and Recreation (tel: 691-6284).

BOATING

École de Voile de Lachine, 2105 blvd St-Joseph, Lachine (west of Montreal), tel: 634-4326. Private or group lessons, approved by the Quebec Sailing Federation. It also rents light sail boats and windsurfers.

Parc Nautique du Cap-Rouge, 4155 chemin de la Plage Jacques-Cartier, Cap-Rouge (west of Quebec City on the St Lawrence), tel: 650-770. Boats can be rented.

FISHING

There are numerous lakes and rivers around Montreal that provide great fishing spots. For specific suggestions, call the Ministère de l'Environnement et Faune (Ministry of Environment and Wildlife) for day-trip ideas, tel: 24–48 hours ahead at 873-3636.

Réserve Faunique des Laurentides is a wildlife reserve with good lakes for fishing approximately 48 km (30 miles) north of Quebec City. Reserve 48 hours ahead, tel: (418) 890-6527.

GOLF

There are many golf courses in Montreal and Quebec City and their surrounding region. The following courses are open to non-members (note that tee-time reservations are often required three days in advance):

Montreal

Brossard Municipal Golf Course, 4705 rue Lapinière. Brossard, autoroute 10 Est, Exit 9, tel: (450) 923-7035.

Fresh Meadows Golf Club, 505 Elm Avenue, Beaconsfield, tel: 697-4036. Nine holes.

Golf Dorval, 2000 rue Reverchon, Dorval and 1455 avenue Cardinal, tel: 631-4653 (both). Reservations needed on weekends, 36 holes.

Golf Municipal de Montréal, Entrance at Viau, north of Sherbrooke, tel: 872-4653. Nine short (par 3) holes, accessible by Métro. Reservations necessary 24 hours in advance.

Quebec City

Club de Golf Saint-Laurent, 758 chemin Royal, Saint-Laurent-de-l'Île d'Orléans on Ile d'Orléans,

Skiing

Cross-country skiing is popular in many parks. The Botanical Garden has a winter trail that is very scenic. Downhill skiing is also available around Montreal. Beginners flock to Mont-Royal, Hirondelles and Ignace-Bourget parks. Experts have unlimited opportunities less than an hour away in the Laurentians or in Estrie. For more details, tel: 872-1111.

In Quebec City, the winter-only HiverExpress bus runs to a number of cross-country skiing centres just outside the city. Within the city, the Plains of Abrham are the most popular area, with plenty of facilities (but not rentals). Contact Domaine Maizerets at 691-2385 for rental information.

tel: 829-2244. Reservations necessary; 18 holes.

Cub de Golf Royal Charbourg, 2180 chemin de la Grande-Ligne, Charlesbourg via Route 73, tel: 841-3000. Reservations necessary, 18 holes.

Club de Golf Albatros, 1418 route de l'Aéroport, Sainte-Foy, tel: 871-1818. Reservations necessary, 18 holes.

HORSEBACK RIDING

For information, contact Québec à Cheval, tel: 252-3002, or the Fédération Equestre du Québec, tel: 252-3053.

JOGGING

Joggers can run in any of either city's parks; Parc du Mont-Royal is splendid for its view over Montreal.

RAFTING

Several companies run excursions:

In the Montreal area
Lachine Rapid Tours Inc., 511 Succursale Champlain, Lasalle, H8P 3J4, tel: 767-2230.
New World River Expeditions, 100 Rouge River, Calumet (90 minutes northwest of Montreal), tel: 1-800-361-5033.

In the Quebec City area
Les Excursions Jacques-Cartier, 978 avenue Jacques-Cariter Nord, Stoneham-et-Tewkesbury (20 minutes north of the city), tel: 848-7238.
Villlages Vacances Valcartier, 1860 blvd Valcartier, St-Gabriel-de-Valcartier, tel: 844-2200.

SWIMMING

There are many indoor and outdoor pools in Montreal open to the public. Listed below are a few of the possibilities:

Skating

Outdoor skating rinks are abundant in Montreal, and there are at least 21 indoor rinks. Ile-Notre-Dame has one of the largest rinks – it is 1.6 km (1 mile) long.

In Quebec City, there are even more choices – including outdoor rinks at Place d'Youville, Domaine Maizerets on boulevard Montmorency, and the skating lane on Dufferin Terrace overlooking the St Lawrence River and the Frontenac, as well as an indoor rink at the City University in Ste-Foy. Most rent skates on-site.

Cégep du Vieux-Montréal (indoor), 255 Rue Ontario Est, tel: 982-3457.
Centre Claude Robillard (indoor), 1000 Rue Emile-Journault, tel: 872-6905
Université de Montréal (indoor), 2100 Blvd Edouard-Montpetit, tel: 343-6150.
John Abbott College (indoor), 21275 Lakeshore Rd, St-Anne de Bellevue, tel: 457-6610, ext. 325.
Olympic Park (indoor), 4141 Avenue du Pierre de Coubertin, tel: 252-4622.
Ile-Sainte-Hélène (outdoor), tel: 872-6093.
For more locations tel: 872-1111.

In Quebec City, the City University pool in Ste-Foy, tel: 656-7377 and the YWCA pool at 865 avenue Holland, tel: 683-2155 – both indoors – are the best bets. There are also two lakes in Ste-Foy on rue Laberge, tel: 654-4641.

TENNIS

Public tennis courts in Montreal are available for hire in Somerled, Lafontaine, Jeanne-Mance and Kent parks. For information and more locations, tel: 872-6211. In Quebec City, Tennisport at 6280 blvd Hamel, Ancienne Lorette has tennis, squash, racquetball and badminton courts. Tel: 872-0111.

Spectator

AUTO RACING

The Air Canada Grand Prix du Canada is part of the world circuit of Formula One racing. The event is held in June in Montreal at Gilles Villeneuve Track, on Ile-Notre-Dame, tel: 350-4731.

BASEBALL

The Montreal Expos presently play at Olympic Stadium, 4141 avenue Pierre de Coubertin, though this may change in the near future. Tel: 253-3434 for information, 790-1245 for tickets. From outside Montreal, tel: 1-800-361-4595, website: www.montrealexpos.com. Admission for adults is $7–28, for children $5–26.

A new Quebec City minor-league baseball team, Les Capitales, plays at 100 rue du Cardinal Maurice-Roy (tickets $5–$12) during the summer.

CANADIAN FOOTBALL

The semi-pro Alouettes play in the Olympic Park stadium from July to November. For more information, tel: 254-2400.

HARNESS RACING

The Hippodrome de Montréal Racetrack at 7440 blvd Decarie hosts major trotting events. The Prix de l'Avenir and the Blue Bonnets Amble are two of the more important. Open Monday, Wednesday, Friday and Saturday at 7.30pm, Sunday from 1.30pm, closed Tuesday and Thursday. Admission for the clubhouse and the stands is $4. For more details, tel: 739-2741.

In Quebec City, there is also a year-round harness racing track called the Hippodrome, on boulevard Wilfrid-Hamel ExpoCité. Races take place each day except Wednesday.

SOCCER

The Montreal Impact Soccer Club was formed in 1993. Games are held on Wednesday and Friday at the Claude Robillard Centre, 100 rue Emile-Journault. The season runs from mid-May to early October. Admission is $8 for adults, $4 for children under 12. Season tickets are $107–205. For information, tel: 328-3668.

TENNIS

The Du Maurier Open at Jarry Park in Montreal attracts the world's best players. Usually held in August. For tickets and information, tel: 273-1515.

Hockey

The legendary Montreal Canadiens have moved from the old Forum to the new Molson Centre. For tours of the new arena tel: 932-2582, for tickets tel: 790-1245; website: www.reseauadmission.com

Language

General

Even if you speak no French at all it is worth trying to master a few simple phrases. The fact that you have made an effort is likely to get you a better response. Pronunciation is key; they really will not understand if you get it very wrong. Remember to emphasise each syllable, not to pronounce the last consonant of a word as a rule (this includes the plural "s") and always to drop your "h"s. Whether to use "vous" or "tu" is a vexed question; increasingly the familiar form of "tu" is used by many people. However, it is better to be too formal, and use "vous" if in doubt. It is very important to be polite; always address people as Madame or Monsieur, and address them by their surnames until you are confident first names are acceptable.

Learning the pronunciation of the French alphabet is a good idea and, in particular, learn how to spell out your name in the French alphabet.

Montreal claims to be the second-largest French-speaking city in the world, after Paris. Some 65 percent of the city's residents and 70 percent of those in the metropolitan area are French-speakers (francophones), with 12 percent and 15 percent English-speakers (anglophones), respectively. Despite nationalistic insistence, the province's French has never been pure. After 300 years of separation from the motherland, how could it be? Québécois and French visitors struggle to find words in common. Over the past decades, as Montrealers acknowledge

differences and gain confidence, this is amusing rather than disconcerting.

Unique to Montreal is *joual*, a *patois* whose name is garbled French for horse: cheval. The earthy dialect flourishes among the city's working class and in the work of playwright Michel Tremblay.

Pronunciation of mainstream French also differs. Accents distinguish French in Quebec from French in Paris or Marseilles. Quebec's francophones form sounds deep in the throat, lisp slightly, voice toward diphthongs, and bend single vowels into exotic shapes. It has also incorporated some English words, such as *chum*, as *in mon chum*, or *ma chumme*, and *blonde*, for girlfriend, while *le fun* is a good time.

Even if you don't speak much French, starting a conversation with 'Bonjour,' is likely to evoke a positive response. Indeed, some shopkeepers in Montreal hedge, with an all-purpose: 'Hi-bonjour.'

In Quebec City fewer people speak English.

French Words and Phrases

How much is it? *C'est combien?*
What is your name? *Comment vous appelez-vous?*
My name is… *Je m'appelle…*
Do you speak English? *Parlez-vous anglais?*
I am English/American *Je suis anglais(e)/américain(e)*
I don't understand *Je ne comprends pas*
Please speak more slowly? *Parlez plus lentement, s'il vous plaît?*
Can you help me? *Pouvez-vous m'aider?*
I'm looking for… *Je cherche*
Where is…? *Où est…?*
I'm sorry *Excusez-moi/Pardon*
I don't know *Je ne sais pas*
No problem *Pas de problème*
Have a good day! *Bonne journée!*
That's it *C'est ça*
Here it is *Voici*
There it is *Voilà*
Let's go *On y va. Allons-y*
See you tomorrow *A demain*
See you soon *A bientôt*

Show me the word in the book *Montrez-moi le mot dans le livre*
At what time? *A quelle heure?*
When? *Quand?*
What time is it? *Quelle heure est-il?*
Note. The *Québécois* sometimes use the 24-hour clock.
yes *oui*
no *non*
please *s'il vous plaît*
thank you *merci*
(very much) *(beaucoup)*
you're welcome *de rien*
excuse me *excusez-moi*
hello *bonjour*
OK *d'accord*
goodbye *au revoir*
good evening *bonsoir*
here *ici*
there *là*
today *aujourd'hui*
yesterday *hier*
tomorrow *demain*
now *maintenant*
later *plus tard*
right away *tout de suite*
this morning *ce matin*
this afternoon *cet après-midi*
this evening *ce soir*

On Arrival

I want to get off at... *Je voudrais descendre à...*
Is there a bus to the museum? *Est-ce qu'il ya un bus pour la musée?*
What street is this? *A quelle rue sommes-nous?*

Emergencies

Help! *Au secours!*
Stop! *Arrêtez!*
Call a doctor *Appelez un médecin*
Call an ambulance *Appelez une ambulance*
Call the police *Appelez la police*
Call the fire brigade *Appelez les pompiers*
Where is the nearest telephone? *Où est le téléphone le plus proche?*
Where is the nearest hospital? *Où est l'hôpital le plus proche?*
I am sick *Je suis malade*
I have lost my passport/purse *j'ai perdu mon passeport/porte-monnaie*

Which line do I take for...? *Quelle ligne dois-je prendre pour...?*
How far is...? *A quelle distance se trouve...?*
Validate your ticket *Compostez votre billet*
airport *l'aéroport*
train station *la gare*
bus station *la gare routière*
Métro stop *la station de Métro*
bus *l'autobus, le car*
bus stop *l'arrêt*
platform *le quai*
ticket *le billet*
return ticket *aller-retour*
hitchhiking *l'autostop*
toilets *les toilettes*
This is the hotel address *C'est l'adresse de l'hôtel*
I'd like a (single/double) room... *Je voudrais une chambre (pour une/deux personnes)...*
...with shower *avec douche*
...with bath *avec salle de bain*
...with a view *avec vue*
Does the price include breakfast? *Le prix comprend-il le petit déjeuner?*
May I see the room? *Je peux voir la chambre?*
washbasin *le lavabo*
bed *le lit*
key *la clé*
elevator *l'ascenseur*
air conditioned *climatisé*

On the telephone

How do I make an outside call? *Comment est-ce que je peux téléphoner à l'exterieur?*
I want to make an international call *Je voudrais une communication pour l'étranger*
local call *une communication locale*
dialling code *l'indicatif*
I'd like an alarm call for 8 tomorrow morning *Je voudrais être réveillé a 8 heures demain matin*
Who's calling? *C'est qui à l'appareil?*
Hold on, please *Ne quittez pas s'il vous plaît*
The line is busy *La ligne est occupée*
I must have dialled the wrong number *J'ai dû faire un faux numéro*

Shopping

Where is the nearest bank (post office)? *Où est la banque/ Poste/PTT la plus proche?*
I'd like to buy *Je voudrais acheter*
How much is it? *C'est combien?*
Do you take credit cards? *Est-ce que vous acceptez les cartes de crédit?*
I'm just looking *Je regarde seulement*
Have you got? *Avez-vous...?*
I'll take it *Je le prends*
I'll take this one/that one *Je prends celui-ci/celui-là*
What size is it? *C'est de quelle taille?*
Anything else? *Avec ça?*
size (clothes) *la taille*
size (shoes) *la pointure*
cheap *bon marché*
expensive *cher*
enough *assez*
too much *trop*
a piece *un morceau de*
each *la pièce (eg ananas, 15F la pièce)*
bill *la note*
chemist *la pharmacie*
bakery *la boulangerie*
bookshop *la librairie*
library *la bibliothèque*
department store *le grand magasin*
delicatessen *la charcuterie/le traiteur*
fishmonger's *la poissonerie*
grocery *l'alimentation/l'épicerie*
tobacconist *tabac (also sells stamps and newspapers)*
market *le marché*
supermarket *le supermarché*
junk shop *la brocante*

On the Road

Where is the spare wheel? *Où est la roue de secours?*
Where is the nearest garage? *Où est le garage le plus proche?*
Our car has broken down *Notre voiture est en panne*
I want to have my car repaired *Je veux faire réparer ma voiture*
It's not your right of way *Vous n'avez pas la priorité*

Sightseeing

town *la ville*
old town *la vieille ville*
cathedral *la cathédrale*
church *l'église*
mansion *l'hôtel*
hospital *l'hôpital*
town hall *l'hôtel de ville/la mairie*
nave *la nef*
stained glass *le vitrail*
staircase *l'escalier*
tower *la tour*
walk *le tour*
museum *le musée*
art gallery *la galerie*
exhibition *l'exposition*
swimming pool *la piscine*
to book *réserver*
tourist information office *l'office du tourisme*
free *gratuit*
open *ouvert*
closed *fermé*
every day *tous les jours*
all year *toute l'année*
all day *toute la journée*

I think I must have put diesel in the car by mistake *Je crois que j'ai mis le gazole dans la voiture par erreur*
the road to... *la route pour...*
left *gauche*
right *droite*
straight on *tout droit*
far *loin*
near *près d'ici*
opposite *en face*
beside *à côté de*
car park *le parking*
over there *là-bas*
at the end *au bout*
on foot *à pied*
by car *en voiture*
town map *le plan*
road map *la carte*
street *la rue*
square *la place*
give way *céder le passage*
dead end *impasse*
no parking *stationnement interdit*
motorway *l'autoroute*
toll *le péage*
speed limit *la limitation de vitesse*
petrol *l'essence*
unleaded *sans plomb*

diesel *le gazole*
water/oil *l'eau/l'huile*
puncture *un pneu crevé*
bulb *l'ampoule*
wipers *les essuies-glace*

Dining Out

Note: *Garçon* is the word for waiter but never used directly; say *Monsieur* or *Madame* to attract their attention.

Table d'hôte (the "host's table") is one set menu served at a set price. **Prix fixé** is a fixed price menu. **A la carte** means dishes from the menu are charged separately.
breakfast *le petit déjeuner*
lunch *le déjeuner*
dinner *le dîner*
meal *le repas*
first course *l'entrée/les hors d'oeuvre*
main course *le plat principal*
made to order *sur commande*
drink included *boisson compris*
wine list *la carte des vins*
the bill *l'addition*
fork *la fourchette*
knife *le couteau*
spoon *la cuillère*
plate *l'assiette*
glass *le verre*
napkin *la serviette*
ashtray *le cendrier*
I am a vegetarian *Je suis végétarien(ne)*
What do you recommend? *Qu'est-ce que vous recommandez?*
Do you have local specialities? *Avez-vous des spécialités locales?*
I'd like to order *Je voudrais commander*
Is service included? *Est-ce que le service est compris?*

BREAKFAST AND SNACKS

baguette **long thin loaf**
pain **bread**
petits pains **rolls**
beurre **butter**
poivre **pepper**
sel **salt**
sucre **sugar**
confiture **jam**
miel **honey**

oeufs **eggs**
...à la coque **boiled eggs**
...au bacon **bacon and eggs**
...au jambon **ham and eggs**
...sur le plat **fried eggs**
...brouillés **scrambled eggs**
tartine **bread with butter**
yaourt **yoghurt**
crêpe **pancake**
croque-monsieur **ham and cheese toasted sandwich**
croque-madame... **with a fried egg on top**
galette **type of pancake**
pan bagna **bread roll stuffed with salade Niçoise**

FIRST COURSE

An *amuse-bouche, amuse-gueule* or appetizer is something to "amuse the mouth", served before the first course
anchoiade **sauce of olive oil, anchovies and garlic, served with raw vegetables**
assiette anglaise **cold meats**
potage **soup**
rillettes **rich fatty paste of shredded duck, rabbit or pork**
tapenade **spread of olives and anchovies**
pissaladière **Provençal pizza with onions, olives and anchovies**

MAIN COURSE

la Viande Meat
bleu **rare**
à point **medium**
bien cuit **well done**
grillé **grilled**
agneau **lamb**
andouille/andouillette **tripe sausage**
bifteck **steak**
boudin **sausage**
boudin noir **black pudding**
boudin blanc **white pudding (chicken or veal)**
blanquette **stew of veal, lamb or chicken with creamy egg sauce**
boeuf à la mode **beef in red wine with carrots, onions and mushrooms**
à la bordelaise **beef with red wine and shallots**

à la Bourguignonne **cooked in red wine, onions and mushrooms**
brochette **kebab**
caille **quail**
canard **duck**
carbonnade **casserole of beef, beer and onions**
carré d'agneau **rack of lamb**
cassoulet **stew of beans, sausages, pork and duck, from southwest France**
cervelle **brains (food)**
chateaubriand **thick steak**
choucroute **Alsace dish of sauerkraut, bacon and sausages**
confit **duck or goose preserved in its own fat**
contre-filet **cut of sirloin steak**
coq au vin **chicken in red wine**
côte d'agneau **lamb chop**
daube **beef stew with red wine, onions and tomatoes**
dinde **turkey**
entrecôte **beef rib steak**
escargot **snail**
faisan **pheasant**
farci **stuffed**
faux-filet **sirloin**
feuilleté **puff pastry**
foie **liver**
foie de veau **calf's liver**
foie gras **goose or duck liver pâté**
gardiane **rich beef stew with olives and garlic, from the Camargue**
cuisses de grenouille **frog's legs**
grillade **grilled meat**
hachis **minced meat**
jambon **ham**
langue **tongue**
lapin **rabbit**
lardon **small pieces of bacon, often added to salads**
magret de canard **breast of duck**
médaillon **round piece of meat**
moelle **beef bone marrow**
navarin d'agneau **stew of lamb with onions, carrots and turnips**
oie **goose**
perdrix **partridge**
petit-gris **small snail**
pieds de cochon **pig's trotters**
pintade **guinea fowl**
pipérade **Basque dish of eggs, ham, peppers, onion**
porc **pork**
pot-au-feu **casserole of beef and vegetables**
poulet **chicken**
poussin **young chicken**

rognons **kidneys**
rôti **roast**
sanglier **wild boar**
saucisse **fresh sausage**
saucisson **salami**
veau **veal**

Poissons Fish

Amoricaine **made with white wine, tomatoes, butter and cognac**
anchois **anchovies**
anguille **eel**
bar (or loup) **sea bass**
barbue **brill**
belon **Brittany oyster**
bigorneau **sea snail**
Bercy **sauce of fish stock, butter, white wine and shallots**
bouillabaisse **fish soup, served with grated cheese, garlic croutons and** *rouille,* **a spicy sauce**
brandade **salt cod purée**
cabillaud **cod**
calmars **squid**
colin **hake**
coquillage **shellfish**
coquilles Saint-Jacques **scallops**
crevette **shrimp**
daurade **sea bream**
flétan **halibut**
fruits de mer **seafood**
hareng **herring**
homard **lobster**
huître **oyster**
langoustine **large prawn**
limande **lemon sole**
lotte **monkfish**
morue **salt cod**
moule **mussel**
moules marinières **mussels in white wine and onions**
oursin **sea urchin**
raie **skate**
saumon **salmon**
thon **tuna**
truite **trout**

Légumes Vegetables

ail **garlic**
artichaut **artichoke**
asperge **asparagus**
aubergine **eggplant**
avocat **avocado**
bolets **boletus mushrooms**
céleri **grated celery**
rémoulade **with mayonnaise**
champignon **mushroom**
cèpes **boletus mushroom**
chanterelle **wild mushroom**

drinks/les boissons
coffee *café*
...with milk/cream *au lait/crème*
...decaffeinated *déca/décaféiné*
...black espresso *express/noir*
...American filtered coffee *filtre*
tea *thé*
...herb infusion *tisane*
...camomile *verveine*
hot chocolate *chocolat chaud*
milk *lait*
mineral water *eau minérale*
fizzy *gazeux*
non-fizzy *non-gazeux*
fizzy lemonade *limonade*
fresh lemon juice served with sugar *citron pressé*
fresh squeezed orange juice *orange pressée*
full (eg full cream milk) *entier*
fresh or cold *frais, fraîche*
beer *bière*
...bottled *en bouteille*
...on tap *à la pression*
pre-dinner drink *apéritif*
aniseed-flavoured apéritif *pastis*
white wine with cassis (blackcurrant liqueur) *kir*
kir **with champagne** *kir royal*
with ice *avec des glaçons*
neat/dry *sec*
red *rouge*
white *blanc*
rose *rosé*
dry *brut*
sweet *doux*
sparkling wine *crémant*
house wine *vin de maison*
local wine *vin de pays*
Where is this wine from? *De quelle région vient ce vin?*
pitcher *carafe/pichet*
...of water/wine *d'eau/de vin*
half litre *demi-carafe*
quarter litre *quart*
mixed *panaché*
after dinner drink *digestif*
brandy from Armagnac region of France *Armagnac*
Normandy apple brandy *calvados*
cheers! *santé!*
May I have more wine? *Encore du vin, s'il vous plaît?*
hangover *gueule de bois*

cornichon **gherkin**
courgette **zucchini**
chips **potato crisps**
chou **cabbage**
chou-fleur **cauliflower**
concombre **cucumber**
cru **raw**
crudités **raw vegetables**
épinard **spinach**
frites **chips, French fries**
gratin dauphinois **sliced potatoes baked with cream**
haricot **dried bean**
haricots verts **green beans**
lentilles **lentils**
maïs **corn**
mange-tout **snow pea**
mesclun **mixed leaf salad**
navet **turnip**
noix **nut, walnut**
noisette **hazelnut**
oignon **onion**
panais **parsnip**
persil **parsley**
pignon **pine nut**
poireau **leek**
pois **pea**
poivron **bell pepper**
pomme de terre **potato**
pommes frites **chips, French fries**
primeurs **early fruit and vegetables**
radis **radish**
roquette **arugula, rocket**
ratatouille **Provençal vegetable stew of aubergines, courgettes, tomatoes and peppers**
riz **rice**
salade Niçoise **egg, tuna, olives, onions and tomato salad**
salade verte **green salad**
truffe **truffle**

Fruit Fruit

ananas **pineapple**
cerise **cherry**
citron **lemon**
citron vert **lime**
figue **fig**
fraise **strawberry**
framboise **raspberry**
groseille **redcurrant**
mangue **mango**
mirabelle **yellow plum**
pamplemousse **grapefruit**
pêche **peach**
poire **pear**
pomme **apple**
raisin **grape**

prune **plum**
reine claude **greengage**

Sauces Sauces

aioli **garlic mayonnaise**
bearnaise **sauce of egg, butter, wine and herbs**
forestière **with mushrooms and bacon**
hollandaise **egg, butter and lemon sauce**
lyonnaise **with onions**
meunière **fried fish with butter, lemon and parsley sauce**
meurette **red wine sauce**
Mornay **sauce of cream, egg and cheese**
Parmentier **served with potatoes**
paysan **rustic style; ingredients depend on the region**
pistou **Provençal sauce of basil, garlic and olive oil; vegetable soup with the sauce**
provençale **sauce of tomatoes, garlic and olive oil**
papillotte **cooked in paper**

Pudding Dessert

Belle Hélène **fruit with ice cream and chocolate sauce**
clafoutis **baked pudding of batter and cherries**
coulis **purée of fruit or vegetables**
gâteau **cake**
Ile flottante **whisked eggs whites in custard sauce**
crème anglaise **custard**
pêche melba **peaches with ice cream and raspberry sauce**
tarte tatin **upside down tart of caramelised apples**
crème caramel **caramelised egg custard**
crème Chantilly **whipped cream**
fromage **cheese**

Days, Months & Seasons

Days of the week and months are not capitalised in French. Dates are indicated thus: "10 juin" or "le 10 jn" (in writing), "le dixième juin" (in speech).

Monday	lundi
Tuesday	mardi
Wednesday	mercredi
Thursday	jeudi
Friday	vendredi
Saturday	samedi
Sunday	dimanche
spring	le printemps
summer	l'été
autumn	l'automne
winter	l'hiver
January	janvier
February	fevrier
March	mars
April	avril
May	mai
June	juin
July	juillet
August	aôut
September	septembre
October	octobre
November	novembre
December	decembre

Numbers

0	zéro
1	un, une
2	deux
3	trois
4	quatre
5	cinq
6	six
7	sept
8	huit
9	neuf
10	dix
11	onze
12	douze
13	treize
14	quatorze
15	quinze
16	seize
17	dix-sept
18	dix-huit
19	dix-neuf
20	vingt
21	vingt-et-un
30	trente
40	quarante
50	cinquante
60	soixante
70	soixante-dix
80	quatre-vingt
90	quatre-vingt-dix
100	cent
1000	mille
1,000,000	un million

Note: The number 1 is often written like an upside down V, and the number 7 is crossed.

Further Reading

Leonard Cohen: Best known for his songwriting, Montreal native Cohen also produced a number of books of poetry and fiction during the 1960s while travelling in Beat-writer circles. Works of his still in print include *Beautiful Losers* (Vintage, 1993), a novel of Montreal and Canadian history that is both disturbing in its portrayal of sexual relations and fascinating for its keen insight into the triangular forces (French, Anglo and Native) that have shaped the city; *Stranger Music: Selected Poems and Songs* (Vintage 1994), collected poetry and song lyrics from the apex of Cohen's career; and *The Favourite Game* (McClelland & Stewart, 1997), a reissue of Cohen's largely autobiographical novel of 1960s, flower power-era Montreal.

Mordecai Richler: This crusty Jewish Montrealer has written dozens of works, everything from children's books to essays to collected newspaper columns to bitingly sarcastic novels. His eye for detailing the hypocracies of Montreal – old and new – is unsurpassed.

Richler's best-known books include *The Apprenticeship of Duddy Kravitz* (Washington Square Press, 1999) about an ambitious, amoral young Jew's ups and downs; *Barney's Version* (Washington Square Press, 1999), a novel of memories and insults from an aging Montreal writer who may or may not have committed a murder – a virtual treatise on hockey, separatists, vegetarians, and the city's old Anglo guard; *Solomon Gursky Was Here* (out of print), about a Jewish bootlegger's family legacy; and *Oh Canada! Oh Quebec!* (out of print), a collection of essays about the schizophrenic Canadian identity taking dead aim at the Quebec separatist movement once again.

Kirk Johnson & David Widgington, *Montreal Up Close* (Cumulus Press, 1998). Thorough walk-through of the city's major architectural and historical sites.

Paul-André Linteau, René Durocher & Jean-Claude Robert, *Quebec: A History* (Jasme Lorimer & Co., 1983). General history of the province, emphasising statistical changes in the evolution of Montreal and Quebec City.

Hugh MacLennan, *The Two Solitudes* (Fitzhenry & Whiteside Ltd, 1997). Novel/love story about a Québécois priest and industrialist battling each other against a backdrop of Anglo-French hatred.

Jean-Claude Marsan, *Montreal in Evolution* (McGill-Queen's University Press, 1990). Decent account of city history, focussing largely on architecture, by the director of the University of Montreal's architecture department.

Kenneth McNaught, *The Penguin History of Canada* (Penguin USA, 1991). Typically comprehensive history of a nation from formation to modern political struggle.

Brian Moore, *Black Robe: A Novel* (Plume, 1997). Sometimes-disturbing novel of a French Jesuit priest's travels in northern Quebec and the brutality he encounters among native peoples there.

Francis Parkman, *The Jesuits in North America* (Corner House Publishing, 1970). History includes background on the religious settlement of Quebec by French orders.

John Sobol, *Montreal Inside Out: A New View of the City* (ECW Press, 1992). Idiosyncratic tour of the city, painting broad overview of Montreal and visiting both well-known places and little-known corners along the way.

Yves Tessier, *An Historical Guide to Québec* (La Société historique de Québec, 1986). Excellent and accessible history of Quebec City, covering both historical events and significant sites.

Feedback

We do our best to ensure the information in our books is as accurate and up-to-date as possible. The books are updated on a regular basis, using local contacts, who painstakingly add, amend and correct as required. However, some mistakes and omissions are inevitable and we are ultimately reliant on our readers to put us in the picture.

We would welcome your feedback on any details related to your experiences using the book "on the road". Maybe we recommended a hotel that you liked (or another that you didn't), as well as interesting new attractions, or facts and figures you have found out about the country itself. The more details you can give us (particularly with regard to addresses, e-mails and telephone numbers), the better.

We will acknowledge all contributions, and we'll offer an Insight Guide to the best letters received. Please write to us at:

Insight Guides
APA Publications
PO Box 7910
London SE1 1WE
Or send e-mail to: **insight@apaguide.demon.co.uk**

Other Insight Guides

Other Insight Guides which highlight destinations in this region include *Insight Guide: Canada* and *Insight Guide: Vancouver.*

Also available are Insight Pocket Guides which provide itineraries devised by local hosts. These are accompanied by a handy pull-out map. Titles include *Insight Pocket Guide Montreal*, *Insight Pocket Guide Quebec* and Insight Pocket Guides to Toronto and British Columbia.

ART & PHOTO CREDITS

Picture Spreads

Index

Numbers in italics refer to photographs

a

Abbaye Cistercienne d'Oka (Laurentians) 228
Abénaquis, Musée des (Odanak) 240
Académie Querbes 199
Act of Union (1843) 44, 46
African Nights Festival *180*
Agouhanna 23
airports 54
Allan, Sir Hugh 48
Allen, Ethan 36
Alpinum 214–15
American occupation 35–6, 43, 247
Amherst, Lord Jeffrey 34
Ancien Bureau de Poste (Quebec City) *248*
anglophone community 67–8
Arcand, Denys 73
Archéologie et d'Histoire de la Pointe-à-Callière, Musée d' 146
architecture 51, 67, *152–3*
d'Arcy McGee, Thomas 43
Armes, Place d' 27, 134–5, 136, 137–8, 142
Art Contemporain, Musée d' 168–9
Artists Alley *146*
arts 173
Arts, Place des *168*
Associates 25
Astor, John Jacob 53
Atwater Avenue 157
Atwater Market *102*
avenues
  Atwater 157
  l'Esplanade *189*
  Greene 198
  Laurier 198
  McGill College 166
  du Musée 158–9
  Sunnyside 197
  Van Horne 198

b

Ballard, Harold 112
ballet 173
Bank of Commerce 141
Bank of Montreal 47, 137, 140, *141*
Banque Royale 141, *142*

baseball 212
Basilique Notre-Dame-de-Québec (Quebec City) 250
Basilique St-Patrick 170
Bassin Bonsecours 150
Bateau Mouche 150
Baxter Block 172
Beaubien family 195
Beauchemin, Yves 73
Beauharnois Generating Station (Montérégie) 237–8
Beaux-Arts, Musée des *158*
Beaver Hall Hill 38
beaver pelts 23, 33
Beebe Plain (Estrie) 232
Beliveau, Big Jean 110
Bellot, Dom Paul 231–2
Beloeil (Montérégie) 236
Belvedere Westmount 198
Benaiah Gibb Pavilion 158
Bibliothèque Nationale du Québec 181
Biodôme 213
Biosphère *208*, 216
Birks 167
BNP Building *57*
Boer War monument *161*
Bonsecours market *133*, *134*
Bonsecours, rue 130
Borgeau, Victor 139
Botanical Garden *213*, 213–15
Bouchard, Lucien 56, 92
boulangeries 100
The Boulevard 197
boulevard St-Laurent 52, 70, *85*, *169*, *171*, 171–2, 173
Bourassa, Robert 92
Bourgeoys, Marguerite 27, 30–31, 133
Bouthillier family 195
Brébeuf, Jean de *29*
brewery 38
British rule 34–9, 245
Brome (Estrie) *230*, 231
  County Historical Museum 229–30
Burns, Robert, statue 161

c

cafés 179
  Outremont 201
calèches 137, *196*
Calumet (Laurentians) 229
Calvet, Pierre du 130
Canada Cement Company 167
Canada, Place du *88*, 161
Canadian Railway Museum (St-Constant) 234

Carré Royal (Sorel) 238–9
Cartier, George-Etienne 48, 131
  monument *198*
Cartier, Jacques 21, *22*, 22–4, *23*
  monument 196
Casino de Montréal 216
Cassons, François Dollier de 28, 31, 33
Cathédrale Christ Church 167
Cathédrale Marie-Reine-du-Monde *152–3*, *162*
Cathédrale Ste-Trinité (Quebec City) 251
Cemetery (Mont-Royal) 196, 200
Centre de Commerce Mondial 142
Centre d'Histoire de Montréal 147
ceremonial gates (Chinatown) 170
Chambly, Captain Jacques 233
Champlain, Samuel de *24*
Champs-de-Bataille Parc (Quebec City) 253–4
Charest, Jean 56
Charlebois, Robert 73
Charlottetown 47
Chasse et de la Nature, Musée de la 196
Château Apartments 157
Château Frontenac (Quebec City) *244*, 247
Châteauguay, battle of 43
Château de Ramezay 28, 128–9, *129*
chemin de la Côte Ste-Catherine 198
Chinatown *87*, *169*, 170–71
Chinese Catholic Church 170
Chinese Garden 215
cholera epidemics 45
Chomedey, Paul de, Sieur de Maisonneuve 25–7, *26*, *124*
  statue 136
Chrétien, Jean 56, 92
Christ Church 167
chronology 18–19
ChuChai 102
churches and cathedrals 27–8
  Chinese Catholic Church 170
  Christ Church 167
  Erskine et Américaine *31*, 158, *159*
  du Gesù 169–70
  Marie-Reine-du-Monde *152–3*, *162*
  Notre-Dame Basilica *46*, 136, 138–9, *139*
  Notre-Dame-de-Bon-Secours 27, *131*, 131, 133, *152*
  Notre-Dame-de-Québec (Quebec City) 250

Notre-Dame-des-Neiges 196
Notre-Dame-des-Victoires
  (Quebec City) 248
St Andrew et St Paul 158
Ste-Brigide 186
St-George 163–4
St-Germain *200*
St-James 167–8
St Joseph's Oratory 200, 203–5
St-Patrick 170
St-Pierre Apôtre 186
St-Pierre-et-St-Paul 186
Ste-Trinité (Quebec City) 251
St-Viateur 200
Vieux Séminaire de St-Sulpice
  139–40, *140*
**Chûte-Montmorency Parc (Quebec
  City) 254**
Cinéma Parallèle 172
Cinémathèque Québécoise 177
Circuit Gilles-Villeneuve 216
Cirque du Soleil *68*
Civilisation Museum (Quebec City)
  249
climate 15
Closse, Lambert 137
clothing industry 104–5
Coeur du Quebec 238–40
Cohen, Leonard *144*
Colborne, Sir John 45
Colonial House 51
Comeau, Baie 92
Commune, rue de la 134
**Company of One Hundred
  Associates** 25
Complexe Desjardins 169
Complexe Guy-Favreau 170
Condor Needle 226
Contemporary Art Museum 168–9
**Côte de la Montagne (Quebec
  City)** 248
Coté, Michel 73
Côte St-Antoine 193–4
**Côte-Ste-Catherine Locks
  (Montérégie)** 235
**Côte-Ste-Catherine Park
  (Montérégie)** 235
**CPR (Canadian Pacific Railway)
  Bill** 48
crime 15, 45–6
Cross, James 54
Customs House 47, 146

d

**Dauversière, Jerome de la Royer de
  la** 25
David M. Stewart Museum 216
Dawson College 198

De La Salle House 28
Desjardins complex 169
Dickens, Charles 134
Dion, Céline 144
Dollier de Cassons, François de
  28, 31, 33
Dominion Square Building 164
Dorchester Square 161, *161*–4
Dorval airport 54
Downtown urban development 155
Drapeau, Jean 55, 209
Ducharme, Réjean 73
Dunlop, Alexandre 168
Duplessis, Maurice 58–9
Durham report 46

e

Ecomusée du Fier Monde 186
Ecurie d'Youville 148
Edifice Ernest-Cormier 128
Edifice Southam 170
Edifice Sun Life 161–2
Edward VII, statue 167
Eglise Erskine et Américaine *31*,
  158, *159*
Eglise du Gesù 169–70
**Eglise Notre-Dame-des-Victoires
  (Quebec City)** 248
Eglise St Andrew et St Paul 158
Eglise St-George 163–4
Eglise St-Germain *200*
Eglise St-James 167–8
Eglise St-Pierre Apôtre 186
Eglise St-Viateur 200
Ernest-Cormier building 128
Erskine et Américaine *31*, 158,
  159
Escalier Casse-Cou (Quebec City)
  248
Esplanade Avenue *189*
Estrie 223, 229–32
ethnic communities 65, 69–70,
  86–7
  Jewish community 69–70, 79–84
Excursion dans le Marais (Sorel)
  239
Expos *212*

f

Fenians 43
festivals
  African Nights Festival *180*
  Cirque du Soleil *68*
  Film Festival 138, 182
  Firework Festival *138*, 216
  Gay Parade *59*
  Jazz Festival 138, 183, *187*

  Just for Laughs Festival 138,
    185
  Mime Festival 173
  Montgolfières *223*
**F.G. Edwards Country Store (West
  Brome)** 231
filles du roi 27, 31
Film Festival 138, 182
Fine Arts Museum *158*
Firework Festival *138*, 216
First World War 52
flea market 150
**FLQ (Front de Libération du
  Québec)** 54
food and drink 41, 65, 69, 101–3
  boulangeries 100
  restaurants 184–5
**Forest Education Centre of the
  Laurentians** 226
Fort Chambly (Montérégie) 233
Fortin, Marc-Aurèle 148
**Fort Lennox National Historic Park
  (Montérégie)** 234
Francis I of France *21*, 22
francophone community 67–8
Franklin, Benjamin 36
Fraser, Simon 37
French Canadians 66, 95
French settlers 22–31, 40–41
Frobisher, Joseph 37, 38
fur trade 23, 33
Fur Trade Museum (Lachine) 237

g

gardens 213–15
Gare Windsor *163*
Gauchetière, rue de la 169
gay community 186
Gay Parade *59*
geodesic dome 216
Geoffrion, Bernie Boom Boom 110
geology 21
Gesù 169–70
Golden Square Mile 157, 158–9
Granche, Pierre 169
Grande-Allée (Quebec City) 252
Grandes-Piles 240
Great Fire 47
Greene Avenue 198
Grey Sisters 27
Griffintown 51
Guy-Favreau complex 170

h

habitants 28, 33, *34*, 40–41, *44–5*
harbour cruises 150
Harrington (Laurentians) 229

Hart, Cory 144
Haskell Free Library and Opera
   House (Rock Island) 232, *233*
Hassidic Jews 82
Hébert, Louis 137
Henry IV of France 24
history
   American occupation 35–6, 43,
      247
   British rule 34–9, 245
   chronology 18–19
   Fenians 43
   French settlers 22–31, 40–41
   Indians 22–8
   modern Montreal 51–6
   Quebec City 245, 247
   Quiet Revolution 53, 58–9
   War of 1812 43
Hôpital des Soeurs Grises 147–8
Hôtel du Parlement (Quebec City)
   252
hotels
   Marriott Château Champlain 163
   de Rasco 134
   Ritz-Carlton 157, *160*
   Windsor hotel 162
Hôtel de Ville *90*, *128*
Hôtel de Ville (Outremont) 199
Hôtel de Ville (Quebec City) 251
Hôtel de Ville (Westmount) 195
House of Wing 170
Hudson (Laurentians) 228, 229
Hudson's Bay Company 37
Hurtubise, Pierre 197
Hutchison, rue 198

i

ice hockey 107–13
Ice Storm *53*
Ile aux Fantômes (Sorel) 239
Ile d'Embarras (Sorel) 239
Ile Notre-Dame 215–16
Ile d'Orléans (Quebec City) 254
Ile Ste-Hélène 24, *54*, *206–7*, 215,
   216
Iles de Sorel (Coeur du Quebec)
   238, 239
Ille-aux-Noix (Montérégie) 234
IMAX theatre 150
independence movement *see*
   separatism
Indians 22–8
Insectarium 215
International Fireworks
   Competition 216
Irish 43
iSci Centre *148*, 150
Italian community 69, *87*

j

Jacques-Cartier, Place *127*, 134
Japanese Garden *214*, 215
Jardin Botanique 213–15
Jazz Festival 138, 183, *187*
Jean-Noël-Desmarais Pavilion 158
Jesuits 24–5, 30
Jewish community 69–70, 79–84
   Hassidic Jews 82
   Immigration Aid Service 84
   Sephardic Jews 83
Johnston, Daniel 56, 92
Joyce Parc 200
Juste pour Rire, Musée 185
Just for Laughs Festival 138, 185

k

Kahnawake (Montérégie) 237
Keeley, Patrick 169
Kingston 108
Knowlton (Estrie) *229*, 229–30
Korean immigrants *86*, 87
Krieghoff, Cornelius 34

l

La Baie 165, 167
Lac-Brome (Knowlton) 229
Lac-des-Deux-Montagnes
   (Laurentians) 227–9, *241*
Lac des Sables (Laurentians) *226*
Lachine Canal 43
Lachine (Montérégie) 236–7
La Citadelle (Quebec City) 251–2
Lac Massawippi *232*
Lac Wapizagonke (Coeur du
   Quebec) 240
La Devoir 143
language 65, 66, 67–8, 132
   laws 56, 67, 94–5
Laporte, Pierre 54
La Presse 143
La Ronde 216, *217*
Latin Quarter *66*, *67*, 177–83
Laumet de Lamonie, Antoine 135
Laureau House (Fort Chambly) 233
Laurentians 223–9
Laurier 189, 198
Laurier, Sir Wilfred, statue 161
Laval, Bishop 30
Le Centre Molson 109
Le Commensal 102
Le Parchemin 167
Les Expos *212*
Lévesque, René 55, 91–3, *92*
Le Village Québécois d'Antan
   (Coeur du Quebec) 239

libraries
   Bibliothèque Nationale du
      Québec 181
   Haskell Free Library and Opera
      House (Rock Island) 232, *233*
   Pettes Memorial Library
      (Lac-Brome) 229
Lieu Historique National Sir
   George-Etienne Cartier 131
Little Italy 69, *87*
Lower Westmount 198
Lumberjack Village (Coeur du
   Quebec) 240

m

McCord Museum *20*, *111*, 166
MacDonald, John A. *43*, 48
McGee, Thomas d'Arcy 43
McGill College Avenue 166
McGillivray, William 37
McGill, James 37, 38
McGill University 67, *166*
McTavish, Simon 37, 38
Magog (Estrie) 231
Mahovlich, Frank *106*
Maigneault House (Fort Chambly)
   233
The Main 172
   see also Jewish community
Maison du Calvet 130
Maison des Coopérants 167
Maison Hurtubise 197
Maisonneuve, Sieur de, Paul de
   Chomedey 25–7, *26*, *124*
   statue 136
Maison Papineau 130
Mance, Jeanne 27, 137
Maple Leafs 112
Marc-Aurèle Fortin, Musée 148
Marguerite Bourgeoys, Musée 133
Marie-Reine-du-Monde cathedral
   152–3, *162*
markets 75
   Atwater Market *102*
   flea market 150
   Marché Bonsecours *133*, *134*
   Marché Ste-Anne 44
Marriott Château Champlain 163
Massawippi *232*
Maurice National Park (Coeur du
   Quebec) 240
Meech Lake Accord 56, 93–4
Melocheville (Montérégie) 238
Men Without Hats 144
Mesplet, Fleury de 36
Métis Rebellion 48
Métro 155, 157
Mile-End *189*

Milton-Parc 188
Mime Festival 173
Mirabel airport 54
Misou, Misou 73
Moishe's Steakhouse 102, 172
Molson Bank 141
Molson, John 38
Monastery Garden 214
Montcalm, Louis-Joseph, Marquis de 34, 253
Mont-Condor 224
Montérégie 232–8
Montgolfières Festival *223*
Montgomery, General Richard 36
Montmorency Parc (Quebec City) 247–8
Mont-Orford Arts Centre (Estrie) 231
Mont-Orford Park (Estrie) 231
Montrealers 73–6
Montreal Gazette 143
Montreal Star 143
Montréal Trust, Place *155, 165,* 165–6
Mont-Royal 21, 23, 189, *192,* 196
Mont-St-Hilaire (Montérégie) 235–6
Mont-Tremblant (Laurentians) 226–7, *227*
monuments *see* statues and monuments
Morenz, Howie 110
Morgan, Henry 51
The Mother House of the Sisters of Notre-Dame 198
Mulroney, Brian 56, 92
Musée Avenue 158–9
museums
des Abénaquis (Odanak) 240
d'Archéologie et d'Histoire de la Pointe-à-Callière 146
d'Art Contemporain 168–9
Bank of Montreal 140
des Beaux-Arts *158*
Brome County Historical (Lac-Brome) 229–30
Canadian Railway (St-Constant) 234
Centre d'Histoire de Montréal 147
de la Chasse et de la Nature 196
de la Civilisation (Quebec City) 249
David M. Stewart 216
Ecomusée du Fier Monde 186
Fort Chambly (Montérégie) 233
Fur Trade (Lachine) 237
Juste pour Rire 185
Lachine Museum (Montérégie) 236–7

McCord Museum *20, 111,* 166
Marc-Aurèle Fortin 148
Marguerite Bourgeoys 133
du Québec (Quebec City) 254
Séminaire de Québec (Quebec City) 250–51
Sutton Heritage (Estrie) 230
l'Universe Maurice-Richard 113
music 135–6, 173
Jazz Festival 138, 183, *187*

n

National Monument 171
Nelson's monument *125,* 127
newspapers 132, 143
New York Insurance Company 137
North-West Company 37
Notre-Dame Basilica *46,* 136, 138–9, *139*
Notre-Dame-de-Bon-Secours 27, *131,* 131, 133, *152*
Notre-Dame-des-Neiges 196
Notre-Dame-de-Québec (Quebec City) 250
Notre-Dame-des-Victoires (Quebec City) 248

o

Odanak Abenaki Reserve (Coeur du Quebec) 239–40
Ogilvy and Sons 165
Oka Park (Laurentians) 227–9
Old Montreal 125
Olier, Jean-Jacques 25
Olmsted, Frederick Law 196
Olympic Stadium 55, 55, *209,* 209–12, *210, 211*
Oratoire St-Joseph 200, *202,* 203–5
Orford (Estrie) 231
Ostwell, John 47
Ottawa River 21
Outremont 193, 194–5, 198–200, *199*
cafés 201

p

Palais de Justice 127–8
Papineau, Louis Joseph 45, 130
parc (parks)
Champs-de-Bataille (Quebec City) 253–4
Chûte-Montmorency (Quebec City) 254
Joyce 200
Montmorency (Quebec City) 247–8

Mont-Orford (Estrie) 231
Mont-Royal *see* Mont-Royal
National de la Maurice (Coeur du Quebec) 240
d'Oka (Laurentians) 227–9, *228*
Outremont 200
Pointe-du-Buisson Archaeological (Melocheville) 238
Pratt 200
Sir-Wilfred-Laurier 189
Parizeau, Jacques *19,* 92, 95
Parliament 44, 46
Patriotes 45, 46
Pensionnat du St-Nom-de-Marie 200
Petit Bastille (Quebec City) 254
Petit-Plateau 189
Pettes Memorial Library (Lac-Brome) 229
Phillips Square 166–7
Phipps, Sir William 248–9
Pierreville (Coeur du Quebec) 239
Place d'Armes 27, 134–5, 136, 137–8, 142
Place d'Armes (Quebec City) 247
Place du Canada *88,* 161
Place des Arts *168*
Place Jacques-Cartier *127,* 134
Place Montréal Trust *155, 165,* 165–6
Place Royale 24, 143, 145–6
Place Royale (Quebec City) 248
Place Vauquelin 127
Place Victoria 142
Place Ville-Marie *164,* 164–5
Place d'Youville 143, *145,* 147
Plains of Abraham 245, *253*
Plateau 188
Pointe-à-Callière 145
Pointe-du-Buisson Archaeological Park (Melocheville) 238
Point St-Charles 51
politics 55–6, 58–9, 89–95
population 51
Poudrière (Quebec City) 251
PQ (Parti Québécois) 55, 56, 92
Pratt Park 200
Price, Bruce 163
Prince-Arthur, rue 183–4

q

Quebec Act (1774) 35, 245
Quebec City 24, 34, 245–54
Ancien Bureau de Poste *248*
Château Frontenac *244,* 247
churches
Notre-Dame-de-Québec 250
Notre-Dame-des-Victoires 248

Ste-Trinité 251
Côte de la Montagne 248
Escalier Casse-Cou 248
Grande-Allée 252
history 245, 247
Hôtel-de-Ville 251
Hôtel du Parlement 252
Ile d'Orléans 254
La Citadelle 251–2
Lower Town *252*
museums
    Civilisation 249
    Québec, Musée du 254
    Séminaire de Québec 250–51
Old Port *249*
Old Post Office *248*
Parc des Champs-de-Bataille
    253–4
Parc de la Chûte-Montmorency
    254
Parc Montmorency 247–8
Petit Bastille 254
Place d'Armes 247
Place Royale 248
Plains of Abraham 245, *253*
Porte Prescott 248
Porte St-Louis 251
Poudrière 251
rue Buade 247
rue Dalhousie 249
rue du Petit-Champlain 248
rue St-Louis *250*
rue du Trésor 247, *251*
Ste-Anne-de-Beaupré *254*
Séminaire de Québec 250–51
Terrasse Dufferin *247*
Vieux-Port *249*
Ville Basse *252*
Québec, Musée du (Quebec City)
    254
Quebec Province 66
    see also politics
Quiet Revolution 53, 58–9

r

rafting (Rouge River) 229
railways 47, 48, *49*
    Windsor Station *163*
rangs 28
Rasco, Francisco 134
Rasco hotel 134
Récollet priests 24
religion 24–31
restaurants 184–5
    see also food and drink
Richard, Henri Pocket Rocket *110*
Richard, Maurice The Rocket 110,
    112, 113, 144

Richelieu, Cardinal (Armand Jean
    du Plessis) *25*
Richler, Mordecai 144
Riel, Louis *48*
Rigaud (Laurentians) 229
Ritz-Carlton 157, *160*
Rock Island (Estrie) 232
Rose Garden 215
Rouge River rafting (Laurentians)
    229
Royal Bank 141, *142*
rue
    Bonsecours 130
    Commune 134
    Gauchetière 169
    Hutchison 198
    Prince-Arthur 183–4
    St-Antoine 157
    Ste-Catherine 165, *172*, *183*
    St-Denis *66*, *67*, 157, 173, *176*,
        177–83
    St-Jacques 47, 140–41
    St-Paul *130*, 131, 135, *137*
    St-Pierre 135
    St-Urbain 172
    St-Vincent 135
    Sherbrooke *157*, *182*

s

Ste-Adèle (Laurentians) 224
Ste-Agathe-des-Monts
    (Laurentians) 226
St Andrew et St Paul 158
Ste-Anne-de-Beaupré 254
Ste-Anne-de-Beaupré (Quebec City)
    254
Ste-Anne-de Sorel (Coeur du
    Quebec) 239
Ste-Anne market 44
St-Antoine, rue 157
St-Benoit-du-Lac (Estrie) 231–2
Ste-Brigide 186
Ste-Catherine (Montérégie) 235
Ste-Catherine, rue 165, *172*, *183*
St-Constant (Montérégie) 234
St-Denis, rue *66*, *67*, 157, 173,
    176, 177–83
St-Faustin (Laurentians) 226–7
St-George 163–4
St-Germain *200*
Ste-Hélène 24, *54*, *206–7*, 215,
    216
St Hubert House (Fort Chambly)
    233
St-Jacques, rue 47, 140–41
St-James 167–8
St-Jean-Baptiste 188–9
St-Jean-Baptiste Day *14*

St-Jean-sur-Richelieu (Montérégie)
    233–4
St Joseph's Oratory 200, 203–5
St-Laurent Boulevard 52, 70, *85*,
    169, *171*, 171–2, 173
St Lawrence River 21, *218–19*
St-Louis Square *152*, 185, 188
St-Patrick Basilica 170
St-Paul, rue *130*, 131, 135, *137*
St-Pierre Apôtre 186
St-Pierre-et-St-Paul 186
St-Pierre, rue 135
St-Sulpice fathers 27, 28, 31,
    139–40, 193, 194–5
Ste-Trinité cathedral (Quebec City)
    251
St-Urbain, rue 172
St-Viateur 200
St-Vincent, rue 135
Salaberry, Lieutenant-Colonel
    Charles de 43
Salutin, Rick 111
Santropol 102, 172
Schwartz's Delicatessen 102,
    172
Scottish Highland Games *65*
Scottish merchants 37–8
Second World War 52
seigneuries 28, 33
Séminaire de Québec (Quebec
    City) 250–51
separatism 53–6, 67, 91
Sephardic Jews 83
Shaar Hashomayim synagogue *80*
Shatner, William 144
Sherbrooke, rue *157*, *182*
Simpsons 165
Sir-Wilfred-Laurier Park 189
slavery 35
snow fences *153*
Sorel (Coeur du Quebec) 238–9
SOS Labyrinthe 150
Southam Building 170
Square Dorchester 161
Square Phillips 166–7
Square St-Louis *152*, 185, 188
Stade Olympique 55, *209*, 209–12,
    210, 211
Stanstead (Estrie) 232
statues and monuments
    Chomedey, Paul de 136
    George-Etienne Cartier *198*
    Jacques Cartier 196
    John Young 146
    King Edward VII 167
    Maurice The Rocket Richard *112*
    National Monument 171
    Nelson's Monument *125*
    Robert Burns 161

Sir Wilfred Laurier 161
Vauquelin 127
war memorial *161*
Stewart Museum 216
Stowe, Harriet Beecher 27
**Sucrerie de la Montagne
(Laurentians)** 229
Sulpician order 27, 28, 31,
139–40, 193, 194–5
Summit Circle 197
Sun Life Building 161–2
Sunnyside Avenue 197
Sutton (Estrie) 230
Symphony Orchestra 173
synagogues 81
Shaar Hashomayim *80*

t

Taillibert, Roger 209
television 65
Terrasse Dufferin (Quebec City)
247
terrorism 54
textile industry 104–5
theatres 168, 173
Centaur 149
IMAX theatre 150
Outremont 199–200
St-Denis 179
Théâtre-de-la-Butte (Val-David)
224
Ticonderoga, battle of 34
Tour d'Horloge 150
Tour Olympique *209*, 209–12
Tremblay, Michel 73
Trudeau, Margaret *97*

Trudeau, Pierre 54, 73, 92, 93, *96*,
96–7
typhus epidemic 47

u

Underground City 155, 157
Union Nationale 58–9
Unity Building 170
**l'Universe Maurice-Richard
(museum)** 113
universities 37–8, 67, 200
McGill University 67, *166*
UQAM 177
urban development 155

v

Val-David (Laurentians) 224
Van Horne Avenue 198
Vauquelin, Place 127
Vauquelin, statue 127
Vélodrome 213
Vezina, Georges 110
Victoria Bridge 47
Victoria Hall 195, 197
Victoria, Place 142
Vieux Palais de Justice 127
Vieux-Port 127, 136, *149*, 150
Vieux Séminaire de St-Sulpice
139–40, *140*
Viger Commission 125
Viger, Jacques 44
Viger Square 44
The Village 186
**Village du Bûcheron (Coeur du
Quebec)** 240

Village de Séraphin (Laurentians)
224
Ville Marie 26–7, 66
Ville-Marie, Place *164*, 164–5
Villeneuve, Gilles 144
Villeneuve, Jacques 144

w

Walker, Sir Hovenden 249
Wapizagonke (Coeur du Quebec)
240
war memorial *161*
War of 1812 43
weather 15
West Brome (Estrie) *230*, 231
Westmount 38, 193–4, 195–8
Shaar Hashomayim synagogue
80
Wills, Frank 167
Windsor hotel 162
Windsor Station *163*
Wolfe, General James 34, *35*, 245,
253
World Trade Centre 142
World Wars 52

y

Young, John 146
youth culture 180
d'Youville, Maria 147
d'Youville, Place 143, *145*, 147

A
C
D
E
F
G
H
I
J
a
c
d
e
f
g
h
i
j
k
l